D0503351

Here's to you Agnes Bane,
from your friend,
Gene Fowler
1950

THE GREAT MOUTHPIECE

A Life Story of William J. Fallon

THE GREAT MOUTHPIECE

A Life Story of

WILLIAM J. FALLON

by

GENE FOWLER

BLUE RIBBON BOOKS, INC.
New York City

First printing, September, 1931
Second printing, September, 1931
Third printing, October, 1931
Fourth printing, November, 1931
Fifth printing, December, 1931
Sixth printing, January, 1932
Seventh printing, February, 1932
Eighth printing, March, 1932
Ninth printing, May, 1932
Tenth printing, July, 1933
Eleventh printing, October, 1933
Twelfth printing, January, 1934
Thirteenth printing, June, 1934
Fourteenth printing, April, 1935

PRINTED AND BOUND BY THE CORNWALL PRESS, INC., FOR
BLUE RIBBON BOOKS, INC., 448 FOURTH AVE., NEW YORK CITY

Printed in the United States of America

TO

BEN HECHT

*We shall all suffer for
what the gods have
given us, suffer terribly.*

—OSCAR WILDE's *Dorian Gray*

THE GREAT MOUTHPIECE

A Life Story of William J. Fallon

CONTENTS

ix

CONTENTS

Chapter One

SIX BARRELS FROM BELLEVUE

OLD DELEHANTY urged his span of ancient geldings across town from the East River. It was January 22, 1886. A low-driving land-breeze swept the soft coal smoke down from New York's chimney pots, freezing one's marrow and scouring the teeth with acid-dust.

The senility of the horses' necks forced them to bow their heads as they pushed against the dirty wind. One horse was rat-gray and a wind-sucker; the other was the color of stale mustard and was blind with cataracts. Their almost bald tails resembled a pair of winter parsnips.

The honest wheels of the canvas-covered truck rumbled over square-cut Belgian paving-blocks in East Twenty-third Street. Old Delehanty—as fat as a brew-master—drove with restrained joy. The harvest had been unexpectedly good. Bellevue Hospital's morgue today had yielded six pauper bodies.

Old Delehanty winked slyly. The hearts of the students at the College of Physicians and Surgeons would leap when they saw the six fat-bellied brine barrels, in each of which was sealed a nameless one.

The January wind had sharp teeth, but Delehanty kept one ear free of his sheepskin collar. A man who loved his work naturally wished to listen to the bass-drum thumpings of the barrels, as truck wheels stumbled against granite paving-blocks. A practiced ear could detect a muted swishing—that sound

would be the futile movement of little waves of brine. Burlap
cowls, tied over the open barrel-heads with Manila-twine nooses,
sagged in the middles; little lakes of brine rocked in the burlap
drum-heads, like washings in placer cradles. The bulges of the
barrels held a clammy dew, like cold sweat on foreheads. The
truck floor was damp with spilled brine and smelled of low tide
at the seashore.

Altogether, it was a day when a man could enjoy a seidel of
Ehret's lager beer and look forward to even richer harvests in a
field where grew a million and a half souls. Delehanty flicked the
liquorice-colored reins and sang a chantey to the rumps of his
horses, without once losing a morsel of his chewing tobacco. The
smell of bilge made him remember the fo'castles of clipper ships.

Seldom had that tobacco tasted so delicious. Seldom had Delehanty garnered six cadavers in one afternoon—and only one
nigger in the whole six brine barrels! Indeed, it was good to be
alive. Fifty cents the body—that was his haulage fee, paid by
the college. Three dollars in a single afternoon! More than
enough for beer—perhaps he would take the old lady to the
Eden Musée, to see Ajaab, the Mysterious Chess Automaton.

The horses plodded along Twenty-third Street, their spavined
bones creaking like masts. Frozen foam on the chin of the off-
horse gave him a weird goatee, like that of a retired lecher.
Delehanty pulled up his team just this side of Fourth Avenue. He
turned into a stable-yard at the rear of a four-story, red-brick
building that was the famous College of Physicians and Surgeons.

Delehanty was too self-esteemed to roar out gloating halloas.
The whole college would know soon enough what a fellow he
was for selecting and transporting bodies. He removed his fur-
lined gauntlets and grunted complacently as he lifted the big
weight, suspended by strap and ring from the dash-board hook.
He let the weight fall against the cobblestones with a brave,
frosty smash. Then he climbed down and waited with a show of
unconcern, kicking with a hob-nail boot against frozen mud of a
rear wheel.

An attendant came lazily from the gaslit basement. "What luck, Delehanty?"

Delehanty chewed his cud non-committally. He was not the sort to let another man discover that a windfall had made him conceited. "It might be I had a little luck today; one must never complain."

The attendant was slapping his hands together and stomping his feet to keep warm. "Come on, let's look. The Old Man is yelling his head off for fresh stiffs."

Delehanty drew back the tarpaulin that curtained the rear of the truck. He stood like a City Father unveiling a statue to The Goddess of Thrift. "Oh, I manage to pick up a stiff here, and a stiff there—enough to keep me and the old lady alive."

The attendant saw the six fat barrels. "Six! Great! They're all spoken for. The Old Man will be tickled pink. Fine work, Delehanty. We'll have a drink on this."

Delehanty pretended interest in the splay feet of the wheel-horse. "I guess I got to get 'em shod soon, what with the slippery weather. . . . Lend me a hand, and we'll carry the barrels to the dissectin' room."

"Six!" repeated the amazed attendant. He called out to the basement: "Jim! Hey, you Jim! Come on out—Delehanty's got *six!*"

"And only one nigger in the lot," said Delehanty.

The attendant stared incredulously. "You don't mean that!"

Delehanty nodded sagely. "Only *one* nigger."

"The Old Man will go insane. Hey, Jim! Where in hell are you? Delehanty's got six stiffs, and only one boogie among 'em. . . . God A'mighty, Delehanty! The Old Man'll kiss you."

"I ought to get seventy-five cents apiece for the hauling," Delehanty said. "It takes a good eye to choose the right ones. The Old Man gets $5 apiece, don't he?"

"Yes, but he's got to pay $3 to the City."

"I ought to get more dough. A whole buck."

Jim came to the stable-yard and looked at the barrels. He was carrying a note. The attendant pointed excitedly. "Jim! He got *six!*"

Jim screwed up his eyes. "That's pretty good."

"Pretty good?" the attendant said. "You can just bet your ass it's pretty good. Where was you all this time?"

Jim showed the note. "A messenger gimme this to deliver to Doc McCreery right away. I don't know what to do."

"Never mind the note. It can wait. Give a hand with these stiffs."

"No, the note can't wait, neither. It's important."

"Well, Doc McCreery can't be bothered when he's lecturin'. You ought to know that by this time."

Jim was worried. "But it's *extra*-important."

"Go ahead an' deliver it then."

"Like hell I will! McCreery trun a spittoon at me last time I busted in." Jim had an inspiration. "Say, let's me an' you carry the stiffs upstairs and send Delehanty with the note. McCreery won't get sore at Delehanty, what with him havin' such a load of stiffs. See?"

"I don't see why the note can't wait. What in hell is it, anyway?"

"Somebody's havin' a kid, the messenger said."

The attendant turned to Delehanty. "We'll hoist the stiffs if you run an errand for us."

Delehanty was meditating aloud. "I ought to get a buck for each stiff. It's tough work."

Jim cut in: "Why don't you take *that* up with the Old Man? See him now, and on your way back you can deliver the note to Doc McCreery. See?"

"Where's he at?"

"He's lecturin' now. You know, the second floor. We'll take care of the stiffs."

"Will you birds back me up when I tell the Old Man how hard I work to pick the best stiffs before others get to 'em?"

"Surest thing, Delehanty," Jim said. "Don't forget the note. See?"

Delehanty took the note and went inside. "I sure ought to get a buck apiece. Only one nigger in the bunch."

The attendant and Jim began to unload the truck. "They put too God-damned much brine in these barrels," the attendant said. "Christ, but this is a heavy one!"

"It must be the nigger."

"I hope we don't get a rupture. . . . Wait till Delehanty busts in on McCreery. He's preachin' about childbirth."

Jim sniggered. "McCreery damn near got me canned last time. I brung him word his house was on fire."

"I never seed such a temper."

The men had to carry the barrels three flights of narrow, winding stairs to the dissecting-room. That room occupied the entire top floor. Wooden slabs were grouped like xylophone bars beneath a big and grimy skylight. The slabs were more or less empty today, there having been a dearth of bodies.

The "Old Man" was professor of anatomy. He oscillated with rapture as he helped Jim and the attendant wrestle the first brine-barrel to a tiled corner and near a bell-trap. He ripped the burlap cowl with the zeal of a Geronimo scalping a missionary.

The Old Man peered into the barrel. "Well, nigger or no nigger, it's better'n nothing. Poor people are getting damned healthy in this town."

The attendant beamed. "Didn't Delehanty tell you?"

"Tell what?"

"All the rest are *white*."

"I didn't talk to Delehanty. I hid in the toilet when I saw him coming. He's always shouting for more money. He's being over-paid now."

"This is a hell of a big nigger, Doctor."

"Yes. Dropsy. Help me hoist him. Take hold of his chin, Jim."

Delehanty was disappointed at not having interviewed the Old Man. He now was at the doors leading to the lecture amphi-theater and was peeking through a crack. He held the note in his hand. He saw tier on tier of steeply-banked benches, at which students of varying ages and nationalities were sprawled. Most of them were chewing tobacco. This reassured Delehanty.

He opened the doors. Before him was a platform, a pit to the rising semicircle of benches. Mysterious designs were chalked on the black slate board facing the class. The tracings represented the inner mechanisms of a lady's torso, but to old Delehanty they looked like a map for buried treasure. The dignified and heavily bearded John McCreery, M.D., was holding a brass-ferruled pointer against the diagram, saying:

"We have two types of premature labor: forced, and natural. The former results in. . . ."

Dr. McCreery had not yet seen the fat messenger. The sleepy class awakened and looked down in wonderment. It was unthinkable—dangerous even—to interrupt the eminent Dr. McCreery. The lecturer, his back to the swinging doors, paused, sensing that something untoward was happening. When his eye caught the messenger, his nose-glasses jiggled with rage.

"Who told *you* to come in here?"

Delehanty was a bit incoherent. "I brung in six bodies, Doc."

"Get out!"

Delehanty all but threw the note at Dr. McCreery and backed away, a sudden pride making him scream: "And only *one* nigger in the bunch!"

"Get the hell out!"

The trembling of the good Doctor's beard silenced a titter in the benches. It was a most celebrated beard, the blackness of which was beginning to suffer an invasion of gray. The beard twisted and swayed like the skirt of a hula dancer. Patients forever remembered the carbolic and iodoform odors that nested in the McCreery whiskers.

There was an uneasy silence while the Doctor read the note. The brass-ferruled pointer slipped from beneath his armpit and clattered to the floor. He began to shout and scream. He paced the platform like a wounded bear, limping—he had suffered hip disease in his childhood—and tearing up the note. He made small wads of the paper fragments. Every time he limped past the blackboard, he shot pellets at the lady's torso, using thumb and forefinger, as one flips marbles.

Finally he grew articulate and faced his class. "What's the use of lecturing? To hell with it! What's the use of practicing medicine? By the classic vesicles of the great Hermes! better you got jobs as ditch-diggers or engineers on the 'El'. I have just received a note from a persistent husband, swearing his wife is taken with labor pains. For one solid month this man has been pestering me with his wife's pregnancy. Me, who has been in practice twenty-five years! Me, who ought to know the period of gestation better than any man alive or dead! And every time I respond to these notes, it's a false alarm!"

The Professor tugged at his beard and glared over the rims of his slanting nose-glasses. He reached over, picked up the pointer and leaned on it like a general on a sword.

"You see in me, my friends, the answer to a life of sacrifice as a disciple of Hippocrates. Think well before you hang out your shingles. I get no sleep. My meals are interrupted until I have had to fortify my gastric mucosa with pepsin. I have contracted the bicarbonate-of-soda habit. The duodenal mucous is washed away, and the stomatogastric nerves of the entire alimentary tract are paralyzed. All because a young man, who doesn't know the difference between child-labor and gas pains, must write me notes. Bah!"

The Doctor removed his eye-glasses, placed them in their shiny little coffin and snapped the lid.

"That's all for today, gentlemen. I leave you with my McCreery recipe for alleviating most of the troubles of this troublous planet. Some day you will look back and thank me for it. It's this: keep the bowels open and the mouth shut. Good afternoon, gentlemen."

Dr. McCreery went to the high stoop of the college. He limped down the right-hand flight of double stairs. His Negro lackey was astonished to see the Doctor so soon. The servant roused himself from the buggy-seat and went to the cast-iron post to unstrap the hitching-rein.

As Dr. McCreery was about to climb into his vehicle, he was hailed by Dr. William T. Bull, the foremost surgeon of the day. Dr. Bull came to the curb, driving his own smart cob.

"Just been over to Fiss, Doerr & Carrol's," Dr. Bull said. "They got in a car of green horses today."

"Thinking of adding to your stable?"

"Sort of, but a man's got to be careful. I hear that glanders was discovered last week in a Twenty-fourth street livery."

"Sounds bad."

"Tell your friends to be careful about letting their horses drink from public troughs in this neighborhood."

"People are getting less sense every day, Bull. No responsibility. Only yesterday some Italians were found carrying a child with smallpox on a Third Avenue car."

Dr. Bull offered his friend a cigar. "What you doing this evening, Doctor?"

Dr. McCreery snorted: "I *was* going to the Union League Club's reception, but I may not be able to make it."

"Another baby?"

"I've got a call from Joe Fallon; his wife is feeling pains."

"Joseph M. Fallon, the contractor, isn't it?"

"Yes. They live in one of those four-story brownstones on the south side of West Forty-seventh Street."

"Oh, yes. I knew her people quite well. She was Ellen Carthy, wasn't she?"

"A fine couple, only Joe Fallon hasn't given me a moment's peace for the last month. It's a question who are the more excitable, the Irish or the Italians."

"We certainly earn our fees, Doctor."

"You're right we do. You know, Bull, fifteen dollars for a first delivery is ridiculous enough, but ten dollars for a subsequent child is stupid."

"But what are we to do? They're calling us robbers for adding the five-dollar fee in forceps cases. Good God! It made me turn over my obstetrical work to Gaillard Thomas."

"The layman doesn't realize that the cost of living is constantly mounting for us as well as for themselves."

"I paid 90 cents the hundred for oats today."

"Our hands are tied, Doctor. Only yesterday I advised a charity case—tuberculosis in both lungs—to eat six fresh eggs a day. She looked at me. 'Fresh eggs! How can I afford fifteen cents a dozen, when I have five children to feed?' Oh, well, I'm sending her the eggs myself. Well, I'll be getting on."

"How's your dyspepsia?"

"How the hell do you suppose, when nearly every meal is knocked on the head?"

"Look here, McCreery, you've got to watch out. Simply *take* time. What you doing tomorrow evening?"

"The usual thing, I suppose. Wait home until somebody's stork stabs me with its beak in the backside. Why?"

"You'll go stale. I've two tickets for the billiard match at Cosmopolitan Hall. Will you come?"

Dr. McCreery played with his watch chain. "If you'll let me stand a dinner at Delmonico's first."

"You're on. Shaefer is playing the fourth of five blocks against Vignaux."

"The Frenchman, eh? I haven't had time to read the papers."

"I've been there every night. No use killing ourselves."

"Well, *you* can do it, seeing you operate in daytime. I hear Vignaux is good."

"He has the hands of a surgeon. Well, I've got to go inside and teach a lot of grave-robbers how to open the belly without leaving an incision as big as Castle Garden. Remember me to the Fallons."

"I'll look for you at Delmonico's a little before seven."

Dr. McCreery tucked a fur-lined woolen lap-robe about his knees. The Negro driver set off at a clipping pace, nosing the cob over to Fifth Avenue and then uptown. The horse's caulks struck sparks from the frozen granite blocks.

They pulled up finally in front of No. 134 West Forty-seventh Street. The Doctor clambered out and looked up and down the thoroughfare. The four-story residences of the well-to-do stood in grim Victorian array, their bay-windows protruding like the pregnancies of squaws; the chimneys rising above square-shouldered roofs in the manner of papooses strapped to the backs of red-brown mothers.

Twilight was thickening and, as the Doctor limped up the stone steps with his black clinical case, his Negro servant lighted the two silver carriage-lamps.

Any of three house-servants usually opened the door for the Doctor; but this time Joe Fallon himself did the honors. He was a straightly built, sinewy man of twenty-eight. He had red hair, a mustache seemingly made of firecracker fuses, and a fine look of Ireland in his face and eyes.

"Glad you've come in time, Doctor."

Mr. Fallon took the Doctor's bag and helped him out of his black great-coat. He was reassured by the enormous strength of carbolic odors that were released. The Doctor grunted, picked up his case and hobbled up the wide stairway. He went familiarly to an ample front bedroom on the second floor. The furniture here, as elsewhere in the warm, hospitable home, was rich and solid, as befitted citizens like the Fallons. The Doctor plopped his case on a night stand of black walnut, which had a mottled marble top.

Of all his patients, Dr. McCreery had the highest regard for the one that now lay in the huge, carved black-walnut bed—a handsome woman of about twenty-seven. She had large blue eyes, dark hair, finely-formed features and the clear complexion that is the gift of Irish blood. Dr. McCreery had delivered two girls heretofore for the Fallons. He was always promising them a son. It would be a ten-dollar case.

The Doctor held the woman's hand with fatherly affection. "So you think it really is your time, eh?"

The woman smiled. She had even, white teeth, and a beautiful mouth. "I don't know, Doctor. Joe seems sure."

After awhile the Doctor turned to Mr. Fallon. "Wrong again, Joe. Irish babies take as much time as any other kind."

At 10 o'clock, a procession of carriages drew up to the curbstone of the Union League Club. One could catch an occasional glimpse of rare gems as dowagers were handed from their vehicles. When the large doors of the clubhouse opened, there came a flood of melody from an orchestra concealed by foliage in the reception hall. A huge limelight burned behind the great stained-glass window that looked down upon the grand staircase.

In the center of the reception hall stood the new president of the club, the Hon. Chauncey M. Depew. He was receiving all comers with *bons mots* that in later days bolstered his reputation as the great-grandfather of the town's wisecrackers. Indeed, the New York *Tribune* of next day declared that "Mr. Depew exercised an official cordiality, meeting the requirements of each case with a brand new joke that *never before* had been uttered."

As the good Doctor left the cloak room, he passed such notables as General Horace Porter, Cornelius M. Bliss, ex-Governor Cornell, W. E. D. Stokes, Generals O. O. Howard and Daniel E. Sickles. The smell of the excellent cigars gave one the illusion that Havana's costliest warehouse was on fire.

There could be seen the city's foremost women. Mrs. Elihu Root was in a rose-pink silk creation with front of rose brocade, pearl fringes, pearl and diamond ornaments. Mrs. I. C. H. Leverich wore white silk, the front and bodice "covered with a lattice-work of pearls; décolleté corsage, a diamond butterfly and clover leaf, and diamond ornaments." She carried a bouquet of lilies of the valley. Mrs. C. P. Huntington "was in silver cloth with a train of pink brocade and. . . ."

Well, the good Doctor was experiencing all these wonderful sights, and was being greeted by the amiable Mr. Depew, who made reference to current bodily ills. Dr. McCreery revealed that insomnia was on the increase among public men, "who are pushing themselves too hard in a materialistic age."

To this, Mr. Depew took issue, observing: "I doubt if it is insomnia, Dr. McCreery. Could it not be a general *revival of conscience?*"

There was a call at the door for Dr. McCreery. A note was handed him on a silver tray. He read it while music floated from the grand ballroom, where a second orchestra (also concealed behind foliage) was playing for a set of *Lanciers.* As he had vaguely divined, the Doctor saw that the note was from Citizen Joseph M. Fallon.

A doctor's life was not his own.

Once again, and this time late in the evening, Dr. McCreery left the home of Joseph M. Fallon. He had laid down the law good and hard. The trembling of righteous indignation still was with his beard.

The obstetrical hand had been placed on Joe Fallon's biceps. "It is possible you are the most worrisome creature in the whole of St. Patrick's Cathedral Parish. It has got to stop. The child won't be here for another week. Now mark you, I'm going home to get some sleep. And tomorrow I'm not to be disturbed, either."

The Doctor amended his words. "Of course, if anything *actually* happens, I'll be dining at Delmonico's. Later on I'll be at the billiard match at Cosmopolitan Hall. But damn it, sir, no more guess work!"

Arrived at his Lexington Avenue home, the Doctor poured himself a neat glass of rare old brandy. He sipped slowly and smacked his lips. Then he undressed, drew on a canton flannel nightgown and a roomy nightcap. His shanks looked waxy in the gas-light as he sat on the edge of his feather-bed and wound his old watch with a key. Then he got under the covers.

The Doctor's man peered in presently to see that the gas-cocks were closed securely. He saw in the moonlight the famous McCreery beard protruding from the bed-covers. The snores sounded like the rattling of five dice in a leather cup.

Chapter Two

A NIGHT AMONG THE CHAMPIONS

DOCTORS MCCREERY AND BULL prepared to set out for the great billiard match. Their white waistcoats and Prince Albert girths were distended by Delmonico's venison pasties. Dr. McCreery brought a round pasteboard box from his side pocket. He chose two capsules filled with white powder and deposited them on his tongue. He chased the capsules down with a sip of white wine and then hoisted a napkin to his lips as though running up a flag of truce.

Dr. Bull voiced academic interest as his colleague closed the box. "Pepsin?"

"No. Rennin, bismuth and bicarbonate of soda. My pyloric glands are screaming because I'm an obstetrician."

"An excess of hydrochloric, no doubt."

"From irregular eating."

"We abuse ourselves beyond reason."

The doctors went by cab uptown. They stopped at The White Elephant in Thirty-first Street and Broadway, where a little rum was had to allay Dr. McCreery's belching. A second application of the same was ordered at George Bullwinkle's Aulic in Thirty-fifth Street. The two gentlemen of the lancet now were ripe for relaxation.

From Mr. Bullwinkle's congenial caravansary, the eminent leeches were driven directly to Cosmopolitan Hall in Forty-first Street and Broadway, where an unruly crowd was milling on the walk. Something out of the ordinary had occurred, as was evident by an onrush of busybodies from the Longacre Square sector. It must be admitted that among those present in the sidewalk congregation were not a few high-busted, narrow-waisted ladies of the once-vaunted profession that—alas!—has degenerated into a catch-as-catch-can parlor game for loutish moderns.

Dr. Bull was diagnosing the scene, over which hung a carnival of noise. "Something has happened, Doctor."

"Maybe they've arrested a pickpocket," Dr. McCreery suggested. He could see police helmets among the silk hats of dudes and curl-brimmed derbies of the sporting fancy.

Dr. Bull paid off the cabby, requesting him to return not later than ten-thirty. "Wait in front of the Vendôme till we come."

The doctors protected their heavy gold watches as they pushed through the crowd. They were jostled about, venison pasties and all, and Dr. McCreery's pill-box was stove in. However, both were fine strategists and used to taking advantage of the slightest openings, so it was not to be marveled at when the two Galens found themselves in a position near the front line of spectators. In the center of that throng, and flanked by bravely mustached policemen, there stood a rather amazing fellow of some five feet ten inches—his 230 pounds teetering on widely rooted, sturdy legs. He wore striped tweeds, a high silk hat which was tilted like the Leaning Tower of Pisa, and a leer such as never before had been seen, except once—and that by John Bunyan during a vision.

According to fragments of conversation supplied by a chance neighbor, the burly man had stepped from his cab not ten minutes since and in high humor. He was—as even the lay eye could tell —comfortably full-up with liquor.

The chance neighbor went on: "He just busted up a shellgame. God, what a man! He beat up the spieler-of-the-nuts."

The statement was literally true. It appeared that the stranger had paused, on alighting from his cab, and had sought in a most peaceful way to take fresh bearings (using the entrance arc-light for a pole star). Inadvertently, and while gazing at the light, he had bumped into the three-shell table, a portable affair on which lay the seductive pods of fortune.

"Watch where y're goin', yah big bum, yah!" the spieler-of-the-nuts was quoted as having said.

Whereupon, the burly stranger unleashed a roar that properly belonged in a lions' den at feeding hour. He caught the spieler by the scruff of the neck, and, using the unhappy hawker's noggin as a ram, proceeded powerfully to demolish the table on which the shells had been resting as snugly as your grandmother's thimbles.

All this had been said and done by the time the two doctors arrived. "Drunk," whispered Dr. McCreery, who was now anxious to get on. "He has a heart look. His face seems familiar, don't you think?"

Dr. Bull left his watch unguarded long enough to pinch his colleague's arm. "Say! That's John L. Sullivan, the Champion of the World!"

Mr. Sullivan's jowls behaved like bellows as he sucked in and blew out the night air of Broadway. His native generosity finally overcame his memory of having been termed a big bum.

The king of the knuckle-smiths called out: "All as wants can follow me to the bar. And to hell with them as don't want!"

The police opened a lane for the great gladiator, and he advanced to the bar entrance, tacking occasionally to recover his course. Many hands fought for the honor of whacking his broad back. A cheering mob followed in the wake of the Boston Strong Boy.

Inside the long bar-room, the Champion began to demonstrate the personality that Albert Edward, Prince of Wales, later found so refreshing. He did standing leaps from floor to bar-top, bent a fire-tong with hands and teeth and danced with a full barrel of beer, which he held aloft on his shoulder, while a blind street-fiddler scraped a tune. This was the evening that preceded the famous morning when John L. sank into deep and drunken slumber in a hotel room, and the night-clerk sold tickets at twenty-five cents each to those who wanted to view "The Champion lying in state." The unscrupulous enterprise was interrupted at dawn. The Champion roused, blinked at the queue of spectators passing through his room, and then got up to hurl the night-clerk at the retreating peepers, halloing as he bowled over four or five of them: "I'll throw this Jew at you!"

The good doctors left the scene of the shell-game debâcle and passed inside the billiard hall. "Too bad," Dr. Bull said rather sadly. "The strongest ones are often the weakest."

Among the celebrities to be seen inside the hall were Dan O'Leary, noted pedestrian; Richard K. Fox, owner of The *Police Gazette*; Adam Forepaugh, the circus man; G. R. Brett, champion hose-coupler; Ed Hanlan, celebrated oarsman; E. C. Stickney, the great dumb-bell lifter; Maurice Daly, renowned billiardist and one-time balkline champion; Billy Madden, mentor to Jack McAuliffe, lightweight pugilist; His Honor, William R. Grace, Mayor of New York City, a group of supervisors and a sprinkling of police officials.

When time for play was called, it was evident that the hall was too small for the match. More than 2,000 persons were trying to occupy 1,400 chairs. There was a large representation from the French colony, and the gallery was packed by noisy sportsmen who presumably favored Jake Schaefer to notch a victory over Maurice Vignaux—called "Lion Face." Bets were being shouted and taken. The air was fogged with tobacco smoke. The babble of sportsmen rose as they caressed their handle-bar mustaches.

It was five minutes after eight when the Wizard, Jake Schaefer, entered. He stood, bowing, beside the green-surfaced billiard table, above which two limelights burned fiercely. Billy Sexton, Jake's elbow-man, was standing beside the Wizard, and was puffed up with reflected importance.

Hardly had the cheers for Schaefer dwindled when bulking Maurice Vignaux waddled in, escorted by Al Smith (not the Oliver Street gentleman, who some years later was denied residence in the White House). The referee was introduced. His name was McCreery; howbeit, he was no relation to our doctor

friend, who had an aisle seat four rows back. The referee inspected the table on which the 14.2 inch balklines were drawn
in chalk. Bud Schofield, the official scorer, took his chair and
lighted a huge cigar.

There was a worrisome argument at the table after the principals were introduced. The rooters began to cat-call and to
stomp their feet. Referee McCreery raised a prayerful hand.
"Gentlemen, there will be a slight delay. M. Vignaux has re-
quested that the balls be weighed."

A more or less polite suggestion descended from the gallery.
"While he's at it, have him weigh his head!"

"Gentlemen! Gentlemen!" cooed Referee McCreery.

M. Vignaux, built on the lines of M. Honoré de Balzac,
shrugged his shoulders and stroked his Van Dyke. He claimed
that the red ball was lighter than the white balls, and that the
most minute discrepancy of such character imperiled his stroke—
the most delicate stroke in the world.

"We ain't got no scales here," Bud Schofield said to Smith.

"Then send to the drugstore for some pans," Smith said. "You
got to weigh them balls before Monsewer Maurice will play."

Referee McCreery endeavored to placate M. Vignaux. The
gallery hooted and offered indelicate and extraordinary suggestions as to what Lion Face should do with his hat. Mr. Fox of
The *Police Gazette*, a recognized arbiter in all matters of true
sport, strode to the scene and lent his good offices.

"Just weigh them balls," Mr. Smith insisted.

"But we *did* weigh them the first night, Al," the Referee
pointed out. "The red one weighed a fraction of a grain under
six and three-quarters ounces. Maurice didn't kick the first night
—why should he complain now?"

"Will you, or won't you weigh them balls?" asked Smith.

Little Jake, leaning on his cue and wearing a mask-like smirk,
put in dryly: "I'll play him with crullers and use a broom-handle
for a cue."

Finally, and at 8:25 o'clock, Lion Face capitulated. It was
Schaefer's break. He went to the table and promptly miscued.

The gallery groaned a Greek chorus as Schofield chalked up a duck's egg for the Wizard. The Frenchman improved this opportunity, running up fifteen and then missing a *massé*, but leaving his opponent comparatively safe. The Frenchman was trying hard to crawl up on Schaefer's total score, which at the beginning of the block was 1,800 to Vignaux's 1,753.

In his second innings, Schaefer again missed after attempting a four-cushion shot that was as close as it was daring. His partisans were sad. The French contingent now called on their Lion Face to accomplish an Austerlitz, but he missed a draw-shot and blanked.

Bud Schofield put up sixteen buttons for Schaefer in the third innings. Jake sat down, twirling his cue with drum-major antics. Vignaux's face was pale beneath his beard. He took the balls from a nice leave and began stroking with amazing skill. He nursed the balls with meticulous precision and calculated nicely the position he wished to be in after each carom. He did everything but play Chopin. The clicks were as brief and sharp as the kisses of frigid women. The audience was strangely still. Then, after 62 points had been made, one of those drunken disturbances jumped out of the silence, and the cry of: "Take off your hat! Sit down!"

The gallery brawl startled M. Vignaux from his concentration. He was unable to continue. He stepped from the table, shrugged his disapproval of American manners and sat down with a deflated expression. An upstairs usher put four adroit knuckles against somebody's chin—possibly hitting the right person—there was the sound of a fall, and then peace. M. Vignaux rose and resumed play. With a series of perfectly mathematical shots, he continued to 136.

"I told you he had the hands of a surgeon," Dr. Bull whispered.

After the 136th shot, it appeared that the balls were frozen. The Frenchman peered at the spheres, leaning over and shading them with his hand from the limelight glare. He smiled a childlike smile and shook his large head in deprecatory fashion.

Schaefer came up, shaded the balls, and looked very grave. The Referee now inspected the balls through a grandmother's reading-glass.

"Not frozen. Proceed, Monsewer."

The audience cheered, and the game went on. The Frenchman faced a most difficult shot, and elected to do it in three cushions. He surveyed the lineup and then distributed his 236 pounds along the rail, pointed one leg at the gallery, poised his cue delicately and gave the stroke. A great cheer was accorded him as he made No. 137. Then, with a simple shot, his for the trying, he missed like a novice.

Runs of 64, 44, and 78 placed Schaefer again in the lead. During this play, a sallow young man was bobbing about in the aisles, peering into many faces and drawing down the ire of spectators when he obstructed their view. Finally, the young man lost his hang-dog look and smiled through his pimples. He hurdled shins that blocked the aisle and hastened to the side of the two doctors.

Dr. McCreery felt a touch on his arm. He looked up wonderingly. "You're needed at the Fallons', Doctor. I come in a cab an hour ago, but they wouldn't let me in till just now."

An outburst of cheering absorbed whatever it was the good Doctor was saying. He turned to Dr. Bull and made his apologies. Dr. Bull said something about understanding "how these things are," to which Dr. McCreery replied tartly: "Then it's a damsite more'n I understand myself!"

As the Doctor and the young man left the hall, the huge and sagging bulk of the great John L. Sullivan could be seen wrestling with a pair of swinging saloon-doors. A multitude of "admirers" were "taking care of the Champion," who was blowing like a whale.

"That's Mr. Sullivan," the young man advised the Doctor.

"To hell with him!" said Dr. McCreery. "Come on."

"If it hadn't been for him, I wouldn't of got in at all."

The Doctor had his good leg hoisted for the carriage step. "What's that you're harping about, young man?"

"The man at the door wouldn't let me in. He said they was full up. I went into the saloon to look for Tim Daly, a friend of my father's. He wasn't in. He's at a wake. Mr. Sullivan, he seen me and says: 'And what's your name, lad?' I says it is Matthew, and he says it's no place for a Matthew in a bar, and he asks me if I drank, and I says 'No,' and he says: 'Don't never do it,' and——"

"Come, come! Don't chatter so much."

"Anyway," the boy went on, "when I told Mr. Sullivan I am looking for you, he give me his own ticket. I wanted to keep the ticket to remember him with, but I was sent to get you. Gee, wasn't it swell of Mr. Sullivan?"

Dr. McCreery made only one comment on the way uptown. "If I was big enough and twenty years younger, I'd punch Mr. Sullivan in the nose!"

An eleven-pound son was born shortly before midnight, January 23, 1886, to Mr. and Mrs. Joseph M. Fallon of No. 134 West Forty-seventh Street, where the Hotel Portland now stands and next door to the mission house of the Church of St. Mary the Virgin.

The baby had red-gold hair, several shades lighter than that of the father, and very fair skin. Dr. McCreery massaged the baby's body with olive oil, bathed it and put it in long flannels—all of which was a physician's duty for a ten-dollar fee. Then the Doctor placed the baby at the breast of the mother whom the boy grew to love beyond any and all other women in this droll world.

He was called William Joseph Fallon.

For those who insist on checking up on their grandfathers (who are notoriously unreliable when referring to great events which they pretend to have witnessed, or concerning women who are represented as having chased them) it should be set down that M. Vignaux won that evening's block of billiards. The following night, however, as recounted by Dr. Bull in a subsequent chat with Dr. McCreery, Jake Schaefer captured the match with a total score of 3,000 to M. Vignaux's 2,838. He won $8,000 in prize money and wagers.

"I regret to report," Dr. Bull added, "that Schaefer went to a gambling house in Broadway and dropped the whole $8,000 at faro-bank. A friend had to lend him $100."

"It is an age of spendthrifts," said Dr. McCreery. He had no way of knowing, of course, that the baby he had delivered to Ellen Fallon would grow up to squander one million five hundred thousand dollars in a period of less than ten years on the same Broadway where Mr. Schaefer dropped what is now popularly known as eight grand. If the good Doctor had been clairvoyant enough to foresee as much, his eyes would have stuck out like the valve-caps of a fire-hydrant.

When Willie Fallon was ten years old, he went with his parents, his two sisters and a younger brother to live at Mamaroneck, Westchester County, New York.

Chapter Three

MANY A STORMY WIND SHALL BLOW

THE bicycles lay on the dry lawn, the frames piping hot; the chain-links oozed black curds in the August sun. The twelve to fourteen-year-old boys raced up from the Sound, their swimming trunks clinging, their matted hair dripping like seaweed. The gray road-dust turned black on their bare, wet ankles. The thin tricklings from their jersey trunk-legs left eccentric piddle-trails as they ran. Their gat teeth were big and buck-like against the blue-pink of noisy throats. The noon sun licked vapor from their naked backs.

The howling racers left the open road; white pickets snatching at their crotches as they hurdled the fence. Like harriers, they swept past the bicycles that lay on gleaming sides, with pedals pushed against the parched sod. The big barn near the tennis court was the goal. Willie Fallon was in the lead, his knees driving teats-high with the six-foot strides of a sprinter. There was a momentary jam at the doorway as the three swiftest runners strove to dash inside. Seven or eight less fleet lads finished the race in varying positions, all babbling and all breathing like donkey-engines as they took their play-clothes from a harness-tree.

The garrulous boys stripped, using their hands for towels on salty skins. A fan-tail pigeon on a lime-streaked rafter wobbled his head like a punch-drunk philosopher. The sun thrust through small windows and chinks of the wainscoting. Barn dust floated in trespassing streaks of sun that emphasized the gangling legs and knobby joints of the adolescents.

The boys dressed hurriedly; an important matter was to be settled. Willie Fallon maintained that he was personally acquainted with a pirate—a real one—over at Mt. Vernon. He was standing, long legs straddled, arms, head and shoulders wriggling into his shirt.

His voice came as though from far away. "I tell you he *is* a pirate! Just wait and see."

Three older boys, Ed, Phil, and Herbie, exchanged glances. "Uh huh," Herbie said, "Mt. Vernon's kinda dry place to keep a ship, ain't it?"

The red head popped through the shirt collar. "Get your pants on, everybody. We'll ride over to Mt. Vernon." Willie had an authoritative manner. "Wait till I get something from the house."

They watched him go, cat-like, toward the kitchen. They saw him climb on an up-ended box to peer through an open kitchen window, from which came the brassy odor of boiling grapes. For several seconds he squinted, and then the upper part of his body was gulped in by the window frame. He hung there with his belly on the sill, then pulled away. He returned to the barn, a basket in his arms.

"He's swiped something to eat," Phil said. "He's usually hungry."

"He'll divvy up," said Herb. "He always does."

The troop mounted their bicycles. The saddle leather felt hot against their squirming bottoms. "We'll ride two-abreast," Willie said. "Phil, you and I will lead. Ed, you and Herb ride behind us."

"What you got?" Phil asked.

"It's a present for the pirate."

"It's a grape basket," Phil said. "I sure like grapes."

"They're for the pirate," Willie said. "They love presents."

"Will he make grape juice?" Herbie asked. "That *would* be funny."

"Grape juice makes 'em think of blood," Willie explained.

Ed and Herbie were carrying on a conversation behind the backs of the leaders. "I bet he ain't a pirate at all," said Herbie.

Willie looked back at the skeptics. "Well, don't let *him* hear you say that!"

"Where is it he lives, Willie?"

"In Mt. Vernon, like I said."

"Whereabouts in Mt. Vernon?"

"Number 243 South Fourth."

"What's his name?" Phil asked. "His pirate name, I mean?"

"Oh, he's just plain 'Mr. Ferris' now."

" '*Now*'," said Herbie. "Then you mean he's *quit* piratin'?"

"He's a pirate all right. A hunderd years old, too."

"Who says?"

"He says."

"This 'Mr. Ferris'?"

"Yes," said Willie. "He's a great pirate. Maybe the best."

"Willie," said Herb, "you can't fool me. It's just old Bill Ferris, and he ain't no more a pirate than your grandmaw. And he ain't no hunderd."

"You know a lot, don't you?" Willie said as he showed the way up a short hill.

"My father told me. He says Old Bill Ferris is a *miser*. He's had the same parasol fifty years."

"Pirates don't use parasols," Willie said. "If he *has* one, it's bound to last all his life."

Herb stood on his pedals to make the pumping more effective up the hill. "I bet he ain't got a map."

"Plenty of maps," said Willie, who didn't rise on his pedals, but went up the hill like a genuine leader. "Just wait."

"Is he rich?"

"He has gold buried. A whole lot."

"Where?"

Willie was having trouble with the grape basket. He made as if the questions, and not the grape basket, worried him. "Did your father tell you that pirates give up their secrets?"

"No," Herb said, "but he told me Old Bill Ferris *walks* all the way to New York; he's that tight."

"You get everything twisted. He walks because he had a fight with the railroad people, and won't use their old railroad. He told my father the railroad people was rival pirates."

The boys finally reached the "pirate's cottage." They found the blinds drawn against the hot August of 1898. The visitors didn't seem in a hurry to advance on the old porch, on which an empty rocking chair stood. Willie leered at his followers, walked boldly to the front door and knocked. The door was opened slowly by a middle-aged woman.

"Well," she said, rather crossly. "What is it?"

"I'm the boy who was here last week with my father," said Willie in a whisper.

"Speak up, boy! Now what is it?"

He held forth the basket. "My father, Mr. Fallon, sent this to your father. And I was to ask him how he is today."

The woman seemed to remember. "Why, what's this? Yes, you're the boy Pappy told all them fool yarns to."

Fortunately the Fallon comrades were beyond ear-shot. Willie was nervous. "I'm supposed to see him *personally*, Miss Ferris. I got a message."

"No, no, boy. Pappy's lyin' down. He's nappin'. The weather's too hot for an old man. No, no. Can't come in."

Willie saw the old man inside the parlor, sitting beside a huge square chimney. "Did you say he was *lying down?*"

The woman became testy. "See here, young man. It's neither here nor there if he's lyin', standin' or sittin'. He's nappin'. Now run along, and thanks to your father."

The voice of the "pirate" interrupted: "Who's that, Frances? I say, who is it?"

"Now run along," Miss Frances said to Willie. "You'll have him all riled up in a minute."

The "pirate" kept calling. "Frances, let him in. Don't keep my visitors away! Let him in. Do you hear?"

"Yes, Pappy. Yes, Pappy." Then to Willie: "Well, don't

stay long." She looked at the grapes. "You can see him a minute."

The Fallon followers were watching from behind trees and fence posts. Herbie had crawled, Indian-fashion, from the side of the Ferris plot, and was lying near the porch. In a few minutes the boys saw their leader re-appear at the door. He had overcome the hot-weather fears of Miss Frances, it seemed. He invited his comrades inside. It was not the first time his eloquence had won—nor by any means the last.

The young citizens of Westchester County advanced from their hiding places, prepared to see a buccaneer of brutish mien. Miss Frances looked at them in a bewildered way. "Why, I thought you said there was 'two or three friends', young man!"

"I guess they all wanted to come in," Willie said.

"Don't tear up nothin'," Miss Frances said, "and don't get Pappy to talkin' too much."

The boys walked falteringly through the darkened room to a chair in which sat a wispy old man. He had white hair and a keen eye. The uremic smell of age was with him, and his knee-joint crackled as he straightened his left leg.

"It's nice of you young 'uns to call," said Mr. Ferris. "If I was ninety year younger, I'd show you some of the games we played."

Willie looked at his comrades triumphantly. He nudged Herbie in the back. "I told you. A hunderd! Maybe more."

Mr. Ferris took Willie's hand. "This young 'un says you boys pitched in an' bought me some grapes. Well, now. That was mighty nice."

Willie's companions were mystified. "They was Willie's grapes," Phil said. "We just helped bring 'em."

"Well," said Mr. Ferris, "I guess that calls for a story. Want to hear a story, lads?"

Willie prompted him quickly. "Tell us about pirates."

"Wouldn't you rather hear about the time I was a secret service man against the smugglers?"

"Is it a pirate story?" Herbie asked.

"I have lotsa stories," said Mr. Ferris. "It's been a *life*, I tell you! I was borned near Tarrytown, almost in Sleepy Holler. I knew Wash Irvin' right well. Splendid man. Too bad he didn't know how to write plainer. Anyhow, I run away when I was six. I was the fifth of eight childern. I went to New York to seek my fortune and lived in a wagon. My first job was drivin' a cow to Catharine Ferry and the man give me six pence——"

Willie interrupted gently: "We'd like to hear a *pirate* story, Mr. Ferris."

"I love grapes," said Mr. Ferris. "I worked in Hibbard's tailor shop, and he was always kind to me. Why, I was eatin' some grapes the very day I shipped on a slaver. They give me a purse of $100."

"Was that the time you were on the smuggler *Jane*?" Willie inquired.

Mr. Ferris called to his daughter for a glass of water. "It's too hot to talk," she said, as she handed him the tumbler. "You should ought to sleep, Pappy."

"In America," said Mr. Ferris, "the *Jane* was a peaceful ship. But in England we was outlaws. We had conflict with a British sloop-of-war, and we escaped in a mist by goin' inter a channel so narrer you could toss a ship's biscuit acrost. The sloop's 'long nine' begun to talk, but our cap'n knew the coast like a man does his pants pocket. It was a matter of seconds——"

"Then you wasn't a *real* pirate?" suggested Herbie, who was kicked in the shin by Willie.

"Lord no, young 'un! I was a freebooter. That was in 1823. Later I was a spy, and then I entered the navy. They was glad enough to get me. I had many excitin' adventures."

"But you were saying," Willie prompted, "well, about the sloop's 'long nine'?"

"It slips my mind a bit. But I recollect the hunt for the West Indian pirates. Originally they was privateers. We had a song: 'The privateers all has big ears, and they wear leather britches' . . . but the song ain't fit for young ears. Anywise, they was men who preyed on American commerce durin' the war of 1812."

"He's probably a hunderd and twenty, if he's a day," Willie whispered to Herbie.

Mr. Ferris took another sip of water. "It was in their blood. They'd become bloodthirsty. The U. S. took means to suppress 'em. Vessels had been attackted by the score. The crews was all slashed to pieces, strong boxes was rifled, and many the ship that come back laden with corpses, and with blood on the bulwarks. I was with Cap'n Davy Porter in 1823, when he was give a fleet and told to clean 'em out. We had in our command five barges, with twenty oars each, to navergate the shaller bays of the West Indies. I was on the *Greyhound*, Leftenant Kearny commandin'. She was sent with the *Beagle* to scour the coasts of Cuba and Santo Domingo."

"There *are* real pirates in this story, aren't there?" Willie asked.

The aged host smiled patronizingly. "Just wait! It's a story of blood-lettin' and no quarter, lad, except in the case of the lady. I'm a-comin' to her in the proper place. Well, lads, off Cape Cruz, boats was seed drawn up on the beach. A landin' party was ordered to investergate. The pirates—for it *was* the famous band of privateers—fired on our dories. At 3 o'clock the follerin' mornin', a party of thirty went ashore to attackt the pirates. And who do you guess was in charge?"

"*You* were," said Willie, fearful because of Mr. Ferris' recent declaration that he was *not* a pirate, and anxious to rebuild the hero.

"Ah, lad, it was someone far greater. Think of it! We was led by David Glasgow Farragut, later the greatest admiral the world ever seed."

"Not greater than Admiral Dewey," said Herbie.

Mr. Ferris jiggered his false teeth with his tongue. "David Glasgow Farragut was the *greatest* admiral the world ever seed. Nelson was next. Drake was the third best. . . . Well, lads, this was the great Farragut's first famous action. We was hours makin' our way through thick underbrush. We was exhausted—that is, all the party was tuckered out except me and Farragut."

The narrator gazed at Herbie warningly. "Presently we come upon the pirate stronghold. It was a series of long, low buildin's adjoinin' some huge caves. 'Why,' says Farragut to me, says he, 'a handful of men could hold an army in check here.' Then he says: 'Bill, what ought we to do?' 'Advance,' I says, says I, 'and remember, we are *Americans!*' 'My sentiments,' says Farragut. We charged with a cheer. The cut-throats was on a hill. They had a four-pounder and two swivel guns. Things looked bad for us, but right then the *Greyhound* and the *Beagle* opened fire. The double attackt stumped the pirates."

Herbie couldn't stay silent. "Wasn't Admiral Dewey there at *all?*" he asked. "Not even a lieutenant?"

Mr. Ferris again had recourse to the water tumbler. "My boy, Admiral Dewey wasn't even borned in 1823. And if he had of been borned and growed a thousand times over, he wouldn't of been chose to go with *that* landin' party. . . . Well, as I was sayin', we begun a desperate hand-to-hand fight, with cutlass, knife and clubbed musket."

"Any swords?" Herbie asked.

"I had *two* swords," Mr. Ferris said. "I had a dirk, too, which I carried in my teeth. . . . Right in the middle of all the shoutin', shootin' and the cuttin', who should show up but the head pirate's *wife!* 'Here's a pretty kettle of fish,' I says to Farragut, who was kneelin' on a big pirate's chest, cuttin' open his throat. The woman, who was a giantess and very bloodthirsty, had a Malay *kris*. She lept for Farragut, and he barely lept up in time to escape the mortal thrust. As she lunged past, the brave Farragut had a chanct to stab her in the back. He shook his head and then winked at me.

" 'Bill,' he says, says he, and I can remember it like it was only yesterday. 'Bill,' he says, sort of bowin', 'she's a *lady*.' I never seed such gallantry, although I've been in the Russian court and drunk mare's milk while a prisoner amongst the Tartars. Well, the woman—who really was the leader of the pirates—attackted six men, clawin' and slashin' 'em with her *kris*. She yelled to her ten childern to run further up the hill and light signal fires to warn other pirates inland. Finally Farragut got mad at her and tripped her up. It took three men to hold her. A bo'sun named Dorsey wanted to bash in her head with a musket-butt, but Farragut stayed his hand, again winkin' at me and bowin'. 'No,' Farragut says, says he, 'She's a *lady*.'"

"Well," said Herbie, "who won the fight?"

The old man drained the tumbler. "Farragut never lost anything he started, son. Well, she was the only one of a band of ninety that we left alive or unhurt. We trussed her up while we searched the caves. We found gold and *bones*. Human bones with bits of rusty chains on 'em. Horrible tortures was evident. We captured and destroyed eight boats, and confiscated a vast quantity of stores that had been took from merchantmen. . . . Later I fought and slew the great Pirate, Diablito, 'The Little Devil.' He had a topsail schooner at Matanzas. We subdued the fiend with pistol and sword——"

"But the woman pirate?" Herbie said, "What become of her?"

Mr. Ferris wrinkled his brow as though recalling a slightly concupiscent interlude. "Oh, well, we left her there."

"Did you untie her?" asked Herbie.

"Now ain't you the persistent young 'un!" said Mr. Ferris. "Why, yes. We untied her when the brave Farragut says to me: 'You see, Bill,' and he winked and bowed, 'You see, Bill, she's a lady.' Myself, I'd been wownded in the leg."

"How bad?" asked Phil.

"They wanted to take off my leg. But I says, says I: 'I'll shoot the first man that comes near my wownded leg.' By the way, boys, I'm the oldest volunteer fireman in the State. I done a lot of work when the Stevens Match Works burned. . . ."

Miss Ferris came into the room. "Now you boys go on home. Pappy'll get all riled up."

As they mounted their bicycles, Herbie looked at Willie and said: "*Pirate*! Huh!"

"He's a pirate all right," Willie said. "He's just modest."

Chapter Four

∗

THE TORMENTS OF A LAY BROTHER

YOU shall learn at once who it was that filched the ginger
ale and chocolate cream bars from the basement shop of
Brother Hooley of the Society of Jesus. This mystery had the
huge, gaunt fellow dithering like ten St. Anthonys as he strove
to balance stock-in-hand with his counter-sales to students of
Fordham University. In fact, he writhed inside his dull, black
cassock until a rumor persisted that Brother Hooley had adopted
a monkish hair-shirt.

The marauder was William J. Fallon, freshman at Fordham,
sergeant of Company B of the Cadet Battalion, and sacristan of
the Parthenian Sodality. It took Brother Hooley five months or
more to make deductions; but work as he did, the best he ever
got was circumstantial evidence. By the time this tall Brother,
of church-candle complexion and ink-well eyes, formed his
conclusions, he was qualified for a position with Scotland Yard.

There are—says Paracelsus—three ways of getting pleasure
of life. One is by eating. Another, by drinking. A third . . .
but so many books are being written about the *third* method that
I shall not even mention it at this time. [Later perhaps]. Master
Fallon, now sixteen, and growing like a bamboo shoot—and
being full of the devil, despite a face of disarming sweetness—
found his happiness in victuals.

Willie Fallon had the most capacious stomach that the Jesuit
Fathers of Fordham had encountered since the graduation of

33

Mr. T. B. Connery of the Class of 1853. It is history that Mr. Connery's mother asked Father Murphy, a man of some merriment, concerning the composition of meals for her ravenous laddie.

The Reverend Father squinted through steel-rimmed spectacles. "Madame," he replied, "we feed them like *princes*. Potatoes and molasses for breakfast; molasses and potatoes for dinner, and *both* for supper. What more could be desired?"

Mr. Connery, who always wore nankeen trousers and was nicknamed "Yellow Breeches," held the all-time eating championship of Fordham until Willie Fallon began to shatter records more than half a century after. Whereas Mr. Connery secreted contraband articles in green-painted boxes of the play-room, Mr. Fallon used the gymnasium. Willie also hit upon the safer plan of dividing his loot, hiding some of it in unused lockers.

Only one thing interfered with Willie's thorough indulgence in stolen delicacies, and that was his abnormal generosity. He was the sort that couldn't say "no" to any charitable plea. Consequently, he gave away so many of his good things that it was necessary that he draw again and again on Brother Hooley's stock. The enormity of Brother Hooley's losses became common scandal.

Brother Paradise, who cobbled shoes in a basement stall, was one of the first to hear of the startling rape of chocolate cream bars and ginger ale. A philosopher, he didn't raise his eyes from the shoe that was on an iron last between his knees. He merely made his awl-holes, plucked pegs from his thin little mouth, grunted and tap-tapped on a half-sole belonging to Loring M. Black (later a Congressman, and a good one, too).

It may be that Brother Paradise knew all the while *who* had broken into Brother Hooley's treasure-chests. It is known that Brother Paradise had been seen of late pulling wisely at ginger-ale bottles and nibbling on chocolate cream bars (when his mouth was unoccupied by brads). It may further be, that Brother Paradise, small and humpty-dumpty and entirely a philosopher, did not relish the daily sight of Brother Hooley, a giant and as strong as six Muldoons (no matter how pale his face or black-ringed his eyes). At any rate, Willie Fallon hob-nobbed frequently with Brother Paradise, sitting in the shoe-shop and eating until his blue eyes stuck out. Willie and Brother Paradise were *pals*.

The hugely-built lay brother of the Society of Jesus tended shop in the basement of the Second Division Building, where first- and second-year men were housed, boarded and schooled. The ginger ale (Exhibit A) was sold at five cents the bottle, with a deposit of five cents added, pending return of the bottle. (Keep the *deposit* well in mind. It is part of a remarkable example of playing both ends against the middle.) In addition to the dewy bottles of ginger pop, one could buy various refreshments of Brother Hooley, particularly the chocolate cream bars. One of these made an amazing sandwich when laid inside a Fordham bun.

Fordham buns, famous in song and story, were passed out by a trusted carrier, who fetched them in a hamper from the bake-shop and distributed them unbuttered, to resident students. The bun-hour was four o'clock in the afternoon and acted as a stomach-ballast until the evening meal. On receiving a bun—and Willie always contrived to have *butter* for his—each student hurried to Brother Hooley's shop for the chocolate filler and perhaps a bottle of ginger ale. Brother Hooley dispensed bars with a hand that would have looked at home on a pick handle. The muscular wrist usually was flecked with snuff, and, like as not, the cream bar would have on it some of the snuff intended for the lay brother's trumpet-toned nose.

The first thing that aroused Brother Hooley's wonderment was the fact that Willie Fallon seldom or never came to the shop to buy a thing. However, he *did* come there almost daily to deliver an *empty* bottle and to claim the nickel *deposit*. Being a trusting soul and utterly wrapped up in the baseball team and matters athletic, Brother Hooley was slow to form suspicions.

When it dawned on Brother Hooley that he was being robbed (and fleeced in the bargain) he changed the lock on the shop door. Still the thievery continued. Then the good Brother plugged the keyhole cleverly with wax. Morning surveys of his stock discovered continued loss, though the wax *remained intact*.

The way Willie—now reinforced by a friend named Finch—got in was this: He waited until Brother Hooley was a-bed and lights were out in the Second Division Dormitory, where Willie slept with some seventy or eighty classmates. Then he would creep downstairs, take the pins from the hinges, removing the door itself, and never *disturbing* the lock.

"Someone has been robbing Brother Hooley," said Brother Paradise between mouthfuls of shoe-nails (or was it chocolate?). "Whoever it is had better watch out, for Brother Hooley is the strongest man alive."

That same day, one of the Prefects happened by the locker-room while Willie was treating a group of pals to candy.

"My, my, Willie," said the Prefect. "You have all manner of good things. Let's look."

"Well, Father, why shouldn't I have?" asked Willie. "Look how many times I'm called to the Parlor." His face had the disarming quality of a May apple. The Prefect pursed his lips and passed on. Willie thereafter hid his booty in the hay-loft of a barn on the old Fordham Farm, north of the Second Division Building and this side of the Bronx Botanical Gardens. Irish immigrant boys, hired as farm-hands, often heard spectral groans emanating from the loft. Willie's ventriloquistic yowls insured privacy as he lay enfolded in the hay-mow, his nostrils tickled by sweet dust of the hay.

The "Parlor" was a reception room, where parents visited their boys. The parents usually brought gifts; a box of candy, a roast chicken, fruit, or the like. When anyone was "called to the Parlor," his friends waited. When the lucky fellow came back, he was besieged. Whatever the present, it soon disappeared, if at all edible, in the stomachs of students.

Willie's mother was not well. Her visits to the "Parlor" became fewer. The Prefect who had looked into Willie's locker hadn't checked on this fact. Even so, he may have liked Willie more than he did Brother Hooley. It was hard not to like him. He was all boy.

The gigantic Brother Hooley had been cudgeled by mystery for five months. His torments were interfering with thoughts of athletics. He was anxious to solve the crime before the baseball season began; to him, the doings of the Fordham team were second in importance only to his spiritual welfare.

Who was the malefactor? How did he work? On the wall, and discreetly shielded by the stalwart Brother's narrow bed, was a glossary written lightly in pencil. At first glance the traceries appeared cabalistic, smacking of an alchemist's recipes. Brother Hooley kept his *criminological reports* on this whitewashed ledger, which was wide and high enough to suit the purposes of the Recording Angel for at least a fortnight.

The wall-entries would have been incomprehensible had not Brother Hooley set down actual *names*. At least fifty names had been written, then penciled through—all except one. The names were followed by comments, dates and other rigmarole. Presumably all this had to do with persons temporarily suspected of the shop-robberies.

Brother Paradise's name appeared *four* times on the wall; and four times *stricken*. The lines that seemed to eliminate the cobbler were wavering and hesitant, unlike the swift, sharp strokes that absolved others. Also, following the shoe-mender's scratched name, were entries in Latin, like grace-notes. One of them read: "*Ne sutor ultra crepidam*" (Let not the shoemaker go beyond his last), and "*Latet anguis in herba*" (A snake lies hidden in the grass).

Eddie Glennon, now a Supreme Court Justice, was the first name struck from Brother Hooley's list. We quote the Brother's phrase, written behind Glennon's name, as an example of his prophetic ability: "Glennon is athletic, brilliant. Will make his mark." Not to give undue credit to Brother Hooley's clairvoyant powers, we add his forecast as penciled after Loring Black's name: "Industrious. Ambitious. Will make a fine physician." [Mr. Black, as the whole world knows, is a lawyer and a Congressman.] For Bobby Graham, later a high officer of the Graham-Paige Motor Company, Brother Hooley foresaw a career as an author. [God congratulate you from His golden throne, Mr. Graham! You were spared a life of pain and poverty.]

Other names crossed out were: "Danny Corcoran," "Vince Seiler," "Tommy Harding," "William J. Murray." Brother Hooley forecast that Murray would "be a priest." Mr. Murray became a corking good newspaper reporter, and is now a successful insurance man. . . . Just what the following phrases may have meant, we can but guess: "December 21, 1902," "Broken water main," "Father Campbell's Lecture on Father Jogues, martyr of the Mohawk Valley," . . . and this entry underscored *thrice*: "One o'clock a.m." There were some figures, too, presumably referring to an athletic event: "Yale 19; Fordham 4."

The one name *not* crossed from the list was that of William J. Fallon. There was no comment accompanying the name; only a question mark in parentheses "(?)."

Brother Hooley's black slouch hat was pushed far back on his puzzled skull. His eye-sockets were sink-holes of despair. His store-room again had been looted. It led one to believe that the Evil Fellow was working full tilt.

The January wind pranked with Brother Hooley's loosehanging habit, whistling impudently up the great-boned calves as his number thirteen brogans crunched the snow. He strode the elm-lined path leading from Fordham Road to the Administration Building.

Cusack, the campus policeman, said: "God and Mary to you, Brother Hooley. And it's a bitter day and all, Brother Hooley, ain't it now?"

Brother Hooley nodded gravely, shouldered the wind and said not a word. He might have put the mystery in the hands of Officer Cusack, but was mindful that the policeman never seemed to accomplish much even in good weather, except read his paper of a morning on a campus bench and then lie back and *sleep* in full view of class rooms. A man who would loll about in fair weather wouldn't be much use in foul. No: an officer called "Sleepy" Cusack by Fordham men was not the person to solve crime.

That very night Brother Hooley wrote the name "Cusack" on his wall. Then he stroked his blue chin, compressed his lips, wetted the tip of his pencil and struck out the name. He added this notation after the cancelled name: "*De mortuis nil nisi bonum.*" [Which, I am informed, is Latin for: "Say nothing but good of the dead." . . . My word! Brother Hooley!]

Brother Hooley paused in the shadow of the old chapel, from the windows of which four saints, Matthew, Mark, Luke, and John, looked down with stained-glass serenity. The Brother turned his back to the wind and arranged a spread of snuff on his right fist. He drew in the brown powder train with a determined nostril, and repeated the dose on the opposite side. Thus fortified, he hastened to the office of the Prefect of Discipline.

The Reverend Father Thomas J. Cryan, lately recovered from a severe illness, listened to the hoarse throatings of the lay brother. "It's five months now, Father, and not a trace of the burglar."

The gentle but firm Prefect raised a thin hand. "It's one of the boys. Well," and he had a reminiscent look, "I was a boy myself in these very halls. When did these pranks begin?"

Brother Hooley mumbled a little in Latin. "Pranks, Father? Did you say 'pranks'?"

The Prefect of Discipline massaged his chin. "Whom do you suspect?"

"I suspect everybody. That is, Father, I *did* suspect everyone. But my main suspicion came with a rush the night of the Glee Club Concert."

"The Christmas Concert? Yes, go on, Hooley."

"One night in November, I saw a tall, swiftly-running lad, and another, shorter boy, sneaking from the vicinity of the shop. I heard the taller boy laugh. I called out. I heard him say something. Well, on the evening of December twenty-first, one of the most warmly-received solos was rendered by Willie Fallon. Englander's 'Cavalier Song.' "

"What has that to do with the robberies?"

"Father, *crede quod habes, et habes*. It was the same voice as that of the tall lad I heard near my shop."

"Willie Fallon is a lively youth. Still, I wouldn't be too sure."

"I am moving with circumspection, Father. *Æquam servare mentem*. But I've been robbed again. Sixteen whole bottles, and a dozen chocolate bars!"

Father Cryan was fidgeting. "When did you say this started?"

"Six bottles were taken the night of September 8, last year. I remember quite well, because it was the first day of school, and also there was the water main."

The Prefect raised his sparse brows. "The water main?"

"I was being driven from the City by my sister's son. The four-foot main on High Bridge viaduct burst. The water poured down in torrents on the speedway. It's 130 feet, Father, from the bridge. I tell you, the report was terrific. The waterfall dug a fifteen-foot hole in the soft earth. The police warned pedestrians, and we took an officer to the pumping station on the west side of the Harlem River. I got home at one o'clock in the morning——"

Father Cryan was not without a mischievous strain. "Did you say 'one o'clock in the *morning*,' Brother Hooley?"

Brother Hooley cleared his throat. "We were delayed at the pumping station. *Tempus fugit*."

"And when was the next looting?"

"I can fix the date of that, also, Father."

"Another trip to the City?" asked the Father drily.

Brother Hooley hesitated. "Why, yes. It was December 7, the night we lost our first basket-ball game of the season to Yale. The score was 19 to 4. Our passing was superior, but Yale has a great reputation. I lost fourteen bottles of ginger ale that night; I don't know how many bars."

"We shall have the place watched nightly," said the priest.

"Thanks," said Brother Hooley. "Who'll watch it?"

"Officer Cusack."

Brother Hooley squirmed. "Just as you say, Father. I think he'll arrest Willie Fallon."

"He'll not arrest anyone," said the Priest. "He'll bring the malefactor to me. I'll discipline him."

Willie Fallon, coming from supper, strolled a path that Edgar Allan Poe used to take during his residence in the Fordham Country. Willie greeted Officer Cusack.

"It's cold, Officer."

"It is that, Willie, my lad."

"They shouldn't make you stay outside in weather like this."

"Ye've a kind heart, lad. I've heard it before. They say ye are eager in givin' things to the poor; that ye are an ornament to the Society of St. Vincent de Paul."

"I wish there was no poverty, Officer."

"It's plain ye are not the lad I'm for lookin' after."

"Then you're looking for someone, Officer?"

"Right ye are, Willie. And I'll catch 'im if it's the last thing I ever do. I was an ornament to the Department; that I was. It was me that kept order in Hell's Kitchen."

"Could I help, Officer?"

"There ye go agin, lad! A fine lad ye are, and kind. No; Officer Cusack looks for his own man."

"What's happened, Officer? You can tell *me*."

"Sleepy" Cusack meditated. "Yes, I can trust you. Remember. It's confidential." He whispered: "Someone's been burglarizin' Brother Hooley's store-room, and I'm to wait for the rascal. Don't even tell your old man."

"You can depend on me, Officer. Well, good luck!"

Officer Cusack beamed on Willie, who that moment decided to quit raiding Brother Hooley's store-room.

Chapter Five

THE BATTLE OF WOUNDED KNEE

ON THE second Wednesday of August, 1903, in his own Cathedral of St. Patrick, the Most Reverend John M. Farley was invested with the pallium—the insignia of his office as Archbishop of the New York See. His own clergy, and distinguished members of the hierarchy, surrounded the plump Archbishop.

Many graduates of Fordham University were in the great congregation. The Archbishop was an alumnus of the Class of 1865. Several undergraduates, among them William J. Fallon, managed to find places among seminarians in the thickly peopled nave, while the organ muttered like a low-rolling sea, and the waxy breath of candles scented the Gothic pile.

The officiating prelate was the Most Reverend Diomede Falconio, Apostolic Delegate to the United States. The Archbishop, his mitre removed, prostrated himself before the Apostolic Delegate and made the profession of faith. The Roman investor arose and lifted the pallium from its silken shield. Over the kneeling Archbishop's head, the Prelate placed the pallium—a circlet of white wool, with pendants hanging from front and back, and on each pendant an embroidered black cross. The Apostolic Delegate then pinned the pallium on the left side, back and breast of the kneeling shepherd.

The Archbishop now arose from his humble posture and administered to priests and people his first blessing as Metropolitan. The *Te Deum* closed the great ceremonial. The successor to Archbishop Corrigan seemed deeply touched. The congregation was stirred with exalted rhythms. William J. Fallon had a sudden desire to be a priest.

Mischievous though he was, he never entirely lost his pious leanings—even in Broadway nights, when the bawdy street itself seemed an altar for infidels. Fallon often drew from a photographic memory the words of the Archbishop (later Cardinal) Farley, uttered on the occasion of investiture:

> "Amid all this solemnity and grand ceremonial, I am not unmindful of one certainty. This scene will pass away like the other figures of this world, and one thing will remain; that is, that even as my predecessors were once the center of just such surroundings, they now sleep beneath this sanctuary, with their mitres on their heads and their palliums on their shoulders. So one day it shall be with him who speaks to you from their former throne. And on that day shall he be asked to give an account of his stewardship. . . ."

When in trouble, Fallon would smile his curiously sapient smile and say:

"This, too, shall pass away."

Sophomore Willie Fallon and his pal, Finch, walked arm-in-arm past Old Rose Hill Manor. They were planning a game of pool in the First Division Building. They passed pairs of conversing Jesuit Fathers—called "Jebbies" by the students. The cassocks of the reverends were raven-black against the gray campus towers.

It was October, and Indian Summer was friendly. The chapel-bell had rung the end of classes. The bouncing of hammers and the whine of dry barrow-wheels was heard from Third Division, where workmen labored at a foundation for the new hall. Captain John A. Lockwood, Professor of Military Science and Tactics, received Sergeant Fallon's salute. The Captain looked meaningly at the Sergeant's unbuttoned blouse and unshined shoes. The Captain, an appointee of Secretary of War Elihu Root, grimaced as he heard Messrs. Fallon and Finch break into song: "Down Where the Bronx River Flows."

"They'll never amount to a good God damn," the Captain muttered, giving his own natty blouse a tug.

As Fallon and Finch neared the First Division Building, they heard shouts. Behind the building, a group of students were gathered about a bloated bay horse. The animal had ambled to the campus and had been interrupted while nibbling collegiate clover. Now he was being ridden haphazardly. Mr. Fallon took immediate charge.

"Let's have a real circus," he said. "Hold his halter, Finch. I'm going to ride bareback."

"Not standing up?" marveled Finch.

"Stand back, everybody. Give me a leg up, Finch."

"You'll break your neck, Willie."

Fallon kicked off his low shoes. "I'm giving 'Brother Hooley' a ride," he said, clutching the mane and planting his soles on the horse's wide rump. "That's the name of this baby. 'Brother Hooley.'"

The students were laughing and howling. "Ride him, Willie!" "Give him some snuff!" "Ride old 'Brother Hooley'."

Attracted by the tumult, the authentic Brother Hooley took a stance behind a basement window. He watched the brazen equestrian, who was having a time of it with the dismayed horse. Brother Hooley thought it imperative to rescue his fair name, but just then a stranger in overalls appeared. The slim stranger jerked the halter from Finch's hands. Willie Fallon lost his balance and fell to the lawn.

"Who in hell do youse fellows think you are?" asked the stranger. "This hoss belongs to me. Giddap, Buck."

"Go sell him for glue," advised Finch. The stranger led his beast across the lawn. Willie Fallon recaptured his wind. "So long, Sancho Panza!"

"Damned fresh college squirt!" the stranger said. "The

damned fresh Micks! Giddap, Buck. The damned fresh flannel-mouths! Come on, Buck. Tin-roof Irish! Whoa, Buck. . . ."

Fallon and Finch made circus-bows and resumed their arm-in-arm march toward the pool game. Brother Hooley was following them at a discreet distance. The boys entered a room where two tables stood. One was a billiard table, much out of repair and seldom used. The pool table, however, was in constant demand and was being monopolized at this moment by a serious, blocky fellow named Eugene F. McGee. He was making practice shots.

McGee, an eighteen-year-old junior from Pittsfield, Mass., had been excused from football practice for the day. He had wrenched a knee. McGee was an excellent scholar. His plodding, deliberate manner concealed an adept mind, a generous nature, but a very quick temper. He had been a mighty baseball fellow, but a collision with the Pittsfield catcher left him an eye-injury that interrupted his diamond days.

Brother Hooley (who now was listening outside the door) thought a great deal of McGee. It was rumored, but never verified, that Brother Hooley once gave McGee a *two-cent-discount* on a chocolate cream bar! The Brother's heart bled when he thought of such a promising baseball man being lost to *his* team. He had a habit of saying to McGee:

"And how's the eye, my son? Do you think it'll mend in time for next spring?"

The inquiry, "How's the eye?" became a campus phrase. Fallon, in particular, used this inquiry to bait McGee. It was merely a question of time when McGee's steam-kettle temper would boil over.

Fallon watched McGee run out the balls. After the Pittsfield man cut the eight-ball into a side pocket, clearing the table, Fallon took a cue and hammered the floor with the butt.

"I'm not through yet," McGee said. "I'm practising."

"You need it," Fallon said. "But we want to play."

"Then go play marbles."

Fallon again began hammering the floor. "You've played all

afternoon," he said. "It's getting dark, and anyone from Pittsfield has got to watch his bed-time."

McGee took the fifteen balls from the gutter-trap and stood like a farmer with a lot of eggs. "Run along now, Gingerbread. And don't be such a wise guy."

"Finch, we've got to take his toys away from him."

McGee racked the balls with a battered triangle. "You're kind of dumb, Fallon. I hear you got forty in French. Well, don't be dumb enough to start anything with me."

"McGee," said Fallon, "how's the eye today?"

McGee addressed his cue-ball, preparing to break. "The eye's not good enough to see a dizzy red-head like you."

Fallon was standing behind McGee. The Pittsfield man began a stroke. It never was finished. Fallon grasped the handle of McGee's cue, jerking it as McGee tried to shoot.

"I wouldn't try *that* again, Brick-Top, if I was you."

McGee crouched once more above the patched green table. Fallon never did know when he was well off; he did the sinister cue-grabbing act over again.

McGee's face was white. "Too bad I'm older than you, and heavier, Fallon. . . ."

Fallon made goat-noises. "Look at Sandow! He bites freight-trains in two."

McGee put down his cue and braced his hips against the table-rail. "Fallon," he said, with a sad sort of rage, "I'm not a bully, so I'm going to lick you *both!*"

Fallon got on one side of McGee and signaled Finch to cover him on the other flank. "When you and I were young-g-g-g, McGee-e-e-e-e-e," sang Mr. Fallon, with more goat-like sounds. McGee lunged at Willie, who turned tail and simulated hasty retreat. Mr. Finch, thoroughly conversant with his friend's manner of thinking and acting, received a signal and promptly booted Mr. McGee in the turned part.

It was the beginning of what Mr. Fallon later described as "The Battle of Wounded Knee."

"*So!*" roared McGee, wheeling on Finch. "Kicks, eh?"

Fallon answered for his partner. "Kicks is right." Whereupon, and with McGee charging on Finch, Willie began kicking goals on the McGee hip-posts with vigor and precision. McGee hurled himself against one and then the other, like a worried bull. His wrenched knee handicapped him, and Brother Hooley, now peering through a crack of the door, was wondering if he hadn't better rescue his favorite.

But McGee was a student who weighed matters. He finally assimilated an overdose of Finch's kicks just to concentrate on Fallon. He worked Willie into a corner. Then he turned promptly and seized Finch's foot at a moment when it was revisiting a now-inflamed cushion. He used a leg-drag and hauled Finch into the same *cul de sac* with Fallon.

Brother Hooley risked opening the door a bit wider. Either he was about to sneeze, or his expression denoted high good humor. One could never tell whether his grimaces were caused by snuff or emotion.

"Kicked me, eh?" asked McGee, as he began to administer the finest lacing ever seen short of a wharf-front.

"Ugh!" said Fallon, as he caught a right first in the stomach. "Ugh!" he repeated, having all but swallowed five knuckle-bones of a left hand.

"Wow!" howled Finch, catching a left-uppercut and a juicy, overhand left-jolt in the eye.

"Want to know how my eye is, eh?" said McGee. "Well, here's how it is!" He sent a fist into Mr. Fallon's right peeper, which began to rise like a popover in a baker's oven. "The eye's just fine, thanks."

There were knock-downs and slip-ups, grunts and heavy breathing. Finch stooped over, as though looking for a lost jaw. He got a rabbit-blow on his neck and went to the floor. He tried to get up but his legs had loose hinges. Fallon endeavored vainly to ward off the practiced jolts. He got in a few taps on his own score, but McGee was as tough as hickory. He hoped Fallon would quit, but Fallon didn't. He stood there, drunk with punches, smiling like a fool and mumbling things about McGee's eye.

Brother Hooley now entered the room to *stop* the fight. He was strangely slow, however; halting beside a bench to see if his cassock had caught on a nail. McGee, convinced he had done a good job, said: "Why don't you admit you've had enough?"

"Come on and fight," mumbled Fallon. "Come on and fight."

McGee dropped his hands. "You're dumber than I thought." Then he saw Brother Hooley and turned red.

Brother Hooley cried out: "You'll get short bounds for this!" He referred to the penalty of confinement to campus limits for breaches of discipline.

McGee spoke up: "I started it, Brother Hooley. It's my fault."

Brother Hooley staggered with astonishment. "It looked as though you were decidedly in the right, Eugene." He quickly amended his words. "Of course, I can't approve of *fighting*."

McGee mumbled something, recalling a tradition that Brother Hooley, in the year 1898, and while coming home from Pain's Pyrotechnics at Manhattan Beach, had been set upon by three thugs. The story had it that the Brother knocked down and *sat* on one thug, then held the two others by the necks, banging their heads together until after the arrival of an ambulance.

"I'm sorry," said McGee, "but I lost my head."

Brother Hooley fixed himself a spread of snuff. Then he went dubiously towards the door. "You understand," he said, pausing at the threshold, *"if I had seen this fight,* it would be my bounden duty to report you." Then he added: "By the way, Eugene, how's the eye coming along?"

Brother Hooley fancied he heard a suppressed titter. He glared at Willie and went out. Fallon and Finch, dusting themselves, decided definitely that they did not want to play pool. Willie held his hand to McGee. "We're sorry," he said.

McGee took Fallon's hand. "Then you're not sore?"

"We had it coming to us," Fallon said. "Why did you take the blame?"

McGee fidgeted. "You better go ahead and use the table."

"No. Some other time. Won't you tell us why you took the blame?"

"Aw, that's all right. Hooley doesn't like you, and anyway, you were damned game. I liked the way you took it."

"Thanks, Gene," Fallon said. "Thanks a lot. And now I'd like to ask you a question, a personal one, if you wouldn't mind."

"Go ahead. Who's stopping you?"

"Maybe I'd better not ask it."

"Go ahead. What in hell is it, anyway?"

"You're sure you won't take it the wrong way?"

"For God's sake! What's eating on you?"

Willie's face was serious. "Well, then," and he edged toward the door, "how's the old eye?"

McGee began laughing. "All right, sap," he said, "I'll never get sore at you again."

In some manner, news of the fight leaked out and Willie was nicknamed "Sap" Fallon.

Chapter Six

*

MR. FALLON'S HORN OF PLENTY

DECEMBER snow was falling on the Fordham country, where Poe once had walked with priests, listening to monastic bells. Junior Willie Fallon sat in Brother Paradise's cobbling-stall, chewing beeswax and reading Lord Byron's *Manfred*. Fallon was becoming more and more popular with his classmates and was described by his preceptors as "alert" and "nimble." He was secretary of the Parthenian Sodality, treasurer of the St. Vincent de Paul Society; secretary of the St. John's Dramatic Association; second tenor of the glee club, member of the board of editors of The *Fordham Monthly*, and first lieutenant of Company A of the cadet battalion.

Brother Paradise scruffed a worn knife-blade against emery paper. He traced a "D" with the knife on an ox-hide scrap, and began paring a heel-tap for the Reverend President Collins' boot.

"My shoes," he said, "have taken people tens of thousands of miles. I sit here always, but my shoes travel like a hundred Marco Polos."

Willie pocketed his Byron and looked out the small basement window. "The refectory food is getting worse and worse. How few *fat* students there are!"

Brother Paradise gave his paring knife a few more swipes on the emery paper. "I can read a man's character by his shoes. When Father Pettit was President, I took special care of his shoes. His heels *never* ran over. They seemed holy to me; just like he was. He always worried whether the boys had their long underwear on in weather like this. Remember?"

Willie rubbed the window-pane and peered through the sleek patch. "I never saw *that* before in all the time I've been here."

Brother Paradise had pegged on the tap and was looking for his rasp. "What you talking about, Willie?"

Willie was pointing to a door that abutted the window, outside. The door was the size of a dog-kennel front. It had a rusty hasp and no lock. A weathered peg was thrust like a mummy's finger through the staple.

"That *door*," Willie said. "Where does it lead to?"

Brother Paradise turned up his alcohol lamp and put an edging-iron on the chimney-rest. "I don't know where it leads to, unless it's the steam pipes between this building and First Division." Brother Paradise ran his hand inside the Reverend President's shoe and found a sharp nail. "So," he said, half to himself, "*that's* why the Reverend President's sermon last Sunday was so sad!"

"No, sir," Willie said, "I never did see *that* door. Funny."

Brother Paradise worked with peg-nippers inside the shoe. Then he slipped a last into the boot and hammered like Vulcan. "I'm going to give him some new laces," he said, "waxed ones. Father Collins has *character*."

"Have you got such a thing as a screw-driver, Brother Paradise?"

"What in the world, Willie? Look in that box; underneath the cement bottle. . . . Well, it will be a great celebration to-morrow. The fiftieth anniversary of the promulgation of the dogma of Immaculate Conception. I was four years old. They say you're to sing the *Ave Maria*, Willie. It's a sweet voice you have."

"There must be a tunnel behind that door," Willie said.

Brother Paradise sighed as he picked up a huge shoe. "I wish Brother Hooley would take his work somewhere else. I'm not saying he is slew-footed, but it takes a lot of material and all kinds of work. And for the same price as another man's half-sole. Look how *run over* the heels are. I can read character, all right."

The cobbler lifted a palmful of pegs. He mouthed the brads like a self-healer taking kidney pills. Willie found the screw-driver and one or two other utensils. He went to the dormitory and sought out the bed of a sophomore, whom it is expedient to call Felix Rasmussen.

[Inasmuch as Felix now is a politican of prominence, it would be a slur on the intelligence of a great electorate to reveal the actual name of one, who, during his Fordham struggles, was as dumb as sixteen Cape Cod oysters.]

Willie Fallon tinkered with Felix's shaky iron bed, as carefully as though it were a rare clock. When he had finished, every screw, nut and bolt was hanging by a hint. The springs were held by something less than a hint—a bare inference of side-bar holding desperately to a slight intimation of rail-rest. And now Willie produced a spool of stout linen thread.

(Brother Paradise this very moment was looking, high, low, and damn-the-luck, for his beeswax-thread.)

Willie made clever nooses, twists, running-knots, loops, cables, tie-'em-ups and hang-me-high-Harrys, until it looked as though a delirious spider had been spinning out his frenzy on bed-post, flange, and bolt-head. Finally Willie attached each strand to a "master" cable of several thread-twists. He coiled this and stowed it for future reference beneath Felix Rasmussen's perilous mattress.

Willie left the dormitory at lunch-time, and as he strolled to the refectory, he could be seen conferring with Finch and other cronies. Boys trooped in noisily from the campus. Several religiously inclined fellows came from a chapel, across the hall, where the more pious ones said prayers before and after meals.

Hardly was the soup finished when Willie tapped a spoon against his tureen. It was a signal. Soon there was a bedlam of plate-rappings. The ring-leaders, followed by students, left the table and assembled on the campus.

Mounting a workman's truck, Willie Fallon gyrated and began to speak: "My comrades, our stomachs have revolted. Shall we stand this treatment? As the immortal Patrick Henry said, shall we lie supinely on our backs while our masters, the Jebbies, pass out slum-gullion in small doses? Are you mice, or are you men?"

There were cries of "Tell 'em, Willie!" "Irishmen never will be slaves!"

Black-robed preceptors, roused from their viands, ran to windows and doors. "Mr. Finch," Willie said, "will you please lead us with a 'Ram'?"

The "Ram," forever a notable college yell, was given with fervor. Instead of the last line, however, which is: "Team! Team! Team!" the word, "Food!" was substituted, giving the affair an atmosphere of the French Revolution. The "Ram," as led by Mr. Finch, went in this fashion:

> "Ram! Ram! Ram!
> F-O-R-D-H-A-M.
> Fordham! Fordham!
> Food! Food! Food!"

Hardly had the "Ram" been finished, than Finch pulled at Fallon's coat-tail. "Nix, Willie! Brother *Hooley!*"

The cadaverous-faced Brother Hooley was advancing with giraffe-like strides, holding his habit above knotty knees to give his legs more freedom. His voice thundered like that of a hoarse Zeus. "Stop it! Stop it! Get down from that truck, Willie Fallon! To your quarters, ye unthankful lads! *Verbum sat sapienti.*"

Although he had no official right to order the boys anywhere, except from his shop, Brother Hooley had great influence on Fordham men. Wasn't he a *part* of Fordham? What would the college be *without* him? Anyway, his intentions were eminently noble. He wished to break up the revolt before the new prefect of discipline, the Reverend Father Brook, S.J., took action. Why? There were six promising *baseball players*, including Jack Coffey, the crack infielder, among the rioters. Had there been no *baseball* men. . . . *Fiat justitia, ruat cælum.*

Willie Fallon, the suddenly deserted Spartacus, stood alone on the truck, his arms folded across his inflated chest, a stance that was to become famous in courtrooms of New York. His shock of apricot hair moved like a flame in the wind.

"Scat, you mischief-maker!" said Brother Hooley.

Willie faced the good lay brother calmly. "I represent a principle."

Brother Hooley uttered several phrases in Gaelic and two in Ciceronian Latin. Then: "You'll be representing a warmed hindend in a minute. Get down!"

Willie always grew rhetorical in a crisis. "I'll never get down, were the earth to open under me."

The gigantic man leaped with amazing agility to the bed of the truck. "Ye won't, eh?" He lifted Willie as though he were a midget. He carried him to the ground. He shoved him ahead with a powerful grip at the collar; in fact, it was the "bum's rush." (*Hobo ejectus.*)

"And no more foolishness from ye," said Brother Hooley.

Willie was called before the Prefect of Discipline and given "short bounds" for a month. Inasmuch as the Prefect was busy with arrangements for next day's Jubilee, and seeing that Willie was to sing the *Ave Maria*, the sentence was suspended.

The dormitory Prefect snoozed in an alcove, separated from the big sleeping-room by dull mulberry portières. Hardly had he drawn his curtains, undressed, and begun to read Thomas à Kempis, when a smashing of crockery and splashing of water brought him back to a material world. Then he heard Willie Fallon's voice: "I'm sorry."

The Prefect, a young and vigorous man, poked his head

through the curtains. Fallon and Felix Rasmussen presented a tableau in the ambulatory between rows of simple iron beds. They had met quite unfortunately (for Rasmussen) while Felix was returning from the water-tap with a full pitcher for his night-stand. Willie had been on his way to the tap with an empty pitcher. Somehow, and while swinging his pitcher gaily, Willie had struck the brimming vessel of Felix Rasmussen. Felix, wetted from the hips down, stood dumbly, a stone-ware handle still gripped; the rest of the vessel in fragments on the puddled floor.

"Yah big fool, yah!" Mr. Rasmussen was saying.

"And the waters covered the face of the earth," said Mr. Fallon.

"Yah big fool!"

"Be more careful boys," the Prefect said, withdrawing his head and closing the curtains with a rattle of brass rings.

Lights were out and the Prefect had put aside his book. He was snoring now, perhaps dreaming of a promised visit to Rome. A rattling, rolling, peppering sound roused the holy young man. He got up, mumbled, felt for his light-switch and looked out. His bare foot protruded from the curtain hem. He felt small, pebble-like objects as he explored with a naked bunion. He reached down and picked up a few BB shots.

The Prefect was of a patient turn of mind. "That's enough for tonight, boys," he said. "Now go to sleep like Christian gentlemen."

Hardly had he re-entered his ecclesiastical slumbers, when another and louder racket dinned through the Prefect's dreams. Willie Fallon, employing his well-known "clear-the-throat-signal," had given the "office" for several conspirators to roll heavy, octagonal salt-cellars, filched from table, across the floor and towards Felix Rasmussen's bed.

The Prefect [and I trust he is now Bishop, for his patience] again thrust his head through the curtains. "Boys," he said, "I warn you once more. It's a cold night; one more breach of discipline, and we'll go to the study room, and *without* heat. Now good-night, like good Christian gentlemen."

On thinking things over, the Prefect slippered himself, drew on his habit, snapped on the lights and went to Willie Fallon's bed. Willie was breathing rhythmically. There was a look of such innate sweetness on his ruddy face that the Prefect leaned over, the better to glimpse the lad who was to sing the *Ave Maria*.

The beloved rogue stirred, opened his blue eyes wonderingly, yawned and sighed. "Is that you, Father?"

"Yes, my son," said the Prefect, who shook his head and pattered back to his alcove.

The Prefect once again was in his dreams. In fact, he reported to the Reverend President next day that he had been dreaming of attending mass at the historic church of *San Pietro in Vincoli*, where the self-same chains that pinioned the wrists of St. Peter are exposed to venerating gaze, and where the tremendous Moses of Michelangelo sits in horned grandeur.

The linen cable that Willie Fallon had coiled and hidden beneath Felix Rasmussen's mattress, and which now was stretched between the bed of the future "People's Choice" and that of the destined leader of New York's criminal bar, was put into play. There was a preliminary tug, and no result. Willie gave another, more emphatic yank. There was a groaning of metal parts, a grinding of springs and a devastating collapse of strut, girder, and beam. And then a horrified shout from the wreckage.

The Prefect sprang from his sleep. It is said that it was the longest leap since the day of the Seven-League-Boots—the Prefect coming in one bound from the outskirts of the Eternal City to Fordham Campus. The Prefect—according to his conversation with the Reverend President—first suffered an illusion that all the churches of Rome had fallen; then awakened to a belief that five New York Central locomotives were fighting for the honor of getting into bed with him.

Willie worked desperately to get rid of the tell-tale threads. He pitched the "master" cable from the window, but that was all. He crawled hastily under his blankets. The Prefect dressed and turned on the lights. The good man at first believed that faulty construction and long usage of the Rasmussen bed had caused the cataclysm. Then he discovered cunning threads attached to screws, posts and bolts.

"I think somebody done this to me," Felix said.

The Prefect was not a man to lose his head. "Get up, all," said he. "We're going to the study room."

The boys marched into the cold hall, there to remain until 2 o'clock in the morning, their heads nodding above Latin texts.

Willie Fallon approached the Prefect, whispering: "If you please, Father," he said, "I've got to sing the *Ave Maria*. I don't want to catch cold in the throat."

The Prefect studied for a time. "You may go back to bed. But the rest of these scallywags will stay right here and suffer."

The new Grecian auditorium was not yet completed, so the Jubilee Celebration was held in the Armory. At 9 o'clock in the morning, the Reverend Father John J. Collins, S.J., President of Fordham, officiated at high mass. The Reverend Father John C. Harmon, S.J., was deacon, and Mr. Coveney, sub-deacon.

The three divisions of the University put the refectory in holiday garb. They decorated with flowers the statue of the Blessed Virgin in the hall. Blue and white bunting was festooned above the dining tables. The college orchestra played, and even Willie Fallon had no complaint to make of the dinner in honor of the Golden Jubilee of Promulgation of the Bull of Immaculate Conception. Ox-joint soup, celery, olives, gherkins, prime roast of beef, Vermont turkey, cranberry sauce, potatoes *au gratin*, Brussels sprouts, French peas, cold smoked beef, jellied tongue, Nesselrode pudding, angel cake, nuts, figs, raisins, assorted fruits, bonbons, cheese, toasted crackers, coffee. . . . Willie Fallon belched and lay back.

Willie said to his friend, John Barry: "Now *this* is more like it."

At half past 4 o'clock, the Armory Hall was crowded. The Prefect of Studies, Father Martin Hollahan, S.J., was in charge of the program, and the Prefect of Discipline supervised the arrangements. The College orchestra played an overture, "Beyond the Gates of Paradise," and then Willie Fallon sang the invocation, Gounod's *Ave Maria*. Even Brother Hooley had a tear in his eye. Edmund J. O'Connor gave a discourse on the Parthenian Sodality, and John W. Clancy recited a poem, "She Shall Crush Thy Head." After the entertainment, the Reverend President addressed his boys, commending them for their loyalty to the Mother of God.

The door near Brother Paradise's cobbling-stall kept worrying Willie Fallon. He took Finch into his confidence. They went together one dark January night of the year 1904 to investigate. Willie had candles and matches.

They removed the peg from the staple. The door moaned as Willie dragged it open. The air inside was warm and caressing. Willie lighted a candle and handed it to Finch.

"Keep the light inside," he said. "We don't want to be interrupted."

He lighted another candle and they looked. They were inside a low tunnel. Overhead and along the walls were steam pipes. The bare ground was damp and musty. The atmosphere was close and mystifying.

"Where does this lead to?" asked Finch.

"It must lead somewhere," Willie said. "Now crawl behind me, and don't burn yourself."

They progressed slowly along a straight line. They paused once beneath a shaft that seemed to lead to the surface. Willie held his light aloft and saw the underside of a man-hole cover. He made a mental note of this, and they crawled on. After fifteen minutes of laborious wriggling, they came to another door, larger than that which had been their entry.

"What's this?" Finch asked.

"Only the gods know," Willie said. He pushed the door.

It yielded. He pushed again and the door swung open and away from him. "Come on, Finch. More light. I've found something."

The boys went through the door. They were on a board floor and in a closet-like chamber. Willie bubbled with rapture. He saw shelves with cans and jars stacked. On the floor were boxes containing all manner of good things. There were cakes, cookies, crackers, jams, dried fruit, and sardines. Beneath a bell-jar there was a cut cheese.

"Let's eat," Finch said.

"No, Finch. Not now." Willie took a key-ring from his pocket and indicated a Yale-lock key. "Take this and go to my locker. Bring back my tennis pants. Be sure the belt is with it."

"It's a long way back, Willie."

"Do as I say, Finch. And hurry. The gods are kind to us tonight."

While Finch was gone, Willie made an invoice of the stock. It was easy to see that he was in the store-room of the faculty. He opened a can of sardines and beamed as he ate oily little fish on crisp crackers. He saw a rat trap, baited with cheese. His prankish nature led him to do an ill-advised thing. He carefully held the trap-spring, took the cheese morsel from the trigger-tray, and put in its place a plump sardine. Finch finally returned with the trousers.

"You hold the pants," Willie said. He tied each leg snugly. "Hold 'em right-side-up, Finch."

Willie began to choose with great care the things he wished to carry in his tennis-pants. The legs stuck out like saddle bags as Willie packed them scientifically. When the improvised duffle-bag could hold no more, Willie tied the top with the belt.

He got on his hands and knees. "You lead the way with a candle, Finch. Be sure the door is closed behind us. I'll crawl with the pants on my back."

The return was laborious. The dummy horseman that strad-dled Willie's back had a way of wedging him against the hot, low pipes of the tunnel. When they came again into the crisp night air, they were sweaty, dirty, but entirely happy. Willie and Finch took their "dummy" to the gymnasium, where Willie stored the loot in an unused locker.

They lived on the fat of the land for a week, but Fallon's free-handed ways again got the better of him. Finch remonstrated, pointing out that discovery was sure to follow if Willie persisted in distributing gifts to so many cronies. Another thing, too, the Jebbie who had baited the rat-trap noticed strange gaps among the neatly stacked cans and jars. He said little about it, however, because of an experience that led him to question his own mental well-being. Indeed, he applied to the Reverend President for a leave of absence the day he found the rat-trap *baited with a sardine.*

"Must you have leave at this time?" the Reverend President asked.

"I think it best, Father," the custodian of the store-room said.

"And may I ask why?"

"I am afraid I have overworked," the good man replied. "I have done one or two *absent-minded* things of late."

"You may go into retreat for a week," said the Reverend President, after hearing about the strange rat-bait. The President of Fordham then was heard to mutter: "For catching cats, yes. For catching rats, *decidedly no.*"

"Dummy" Rasmussen participated in the contents of the Fallon tennis pants, which, as may be assumed, were filled on an average of once each week. But Fallon would not disclose the source of the booty.

"This is my horn of plenty," he would say, patting the tennis pants. "Never you mind, Rasmussen, *how* things happen. Be grateful that they *do* happen."

Rasmussen and three others decided to do some sleuthing. One night, when Fallon and Finch were creeping back from the store-room, and with the headless horsemen astride Willie's back, there was an *impasse* at that part of the tunnel beneath the man-hole.

Finch's lighted face met Felix Rasmussen's lighted face. They looked at each other mutely.

Willie broke the silence: "Give way there, Rasmussen. Back up. We got a load."

"I'll not back up," Felix said. "You've got to back up yourself."

"Rasmussen," said Fallon, "if you ever amount to anything, it won't be because of your brains. Now back up and let us out."

Felix was stubborn. Fallon, sweating and cramped and ridden into the ground by his headless horseman, now launched a plea as eloquent and as stirring as any he was destined to make before twelve men in a jury box. He piled up, point on point, the law of priority, the law of possession, the law of discovery. He called on "Dummy" Rasmussen's manhood, his sense of fair play, his appetite, and his chance of success in the world beyond this vale. Then he painted such glowing pictures of the treasures that lay concealed in the store-room that Rasmussen's salivary glands began to spout like geysers.

"Eye hath not seen, and ear hath not heard the wonders that await you there," said Willie. "Back up, Rasmussen, my good fellow, and there'll be *twice* the room, and *half* the interference, for *you* and your men."

Swayed by Fallon's eloquence, Rasmussen finally consented to the retreat. Fallon and Finch went to their basement hide-out. They were upset concerning Rasmussen's discovery.

"He'll be sure to get the wrong things," Willie said. "He'll bring back a load of dried herrings and cans of tomatoes."

"Too bad we had to let him in," Finch said.

Willie had a mouthful of crackers and jam. "I fear the worst."

Rasmussen's technique was faulty, in that he made larger hauls than Fallon, and gave away less to hungry colleagues. It was inevitable that the Jebbies find they were being robbed. They placed the mystery in the hands of Officer Cusack. He deduced in a week that the avenue of robbery was by the tunnel. He took up a night-watch at the man-hole cover.

Fallon saw Sleepy Cusack on night-duty and sensed that all was not well. He gained Cusack's confidence. "It's a hell of a whopping big robbery," the officer said.

"But they can't fool *you*," said Willie.

"And remember, Willie," said the officer, "don't breathe a word of this to anyone."

"The thief is as good as caught," said Willie.

"I know, my boy, but it's a whopping case. It already has drove one Jebbie off his nut until he tried to catch a mouse with a sardine."

"You don't tell me!" said Willie.

The officer crossed himself. "May the saints preserve us."

Willie and Finch held a conference. It was plain they should quit operations immediately. But Rasmussen? Finch was for letting him go unwarned, but Willie said No. He sought Rasmussen: "You ought to quit going to the store-room for a while."

"Oh," said Rasmussen, "you want it all to yourselves, eh?"

"That's not it. They're getting ready to catch us."

"I don't believe a word. You're too full of tricks."

"Well," said Fallon, "I'm warning you. If you get caught, you'd better keep shut about anyone else being in it. See?"

One night in February, Officer Cusack thought he heard voices beneath his feet. He leaned close to the manhole cover. He heard the voices, but couldn't make out the words. He ran to the door beside Brother Paradise's window and shut it. He found a stout twig and thrust it through the staple. Next he went to the First Division Building, descended to the basement store-room, went inside and piled full boxes of canned goods against it, bracing them so that the door could not be opened with anything less than a ram.

The officer beamed as he returned to the outside tunnel door. He heard the voices again. Then the sound of someone trying to open the door. Then silence. Then more vocals; a conversation. "What in the devil?" "It's locked, I tell you!" "Well, try it again." "Kick it!" "Should we go back?"

The officer went for the Prefect of Discipline. He escorted the Prefect to the door. Officer Cusack now pulled out the twig. He flashed his bullseye inside. He saw the gaping face of Felix Rasmussen, and behind him three other lads.

"Come out, ye robbin', desp'rate laddies!" he said.

The Prefect looked sternly at the boys. "Come to my office."

There was a general confession. The followers of Felix refused to implicate anyone else. Felix informed on Willie Fallon. Officer Cusack rallied to the defense.

"It's bosh he's talkin', Father. Don't believe a word of it. There nivver was a more kindly lad in the world than this same Willie Fallon. It's bosh, I tell you."

The Prefect sent for Willie. "Is it true that you are involved in this?" he asked.

"Yes, Father," said Willie. "I planned the whole thing."

Felix Rasmussen turned red. His better side appeared. "He's no more to blame than me, Father."

The Prefect said: "This is very serious. It calls for drastic punishment. However, you both have made a clean confession. I shall put you on probation. Let me see by your future conduct and your marks that you have decided to be real Fordham men."

From that time on, Willie Fallon's rise was sensational. Various reasons were assigned for this change. The fact that in his junior year he underwent oral tests instead of so many written examinations, may have been one reason. He proved himself best when on his feet; meeting rapid-fire questions that necessitated shrewd and quick thinking. He had a phenomenal memory, which cut down his hours of study and permitted his reading an enormous number of books.

It was the Rev. Father Mahoney (pronounced *Mä'honey*) who really discovered Fallon's latent talents and predicted for him a brilliant future in the law. The good Father, one of the foremost educators in America, was watching the annual St. Patrick's Day game between Fordham's Spanish and Irish students, when he heard Willie spouting philosophy to a group of cronies.

At the close of his extemporaneous oration, Willie said: "And when I am ordained a priest, I shall be broad-minded and liberal."

Father Mahoney later told Willie: "I think you should go to law school after your graduation."

Eugene McGee took Fallon aside one evening, after hymns had been sung and speeches made before the campus statue of the Virgin. It was during the historic May Devotions.

"Bill," said McGee, "I have only one more year. I go to law school next. Why don't you fix your eye on the law?"

"I can't make up my mind. Sometimes I think I'll take orders."

McGee grunted. "You'd make a hell of a priest!"

"You mean I'm not good enough?"

"I guess you're moral. At least they say you don't smoke, drink, swear, or chase women."

"No, not that I want any credit."

"I don't know, Willie. But I think a priest couldn't be so hellishingly full of mischief as you. Anyhow, you'd be better off as a lawyer."

"I'd sort of like to be an actor."

"Why not something substantial?"

"Shakespearean actors are substantial."

"And poor as hell. You ought to go in for the law."

"I don't think I'd make a go of it."

"I think you would, and later on, I'd like to have you for a partner."

"You don't mean that, Gene?"

"I think we could make a go of it. I've had my mind on it ever since you took that licking I handed you."

"It surely was a peach of a licking."

"I hope it did you some good."

"I think it did."

McGee had to run along. "Nothing ever will do you any good until you settle down."

"I'll settle down when I'm an old man," said Fallon.

"I doubt it to beat hell," said McGee.

Chapter Seven

BROTHER HOOLEY GIVES 'THE RAM'

FORDHAM's student body felt bereaved when the order came for Brother Hooley's transfer to Holy Cross. It was hard enough to lose this fabulous character, but to see him given to an ancient foe was as wet ashes in the mouth. The baseball men considered wearing crêpe brassards, and a person, or persons unidentified, tolled the bell at midnight as if for the repose of a soul.

E. Franklin Smith, M.D., Professor of Physiology, was experimenting on a Maltese cat, registering its reactions to galvanic stimulation. The cat worked loose from its truss and leaped hissingly against the face of Willie Fallon, scaring him half to death and making him forever afterward chary of cats.

The transfer of Brother Hooley was believed responsible for this and other weird enigmas.

It was hard to say good-by to one who was as truly part of the campus as were the ancient elms, beneath which Poe had muttered his melancholy strophes. Indeed, Brother Hooley refused to say farewell in English. He chose the Latin, *"Vale,"* and quoted excerpts from Aristotle.

If anyone bore Brother Hooley ill will, it was not manifest by the behavior of supposedly less enthusiastic colleagues or students. For example, Brother Paradise awaited a propitious moment to deposit a huge package on Brother Hooley's counter.

"Oh, it's you, Paradise," Hooley said, glancing up from his final invoice of stock.

Brother Paradise ran a finger-nail beneath the twine of the package, snapping it as one does a banjo string. "This belongs to you, I guess."

Brother Hooley's great back was bowed as he sat with his memorandum pad at a packing-case. "Sixty-one bottles," he counted aloud. "In all, that makes five cases and seven bottles on hand. . . . Just leave the bundle there, Paradise. *Finis est.*"

Brother Hooley waited until the cobbler had departed with penguin-like steps. He rose and began to undo the package as though it were a bomb. He saw a pair of *brand-new hand-made brogans!*

Brother Paradise was fitting a felt insole in the boot of a workman named Gregg, designated as Brother Hooley's successor in the candy shop. The new shop-keeper had a wooden leg. He needed but one insole. Brother Paradise wore a solemn expression, like that of a fellow having swallowed a peach-stone. He heard Brother Hooley's elephantine step and the familiar, hoarse voice. He looked up.

"Brother Paradise, your hand. That was a Christian act, and I thank you for the fine boots."

Brother Paradise got up, rubbed his right hand on his apron and extended it. "The paths at Holy Cross are not as pleasant to walk upon as ours." He sniffled in an unmanly fashion. "I have taken cold. There's a draft."

Brother Hooley's Adam's apple bounced like a baseball. He stalked off, smothering his emotion with snuff and Latin. "*Dominus vobiscum.*"

Brother Reppard, in charge of the college bake-shop, had been at work before his brick oven since cock-crow. He plucked fistfuls from a mound of dough as puffy as a retired police-inspector's buttock. He molded the sponges with expert fingers, and soon had a great pan of rolls. This he introduced to the fire-brick hearth with a wooden peel shaped like an ancient Egyptian oar. At noon he brought to Brother Hooley's shop four dozen rolls which had almond-dust, allspice and powdered sugar scalps. They were as fat as puppies.

"A little snack for your journey, Brother Hooley."

"Do they have buns at Holy Cross?"

The baker was pale with flour. "I'm told they eat bread made by a Slav, whose barrels are full of moth-webs. Too bad."

Brother Hooley snuffed himself right lustily. "Will you have a bottle of ginger ale?"

"We'll both have one. I'll pay for it."

"Tut, man! This is a special occasion; or, as the masters would have said: '*pro re nata*'."

"My Latin has been sweated out of me over the kneading-troughs. I must brush up."

Brother Hooley sighed. "What a fine day for baseball! I'll miss my team."

"I'll send you some French pound-cake for Christmas. Only the yolks of eggs are used. The Slav wouldn't know enough for that."

"We shall pray for each other in humility and gratitude."

"I'll burn a candle for you."

"The cake need not be a huge one."

"It will weigh ten pounds. The use of yolks keeps it from growing stale and rancid. The Slav wouldn't know that."

The deep-set eyes of Brother Hooley seemed to follow Willie Fallon here, there, and everywhere, their light fueled by unspoken accusations. Each honor—and they were many for Willie in his senior year—somehow seemed to find Brother Hooley in the offing . . . just looking on.

When Willie was manager of the track team and was promoting Fordham's first indoor meet, he glanced up, while checking the running-trunks and shorts, to find Brother Hooley at the dressing-room door . . . just looking on.

"He must think I'm taking these things for underwear," Willie said to his friend, Bill Murray.

As President of the St. John's Debating Society, Fallon was chairman the night when J. Ignatius Conveney and Francis V. Oliver took the affirmative, and Dick Baker and T. F. Connolly, the negative, on the resolution: "That the policy of President Roosevelt regarding San Domingo is commendable." While announcing the question, Willie caught the stare of Brother Hooley, and almost said "ginger ale" instead of "San Domingo."

As business manager of The *Fordham Monthly*, with Thomas J. Gallon, Jr., Willie procured many advertisements for the college magazine, then edited by the accomplished Loring M. Black. He wasn't a business man *per se*, but his genial, happy-hearted manner earned him a brisk response from tradesmen. Brother Hooley always seemed to be near-by whenever Willie came down the campus paths, his pockets jingling with magazine cash.

When Willie became part owner of a touring car, together with his friends, Hubert McNally and Jack Barry, and it balked at being cranked, it had to be Brother Hooley who came to the fore. He seized the crank-handle, giving it a mighty spin that threatened to wrench crank-shaft, cylinders, and radiator from their moorings. He looked so *knowing* as he watched the car snort away.

There were little revenges undertaken by Willie. At the great sham battle of the cadet battalion, in which were illustrated the principles of attack and defense, and with General O'Beirne himself looking on, Willie deployed to a clump of bushes where Brother Hooley stood. Lieutenant though he was, Willie nevertheless had managed to borrow a musket, which he discharged near the good lay brother. The Hooley cassock behaved like a faulty parachute as he gave a leap.

All in all, Brother Hooley's surveillance threatened to deflate Willie, who was beginning to show a streak of vanity. It was rather hard to strut before eyes that looked one through.

Willie was modest enough concerning his scholarly accomplishments; his almost perfect scores in logic, rhetoric, and philosophy; his successes in oral bouts, even against learned Jebbies. But he loved the sound of his own voice. He discovered that he was handsome. Let him win at tennis, skating, or swimming, and he put out his chest like a pigeon. His apricot hair also had captured his fancy, and he would allow no barber to touch it, much to the disgust of Peter Stieb.

Mr. Stieb, one-time ace of the Fifth Avenue Hotel tonsorial stools, and now owner of a shop outside the Fordham Gate, declared that Willie cut his own hair because he didn't want to run into Brother Hooley. The latter called daily on Mr. Stieb to battle with blue stubble that shadowed monastic jowls.

Willie devised a system of triple mirrors whereat he trimmed his apricot hair. All through life he let no barber hair-cut him, shave him, or do anything else to him.

Mr. Stieb, as bald as a fence post, concocted and sold a hair restorer called "Artophylax." He told Fallon he would not advertise with The *Fordham Monthly* as long as he refused to let Stieb cut his hair. By dint of great argument concerning "Artophylax," Willie succeeded in selling Mr. Stieb an inch of space.

" 'Artophylax' really is its own best ad," Mr. Stieb declared, putting talcum on a towel and dusting his own naked scalp. He blundered against a razor-box, upsetting it, saving all but one razor from falling. "There, damn it!" He picked up the razor, which was half-opened, like the bill of a dying duck. "It's the only blade that can polish Brother Hooley's chin. Cripes, what a beard! Three times over, and he won't stand for no hot towels."

"Brother Hooley's razor?" Willie asked.

"Thank God it ain't nicked. Stroppin' don't do it no good. Have to *hone* it each time for him."

"How much do you want for it?"

"I wouldn't sell it. How the hell would I shave Brother Hooley?"

"But he's going to Holy Cross."

"That's right."

Willie then set forth a proposition.

The Fallon touring car hiccoughed and skidded beside the basement window of Brother Hooley's shop. Willie, wearing a straw hat with a dazzling blue band, got out and pressed his face against the burglar-proof wire of the open window. He had just rolled 130 pins against Bobby Graham at Müller's Bowling Alleys. He was feeling very cocky, indeed.

"Got a surprise for you, Brother Hooley," he called.

The meditating brother couldn't have looked more put out, had he beheld the face of Lucifer himself framed in the window. He was trying on his new boots, massaging the vamp of the left one to see if Brother Paradise had taken into account the difference in size between the left and right feet.

"My shop has a *door* for all that have business with me," said Brother Hooley.

Willie got a package from the tonneau and went to the shop. He opened the bundle enthusiastically and showed six pairs of black woolen socks. "They're for you. A going-away present."

Brother Hooley feared some trick, remembering that Willie only yesterday had put a ripe tomato in the pocket of the glee-club coach. He fingered the socks, however, and noted the fine quality of the wool. "Ummmmmmm," said Brother Hooley.

"That's not all," Willie said. He brought a razor from his pocket. "Look at this!"

Brother Hooley at once recognized the massive tool on account of its horn handle and the saber-like blade.

"My son," he said, "this is indeed kind. But, I must ask: Where did you *get* it?"

"I bought it for you."

"*Bought* it?"

"Why, sure. For you."

Brother Hooley hemmed again, turned the razor over and

over, then opened it and leveled the blade against weedy hairs of his knuckles. "Willie, this is the living image of a razor that Peter Stieb has used on me these five years. You *bought* it?"

"From Pete Stieb. He said it was your favorite."

Brother Hooley's snuffy nostrils dilated. "'Tis a fine instrument, lad. I'll be remembering you at Holy Cross."

When Brother Hooley shut up shop, he visited the place of Peter Stieb outside the Fordham Gate.

"Good evening," he said, putting down the razor on a marble shelf, beside a half-empty bottle of "Artophylax."

Mr. Stieb was bundling the day's laundry in a striped apron. "And what may that be, Brother?"

Brother Hooley's hand was half upraised, as though in exorcism. "If there's been a mistake, Stieb, it's rectified. Someone must have dropped this razor in my shop."

"Didn't Willie Fallon——"

Brother Hooley seemed in pain. "And *what* about Willie Fallon?"

"Why . . . it's his, I guess."

"*Guess?*"

"Well, he got it from me to give to you."

Hooley's face was less grim than Stieb had seen it in five years. "Then he *bought* it from you?"

"Bought hell! Saving your presence, Brother Hooley. . . . Bought nothing! He won it from me at dice."

Brother Hooley hemmed and snuffed himself. "In that case," he said, "I want none of it."

"Then I make you a present of it myself," said Stieb.

Brother Hooley picked up the gallant razor. "That alters matters. I shall burn a candle for you, Stieb."

The Friday of Brother Hooley's departure, students wore their brightest scarves and hat-bands, so as not to depress the departing brother. At the campus gate the Brother was pushed into Willie

Fallon's car. He stood and bowed as the boys gave him "The Ram." He was unable to speak, even in Latin, as Willie drove to the station with his throttle wide open and a banner flapping at the rear of the car, like a campaign plea, reading: "God Speed, Brother Hooley."

As the good Brother got out, he held Willie's hand. "As soon as you quit your monkey business, Willie Fallon, there's a great world awaiting you."

"Brother Hooley, now that you're going, I want to tell you something."

Brother Hooley raised his ham-like hand. "Tell it to your confessor, my son. I know all about the boy that broke into my shop some years ago. I lost 286 bottles of ginger ale and 461 chocolate cream bars. Tell it to your confessor. *Vale, Willibus, et pax vobiscum.*"

Could it be humanly possible that Brother Hooley was weeping?

A number of students were drinking Brother Hooley's health. Some of them congregated at Pat Nolan's. Others gathered for high ones at Mark Simon's Place. It is with the utmost delight I am able to chronicle that the departure of a dear friend, the winning of a football or baseball game, the visit of a distinguished alumnus—in short, any important happening whatsoever could be emphasized by a "tall one" at either of these two decent saloons. Hip flasks and collegiate misuse of liquor is of a later era.

Pat Nolan had a frame building set back from Fordham Road and Webster Avenue. It was a northwest corner; a stiff nor'easter of winter would blow you right into a barroom of hospitable warmth; and one also might find there a shadowed coolness on hot Commencement days. There were wide steps leading to the saloon-porch, easy steps that almost helped you into a place where clean sawdust was on the floor. The brass bar-rail was polished like the Kaiser's coach-lamps. A fourteen-inch cheese was on the free-lunch table, with brittle oyster crackers piled in a huge bowl. The yeasty smell of honest lager made the nose believe that heaven was nearer earth than many folk suspected.

The reputation of the eminent Pat Nolan, who wore a black derby and a white Van Dyke beard, may be inferred from remarks of the Rev. Father Harry Lyons, S.J. (called "Silk Hat Harry" by admiring students).

"I don't approve of careless drinking," he said. "But if you *must* drink, drink at Pat Nolan's."

[What this country needs is more "Jebbies".]

Mr. Nolan was taciturn, shortly built, and stately. What he lacked in talkative qualities, however, was compensated by his nephew, John O'Leary. Mr. O'Leary presided efficiently at the bar and always was eager to recount his doings in the woods, in pursuit of big game. It was confidently believed that Mr. O'Leary's moose were jack rabbits; yet he told of gallant hunts, camp fires, mountain lions, and of one time when he leaped from a canoe to the back of an eight-pronged bull moose and *rode* him, by gad! Rode him to shore! All in all, Pat Nolan's was a place of fellowship. No one was over-served there at any time, and if there was a mission in the Church of Our Lady of Mercy, Pat always closed his saloon at 7:30 o'clock. He was well-to-do, respected and trusted. He had no tribute to pay to hoodlums; he was not in fear of being taken for a ride; he gave to the constituted authorities whatever fees there were to be given, and not to the underworld. Pat Nolan lived, worked, and died in a *civilized* age.

As for Mark Simmons, his place was not as convivial perhaps as Nolan's. It was cleaner and more business-like. It was on the southeast corner of Fordham Road and Third Avenue. Joe McCarthy was the bar-man and he had a strong following, especially among the football men, who dropped in after practice to sip beer. Joe was thin. He had bulging eyes and a cough. He was an expert at telling when you had had enough. And that's all you *could* get from him.

After Brother Hooley's health had been drunk, the boys came from both saloons and gathered in John F. DeGroot's "College

Restaurant" near the Fordham Gate. They had an impromptu banquet, at which speeches were made extolling the virtues of the departed Brother. DeGroot, his wife, and their daughter, Annie, heard amazing tales of Brother Hooley's prodigious strength. It was said he once had wrestled in private with Farmer Burns and *threw* him with a full nelson.

It was decided that a strong delegation of rooters go to Holy Cross, Worcester, Mass., in honor of Brother Hooley, and to support the Fordham baseball team in its scheduled game there. Then the boys began steaming up Mr. DeGroot, who, it seems, had a long-time feud with his next-door neighbor, Barber Stieb.

In matters of this sort, Willie Fallon was a master. He began by telling Mr. DeGroot that Barber Stieb had said the food at the "College Restaurant" was not fit for the lowliest swine.

Mr. Fallon utilized a classic jest. "I stuck up for you. I told Stieb that your food *was* fit for swine."

"Bah," said Mr. DeGroot, "Stieb has a hair-tonic that would burn the rust off of old nails."

Mr. Fallon went to Mr. Stieb and reported that "Artophylax" was being impugned in DeGroot's restaurant. Soon the two rivals were at their respective doors, uttering challenges and threatening to go to law. The students finally gave each sputtering proprietor "The Ram" and went to the campus. They heard behind them cries of "You lie, Stieb!" and "The truth is not in you, De-Groot!"

Brother Hooley and the manager of the Holy Cross baseball team met the Fordham delegation at the Worcester station. They drove to the campus. Brother Hooley—looking years older—wouldn't let the players out of his sight. When the manager had gone to see that quarters were ready for the team, Brother Hooley beckoned the Fordham squad with a mysterious forefinger. He drew them to a secluded spot, far from the campus buildings.

He didn't make a speech, nor did he offer any explanation of his dramatic act. He looked about furtively, as though to make sure that he—now a member of Holy Cross's personnel—was not being spied upon. Then he gave a low, hoarse, "Ram!"

After the Brother had completed his solo "Ram," he turned and walked alone along the winding path of Holy Cross.

When it is considered that Willie Fallon—in St. John's Preparatory School (Fordham) and during his first two years in the college itself—was regarded as lazy and indifferent, his position at time of graduation is something to remark.

On June 20, 1906, gaining a degree of Bachelor of Arts, Willie Fallon was valedictorian of his class, and recipient of the Hughes Medal for the highest mark in philosophy. This medal, instituted in honor of Archbishop Hughes, is one of the most coveted of Fordham prizes.

Fallon's exceedingly acute mind, his tremendous memory—he could read an average book in two hours and repeat almost word-for-word the *entire text*—were undoubted factors in his so-called awakening. It is generally believed, however, that the extemporaneous oral drills of the Jesuits, requiring shrewd and ready reasoning, and occurring in the third collegiate year, were the principal stimuli for one of the brightest minds that was to come to the law.

Willie was twenty years and five months old; five feet ten and a half inches tall; weighed 170 pounds, and was handsome in his cap and gown. Here was a clean, alive fellow, by all accounts (including his own), a boy who had had absolutely no sex life, a boy who never had smoked or tasted liquor (he was a teetotaler until he was twenty-nine), and who never cursed, told, or listened to an off-color story. His principal physical outlet was strenuous play. He showed a mischievous but never vicious disposition that constantly led him into scrapes. He never had known hardship; his parentage was of the best; his home life wholesome, and his future without a discernible shadow.

Willie stood on the campus on a May evening prior to commencement month and before the statue of the Blessed Virgin.

He delivered an address that gained him fame. Each evening in May, an upper-classman is designated to address the Holy Effigy, after hymns have been sung by assembled students. This statue of Our Lady was dedicated on February 2, 1887, by the Sodalities of the College, and since then, May-time hymns have been sung around it, and addresses given. It is one of the most beautiful and impressive of Fordham's traditions.

As time grew near for the farewell, Willie Fallon became more serious in manner and in action. He participated in a play, "A Night Off," taking the part of "Jack Mulberry," a chap that liked a good time. He sang "Rosemary," "The Message of the Shamrock," and "I Shall Sing Thee Songs of Araby" in the final glee-club concert. He successfully debated the question: "Resolved, that the present attitude of labor unions towards the 'open shop' is unjustifiable."

At 2:30 o'clock the afternoon of Wednesday, June 20, 1906, Fordham's Commencement exercises were held indoors for the first time. The modern clatter of the elevated, the increase of near-by railroad traffic, and street-car clangor had invaded the former rural peace of the Fordham country. The faculty decided to abandon the custom of holding Commencement on the wide lawn. The new College theater was the place of ceremony. It was the sixty-first annual Commencement.

After three days of heavy rain, Commencement afternoon was brilliant with sunshine. The campus was fragrant with the mid-summer breath of full-blown flowers. Visitors walked beneath the old elms and beach trees of this first Catholic center of higher education chartered in New York City.

The Reverend President, Daniel J. Quinn, S.J., left the administration building at 2:30 o'clock and led the guests, faculty, and graduates to the new theater. They filled the stage. The Right Reverend Monsignor Joseph Mooney, (Fordham '67) presided. The Reverend President sat at the right hand of the master of ceremonies. To his left sat the Right Reverend Monsignor M. J. Lavelle, Rector of St. Patrick's. As they took their places, the "March of the Prophet" was played as a processional. After four addresses, William J. Fallon gave the valedictory.

"And often in fancy we shall return to these elm-lined paths, to relive the days we spent among beloved comrades."

Often did he return to wander over familiar ground, in times when he was maligned, hungered, and spent.

Mr. Fallon was in retreat in June, 1906, at St. Andrew-on-Hudson. He had five days in which to meditate on his past and his future. He went with fourteen other seniors, arriving at Poughkeepsie at 6 o'clock in the evening. They traveled in carriages to the Novitiate, two miles from town, on the Old Albany Post Road. The horses pulled earnestly up the winding road. It was thickly wooded. Occasionally, through oak-openings, Willie could see the bland Hudson, cool with silver solitude.

The party came at last to an ancient building, sheltered by trees. They paused at a small chapel, Our Lady of the Wayside, kneeling there before proceeding to the monastic building. The Reverend Father Dillon welcomed the party and showed them to their rooms.

Willie Fallon brushed the dust from his clothes, washed at a white stoneware bowl and joined the others in the cloister, where Mr. Dean, a Fordham graduate and novice at St. Andrew's (now a Father, and Dean of Studies at Fordham), shook hands with the seniors. It was then that the benign little Father Pettit, once President of Fordham, greeted the boys.

"It will soon again be time for you to put on your long underwear," he said. He took them to see the Reverend Rector of St. Andrew's, Father Richards, ex-rector of Georgetown University. Father Richards later visited each room and gave the retreat.

It was here that Fallon remembered his talk with Eugene F. McGee, now at Fordham Law School, downtown Manhattan. Fallon decided definitely to take up the study of law.

On Saturday morning, the boys gathered on the front stoop of the Novitiate and startled everyone by giving loud cheers for their hosts. The horses danced at the carriages as the "Ram" was sounded.

The next year, Willie Fallon entered Fordham Law School, where he carried his preceptors away with his brilliance and his "feeling" for the law. Dean Paul Fuller said of the personable youth with the apricot hair:

"Here is a new star in the constellation of the law."

With three years of unbroken high marks, Willie Fallon was graduated from the Fordham Law School, receiving an LL.B. degree. He now was ready for the world . . . and the world was ready for him.

Chapter Eight

AT THE SIGN OF THE ADMIRAL DOT

ADMIRAL DOT was neither an admiral nor a seafaring gentleman of any sort. He traveled far and long as a midget with Barnum & Bailey's Greatest Show on Earth. Circus life eventually palled on this successor to General Tom Thumb. Night journeys, morning parades in a howdah aboard the back of Schneider, a sensual bull elephant; sweltering matinées beneath the Big Top; the drudgery of hawking postcard photographs portraying himself in chapeau, tunic, epaulets, and side-arms of the Queen's Navee-ee-eeee all these rituals began to bore the Admiral. An ennui possessed him. He became irascible and dreamed of trolls.

A horn-voiced Omaha physician mumbled something about glandular frustration and recommended organotherapy. The Admiral's glands hardly accounted for his ungentlemanly behavior toward the Bearded Lady.

"Maybe I got a beard," the hirsute wench complained to her husband, "but I'm a lady." Her husband was a clown, who disputed the great Slivers' claim to invention of baseball pantomime. His principal ambition, however, was to be an undertaker. He was taking a correspondence school test in embalming the moment his wife's tears began to be-trickle her beard.

"Nix!" he said, "You'll get me all balled up." He put pencil-point to tongue. "This is my mid-term exams. Nix!"

"You and your *embalmin'!*" she said. "Are you gonna let a midge say them nasty things?"

"Well," said the clown, (who was trying to cudgel an answer to question six: What is the correct technique when the body begins to turn blue?) "Well," he said, "get one of our kids to lick him."

The circus one day spread its canopies in the Admiral's home town of White Plains, Westchester County, New York. At Grand Entrance time, Admiral Dot drew himself to his full height (thirty-eight inches) and quit. Lacking a handier object for his spleen, the Admiral spat on the whitewashed toe-nails of the elephant, Schneider.

The trainer of the bulls took this as a personal affront. "Wot the hell, Admiral! Ain't they room enough for you to use as a gaboon? You ain't got no sense of proportions!"

The Admiral told the trainer what to do with his sjambok. "And keep it there," added the Admiral, quitting the lot.

The canvas boss overheard the Admiral's amazing suggestion concerning the steel-sharded sjambok. "It's temp'rament," he said to the elephant trainer. "It's temp'rament, Ralph."

"By God!" said Ralph. "By God!"

"I heard him tell the Bearded Lady to do the very same t'ing wid her side-burns, Ralph. It's got me stopped."

The trainer of the bulls began hacking Schneider's armpit with the sjambok. "Them midges ain't got no sense of proportions. I would of socked anybody else if they'd of told me wot he just did."

"I hear he's quittin', Ralph. It's a godsend if he is."

Ralph grunted. "He'll never blow this soft job. It's too much of a graft. Anyway, wot in hell could a runt like him do? Rustle cheese for a mouse?"

"I don't blame the Bearded Lady for gettin' sore, Ralph. He shouldn't ought to of yanked her beard."

"He ain't got no sense of proportions. Like I said."

"The Five Flyin' Strongforts had an argyment wid him las'

season. Same t'ing. He told Frank Strongfort wear to shove his trapeeze. It's got me stopped."

"Five'll getcha ten if he quits," Ralph said. "Why, wot could a runt like him do? He ain't got no stren'th."

"He'll get run outa town for tellin' the Mayor wot to do wid the City Hall. Too much temp'rament, Ralph."

"Midges ain't got no sense of proportions, like I said. You know? I would of socked anybody else if they had of said what he did to me about the hook. The Goddam cloze-pin!"

"Ralph, it's got me stopped."

The circus left White Plains in the early morning—without Admiral Dot. The side-show banners were struck, including the faded one depicting Admiral Dot in British Naval regalia and standing on a human hand. Razor-backs sweated beneath the flood of gasoline torches. The Admiral dreamed that he heard a far-away trumpeting of the bull-herd and the creaking of bravely painted wagons. At dawn he walked to the lot. Only a great patch of soggy sawdust, strewn with crumpled papers, peanut husks, bottles and ticket stubs, met his eye. He wrinkled his button-nose at the weird smell of stale animal-litter, all that remained of the mighty spectacle.

The Admiral had a wife, Lottie Swartwood, no bigger than a whisk-broom. She was as thrifty as a concièrge. They invested their savings in a hotel in Orawaupum Street, across the way from the railroad station. The hotel had a bar. The Admiral glowed all over; his glands returned to normal and he was indeed happy to have bearded the circus lady. He called his place "The Hotel Peewee," and joined the Elks Lodge.

He felt inflated. Yesterday the acknowledged smallest man in the world (at least the barkers claimed as much), he was today the biggest. In a moment of fine animal spirits, the Admiral revealed to his wife where Barnum & Bailey could put their circus, for all of him. "And that goes for the winter quarters, too," he added for good measure. He even went further with his idea of a warehouse: "And they can put the whole town of Bridgeport there. The hell with 'em!"

"You got to be more pleasanter with our trade," warned Mrs. Dot. "That is, when we get some."

The Admiral opened a box of postcards of himself. He stood on a packing case and called for a hammer and some tacks. Mrs. Dot couldn't find a tack-hammer but brought him a claw-hammer. Her husband used both hands, swinging the claw-hammer as though it were a sledge. He kept tacking up pictures of himself until he broke into a sweat. Then he got down and surveyed the room, almost exploding with pride. "I'm going to tend bar myself," he announced.

Mrs. Dot looked up at the bar. "Maybe we ought to get it sawn down to our size."

"The hell!" said the Admiral. "Bars are made for them that buys; not for them that sells. I got a scheme."

"You may get a crick in your neck reaching up the drinks."

"Don't you worry none, Lottie."

The Admiral called for carpenters. They built a platform running parallel to the bar and behind it. There was a flight of shallow steps leading to the platform. The Admiral strode the runway like a real quarter-decker. He opened shop and immediately became popular. He had to do a deal of getting up and down for this and that, and it was out of the question for him to handle beer-kegs. He hired a bar-fly to do the bung-starting. The Admiral abused the poor fellow, accusing him of drinking the profits, and occasionally climbing up to smell his breath; but the bar-fly long ago had learned to submit meekly to the axiom that the most one can expect of Life is a draw-decision.

Thirsty men came from as far away as Mamaroneck to hold wassail at the Admiral's mahogany. In holiday season his Tom & Jerry was accounted the finest. The good folk of White Plains were proud of their fellow citizen. Only one bit of adverse criticism was heard, and that from a soused stranger. This man, unmistakably a sot, appeared at the Dot bar one slow Monday forenoon. He found the place deserted, except for the bar-fly, asleep in a tilted chair. The stranger helped himself to numerous snifters of Highland Queen and didn't bother about chasers.

On leaving the place, the stranger heard a squeaky voice. He looked at the bar-fly, whose chin was married to his chest in sleep. Then he glanced at the bar and saw standing on it, his arms wildly flailing, an aproned elf. The stranger whooped with terror, shouted something about "quitting this damned stuff for good" and loped into the street. In crashing through the swinging doors, the stranger's watch and chain were snared, but he never stopped. The Admiral appropriated this souvenir as payment for the Scotch.

It was the sort of watch that light-fingered gentlemen called a "kettle" or a "super." It beat like a lion's heart and looked like a snare drum when in the Admiral's admiring hands. Nothing pleased the Admiral more than having a patron ask him the correct time. It gave him opportunity to display his big watch and tell a story or two concerning its supposed history.

"This watch," he would say, "was give to me by the Prince. We was playing London, and the Prince had come from Ascot, a heavy winner on the horses. He commanded me to his presence. 'Take this watch,' he says, 'to remember me by.' I took it, and we drunk a few balls together like bunkies. Fine fellow, the Prince."

In the early part of our dizzy century, White Plains was not the thriving center it is now. There was a volunteer fire department, and it was a matter of national interest when Admiral Dot was named honorary chief. He long since had forsworn all manner of pageantry calculated to remind him of circus parades. In fact he often was heard to specify where the calliope player could secrete the steam-organ. But when he donned his fire-eating regalia, the Admiral's chest rose like an actor to his cue. He appeared on parade, his helmet gleaming and his silver trumpet polished until it seemed it might have dazed a blind man. Press notices concerning the Fire Department were pasted in the Admiral's hotel and bar-windows for all to see.

There is some question concerning the Admiral's actual skill in combating conflagrations. A more or less apocryphal tale is still told regarding the destruction of a grocery and meat store in White Plains. It burned to the ground before the eyes of the Admiral and his men. The Admiral, however,—an arrant foe of waste—salvaged some bread, a necklace of sausages, and a cannister of ground coffee. He filled the cannister from the dribbling hose-cart nozzle. He set it with the sausages on embers that lately had been a meat-block. When the fire laddies scented the Admiral's steaming coffee, they interpreted it as a fire-out signal, shut off the water and gathered 'round their leader. It was a real feast, what with other viands being rescued in time for kitchen-treatment.

The Admiral, glowing with coffee, sausages, and compliments, was inspired to story-telling heights. The sampling of marmalade reminded him of experiences in the British Isles.

"I sat on the Queen's lap," he said, his face looking chubby and infantile. His cheeks were pouched with bread, and his mouth smeared with marmalade. "The finest woman in the world! Not fresh like some of our society jinny-winks. I'll never forget when I was in South Carolina. A society jane tried to make me. Her husband was watching the sword-swallower at the time, and I felt awful sorry for him."

One of the company wanted to know if sword-swallowing was a fake. Before the Admiral could deny that it was, another man asked concerning the love-life of elephants. This subject kept the Admiral busy until the grocery and meat store was a heap of charcoal and ashes.

"You never seen nothing like it," the Admiral concluded. "I'll take the whole company to Bridgeport some time. We'll have a picnic with beer."

"Three cheers for the Chief," proposed one of the hose-couplers.

" 'Ray! 'Ray! 'Ray!' "

"And three cheers for the elephants."

" 'Ray! 'Ray! 'Ray!' "

On the way home, one of the bashful members of the company whispered to the Admiral: "Was that the truth what you told us about the elephants?"

"As God is my judge," said the Admiral, lighting a huge cigar.

Although most of the lawyers of White Plains braced themselves at a saloon across from the old courthouse, not a few patronized Admiral Dot. He was particularly fond of attorneys, and his favorite was David Hunt.

Lawyer Hunt was a veteran leader of the Westchester criminal bar. He was learned in the law, picturesque, thick-set and sloppy. During a course of lectures at Fordham Law School, he had become acquainted with William J. Fallon. At the outset he regarded that young man as a prodigy. They had clashed during a quiz, and Fallon had held his own with the Westchester veteran. Fallon—intrigued by Hunt's personality and ability— listened to the Westchester attorney's urgings that he begin the practice of law in White Plains.

"I always wanted to practice in New York City," Fallon said.

"Get a reputation and experience in a small town first," Hunt said. "You don't want to wind up chasing ambulances."

"I'll think it over," Fallon said. "Somehow, I feel my place is in New York."

"Wait until you're married, settled down, and have made political connections."

"Marriage and politics are the two things that bother me least."

"Don't you know a nice girl?"

"All girls are nice, I guess," Fallon said. "I've got only one girl. She lives in Mamaroneck."

"You mean your mother?"

"Yes. She's girl enough for me."

"Well, if you practice in White Plains, you could be closer to her. I'll make you a member of my firm."

"I'll think it over," Fallon said.

Although Fallon came to no immediate decision, Lawyer Hunt spread word in White Plains that he was taking a new partner into his firm. He visited the Mamaroneck home.

Lawyer Hunt looked at the fine old chairs, upholstered in yellow plush; the well-bound books in tall shelves, inset in a walled-up double-doorway; the discreet bronzes, and the black upright piano. Bill sang for him and then they went boating on the Sound. Bill was an expert sailor. He seemed entirely happy as the wind and sun reddened his face.

"You'd be a fool to leave such surroundings," Lawyer Hunt said. "When you coming to White Plains?"

"I'll come over soon," Bill said. "I want to hear you address a jury."

"There's only one thing for fellows like us to do," the attorney said. "I mean fellows with personality. You've got a front, and I'm told I have, too."

"You surely have," Bill said. "Well, what should we do?"

Bill's two bird-dogs ran to greet him as he came ashore. The lawyer patted one of the dogs. "Most lawyers break their necks trying to get a jury to be favorable to a client. The thing to do is make them *favorable to you, yourself*. After they are won to you, the rest is easy. It's like shooting fish in a barrel."

"Maybe you're right," Bill said.

"I don't deal in maybe's," Lawyer Hunt said. "I know."

Bill as yet had not shone in the presence of girls. His companions had been boys mostly. He attended dances of the Fordham alumni, and when he proved graceful, rhythmic and strong, he began to pay more attention to girls than formerly. He became vain about his dancing.

Fallon met girls of good family. They thought him somewhat reserved, but romantic. He was judged the handsomest boy in Westchester County and soon was aware of that fact. He allowed his hair to grow almost to poetic length and continued to barber it himself. He paid no particular attention to clothes, aside from showing a partiality to blue serges and wine-colored neckties. This combination, he believed, set off the value of his hair and the flush of his cheeks. The girls said he had a "bow-knot mouth." He tried kissing a few of them.

At one of the Fordham dances he met Agnes Rafter. Her father owned a chain of grocery stores. She was a quiet girl. Fallon blossomed verbally in her presence. He even ventured to brag, in a left-handed manner, telling stories of Fordham that showed his companions to have been worthy fellows, and by inference portraying himself the biggest personality of all. Miss Rafter listened attentively to his aims and ambitions.

Fallon's vanity never was offensive. Rather, it added to his charm. It has been said that he actually suffered a feeling of inferiority; that he indulged in emphatic gestures and romantic forays more to bolster his own soul than to impress anyone else. In Miss Rafter he found not only a friend, but one to love whole-heartedly. She wasn't always asking him to explain himself. He was bold sometimes. Again he was inexplicably shy. Miss Rafter didn't bludgeon him with questions.

They were married at the Church of the Holy Trinity, New York City, June 3, 1912. Mr. Fallon felt quite a fellow. He said he wouldn't be astonished if he were to become Chief Justice of the United States Supreme Court. He was full of Irish songs and Irish laughter in those days. Here was a couple envied by everyone. Their home life was said to be ideal. Two daughters were born; first Ruth, and then Barbara.

Eddie Foy was the only actor Fallon knew at the time. Fallon's visit to the Foy home at New Rochelle later became a famous story along Broadway.

"I went to visit Eddie," Fallon used to say. "I never expect to see such a father again. His seven children were there. Eddie was *trying* to read the sports pages. We both were friends of John McGraw as ardent rooters for the Giants. Eddie was sitting with his feet propped up.

"I never heard so much noise. The kids apparently were trying to tear down the house. Bryan Foy had a croquet mallet, with which he was hammering nails into the door-jambs and window-frames. Eddie took his feet from the chair and said in his wheezy way:

" 'Sit down, Bill, but watch yourself. Them kids like to murder visitors.'

"I wondered how the house had stood up so long. Eddie, Jr., was removing handfuls of stuffing from a davenport, and was making wigs and false-beards. Irving Foy was sawing the leg of a reading-table. I forget what Charlie and Dick were doing; possibly chipping porcelain from the kitchen sink.

"We were trying to discuss Christy Mathewson's shutout game, but it was no use. You couldn't have heard a cannon. Finally Eddie looked at Bryan, who was driving big nails in the door. I thought the old man was going to put a stop to it. Imagine my feeling when he yelled:

" 'For God's sake, fellow, drive them nails *clear in!* Don't let 'em stick out to catch people's pants!'

"After another deafening interlude, Eddie shouted to Eddie, Jr., who was wearing a ferocious beard made from davenport-stuffing: 'Lord, Eddie! why don't you take some hair out of the *middle* of the sofa? What you want to do? Make it lopsided?'

"Eddie, Sr., then criticized the work of Irving, who was looking around the room for something else to saw. 'Hey, you!' Foy shouted to Irving, 'You goin' to leave the table that way? Don't be a sap! Saw the *other* legs down so they'll be even. A lamp's liable to fall off or something.'

"It was *some* family! And how they loved that great old man! He beamed when they did something especially devilish. On my way out, Eddie shook my hand and I thought he was going to cry.

" 'Ain't they the damnedest, finest kids?' he asked.

" 'They're full of life,' I suggested.

" 'They're understudying the 'Katzenjammers,' he said."

Fallon visited Lawyer Hunt at White Plains. They sat at a table in Admiral Dot's place. Fallon drank ginger ale. Lawyer Hunt opened a bottle of wine in honor of Bill's wedding. Fallon was particularly impressed by the Admiral and got his entire history from him. The Admiral "took" to Bill, who could blarney anyone out of his eye-teeth. Admiral Dot said he wanted Fallon to act as his attorney. He had nothing of a legal nature pending at present, he explained, but offered a suggestion that a certain bar-fly "might be up soon on a charge of grand larceny."

"I'm thinking of getting a cash register," the Admiral said. "My money-till is too much temptation. Anyway, it's hard as hell for me to work them keys underneath. My hands ain't as strong as they was when I cracked the lion-whip under the Big Top."

"So somebody's been knocking down on you, eh?" asked Lawyer Hunt.

The Admiral stood on a chair to wipe wine-pools from Lawyer Hunt's table-top. "It's a very crooked world," he said. "The cash register salesman was in yesterday. I ain't exactly bought it yet. He's leaving it here Monday for a week's trial. Would you both come Monday to advise me about it?"

"We'll sure come, Admiral," said Hunt.

Lawyer Hunt was in particularly fine mood Monday forenoon. Fallon had consented to become a partner in his firm. A sign-painter was lettering the door with gold-leaf: "Hunt, Fallon & Smith, Counselors at Law".

Hunt and Fallon went to Admiral Dot's to see the new cash register. The Admiral couldn't wait to have it installed properly behind the bar. He stood on a keg before the bright glass mechanism, peering like a Peeping Tom into the indicator-glass.

The cash register salesman acted as though it were his own invention. "Gentlemen," he said, "the Adm'ral has a license to be hopped-up over this register. It's a new departure. It's aces, back-to-back. The Adm'ral wants it demonstrated for youse. It works like a watch. No effort. One press of the keys, and the drawer comes out like nothing at all. Records everything. Not a chanct for no crooked stew-bum. . . ." The salesman looked nervous. He half-whispered as he saw the Admiral's bar-fly slinking with a mop-bucket into the wash-room. He waited until he could read the sign, "Gents," on the closing door before continuing. "As I was sayin', no louse can knock down on youse, Adm'ral, with this machine."

The Admiral straightened on his keg. "They better not! . . . Well, Mister, let's see it work. Watch it, Mr. Hunt, and Mr. Fallon."

The salesman rubbed his hands joyously. He had the sadistic eyes of a painless dentist. "I'll do that little thing, Adm'ral. Honest to God, gents, youse won't believe your eyes. Here, Adm'ral! Here you are, Ad! Just stand natural on your keg. Press the No-Sale key, Ad. Just barely tap it. You won't believe your eyes, Gents. Works like a watch. Here, Ad. Just press the No-Sale key. Now watch, ev'body!"

The Admiral, a bit self-conscious, pressed the key. The door popped out like a cork from a champagne bottle. It caught the Admiral flush on the chin. He literally sailed from his barrel and crashed to the floor. He was knocked as cold as a Bismarck herring. The salesman's eyes seemed as big as croquet balls.

"Holy Jeez!" said the salesman. "It sure crocked him! Adm'ral! Hey, Ad, did it hurt youse? I never knowed it to behave thataway before. Jeez!"

Mr. Fallon was picking the Admiral from the floor. "Get some water, you."

"Hadn't it ought to be booze?" asked the salesman. "Jeez!"

"Some water and a towel."

The Admiral's bar-fly came shuffling from the wash-room. He seemed to think there had been a hold-up. He ran back to the wash-room and sat down, holding the mop-handle as though trying to hide behind a post.

The Admiral finally came to a bit. He had trouble getting his legs under him. He had a dreamy, love-sick expression.

"I sat in the Queen's lap," the Admiral said.

The salesman was dabbing the Admiral's forehead with a bar-towel. "Jeez! I never knowed it to behave thataway before."

The Admiral returned to full consciousness, but still walked on his heels. "Sue him!" he squealed as the salesman leaned over to give him another dab of the wet towel. "Sue him!"

"I'm awfully sorry, Ad," said the salesman, who meanwhile had shut the knock-out drawer slyly. "I never knowed it to——"

The Admiral was an apoplectic red. "Take that damned thing and stick it——"

"Now don't lose your temper, Adm'ral," said the salesman.

The Admiral screamed a repetition as to the cash register's placement. "And put your horse and buggy there, too!" said the Admiral.

"Now, is that a nice thing to say?" asked the salesman.

The Admiral was hunting for the bung-starter. Mr. Hunt advised the salesman to take his machine and depart at once. "He doesn't want you or *it*," said Mr. Hunt.

"I never knowed it to behave thataway before," the salesman said, wheeling the machine to the door.

After he had recovered from the No-Sale punch, the Admiral announced he was going to stick to his antiquated money-drawer. "The old-fashioned things is the best," he said. The bar-fly came hesitantly from the wash-room. The Admiral looked at him and added: "God help any lunkhead that tampers with my cash-drawer!"

"Should I mop up the donniker now?" the bar-fly asked. "Or should I ought to clean the windows and lay fresh sawdust?"

"God help any bloke that ever holds out on me!" said Admiral Dot, walking tidlump-tidlump, up and down his platform. "P. T. Barnum, hisself, saved me in a terrible storm in 1884," he said to his guests. "The tents all fell down. I hate storms."

The courthouse at White Plains must be very old—the core of it, I mean. They've built an imposing shell of creamy stone about the ancient, dull gray walls that James Fenimore Cooper knew. Someone with feeling managed to preserve the historic court-chamber, hidden though it is by high corridors lined with the pale sweatings of Mt. Vesuvius.

Architects come from many lands to see this ancient room, with its narrow, tall windows—the tiny panes surmounted by eloquent arches. The walls are a pale blue, with saffron scrolls of the old order. There are aged oil-paintings of tawny-whiskered jurists on the high wall, and behind the bench where sits the learned court.

From the center of the chamber ceiling, there hangs a solidly-wrought chandelier, now electrified. It has formal bosses of brass on the hoop. These may represent fleurs-de-lis, three-leaf clovers, or, (Heaven forbid), aces of clubs. This room is the soul of the building, no matter how costly or ornate the modern envelope of stone, with ranks of columns and elaborate architraves.

It was in this room and in this old courthouse that William J. Fallon began the practice of law as a member of the firm of Hunt, Fallon & Smith. It was concerning this court that James Fenimore Cooper coined the phrase: "Horse-shedding the witness." There were carriage sheds near the courthouse in Cooper's day, where attorneys lingered to rehearse witnesses. Mr. Hunt could remember the sheds right well, and if he had had a mind to do so, could have told of indulging in no little "horse-shedding" himself. The courthouse was on Railroad Avenue (now Main Street).

Mr. Fallon's start as a trial lawyer was not impressive. He grew, however, in knowledge and in artifice under the guidance of the old master, Hunt. Many of his early cases were tried before Judge William Popham Platt, of the Westchester Pophams.

"The Pophams were one of the oldest families," said Hunt to Admiral Dot.

"How old?" asked the Admiral.

"Why," said Hunt, "some of the Pophams spent a hundred and fifty years, standing on one foot."

Lawyer Hunt advised Bill to be a candidate for the State

Legislature. Much against his personal desire in the matter, Fallon became Republican candidate for Assemblyman and was elected. He made only two trips to Albany as a legislator.

"It's no use," he told Hunt, who remonstrated with him for slighting his public work. "I can't stand that kind of life. Everything up there is cut and dried."

"I know," said Hunt, "but it will give you background and connections."

"It's no use," Fallon repeated. "It bores me. And anything that bores me, I'm never going to do."

This statement, if taken at full value, may throw light on Fallon's later activities. He already was proving restless. If he were interested in a case, he was superb. If he weren't, he gave it little thought or attention. This, I believe, was one of his major weaknesses. He was incapable of prosaic drudgery. But given a case that captured his fancy, no matter how complicated, he would work with enormous power and insight. This will be demonstrated—I trust—in the famous Fritz case. It will be shown how he studied, and apparently mastered, four highly technical books on gynecology in one evening, and confounded medical experts when they took the stand for the prosecution.

Things, in a manner of speaking, came to Fallon. Although he was indifferent to political hook-ups, such was his local popularity and ability that he was named assistant prosecuting attorney by Frederick E. Weeks, District Attorney of Westchester County.

Mr. Weeks was a printer's devil in his youth, and later a reporter, for William H. H. Ely of the Tarrytown *Press Record*. In the Spanish-American War he served as a corporal with Company C, 71st Regiment, New York National Guard. He was cited for bravery at San Juan Hill, and in December, 1898, was appointed Assistant Adjutant General of New York by Governor Black. Mr. Weeks, a tall, powerful man with a gentle and reserved manner, retired from public office in January, 1923, after twenty-three years of notable endeavor. He served twice as Mayor of White Plains.

Under such an able, reticent man, Fallon received another sort of experience than that which he had gained with the picturesque David Hunt. He was notified of his appointment on a Thursday, January 1, 1914. New York politics were taking all manner of strange somersaults at the time. Mayor Mitchell, newly installed in Gotham's City Hall, announced the members of his cabinet. The deposed Governor, William Sulzer, knifed by Tammany Hall, said he was going to sit once again in the Executive Mansion at Albany, and that it would be the "People's House." That, however, never materialized.

One of Fallon's favorite stories concerned Governor Sulzer, who, as a nine-times member of Congress, had made numerous speeches in behalf of Russian Jews (as well as for the Cubans and the Boers).

"Every night," bellowed Sulzer, during a political campaign, "a hundred million Jews in Russia kneel to pray for William Sulzer."

"Jews don't *kneel* when they pray," a heckler called out.

The Hon. Mr. Sulzer fixed the audience with his Henry Clay eyes. "They do," he shouted, "when they pray for William Sulzer!"

Citizen Sulzer was not the only disgruntled gentleman of sandy complexion in New York on this New Year's Day. Freckled Bob Fitzsimmons, debarred on account of advanced age from boxing in New York State, left the commonwealth flat on its back. With his manager, Johnny Meek, he entrained for Pennsylvania, shouting New York's motto: "Excelsior!"

"Excelsior!" yelled the spotted Cornishman. "The bloomin' State is stuffed with it!" He denied that he was an old man. "H'I'm so young," he declared, "that they ought to bring me before the Children's Court."

District Attorney Weeks shunned publicity. He did not stand in the way of his brilliant young Assistant, who decidedly *did* like publicity. Mr. Fallon soon piled up a long list of convictions, among them eight Black Handers. For years this gang had terrorized workmen employed on the Croton water system.

Between cases—and he worked hard—Fallon spent much time at the Polo Grounds. He often ran into his old friend, Eugene McGee, who was just plodding along.

"Do you still want me for a partner?" Fallon would ask.

"Whenever you get good and ready," was McGee's unvarying reply.

"Well, it may not be long, Gene. I'm not a prosecutor at heart."

"You're doing a fine job."

"I know, but my sympathies are with the fellow who is up against it. Most of them are sick mentally."

It is said that Fallon gave his earnings as Assistant District Attorney to families of men he sent to prison. He enjoyed the fury of his own eloquence and the combat of the court-room, but when the battle was over and the victim sentenced to servitude—or perhaps to the electric chair—Fallon found no pleasure in retrospect.

Fallon's wide acquaintance with people of the stage began at this time. Many theatrical folk believed that Fallon, after all, was more actor than lawyer. It was not uncommon to find a Broadway performer in the White Plains court-room, studying Fallon as he addressed a jury. Already he was a master in that respect.

Willie Collier, then playing "A Little Water on the Side" at the Hudson, was one of Fallon's favorite actor-friends. Another was Louis Mann, who found in Fallon the thing that he appreciated most—a good listener. While Mr. Mann was playing "The Bubble," Edward Locke's three-act comedy, at the Booth, Fallon often called at his dressing-room. Fallon regarded Mann as one of America's most intelligent actors.

Mann had an inflated ego. He had been everywhere and had seen everything. He had a memory that was almost as good as Fallon's. Sometimes, when they argued a point—whether about

Chaucer or the name of a hotel in Buffalo—Mann would become characteristically excited. He was, in reality, as gentle as a child, and always loyal to his art.

Among the things on which Mann prided himself most was his ability to imitate animals, domestic and wild. In one play—the name escapes me—he insisted on doing the duck-calls and cock-crows that went with the piece. He worked even harder behind the scenes, quacking and crowing, than he did when on stage as the star. It was not safe to kid him about it, either, for Mann was surprisingly strong. He even believed he could out-tussle Gentleman Jim Corbett. They clashed in a Palace Theater dressing-room one night. (Jim prolonged the contest until Mann's tongue stuck out like a red sock: "For God's sake, Jim!" gasped Mann, holding tight, *"Let's quit before we kill each other!"*)

At the play in which Mann doubled as star and duck-rooster, he invited a gallery of friends backstage to hear him give the barnyard calls. The waggish Walter Kelly, the Virginia Judge, had inferred that Mann's imitations were fake; that he used special whistles. Fallon was one of the backstage group. Joe Laurie, Jr., then a rising young vaudevillian; Raymond Hitchcock, Freddie Block, the burlesque official; Ren Wolfe, dramatic critic of the *Morning Telegraph;* Bill Collier, who was constantly baiting Mann about his super-high winged collars, and other sceptics from the *Friars* and *Lambs* Clubs, crowded about Mann as he awaited the farm-cues.

"I've added a dog-bit tonight for your benefit," said Mann, proudly. "I'll bark and growl especially for you. Also a *cat*-part. No one can me-eow like I can."

As the curtain rose, a bill-collector arrived backstage, taking advantage of the crowd of visitors to slip past the doorman. While Mann stood in the wings, waiting for the barnyard cue, the bill-collector, unused to backstage procedure, crossed over, behind the back-drop. The stranger brushed against the drop, making it shudder. Mann was furious.

"Who in hell can that be?" he whispered hoarsely.

"It's your rooster, or your duck," said Collier.

"I'll kill whoever it is," rasped Mann.

The bill-collector crossed back again. Once more he jiggled the back-drop. The poor chap, blundering in the semi-darkness, was unprepared for the attack. Mann sprang, clapping a low head-lock on him. Mann let his forearm and wrist settle across the collector's guzzler, shutting off his wind. He began to mop up the floor with the stranger.

In the middle of this scramble, Man's cue came for a rooster-crow. Without loosening his hold, Mann thrust out his chin and crowed: "Cockle-doodle-do-o-o-o-oooooo!" He returned at once to the business of pulling the collector limb-from-limb. Then came the duck-cue.

"Quack! Quack! Quack!" said Mann, pausing only long enough to respond to the cue. He resumed work on the half-strangled fellow, then stopped to answer the special dog- and cat-cues. "Bow, wow-wow-wow. G-r-r-r-r-rrrr." He whispered to the barely conscious collector: "You *will* rustle the back-drop, will you?" Then to the unseen audience: "Mee-e-e-eee-owwwww!"

The gallery of Mann friends rescued the sadly used stranger. He staggered to the stage-door and into the alley. Outside, the stranger found a policeman.

"For God's sake!" he gasped. "For God's sake, go inside!"

The officer made a pendulum of his night-stick. "What's eatin' on you?"

"Go inside," the stranger panted. "Or you'll be too late!"

"What in hell?" asked the patrolman.

"An actor's gone crazy in there, officer. He just tried to kill me, and now he's attacking the audience. He's making noises like eagles and lions. He's plumb nuts. I swear to God!"

Fallon's actor-friends kept insisting that he "belonged" in New York City. He smiled and said nothing. He served as Assistant District Attorney during the years 1914, 1915, and 1916.

Chapter Nine

AN ALLEGATION IN LAVENDER

THOMAS MOTT OSBORNE, stormy penologist, was born in Auburn, New York, September 23, 1859. His father was a figure in the so-called Harvester Trust; his mother a leader of the women's suffrage movement. The Osbornes lived in an ivy-covered mansion of the roomy Cambridge type, with a brick-walk approach, bordered by boxwood hedges and tall poplar trees. The South Street house was not far from Auburn State Prison. It was inevitable that Osborne become interested in prison affairs.

Tom Osborne attended Hobart College, and later was graduated from Harvard. He was tall and athletic. He was interested in art and music and could play the piano well. Sometimes he gave recitals. Mr. Osborne was married once, his wife dying in 1886. They had four sons.

Like another Harvard product, Big Bill Thompson of Chicago, Osborne reveled in the dramatic and the spectacular. Unlike Big-Bill-the-Builder, Osborne was cultured and articulate, and never even thought of "busting King George on the snoot." It is reasonable to assume that King George, barred from Chicago, might have come safely to Auburn at any time, and that Mr. Osborne himself would have captained the reception committee—perhaps carrying His Majesty's crown and scepter. Of course it would not have been advisable for the King to visit Auburn during a prison riot. Nobody's snoot is safe at such a time.

On graduating from Harvard, Osborne entered his father's reaper-works, eventually succeeding to the presidency of a concern employing 3,500 men. He proved a splendid organizer, a humane employer, and his men spoke well of him. Osborne, however, had a penchant for public service. He became Commissioner of the Board of Education. He enjoyed a close friendship with President Eliot of Harvard, sending many indigent boys to that University, paying all their expenses. Another friend and admirer was Dean George S. Kirchwey of Columbia Law School.

Osborne began his political life as a Democrat and subsequently became a leader up-state. He was unstable in his party affiliations, however, bolting the ticket that supported William Jennings Bryan in '96. Later he returned to the fold, in which the Grapejuice Commoner was silverplating his followers.

Osborne decided to run for mayor of Auburn. He organized an overall brigade and campaigned among the lunchbuckets of the workingmen. He was elected then, as well as a second time, in a community that hitherto had produced a Republican majority of 2,500. He was defeated a third time out.

Osborne's speeches were rip-roarers. His attacks were vigorous. He did not, at any time, however, dip into the gutter for political syllables.

Together with Henry George, Jr., and William Randolph Hearst, the publicist, Osborne became interested in the George Junior Republic. This was a self-governing institution for city boys—usually street waifs. The republic was at Freeville, New York, thirty miles south of Auburn. Osborne eventually became president of the association controlling the republic. He took many of the boys into his employ and sent some of them to Harvard. Before long he had differences with Mr. Hearst. He charged that the publicist sought to use his connection with the boys' institution as advertising promotion for his newspapers. This breach widened later in political conventions.

Osborne organized a Beethoven Orchestra in Auburn and frequently took the baton himself. He was not without critics in his home town. There were charges that Tom Osborne was "conceited" and "too smart." Certain of his detractors held it "a pity he should waste his father's money on his personal vanity." He had plenty of money, and just whose business it was what he did with it is not clear. As mayor he refused to accept a salary. Although gubernatorial sparks crackled in the Osborne skull, it is certain that he was charitable and no grafter.

He was fond of motoring. He toured Europe with his four sons in a machine called "The Green Dragon." This led him to turn literary, and he wrote a travel-book entitled "The Green Dragon."

Osborne hoped to be candidate for governor in the Democratic convention of 1906 that nominated the then Congressman William Randolph Hearst. He was outspoken against the publicist at the Buffalo conclave. He denounced the methods of State Chairman "Fingey" Connors, politician and Buffalo newspaper proprietor; also Tammany leader Charles Murphy. Osborne claimed these men favored and forced the Hearst nomination through ulterior motives.

State Chairman "Fingey" Connors was quite a boy. As a politician he was cagey and picturesque. His newspaper training was a bit ragged, but he made a go of his properties. Certain functions of newspaper-making were Greek to "Fingey." For example, he never could grasp the reason for an exchange editor. In case you don't know, an exchange editor sits at a paper-littered desk, reading public prints from other cities, clipping for fillers such whimsies as "When to Move Bees" and "Three-legged Donkey Born in the Bahamas."

"Fingey" passed the exchange editor's desk, day after day, and finally could stand the sight no longer.

"Who the hell is *that* guy?" he asked the managing editor.

"It's the exchange editor," was the reply.

"Well," said Mr. Connors, " '*It's*' goin' to be fired."

"Fired?"

"You heard me."

"O. K., Mr. Connors, but may I ask on what grounds?"

"Fire him," repeated Fingey. "I've seen him every day for a month, and all he ever does is *read newspapers!*"

Osborne bolted the Democratic ticket on account of the Hearst nomination. He turned whole-heartedly to prison affairs. He commenced an intensive study of penal conditions, and his opinions began to be quoted widely.

In 1913, Thomas Mott Osborne—as special investigator— voluntarily served a "sentence" at Auburn Prison. He was there a week. Warden Rattigan—an old friend—and one or two members of the prison board were the only persons supposed to know that the new "convict," Tom Brown, Number 33,333, was Thomas Mott Osborne.

Osborne, as Tom Brown, was placed at his request in the prison basket-shop. There had been complaints by convicts regarding the inferior grade of rattan rods. The rattans were too thick, they said, and too hard. Sore fingers became infected. Prison officers steamed the rods and otherwise treated them, but they were admittedly not up to standard.

On October 3, 1913, Tom Brown worked a short time on the afternoon shift. He put down a half-completed basket and nodded to Officer Otto Stitt, the basket-shop guard. Then he went to the toilet.

When Tom Brown returned, Officer Stitt said: "Whatcha go away for without askin'?"

"Why, officer," said Brown, "I looked toward you, and I thought I saw you nod that it was all right."

OFFICER: Well, I didn't see you, and I didn't nod.

BROWN: Oh, well, officer, it makes no difference. These rattans are too thick, and they hurt my fingers.

OFFICER: The hell they do! Well, you're the biggest guy here, and if the rest can work 'em, you ought to. Now let's not have none of your lip. Get busy, see!

BROWN: No, Mr. Stitt, I'm not going to work with these rattans any more.

OFFICER: Don't "Mr. Stitt" me, and cut out puttin' on airs. Remember, you're just a con, and you'll do as you're told, see?

BROWN: I'm through for today.

OFFICER: Do you mean you won't work no more?

BROWN: Precisely.

OFFICER: Oho! So you're pullin' big words on me, hey? "Precisely," hey? So that's it? Well, take your "precisely" over to that bench, and do it God damn quick, see?

BROWN: You mean you'll strike me if I refuse?

OFFICER: You fresh bastard! Get your hat and coat and come to the P. K.'s office. You fresh bastard, you!

BROWN: I'll go anywhere except back to the bench. Is that clear?

OFFICER: I ought to push in your face. Come on. You'll get yours!

Tom Brown got his gray coat and prison cap. Officer Stitt took him to the quarters of the Principal Keeper. There he repeated his refusal to work.

PRINCIPAL KEEPER: Then you'll have to go to the dungeons.

BROWN: Just as you say, sir.

KEEPER: I don't like to do it. You look like a sensible man.

BROWN: I won't work with those inferior rattans.

KEEPER: You use pretty good language for a con. I'll give you one more chance to comply, Brown. What say?

BROWN: My mind is made up.

OFFICER: He's settin' a bad example for the others.

BROWN: I'm thinking of the others when I choose to quit. Conditions are intolerable.

OFFICER: Who the hell do you think *you* are? Maybe you have a pull with the Gov'nor.

BROWN: That may be, too.

OFFICER: Haw! Haw! Give the Govvie my regards when you see him.

BROWN: I shall be delighted to do so, officer.

KEEPER: Well, how about you, Brown? Will it be back to work, or solitary confinement? It's no picnic in the dungeon.

BROWN: It's no picnic anywhere here, sir.

OFFICER: He's a philosopher. That's how he got to be a bunkie of His Knobs, the Gov'nor.

KEEPER: I've no alternative, Brown. (To officer) Take him to the dungeon. No convict can run this prison.

BROWN: Some day the convicts *will* have a voice.

OFFICER: He's screwy. Come on, Brown. It's nice and dark where you're goin'.

BROWN: Wouldn't you be surprised to wake up and find you'd made a mistake, officer?

OFFICER: Wouldn't you be surprised if I took a good swift kick at your pratt?

The guards stripped Tom Brown at 3 o'clock in the afternoon. "He's built like a horse," said Guard Raymond to Guard Cummings.

"What's he in for?" asked Cummings.

"Damned if I know. Somethin' desp'rate. I hear he tried to kill Stitt."

"Yeah. They say he smuggled in a gun or somethin'."

A special suit without pockets or metal fittings was put on Brown. Everything, including his pocket handkerchief, was taken away. They thrust him into a dungeon-cell. He had five neighbors, whom he could hear but could not see. The place smelled like a cabbage-cellar. Two of the five others were mental cases. There was neither bed nor chair. Brown lay on the floor, but he had to get to his feet when a rat and wife wanted to share his stone bed. He was nauseated.

Three gills of water and three slices of coarse-grained bread, cut thin, were put in his cell. "What time is it?" Brown asked the guard who placed the rations on the cell-floor.

"Shut your mouth," the guard said. "And keep it shut."

"Then you won't even tell me the time?"

"If you want the strait-jacket, just keep on crackin'."

The two feeble-minded prisoners began to gibber obscenely. When it became quiet again, the rats started to fight for Tom Brown's neglected bread. He kicked them away, knocking over his water. His throat was dry all night long. He had no way of knowing when dawn came, but at 6 o'clock there was a noise outside his cell. A guard with a flash-lamp told him to come along. Tom Brown returned to his regular cell. He was pale and dazed. His big body shook. He flopped on his cell-cot and lay face downward.

At 7 o'clock a keeper said: "Get up from there, Brown. The warden wants to see you."

When Warden Rattigan and Tom Brown were alone in the main office, Rattigan said: "Well, Tom, how about you? Don't you think you've had enough of this?"

"I have got what I came after," said Tom.

"The newspapers have got wind of it. Some of the boys are waiting to see you. Well?"

"I notified the newspapers myself, but I didn't know I'd be so upset. Tell them I'll give out a statement later."

At chapel the Rev. Arthur Copeland announced that Convict Tom Brown would make a speech. In his address, Tom Brown revealed himself as Thomas Mott Osborne. He received an ovation when he said he had undergone convict-treatment to familiarize himself with the problems of prisoners. He promised to work unceasingly for the betterment of convicts. When he left chapel, he was solicited by several separate guards, all of whom hoped their jobs were not jeopardized by their handling of him as Tom Brown.

"Don't worry," he said to each one individually, "it's not your fault. It's the fault of a barbarous system. You did your duty as you saw it."

"He's O. K.," said one "screw."

"He's batty," said another. "This ain't no kindy-garden."

Brown had a light lunch with the warden. On his way to the prison gate and to freedom, he was stopped by newspaper men. "I'll publish my findings later, boys. Right now I am too thrilled—in a horrible way, of course—by my recent experience in solitary. I am more confirmed than ever that the prison system is singularly unintelligent. It is a form of slavery."

Osborne's electric automobile was awaiting him at the gate. He drove to his home in South Street. The first thing he did was to eat a good meal. Then he began writing his book: "Within Prison Walls." In it, he described the prison system as "the organized lunacy of the people."

One passage read: "An aching, overwhelming sense of the hideous cruelty of the whole barbaric, brutal business sweeps over me; the feeling of moral, physical and mental outrage; the monumental imbecility of it all; the horrible darkness, the cruel iron walls at our backs; the nerve-racking routine; the whirring dynamo through the other wall; the filth, the vermin, the bad air; the insufficient food, the denial of water and the overpowering, sickening sense of accumulated misery—of madness and suicide—haunting the place."

On December 1, 1914, Thomas Mott Osborne assumed office as Warden of Sing Sing Prison. He succeeded Acting-Warden George S. Weed. Weed had been appointed temporarily, following the dismissal of Warden Thomas J. McCormick. The latter had been stripped of office for granting unusual liberties to David A. Sullivan, former Brooklyn banker.

Mr. Osborne, now a man with iron-gray hair, inspected the entire prison plant. As he was visiting the shoe-factory, an elderly convict stepped from the line-up, tipped his gray cap and said: "Good morning, Mr. Osborne."

Warden Osborne's guard-escort got ready to sock the too-familiar convict, but the big warden smiled and pumped the hand of the convict. The guard-escort's eyes bulged. It is believed it cut his life-span by at least ten years.

"Why, hello, Bill," said the Warden. "I didn't expect to see you here."

"Oh, yes," said Bill, "I'm here for a six-months' bit."

"I remember you well at Auburn," said the warden. He had an uncanny memory for names and faces.

The new warden tasted the coffee and proclaimed it "rotten." He condemned the medieval bucket-system. He began to make wholesale changes at Sing Sing.

"The State has a right to punish a prisoner," he said. "But it has no right, constitutional or otherwise, to rob him of his health."

Men, diseased or well, washed from the same bucket. There was little running water anywhere in the prison. The fire hazard was great. The cells were antiquated. There were 1,200 cells, each one seven feet long, six feet six inches high and three feet four inches wide. Two men sometimes occupied one cell.

There was a society of prisoners known as The Golden Rule Brotherhood. Osborne interviewed fifty of the so-called delegates of this society.

"There's one grave slip in your organization, boys," he said. "You have no way of disciplining members except by sending them to prison authorities. That's bad. You should be self-governing and self-disciplining. You must have the power to suspend offenders after a trial. Your punishment should consist of taking away the afternoon privileges and recreational hours of an offender."

Osborne had broken up the drug-traffic at Auburn Prison. He now undertook to do likewise at Sing Sing. Certain guards were said to be carrying on a lucrative business, supplying convicts with narcotics. It also was charged that prostitutes were brought into the prison for the entertainment of moneyed inmates. Osborne's drive against these abuses stirred the ire of petty grafters, who presumably were shielded by politicians. The warden began to be praised by some and attacked by others as a "faddist" and a "show-off."

"Out of every ten convicts," Osborne said, "there are nine who want to behave, and one who doesn't. It is up to the nine well-behaved ones to take care of the one dissenter. There must be less 'guarding' and so-called supervision. The men work better if they are not constantly reminded that they are rats in a trap. We will increase their recreational periods."

"But it will make them lazy," said a prison commissioner.

"No. I'd rather have the men work two hours than putter around, cheat and loaf for eight. One of the worst things the State can teach the men is to work badly."

"But these are men of the criminal type."

"There is no criminal type."

"They won't feel they are being punished if you allow so many liberties."

"Nonsense, Commissioner. Prison always will be prison. Punishment consists of curtailing a man's liberty."

Warden Osborne founded the Mutual Welfare League, in which the prisoners virtually governed themselves. Although that system since has been modified and parts of it rejected, it marked the beginning of more intelligent treatment of prisoners all over the country. Osborne shelved the old "silence" rule. Prisoners now might speak to one another under certain conditions. Production in the shops increased when guards were withdrawn. There were abuses, however, and it was said that perverted practices increased among the convicts.

Warden Osborne organized an orchestra in Sing Sing. He allowed baseball games and asked Battling Nelson, the famous lightweight, to promote boxing-bouts inside the prison walls. Superintendent of State Prisons, John B. Riley, refused to sanction these bouts, scheduled for July 4, 1915. Osborne otherwise met with outside interference. But he continued to modernize the prison. He delivered lectures before groups of prominent citizens.

On October 5, 1915, twenty-five ex-convicts tendered a

private party to Osborne at the Park Avenue Hotel. They ate a fine dinner and made speeches. All of them had returned to the free world and to good jobs. They raised their glasses to "Tom Brown," who made one of his emotional speeches. He called them "his boys" and would not consent to sitting on a dais. The men sang, talked, and hoisted wine until a late hour. The big, gray-haired warden beamed.

"It's getting late," said one ex-con to another.

"That's O.K.," was the reply. "We got an A-1 alibi while we're here."

Nearly every speech, including "Tom Brown's", began with the preamble: "I'm proud to be an ex-convict. . . ."

Warden Osborne permitted the men to ornament their cells with pictures and knickknacks. Most of the pictures either were of a sacred sort or family portraits. He gave each man two suits of underwear, so that one suit could be kept clean. Before Osborne took charge, the correspondence privilege was confined to one out-going letter a week. However, if a convict had a bit of graft-money, he could write oftener. The new warden increased the number of letters allowed.

One convict—in the pre-Osborne régime—received word that his wife was dying. "Would you let me write to her?" the convict asked the "screw."

"You already have wrote one letter this week."

"Please let me write. She's dyin'."

"Well, wait till she dies and I'll give you some paper."

State officials warned Osborne that he was smashing too many rules. He said: "I like to smash rules."

There was a great concert in October, 1915, by the "Tom Brown Band." A lifer played the flute, and a fellow whose sentence had been commuted from death in the electric chair to life imprisonment, banged the drum. The boys rendered "Poet and Peasant" for Osborne. He finally had obtained sanction for the Battling Nelson boxing-program, and it was given with the band concert. Mr. A. J. Drexel Biddle, of the Philadelphia Biddles, a doughty man with the gloves, showed the Sing Sing boys how it should be done. He used the ring-worn chin of Philadelphia Jack O'Brien for his anvil-shots. There were several well-known boxers in the group that performed for the Sing Sing audience, among them Leach Cross (now a dentist), Young Ahearn, Ted Kid Lewis, Eddie Morgan and Freddie Welsh, the pride of Pontypridd, Wales.

Osborne rectified abuses, one by one. There was the laundry situation. Owing to graft in the shirt-tail emporium, it was impossible for a convict to get his handkerchiefs or socks returned unless he paid a fee for "protection." Osborne discovered one case in which a convict's wife sent a weekly cash-dribble from her pitiful earnings to insure her husband's socks.

For good behavior, Osborne distributed presents. He gave away oranges, apples, and bananas, and occasionally tobacco. He was criticised for this by smug gentlemen, who never had breathed the air of incarceration. Several guards, discharged by Osborne, found willing ears for gossip concerning the Warden and his alleged relations with convicts. Word went round that the big, gray-haired man was an epicene.

The Westchester grand jury at White Plains indicted Osborne on December 28, 1915. The accusations charged him with perjury, and neglect of duty. Two indictments, containing seven counts—one of which alleged personal immorality with prisoners—were handed up to Justice Morschauser.

On the question of indicting, the jury stood fourteen for and six against, the affirmative having two more votes than the number needed. The charges may be summarized as follows:

1—That he (Osborne) absented himself from prison, being on duty but four days a week.

2—That he was neglectful in performing his duties, so that there were assaults within the prison.

3—That he neglected to report such assaults.

4—That he permitted at least four persons to visit the death-house in violation of the law, when Police Lieutenant Charles Becker (electrocuted for the murder of Gambler Herman Rosenthal by Gyp-the-Blood, Leftie Louie and other gangsters) was there confined.

5—That he allowed certain unfit inmates of Sing Sing to control the discipline of the prison, its management, and its policies.

6—That he failed properly to protect the convicts under his control and permitted lax discipline generally.

7—That he personally was guilty of gross immorality with Paul Vogel, James Connelly, Max Kleinberg, Henry Delara, Sidney Walsh, and others.

The perjury indictment charged that one month after a convict named Harvey had told Osborne that immorality was common in the prison, the warden had sworn before the authorities that there was no immorality.

District Attorney Weeks, in conjunction with his now noteworthy assistant, William J. Fallon, announced he would not ask for a warrant if Osborne would agree to appear the next court-day, December 31.

Mr. Osborne had been expecting adverse action by the grand jury. "It had to come. The politicians are after me. They will leave no vile charge out of their attacks."

The warden simulated serenity. The prison wireless conveyed the news. The "boys" were despondent. The warden assembled the convicts in the mess hall after supper, the day of the indictments. They began filing in from the cell-blocks; not a few were crying.

"They're givin' the old man the business," was the plaint.

Most of the men understood the full weight of the indictments, including the lavender implication. A rousing cheer greeted the warden as he stood before the convicts.

"I have just received one of the greatest honors of my career, boys," he began in a melodious voice. "I have just heard that I've been indicted by the Westchester grand jury. I presume you will all congratulate me."

The sad atmosphere dissolved beneath the warden's dulcet tones. The boys laughed at his sally. He went on:

"But I'm Warden of Sing Sing. I'll be Warden of Sing Sing until they kick me out."

There were cheers and cries of: "The hell with them, Warden!" "We're with you to a man!"

"These indictments," the Warden said, "will make friends for our Mutual Welfare League. I am glad to be attacked for bringing you baseball and movies. I'll fight for you always."

On October 9, 1916, Warden Osborne resigned in a letter to Governor Charles S. Whitman. The letter charged Whitman with having acquiesced in "shameful attacks made upon me in Westchester County." On October 15, 1916, Osborne bid farewell to Sing Sing Prison. He shook hands with the 1,600 convicts. The prisoners almost rioted in an effort to demonstrate their affection. There was a gray line extending from the mess hall into the yard. The line broke suddenly. The men swarmed about the big figure in the light coat and soft hat.

"It's the boss!" they yelled.

The warden's lunch grew cold while he held a long farewell in the prison yard. He called the convicts by name and recounted some personal incident concerning each one. The prisoners God-blessed him. Some of the afternoon newspapers in New York City God-damned him. There were three great cheers for "Tom Brown" as he walked away from his "boys."

The Osborne case added to Fallon's stature, despite the outcome. It gave him greater self-assurance, and it focused the attention of the bar on the young prosecutor. District Attorney Weeks, never a show-off, permitted his brilliant assistant to take whatever credit there was for entering the lists against some of the foremost legal minds of the day.

Osborne may have posed as a martyr before his Sing Sing "boys"; it is true he joked in some of his talks with them. But he was cut deeply. He was, after all, a sensitive big man. So fearful had he been of the outcome of the grand jury inquiry that he had visited the District Attorney's offices in White Plains and pleaded with Weeks not to call any convicts before that body.

Osborne saw on Weeks' desk a long letter from Superintendent of Prisons John B. Riley. "I wish you'd ignore that," Osborne said.

"It contains a list of fights and assaults at the prison," replied Weeks. "Some of them have resulted in serious injuries. The grand jury's investigation is based on this letter."

"I beg you not to call the convicts," Osborne said.

"How about these alleged assaults?"

"Pooh! Pooh! Just talk. They are incidents that I, as warden, ought to deal with. Just incidents."

"Well," said Weeks, "what would *you* do with the Riley letter?"

"Ignore it."

"What! Would you have me disregard a letter from your superior, and on your say-so?"

Weeks showed Osborne a list of cases. He read off six or seven, each one an instance of first- or second-degree assault.

"I'm no surgeon," said the District Attorney, "but when I see that so-and-so had five stitches taken in his head, I know it was an assault."

Osborne interrupted quickly. "I didn't say to ignore the letter."

"Then I don't understand English," said the D.A.

Osborne's friends engaged George Gordon Battle and a number of other prominent attorneys. His long-time friend, Dean Kirchwey of Columbia, acted in an advisory capacity. Not only was it a crisis in the warden's experiment in prison management; it was undoubtedly the climacteric of his political life.

Osborne was a Democrat, serving under a Republican administration. He had made enemies among discharged guards. He had put his heel on peculating contractors, insisting on an economic basis of repair and building-bills and on fair prices for good food, instead of enormous prices for bad food. He had four stalwart sons. These factors must be taken into account when considering the thread of lavender that ran the whole length of the mantle of accusation.

Osborne, through his sensational reforms, his undoubted economical practices, his self-evident culture, and his power for organization, up to now looked the sure Democratic candidate for Governor. Mr. Whitman, the Republican incumbent, had come to high office, Osborne charged, over the body of the executed Lieutenant Becker. Gov. Whitman appeared to be entertaining White House aspirations. If he didn't have them, then his friends surely had such hopes for their leader. If Whitman were to miss out at the coming election, the White House dream would become a Willie's-lost-lollipop. Certain Republican leaders believed it was necessary to "get" Osborne.

[The irony of life, love and plug-hats is a bitter dish of tea, when we consider that Mr. Whitman later was sounded out for the candidacy for Vice-President of the United States. He scorned it. Mr. Coolidge accepted. Warren Harding died. Heigho! Set 'em up in the next alley.]

Osborne's influential friends endeavored to block the removal of convicts from Sing Sing as witnesses. The first act by the District Attorney's office—Mr. Fallon working like a bunch of fire-crackers in a kettle—was the transfer of ex-Congressman William Willett of Queens from Sing Sing to the White Plains jail. Mr. Willett had been convicted of trying to buy a Supreme Court nomination. Now he was "chief justice" of the convict-court at Ossining.

Mr. Willett moved from Sing Sing to White Plains on a Friday night in November, 1915, on a writ of *habeas corpus* granted by Justice Morschauser, there to remain at the District Attorney's instructions and until the grand jury inquiry's end. Nearly all assaults and other cases mentioned in Superintendent Riley's letter had been "tried" before Willett as a Mutual Welfare justice. In fact, Willett was himself one of those assaulted.

Willett was one of two principal witnesses against Osborne. The other (not a convict) was a Rochester physician. The latter was said to be ready to go into the lavender implication with medical authority.

Mr. Fallon announced that he would prosecute the twenty or more assault cases, and added:

"But I don't know just *where* this thing will lead."

Bill had an inferential way of making such statements. His phraseology, "not knowing just where it will lead," aroused publicity and speculation.

"It will be useless for anybody but myself to question these men," Osborne said in reference to the convicts. "I am the only one that knows how to get the truth out of them."

"I'll get the truth," said Fallon. "In fact, I *have* the truth. I'll show how you pinched the cheek of one convict, a young chap, and said: 'Why, you have the face of a girl!'"

The Osborne case was destined to drag for months. Dean Kirchwey was Osborne's companion throughout the uncertain days.

The insinuations against the morals of Osborne flared into the wide-open when Fallon read the affidavit of one, Paul Vogel, a convict, charging that Sing Sing love had laughed at locksmiths. The reading occurred on December 13, 1915, in Justice Morschauser's court, White Plains, and during the sitting of the grand jury.

"I'll offer to make *all* the testimony and numerous affidavits public," said Mr. Fallon. His powers of insinuation already were developed to a high degree. "That is," he added, "if Mr. Osborne will *consent*."

Mr. Battle and Huntington W. Merchant, of Osborne's counsel, surprised Mr. Fallon. "We consent to that," said Mr. Battle. The shrewd Battle was anxious to get his hands on the grand jury minutes. He sensed that Fallon was bluffing. It was to be a long, hard pull before anyone got those minutes. Fallon, then, as later, made daring moves and created exaggerated effects to gain immediate objectives. Right now he was seeking to prejudice Osborne's case with court and political public.

The Osborne counsel alleged they had been trying—without avail—to induce the District Attorney's office to bring the charges into the open.

In this case, Mr. Merchant nominally was Osborne's counsel, Mr. Battle acting for the National Prison Reform Association. They filed with Justice Morschauser a twenty-four-page brief, charging the District Attorney's office with attempting to prejudice Osborne before the grand jury; of forcing convicts (with promises of immunity and pruning-down of sentences, as well as by threats) to testify against the warden; of refusing to call witnesses that Osborne asked to be called; of allowing ex-Congressman Willett to conduct the inquiry, and seeking to compel Osborne to testify to confessions made to him by prisoners—confessions he had believed confidential.

The witnesses whom Osborne had asked the District Attorney to bring before the grand jury were: Dean Kirchwey, George W. Wickersham, former Attorney General of the United States; Charles F. Rattigan, Warden of Auburn Prison; Richard M. Hurd, president of the Lawyer's Mortgage Company and State Prison Commissioner; Clifford E. Harmon, Dr. E. Stagg Whitin, of the National Prison Labor Commission; Miss Madeline Z. Doty and Miss Emily Seaman, both women investigators of the Prison Commission.

Mr. Fallon told the court: "Osborne has evaded answering questions. Here is the testimony of Paul Vogel, a convict. He swore Osborne told him: 'You are a good-looking boy; if I were a girl, I would fall in love with you.' The warden was asked if he knew a boy named Connolly. He said he did. He was asked if Connolly was truthful. His answer was 'yes.' When we read him Connolly's testimony charging him with a crime, Osborne's answer was: 'He's a damned liar.'" Mr. Fallon's voice rose. "Osborne also called District Attorney Weeks a damned liar."

The court interjected: "There is no need of becoming hysterical. Everybody will get his rights here if it takes until next summer."

"Your Honor," said Mr. Battle, "coercion has been used to compel convicts to give testimony, to compel them to make affidavits against the warden."

Mr. Fallon folded his arms. "We have affidavits; yes, innumerable affidavits, showing that this man is the worst kind of degenerate, and for that reason he should not be in the management of Sing Sing Prison."

The court hemmed. "He may be ever so bad a man, and all that you say may be true, Mr. Fallon, but that is not the question before me at this time. The question now is: shall he divulge privileged statements made to him by convicts?"

"I have here an affidavit of Sidney L. Welsh," declared Mr. Fallon. "It was obtained in another prison. This man has not been here. He charges him with the vilest crimes. Shall I read it?"

"No."

"Has Mr. Osborne the right to refuse to answer the questions before the grand jury?" asked Mr. Fallon.

"I refuse to answer that question," said the court.

The lawyers then went to the grand jury room, where ex-Congressman Willett was telling about the Mutual Welfare League. The warden was jubilant and expressed himself confident of clearing himself of all charges.

The case was fated to limp along, however, with political ramifications that at times cloaked the real issue. The trial itself finally was set, but was delayed because of Mr. Weeks' application for a writ of prohibition to prevent Osborne's counsel from moving to strike from the indictment the count charging immorality. M. J. Tierney and others had joined the defendant's counsel.

Justice Arthur S. Tomkins threw the perjury indictment out of court. Mr. Battle kept thundering for a trial and Justice Martin J. Keogh set it for March 30. Fallon reported the People as not ready. He explained that some of the convicts had recanted their grand jury testimony. Other defections were reported. One of the convict-witnesses proved to be a man disciplined by Osborne. After a baseball game at the prison yard, this man had put on the wrong coat. Another convict-player put on the first convict's coat. In the pocket was a memorandum showing the owner's plan to escape. The finder of the coat turned this memorandum over to the warden. The owner of the coat was called to the warden's office and disciplined.

Osborne appeared before Justice Morschauser early in 1916 with a demand for permission to plead to the indictment charging mismanagement and immorality. He also made a new demand for the grand jury minutes. Mr. Fallon refused to surrender the minutes. Osborne's attorneys then went before Justice Tomkins, who ordered all evidence that had been transcribed to be delivered forthwith. When this order was shown to Fallon, he refused to comply. Contempt proceedings were talked of, the first of such proceedings that often threatened Bill later in his career. Even as a prosecutor he was beginning to "get on the nerves of the courts."

Lawyer Huntington W. Merchant visited the District Attorney's office with the Tomkins order at noon, January 21, 1916. "I want the minutes," he told Fallon.

"What minutes?" asked Fallon.

"Come now, Fallon. You know what minutes."

"I certainly don't know, unless you tell me."

Lawyer Merchant was fuming. "I want the minutes of the Osborne case."

"Oh!" said Fallon. "*Those* minutes."

"Yes, *those* minutes."

Fallon could be most annoying. "We have but one copy. But if you really *want* the minutes, you'll have to bring a stenographer to copy our set."

"Oh, no," said Merchant. "Not at all. The court order is that all the testimony, except that of Stenographer Young, be delivered to us at once; the rest in a few days. Now we want 'em, Bill."

"Wanting them is not getting them," Bill said. "Anyway, how *could* we give you the originals? Our typist is away, sick, and you'll have to wait until she gets well. It may be a year."

"Sick or no sick, Bill. Here's the order."

Bill looked at the order. "That won't do. I don't recognize some of the writing. I'll have to see Judge Tomkins to verify it."

Mr. Merchant was beside himself.

A messenger arrived with a notice of intent to ask for an order compelling the District Attorney to permit Osborne to plead to the indictment. The notice was presented to Mr. Fallon in the presence of the inflamed Mr. Merchant.

Fallon pursed his lips and made clucking sounds. "No-o-o," he drawled, "I can't sign this notice 'copy received'."

"Oh, for God's sake, Fallon, go ahead and sign it," said Merchant. "It will save me the necessity of making an affidavit that the notice has been served."

"No," said Fallon, "we'll have to have five days' notice."

"Come on, Bill."

"No," Fallon said. "You'll have to make out the affidavit."

Mr. Merchant, very hungry by now, retired to an anteroom where he made out the affidavit and wrote a formal demand for the grand jury minutes. Fallon went to lunch. When Mr. Merchant appeared an hour later, he couldn't find Fallon. He had to wait three hours. Bill said he was exceptionally hungry that day.

"I had the finest steak you ever saw," Bill told Merchant. "You don't mean to say you have been *waiting* all this time? Oh, *what* a steak it was! Mushrooms and butter-gravy. French fried potatoes and——"

"Oh, for God's sake!" pleaded the starved counselor.

Among the convict-witnesses held at White Plains jail were Kid Dropper, Joe Rotala, James Connelly, "Mayor" of Sing Sing Prison, and Bill Trefry, pitcher on the Mutual Welfare Team and operator of the telephone switchboard in the prison office. They told Fallon many tales of alleged mismanagement and sexual aberration. Kid Dropper came to the District Attorney's office by a rear entrance to avoid an appearance of violating the gangster's anti-squealing code. Later he asked for a transfer to Great Meadows Prison, fearing reprisal.

Inasmuch as the new courthouse was being built, the District Attorney's offices were located temporarily in the Realty Building across the street. And here occurred one of the two important behind-the-scenes events that outmaneuvered Bill Fallon for the first and perhaps the last time in his career.

"I'm desperate," Osborne told Mr. Battle. "I'm being jobbed. What would you suggest?"

Mr. Battle said: "I want you to tell your whole story, omitting nothing, to Val O'Farrell."

"A detective, isn't he?"

"One of the best."

Mr. Battle put in a call for Val O'Farrell, former lieutenant of detectives of the New York Police Department, and the nimblest Sherlock in private practice.

"I'll be down as soon as the palm is crossed with silver," said Mr. O'Farrell, who is a good business man.

"Come ahead," said Battle.

O'Farrell brought with him his able assistant, Archie Owen. They listened to Osborne's story. O'Farrell said he believed that a conspiracy was evident. Not only were convicts being forced to testify, he was told, but a certain physician in Rochester—a man of fine professional standing—was being groomed to take the stand against Osborne. The doctor and ex-Congressman Willett were to be the "star" witnesses for the State.

"I'll get my operative, Valentine, to handle the Rochester angle," said O'Farrell. "I'll tend to this end."

In despatching Valentine to Rochester, Mr. O'Farrell purchased twelve of the new and much-discussed violet-ray lamps. "What in the devil?" asked Battle.

"Never mind," said O'Farrell. "We want violet-rays."

As O'Farrell said good-by to Valentine, he called out: "Don't get sun-burned."

It was an inclement spring and very cold. Mr. O'Farrell appeared incognito in White Plains as "Col. Trout," late of the British Infantry. He engaged offices in the Realty Building through a "remove," or intermediary, so as not to be discovered. These offices were four floors below the District Attorney's temporary offices, which were on the seventh floor.

Archie Owen, an expert electrician and linesman, set-up a detectaphone apparatus in "Col. Trout's" office. "You might have chosen a warmer night," Owen said to O'Farrell as they "shinnied up" the face of the building with scaling ladders. It was necessary for them to get a night watchman drunk and to put a wire over the top of the building, bringing it down the other side.

On the flat roof of the building, Archie selected a hammer and some staples to make the wire fast. A gale was blowing and it was zero weather. He had been pounding for half a minute, thinking he was driving the staple into mortar. It was very dark. O'Farrell finally risked a flash-lamp to see what was delaying Archie.

"Good God!" O'Farrell said, "don't you know that you're pounding your *finger*?"

"The hell!" said Archie. He had hammered the first joint of his left forefinger to a frozen jelly. A week later it was necessary to amputate it. But the detectaphone was installed.

For some weeks, the O'Farrell stenographers took down everything that was said, not only in the Fallon offices, but in the grand jury room. From that time on, the District Attorney began to be worried by check-matings and counter-moves.

"I think we've got enough to prove a conspiracy," said O'Farrell in March.

"I guess so," Battle said. "But what about that physician in Rochester?"

"We'll hear from Valentine soon."

O'Farrell took from his office the entire detectaphone force and all records. Through his "removes" he hired a complete new staff. Then he deliberately tipped-off Fallon that a detectaphone had been employed wherewith to find out what had been going on. Meanwhile O'Farrell dictated a *new* set of records. He set down tremendous exaggerations, in what purported to be the detectaphone notes. Val became so imaginative that for a time he believed himself related to the late Jules Verne. Val scattered the trumped-up records all over the place.

Fallon's men descended on the office, tracing it through the wire that had cost Archie Owen his pie-finger. They gloated. They seized the "records" and pinched the office force. The members of the new outfit had no more idea of what they had been doing for "Col. Trout" than had Mrs. O'Leary's cow that time in Chicago. The more Fallon questioned the "staff," the more he was at sea. He got the funniest sort of answers.

Sheriff Wiesendanger and a deputy found two young men and a young woman in the "Col. Trout" office. They said they had been employed by Colonel Trout and knew nothing whatsoever about a detectaphone. These bewildered persons were subpoenaed and told to be in court the following Monday, when Mr. Osborne was scheduled to go on trial.

When the anti-Osborne forces read O'Farrell's imaginative records, they were frantic. Mr. O'Farrell chuckled and regarded himself as a modern Charles Dickens. It all sounded true—and very damning. Fallon raised a shout that O'Farrell would be prosecuted for eavesdropping.

"Go ahead and prosecute me," O'Farrell told Fallon. "Eavesdropping has something to do with an ear to the keyhole. We didn't bother about keyholes."

The boys at Albany rushed a bill through, making the installation of a detectaphone a serious offense.

Valentine took his violet-ray machines to Rochester. Inasmuch as he was selling these expensive contraptions at one-third the market-price, he found ready buyers. When he had disposed of several, with appropriate lectures on "Let the sun's own rays cure you of that lost manhood," he visited the offices of the physician who was to be the anti-Osborne star witness.

"It's a marvelous machine," Valentine said. "I've sold them to so-and-so and to so-and-so. They gave me your name. Now, you can help me sell more of them. If you want to come in with me, there's a fortune in it."

"I think they really are good things," said the physician.

"Well, as a starter," said Valentine, "I'll give you one *free*, if you'll write me a testimonial."

The physician was delighted. He went to his desk and wrote the testimonial.

Mr. Fallon had sporadic attacks of sinus trouble during the winter of the Osborne case. At times it was so painful as to threaten his turning over the work to a second assistant. A surgeon removed a small bone from the nasal cavity. Mr. Fallon, in this, his first real illness, refused to quit work.

"Can't you rest a few days?" the surgeon asked.

"I've got to be on the job," said Fallon.

"But you will be in pain for a while."

"I don't need a doctor to tell me that. I'm in pain now."

The doctor poured a drink of rye. "Here. This may brace you up."

"No, thanks," Fallon said. "I don't drink."

"This won't hurt you; but of course, if you have scruples about drinking. . . ."

"Well, give it to me. I guess it won't do any harm."

Mr. Fallon took his first drink. He was twenty-nine years old, almost thirty. He downed other bracers in the busy months that followed. He became what is known as a moderate drinker.

"There is no question in my mind," said District Attorney Weeks, "that efforts are being made to intimidate the State's witnesses. "Not only has a detectaphone been used to anticipate the State's case, but I hear that wives of convicts are being told that if their husbands testify for the State, they will never get a parole, and will be rearrested when their terms expire."

Convicts watching the newspapers noticed that ex-Congressman Willett didn't get his parole for ninety days after he was eligible.

The big trial finally came off before judge and jury. Many political personages were in the doldrums, largely because of the detectaphone records. No one among them knew exactly *what* had been recorded or *to whom* it had been said. The State now depended, it was believed, on the Rochester physician to weave the lavender thread in the rope that was allegedly fashioned to hang Osborne politically. Mr. Battle, supplied with a second round of Val O'Farrell's ammunition, awaited the enemy's charge.

The physician took the stand and qualified as an expert witness. Mr. Battle led him on, calmly. He inquired into all manner of medical matters that at first appeared immaterial. Then finally:

Q: Do you have any faith in the new appliances? the electrical ones, such as the fluoroscope? A: Yes, indeed.

Q: And what is your opinion of the violet-ray lamp? A: Why, I think it beneficial in certain cases.

Q: What kind of cases? A: In the treatment of rickets and other maladies that are alleviated by the sun's rays.

Q: Then this machine duplicates the sun's rays?

Mr. Fallon: Your Honor, I object. What has the sun's rays to do with this witness or this case?

Mr. Battle: The sun is an enlightening medium.

The Court: What is the purpose of this line of inquiry, Mr. Battle?

Mr. Battle: Your Honor, I intend to impeach this witness.

Mr. Fallon: With the sun's rays? Your Honor, Mr. Battle thinks he is a Joshua and will make the sun stand still.

The Court: I shall permit the questioning until it is shown what counsel is aiming at. Be more explicit, Mr. Battle. This case already has lagged.

Mr. Battle now asked the witness: "Did you ever write a testimonial in behalf of a violet-ray lamp?"

The witness seemed to be fearing some sort of trap.

"Come," Mr. Battle said. "Answer yes or no."

"Yes. I recommended such a lamp."

Mr. Battle produced the testimonial written for Valentine, the day the free lamp was promised. "Is this the letter?"

The witness read it. "Yes."

Mr. Battle entered the letter in the record, and over the objection of Mr. Fallon, who shouted: "What do we care about a man's correspondence concerning violet-rays? Mr. Osborne is not charged with being a bad electrician. His conduct at the electric chair is not being impugned."

The court allowed the letter. Mr. Battle read it into the record. The document testified to benefits obtained by use of the violet-ray. The letter said, in substance, that the doctor had used this apparatus for several years and had arrived at pleasing results. No one could go far wrong in owning one, especially at such low cost.

"And now," said Mr. Battle, roaring, "this man appears here, swearing to tell the truth. He admits this is his letter. Your Honor, and gentlemen of the jury——"

"Are you summing up?" asked Mr. Fallon.

The Court: Sit down, Mr. Fallon. If you have an objection, make it in the prescribed form.

Mr. Fallon: I make such an objection now.

The Court: Overruled.

Mr. Battle: He writes this letter as a testimonial. This witness says he has—mark the words—*used it for several years*. Your Honor, we shall show that this lamp has not only *not* been on the

market for several years; it has been before the public for only
six months!

Mr. Fallon whispered to Eugene McGee, who had come to
hear his Fordham friend in action: "There goes the old ball
game!"

It was the theoretical end of the witness and the virtual close
of the famous case. The Court granted Mr. Battle's motion
to dismiss the charges for lack of evidence. The case did not go
to the jury. The gray-haired penologist was absolved of illegal
acts as charged in the indictment alleging mismanagement and
immorality.

"This defeat," Fallon said, "did me more good than anything that ever happened to me. I learned much. I had the most
brilliant opposition. If I had won, perhaps I should have grown
too sure of myself."

"The mistake I made," he said at another time, "was being
too aggressive at the wrong time. I turned a prosecution into a
persecution. And that is always bad."

He was destined to escape a serious charge himself one future
day, largely because a prosecution became a persecution.

Thomas Mott Osborne's gubernatorial chances had dimmed,
no matter what his legal victory had done to clear his record
or his name. He plunged, as usual, into prison work. He returned
to Sing Sing as warden in July, 1916. He was promised he would
meet with no further interference.

There were gay ceremonies marking "Tom Brown's" return
to his "boys." Only one thing marred the reunion. Mr. Osborne's
former convict-secretary, Dick Richards, had been paroled during the Osborne absence and had forged a check in Osborne's
name for $2,000. His parole was revoked. On the day Osborne
returned as warden, members of the Mutual Welfare League
stood guard over Richards.

Mr. Osborne's reappearance at Sing Sing was brief. He
resigned soon, bitterly attacking Whitman and others, charging

that every sort of masked interference had been set against him. When he left, he was commanded by a high prison official "never to set foot again in any State institution."

In June, 1920, Lieutenant-Commander Thomas Mott Osborne of the United States Navy, not only set foot inside Sing Sing's walls, but aroused an enthusiasm said to have surpassed ovations accorded John L. Sullivan, the Hon. William Jennings Bryan, and the Reverend Evangelist William Ashley Sunday on their respective visits to the Big House. Osborne now was commanding the Naval prison at Portsmouth.

The Lieutenant-Commander received the "freedom of Sing Sing." Warden Lewis E. Lawes permitted him to go alone among the inmates. Osborne met "O.K." Bill Myers, the bank burglar, one of the former warden's right-hand men in the old days.

"We miss you a lot, boss," said Myers, "but Major Lawes is a fine man, too."

"I'm sure he is," said the Lieutenant-Commander. "And you can all do me a favor by playing square with him."

The former warden then called on a gangster in the prison hospital. The man was convalescing from an operation for stomach trouble.

"How's your stomach now?" asked Osborne.

"I et too much lead when I was a gun," said the gangster.

"You'll have to go on a diet," said Osborne.

The Fire Island Baker ferried me across Great South Bay in his good white dory. It was late winter and the sheet ice still floated in thin islands on the dark waters. I never knew such a neighborly fellow. He said he would help me write the book. In return, I helped grease his cake-pans. We spent the early mornings together beside the hot oven, and the smell of warm dough was satisfying. The city seemed so far away.

It is sure that certain prosecuting officers believed Osborne guilty of the lavender charge. Fallon maintained as much until the last. After a diligent inquiry into the man's life and into the case itself, I cannot share this belief. I am told that a biographer should not inject editorial opinions into a story, but the Baker on Fire Island wanted to know about this phase, and I think more of him and his cinnamon buns than I do of ten thousand technicians, smug-mugs and literary architects. . . . Only yesterday we rode through a gale to Lonleyville and the Baker said:

"I wish'd to God Admiral Dot was here to tell us about them elephants."

If, however, Mr. Osborne were given to secret practices of the sort alleged, I fall back immediately on the position taken by Captain Jeremiah Dorcas, skipper of *The Four Brothers* out of Halifax.

"And what happened?" the Baker asked.

"Wait until I get this fire-place going," I said, pouring kerosene on the damp wood. It took a long time. There were pale yellow flames. That was the sea-salt. There was a clear, jade flame licking through the yellow. That's where corroded brass was being heated. Rust-caked iron gives off a purple flame, and that's what brought about the whole discussion.

"For the love of God," the Baker said, "hurry up with the Captain's story."

"It was in a gale like this very one," I said, "when *The Four Brothers* finally stopped walking on her heels and the Old Man turned in for some well-earned rest. As was his custom, fair weather or foul, he did a bit of reading from his favorite story —the account of the death of King Solomon. He was smoking a dingy briar pipe and was at the favorite part of his favorite story, the portion that tells *how* the people of Solomon's court tried to revive His Majesty."

"How did they?" the Baker asked.

"We'll get the book and read it after we've had our gin. . . . The captain looked up from his book as the second mate came in and stood with his back against a bulkhead. The captain kept his place with the stub of his left thumb. It had been bitten off in 1892 in a fight over a Lascar woman.

" 'And if you please, sir,' the second mate says, says he, 'if you please, Cap'n Dorcas.'

" 'Out with it, man,' the Cap'n says, keeping his thumb-stub glued to the place in his book. 'Out with it.'

"The second mate was gasping and had a horrified look. 'It's the Chink we shipped the last v'yage outa Rio.'

" 'Quit luffin', man,' the Cap'n says. 'Out with it ****** ******** **** and say your piece, and ***** ***** ****** afore I ****** ******* your ****** ***** .'

" 'Well, Cap'n Dorcas,' the mate says, says he, 'you remember the pet duck the Chink brung aboard?'

" 'Ay, ****** ******** ****** and I do,' says Cap'n Dorcas.

" 'Well, Cap'n Dorcas,' the mate says, says he, turning as red as a fast lady's hat, 'I just come from the fo'castle and ******* ******** ******** ******* because I thought you ought to know.'

"The Old Man put down his briar and rubbed his nose with his thumb-stub, losing the place in the book. 'Mr. Spencer,' the Cap'n says, says he, calling the mate by name, 'Mr. Spencer, ********** ********** ********** ************ ********** in the Barbadoes in 1897, and ******** *********** ************** ******** ******** his wife's mother; but I ****** ******** ********** ******* began to fire on me with a pistol until ********* ******** ************* .'

"The mate didn't know what to say to this, and Cap'n Dorcas continued: 'And ever since that time, Mr. Spencer, I never have interfered in a man's love affairs.'

" 'Ay, ay, sir,' says Mr. Spencer, saluting."

On October 20, 1926, the body of a huge man with iron-gray hair was found. A difference of opinion arose as to where it was discovered. Some said in a box-car. Others held that it had lain beside the railroad right-of-way. Still others insisted that the body was picked up from a deserted street in Auburn. The clothes were shabby and the face unshaven—indicating that the man had been wandering for a time, perhaps going incognito among the less prosperous citizens of the open road.

"Why!" the Coroner said, returning from his vacation and after the body had remained unidentified for some time, "I'm damned if it ain't Tom Osborne! He was the picture of health a month ago."

Osborne had died of a heart attack.

On October 23, 1926, services for Thomas Mott Osborne were held in the Unitarian Church in Auburn. There were many messages of condolence from prominent persons. The body was taken to Auburn Prison. There were 1,200 inmates in the line filing past the bier. One convict wrote a song, but it was not sung. It began:

"Tom Brown's body lies a-moldering in the grave,
But the Welfare League goes marching on."

Chapter Ten

CHILDE HAROLD ON BROADWAY

THE rain came down with swift, slanting strokes, like the penmanship of an old school-master. The street had the smell of a wet dog. People everywhere were stooped, their eyes fixed on the ground, as though shopping for graves. It was good to have on old clothes; the honesty of English weave and the grease of long wear helped shed Manhattan's April rain.

The blows of riveters hurried through the tumult of the sky. Behind the curtain of gray rain, pneumatic hammers drummed upon the framework of some new, huge coffin for the stumbling, dispirited folk. They seemed corpses walking to their own interment, bent on saving expense of sexton, undertaker, and hearse-driver. Were they going to the tomb? Or coming *from* the tomb? A wet rehearsal for Judgment Day.

When will the sophisticated ones learn that it is a fine, brave thing to lift one's face to the sky, letting the cool, sweet fingers of the rain caress the lips? A man is a fool to hunch his shoulders, quivering and sniveling like an animal being house-broken. You have but to stand erect; letting virginal little fists of rain beat bitterness from your teeth, bringing memories of long-ago kisses. "For Jesus' sake!" I felt like saying. "For Jesus' sake, stand up! Don't kick your own wet noses."

In fair weather, all this is changed; the sophisticated ones escape the cowardice of the storm. Their lately limp spines come back from God's laundry, nicely starched and stiff.

The parching wind drives across the prairie, and the sun

scorches the farmer's grain. His cattle lie in the corral, licking feebly at shaded boards; their ribs stand out with hunger, and their bowels are griped by drought. When the first thunder comes, the farmer thinks it is the voice of God. When the rain pours from black heaven, he calls to his wife, to his hired hands, to his world:

"Thank God! Water."

But the city-cadaver looks from his apartment-sepulchre. "There's that lousy, stinking rain again!"

On Broadway, the walkers have no time to answer questions (except carnal or commercial ones). On Fifth Avenue, pedestrians are too excellent for anything. I like Sixth Avenue best—there you find unemployed men in front of bulletin-boards. They wear no masks as they read the bulletins: "Ditch-digger wanted." "Cook wanted." "Logger wanted." When I look into the faces of these men, I am not confused. On other streets—and on clement, cloudless days—I am confused; the dandified, restless men and women appear to be tracking down something that will be most precious to them, if they can but find it. What is it they are seeking?

On Sixth Avenue, the men seek but one thing—bread.

I returned to Fire Island and drank in the eloquent silence that followed the gale. The Baker ferried me across the Great South Bay. There was a sunset of scarlet. I put three stump-logs on the hearth; an oak back-log, a bilious locust, and a quick-tempered spruce. I made tea with mellow well-water. It was time to write concerning Broadway.

["You ought to do it right away," the Baker said. "People will be sore if they buy a book and don't find no dames in it for 132 pages. No, I don't think they'd be so hot for a book about Sixth Avenue."]

When William J. Fallon left the District Attorney's office

in White Plains he entered partnership with Edward J. Glennon, a Fordham classmate. Their law-firm in the Bronx was short-lived. They were temperamentally unsuited to each other.

Glennon was studious, painstaking, and dependable. Fallon scoffed at routine. He never bothered, then or thereafter, to prepare cases in the accepted manner. He relied on court-room stimulus. His phenomenal memory, his ability to take the dregs of a cross-examination and build a spontaneous defense, his genius for summation and his personal magnetism all led him to neglect slow, constructive practice.

Mr. Fallon had a tendency to forget his Yesterdays and to pawn his Tomorrows. He was perhaps one of the world's foremost collectors of Todays. His philosophy was that the Past was a spilled sack of meal; the Future a maybe-so; the Present a real and tangible asset. . . .

["He might of been right at that," the Baker said. "We was rammed by a British collier off Cardiff, Wales, in 1917. I and two others found ourselves with a hatchway door in the open sea. We spent nine hours in the water, and I got to thinking things over."]

On dissolution of the Glennon-Fallon law-firm, Mr. Glennon became City Chamberlain; later District Attorney of the Bronx, and finally Supreme Court Justice. Mr. Fallon went to Broadway. He took with him a brief-bag containing his shaving and hair-cutting tools, a burgundy-colored neck-tie, and a limp-leather volume of Byron's "Childe Harold."

He invaded the city on Saturday, January 12, 1918, a heatless day of a war year. When he visited the offices of the Metropolitan Trust Company to cash a check, he saw the cashiers and tellers in hats, overcoats, and mufflers as they shivered at their wickets. A blizzard was swirling eastward, tying up railroad traffic, delaying shipments of coal. The Twentieth Century Limited was snowbound near Elkhart, Indiana. Aid was being despatched to hungry passengers as they tried to sleep with baggage for pillows. The coal famine aroused talk of shutting down industry for three days a week. Democracy was being saved. It was anything but an auspicious time for a play-loving man to invade New York City.

Mr. Fallon's capacity for worry was small. He attended a matinee of "Blind Youth," a play in which Lou Tellegen was star. In the evening he surfeited himself on steak at Luchow's in Fourteenth Street. He called ceremoniously for oil, vinegar, English mustard, and paprika, and made a salad-dressing for a whole head of lettuce.

Fallon had an appointment next day with his friend, Eugene F. McGee. Fallon, as usual, was late; his attitude toward temporal matters being one of pure indifference.

"When mankind had nothing better to do," he said, "it fashioned sun-dials. A later civilization, desiring to be bored by night, as well as by day, devised clocks. As for myself, the best way to waste time is to save it. Eternity is a great ship that springs tiny leaks. Men run with their frantic tin-cups, their childish pails and their dippers, catching drops of water that dribble from the great ship's seams—and they call out proudly: 'Look at the minutes I have saved! Soon I'll have a whole hour!' Then they squat smugly beside their tin-cups and their pails, to contemplate their labors. Meanwhile the water evaporates and the watchers rouse from a stupid, waking-sleep, muttering: 'Great guns! I must hurry and save some more time!' Well, let them go ahead and save it. Every man to his own pleasure."

Fallon sauntered into the Astor grill, where McGee was gagging over a fifth cup of coffee. Most of the midday diners had gone, leaving only the sports crowd lingering in the room overlooking Broadway. At tables adjoining that of the long-suffering McGee, sat various notables of the muscular world, bemoaning the effects of the war on cauliflower ears and charley-horse legs. At one table, Mr. James J. Johnston was telling Mr. George L. ("Tex") Rickard how to promote prize fights, and to hell with the Kaiser. At another, the pink-cheeked and huge Mr. Jack Curley was feeding "Strangler" Lewis into a mood for signing articles to wrestle Wladek Zbyszko. William A. Brady, the theatrical producer, was sitting with a group of stage-people. Mr. Morris Gest was in the cloak-room, putting on an ancient black velour hat. He tugged at his Windsor tie and mumbled about "the death of art in the theater."

"I've rented an office," McGee said. "We start Monday."

"Fine," Fallon said. "Where is it to be?"

"Singer Building. No. 149 Broadway."

"Great," said Fallon. "We'll begin at the bottom of Broadway and work our way up the street."

"It's a good location, lower Broadway."

"That's what the Standard Oil people thought."

"I've waited a long time for this partnership, Bill."

"I hope you won't be disappointed."

"There's no limit for us. You have court-presence. I haven't."

"I wouldn't say that, Gene."

"I'm O.K. in a chair, but not so many on my feet. I *will* say, though, you're the worst picker of jurors I ever saw. You take *anybody*."

"What's the difference?"

"A whole lot. You should be more critical."

"I don't think so. When I accept a jury right off, it makes them think I am some pumpkins. They are psychologically *for me*. Later on, when I *do* object to something, they think I have a solid, worth-while reason."

"Well, after you get a jury, you certainly *handle* them."

The law-firm of Fallon & McGee was ready for business the next Monday. The partners owned three chairs and a desk. They had no law-library.

"We don't need one," Fallon said. "The place for the law is in the skull, not on a shelf. Anyway, what's wrong with the Public Library?"

Fallon was a mediocre business-getter; McGee a first-rate one. The latter began immediately to "build up" his partner, directing attention, through press and court-room behavior, to this new and picturesque "flame" from Westchester. With McGee as his

Warwick, Fallon soon was on his way toward legal kingship. Part of the McGee method included prima donna tactics by Fallon. Mr. Fallon could not be "disturbed" by anything less than "important" consultations. McGee simulated an exaggerated respect for Fallon when in court, giving a jury the impression that here was a counselor to be reckoned with.

Fallon baited judges and prosecutors in a most brazen manner. This focused attention on him, no matter how trivial the case. The press found in him superior material for stories. The newspaper men—and they were a gifted group—discovered that Fallon, out of court, was a most charming and genial companion. Other attorneys often were mysterious, reticent, and disinclined to trust a reporter with a defendant. Mr. Fallon permitted his clients to be interviewed at any and all times—the oftener, the better.

In one of his early, minor cases, tried before the late Judge Malone, Fallon's only chance for victory lay in confusing the prosecution's witnesses. He was an adept at making a truthful witness seem to be lying, or utterly mistaken. He accomplished this partly because of his sure, confident manner, and partly by relying on the failure of human memory for details.

It is certain that many, if not all of us, go for random walks; that in leaving home to buy a loaf of bread, we are apt to take a turn of the block, and for no particular reason. Mr. Fallon, however, would apply a sinister motive to your stroll.

"And you mean to say—remember, now, you are sworn to tell the truth—you mean to say, Mr. Sturdevant, that you live only three doors from the bakery, yet you went around the entire block to buy a loaf of bread? Think back carefully. You had to go *only three doors* for that loaf of bread; but you actually went *clear around the block*."

His habit, after asking such a question, was to look terribly pained; to turn away swiftly after putting the question. To act as though he dreaded to hear the "lying" answer. To gaze knowingly at the jury as Mr. Sturdevant replied:

"Yes, I went around the block."

Then he would wheel suddenly, moving on the balls of his feet, charging at the witness, pointing his forefinger as though it were a pistol. "Then *why* did you go around the block? Tell us *that* if you can!"

In the case referred to (and before the author went around the block), Fallon muddled several witnesses and clashed with court and prosecution. "I object," said the prosecutor. "Mr. Fallon is charging on the witness and poking his finger almost in the man's face."

"You will stop all threatening gestures," the court said.

Mr. Fallon cupped his ear with his palm. "I didn't hear what your Honor just said."

The court repeated: "I said to cease pointing your finger."

Mr. Fallon folded his arms and stood unnecessarily close to the witness as he continued the cross-examination.

The Assistant District Attorney again rose to object. "I ask the court to instruct counsel to move back from the witness stand."

"You will please stand in the proper place," the court directed.

Mr. Fallon didn't stir as he continued the cross-examination. The court was wrathy. "I again direct counsel to stand back!"

Mr. Fallon cupped his ear. "I beg your Honor's pardon. I didn't quite catch the court's last remark."

"Mr. Fallon," the judge asked, "are you hard of hearing?"

"Will your Honor please repeat the question?"

The court roared: "I said: 'Are you hard of hearing?'"

"I am sorry to say, I am, your Honor. And I maintain that I have a right to stand close to the witness."

The court was astonished. "On what ground do you make such an assertion, Mr. Fallon?"

"On the ground that my client is entitled to the services of his attorney—one hundred per cent services, and not sixty or seventy per cent. If, as happens to be the case, counsel is suffering any ailment that impairs the sense of sight or hearing, counsel cannot give the service guaranteed a defendant under the law. That is, if counsel is thwarted by court or prosecution from standing where the full import of question and answer, or of court ruling, may be had. The prosecutor here would seek to have counsel for the defense stand in a position where he cannot hear——"

"That is not so," said the Assistant District Attorney. "We object principally to the threatening manner of counsel."

"My impaired hearing," said Mr. Fallon, who virtually had the ears of a lynx, "may or may not cause me to appear threatening. I certainly hope not. There are certain grimaces that accompany defective hearing. Need I apologize for nerve-reflexes?"

"Counsel needn't gesture, lean forward, and clear his throat meaningly while a witness is answering," said the Assistant District Attorney.

"Mankind cannot well govern his sneezes, his coughs or the alleged clearing of the throat," Mr. Fallon said.

"We shall not go into that," said the court. "However, you may stand reasonably close, so as not to prejudice your client's case. But keep within limits."

"My client and I thank your Honor." Then to the witness, gently and with great courtesy: "I merely am trying to help you recall certain details which seem to be hazy in your mind."

"I object," the Assistant District Attorney said. . . . And so on for an hour.

McGee prepared the ammunition and loaded the piece for Fallon's sieges. Fallon stepped forward and jerked the lanyard. And each time the legal gun roared, Broadway said:

"That's Bill Fallon."

No one ever said: "That's Gene McGee."

This condition was acceptable to McGee. He didn't have a jealous fiber in his big body. He loved Fallon like a brother, and he enjoyed seeing his partner dash into action. Brilliant though he was, and the most ingenious trial lawyer at the criminal bar, Fallon never could have flared so dazzlingly had there been no McGee.

Fallon was at the morning of his thirty-second year when he arrived on the Broadway scene. He was passably interested in beautiful women. He had game-cock mannerisms when in their presence; but infidelities as yet had not saddened his home. He was in the full flower of his manhood, sturdy and handsome. He moved with the grace and sure rhythm of a trained boxer, in court or in drawing-room. Already he enjoyed the flatteries of women, spoken or unspoken, as they twittered at his elbow.

Fallon seemed taller than he actually was. His erect bearing, his squared shoulders, inflated chest, large head, and the tangle of apricot-colored hair, made him appear six feet two inches, instead of five feet eleven. He seemed to know that he looked his best when standing. So whenever possible, Fallon stayed on his feet. A certain restlessness had something to do with his aversion to sitting.

Fallon's remarkably resonant voice soon became known in Manhattan's courts and along Broadway. However, he never raved or bellowed like a ward-heeler who has been asked to *pay* for his beer. His diction was faultless; his choice of words excellent. He seldom resorted to slang. He had a wit that danced.

Mr. Fallon has been classed by some as a sex-maniac. It is said that his blanket covered all women. A survey of the record does not wholly justify this charge. He seems to have been moved by women through channels other than the one usually associated with appetites of sensualists. He, in turn, appears to have inspired women in a variety of ways not altogether physical. He may have strayed at first because of fancied biological needs. Later, it is apparent, he succumbed more readily to flatteries attendant on sex-adventures—to the vanities of the flesh—than to strictly primitive urges.

Fallon attracted immediate attention in any environment which was more or less colorful. He required background for his best performances. The underworld was a ready-made easel on which to set the Fallon portrait, and Broadway placed it there. As Fallon grew in importance, the Big Parade of women began. He became more and more Byronic—a Childe Harold on a Broadway pilgrimage.

I called on Johnny O'Connor in the Hammerstein Building. No one knows more than he concerning Broadway and its folk. Mr. O'Connor was feeling fine. He had booked Waring's Pennsylvanians for "The New Yorkers," and it was a hit-show. Still, he always feels fine. He felt that way the night of the actors' strike, when someone in a club washroom said that George M. Cohan was a heel. Mr. O'Connor knocked the man down. That was his way of resigning from the club. Mr. O'Connor was employed at that time on Sime Silverman's *Variety*. He wiped his knuckles on a towel and went to his office. He wrote a story about George M. Cohan that wasn't just a story. It made several mummers weep. Others were ashamed. The Cohan critics got wise to themselves and laid off the greatest little fellow that ever talked out of one side of his face.

"They tell me," Mr. O'Connor said, "that Fire Island is so cold it would freeze the whatzis off a brass monkey."

"The world is full of error."

"It has me licked," said Mr. O'Connor, "how anybody can bury himself in a lot of sand in the winter. What brings you to town?"

"I'm trying to find a set of Scotch bagpipes. I thought you could get them wholesale."

Mr. O'Connor considered. "I hear they are tough to get. If I remember right, those things are handed down from one oatmeal addict to another."

"Then you don't know of any?"

"Well, this is kind of sudden. You wouldn't take Irish pipes, would you?"

"My heart is set on the Scotch."

"I once pulled a prize boner," Mr. O'Connor said. "I was working for The *Morning Telegraph*, getting ads for the Santa Claus number. Some of the kilted boys were entertaining Harry

Lauder, and invited me to clan headquarters. They had a lot of pool tables there, with the balls racked, and when the head guy asked me if I liked the place, I said I was surprised they had regular-sized pockets on the pool tables. That one didn't go over so well. When it came my turn to speak, I began with some Scotch stories. Things got cooler and cooler, and then hotter. I told the one about the Scotchman who killed his wife before breakfast, so that he could have two portions of porridge. Somebody began throwing pool balls. I picked up the thirteen-ball and let her go. It crocked a Highland-flinger on the bearded gadget he wore at his belt. He went down yelling! 'Foul!' Then the police came. . . . Say, will they let you practice on the pipes out at Fire Island?"

"Practice, hell! I'm a good player."

"If you'd take the Irish pipes, I think I could swing it right away."

"I want the Scotch."

"I'll get busy. . . . That wasn't all that brought you out of hiding?"

"I'm doing a book about Bill Fallon."

"There *was* a man! You should have seen Frank Gerety at Billy La Hiff's Tavern. He knew everybody. He was Fallon's special friend."

"I'm going to see Frank."

"No," said O'Connor. "You'll not get anything from him now."

"What do you mean?"

"Gerety died yesterday."

"You wouldn't kid me?"

"In his sleep. They found him propped up in bed."

"I guess he was pretty old."

"Eighty, but he never looked it. Gerety was a part of New York—the old New York. Never asked a favor. Did a million. He and 'Big Tim' Sullivan were boyhood friends. Nobody knew more about sports—especially racing and boxing. From Sullivan to Mickey Walker. He knew them all. One of the best saloon and restaurant men in the world. Worked at Martin's in Four-teenth Street, and a lot of other places. Did you know he once worked for Jim Corbett?"

"When Jim had the Herald Square saloon?"

"Yes. 'Diamond' Jim Brady was one of Frank's closest friends. Remind me some time to tell you that story of Brady, and how he used to lock up his rocks each night after his broad had worn them to the show. When they got home one night, Diamond Jim opened the safe-door, saying: 'Come on, sweet-heart, take them off.' The broad said she was sick, and had to go to the bathroom. 'Diamond Jim' waited there a long time, his hand on the pete-door. He got tired waiting, and went to the bathroom to reconnoiter. All he saw was an open window. There was a ladder under it. The frail never came back. Among the missing was a platinum breast-plate, made like a bar of music and with the notes done in diamonds. That was the only time any dame trimmed Brady."

"When is the Gerety funeral?"

"They haven't announced it yet." Mr. O'Connor chewed a cigar-butt. "You know? I think you could get along with Irish pipes O.K."

"I only want the Scotch."

"I guess I can swing it. . . . Speaking of Gerety, he was the man who introduced the miniature welsh-rabbit. Had them on his free-lunch counter. Little bits of things, with laughing dabs of cheese on squares of toast. No one knew how they kept so fresh. . . . Gerety never missed a big race. He knew horses. You'd see him at Belmont, Havre de Grace, Saratoga and Churchill Downs every year. Always immaculate, his gray mus-tache neatly waxed, and white-piping on his waist-coat. His hair had the finest bartender's lick I ever saw. Wore it that way as a souvenir of civilized times. Was a great plunger, too. Lived high and handsome when he had it. When broke, he never asked anyone for a chip. Just went back to work until next time."

"Fallon thought Gerety the most charming man on Broad-way."

"Frank had the same barber thirty-seven years. Wonder what the barber thinks this minute? Eleven o'clock. That's the time to the dot when Frank showed up for his daily shave. . . . Yes, Frank cashed plenty of Bill Fallon's checks in the late days. The paper was pre-dated. But Frank never said a thing. Just cashed the checks and held them until they were made good. . . . You wouldn't hear to the Irish pipes, eh?"

"Scotch."

"They tell me you have a deaf dog?"

"A pit bull. He was killed by a taxi. I was just breaking him in to signs, too."

"What kind of signs?"

"All kinds in daylight; in the dark, I'd stomp my foot on the floor."

"He couldn't hear it, though?"

"He felt the vibrations up his leg."

"You should have taken him to Fire Island. This town's tough even on a dog *with* hearing. Was it malarkey, that yarn about you ordering some ear-phones for the dog?"

"The Westinghouse people were building a set."

"For God's sake! How would you work it?"

"Hitch it to his muzzle, and put the batteries on a saddle, with a belly-band."

"Oh, well, if he's dead the Westinghouse people can call it a day, can't they? . . . I suppose you'll have some Broadway stuff in your book?"

"The Broadway I know is so different from the one they show in the movies. Nobody would believe it."

"I'm monkeying with a Broadway book myself."

"You ought to. Your 'Broadway Racketeers' was a topper, but I felt that you were holding out on the reader."

Mr. O'Connor looked his wisest. "A fellow can't be a whistle-blower. Say, would you like to see some of the stuff I've written?"

"Read me some."

"I know at least two Micks who have Irish pipes," he said,

going to a cabinet. He rummaged for a time among contracts, and then put down his cigar. He began reading:

"Broadway. A big, beautiful dame. Her head is up there at Columbus Circle. She sits straddling Longacre Square, with her two legs dangling down on either side. In the morning, with the busy business men buzzing in and out of her pockets, she looks like a spectacled old spinster on her way to market. At midday, she's like a school kid at recess hour. In the evening, all dolled up in her diamonds, sapphires and rubies, she's a typical *grande dame*, ruling until eleven o'clock. Then, in the cold, friendless dawn, she flops there, scowling and alone, deserted by all but the scavengers of the night—they are her own illegitimate children. She is stretched out, waist-deep in tarnished tinsel and the muck of her daily debauch; and she looks like a naked whore after a tough night."

Mr. O'Connor rang for his secretary. "Miss Gordon, remind me to look into the bagpipe situation." When Miss Gordon went out, Mr. O'Connor said: "The minute I get some action I'll give you a ring."

"But we haven't any 'phones on Fire Island."

Mr. O'Connor seemed dismayed. "Good God! You're worse off than Robinson Crusoe. Good God!"

There are three Broadways within the memory of men. There was the street of Frank Gerety, a pre-war promenade for all the world. The war created a second Broadway that had a cycle of some ten years—a dizzy, sensual, pointless Broadway. A third Broadway—the Broadway of now—had its inception at approximately the time when the talking picture began to squawk like a lad whose voice is changing. This last Broadway was a merger of Los Angeles and Coney Island, retaining the worst features of both.

Mr. Fallon came to Broadway on the heels of the old order. The grand Broadway tradition was crumbling, but all was not entirely lost. His career was concurrent with the second, war-whelped Broadway, in a decade of national deterioration.

Each of the three Broadways had its corresponding under-world. The first had its gangs, cliques, and rings of plug-uglies. These were muscled pioneers, the forebears of modern mobsters. They were the servants of politicians; not yet the masters. Mr. Fallon arrived during the intermediate period that bridged two milieus of crime. He found the underworld in flux. Crime was ceasing to be mere enterprise. It was becoming an industry.

With an entire nation gibbering over easy money, the Fallon Broadway became a wild and vulgar spending-ground. Fallon's fees were the first tremendous ones paid by captains of modern crime-syndicates for legal advice. He became, in fact, a corporation counsel for the underworld. He did not seek this condition; it was thrust upon him. After a few successes, Fallon was deeply involved, and his services were virtually commanded by men powerful in politics and in criminal circles.

The World War killed more than men. It bred a new and more stinking fanaticism in the holy prophets. It made the virtue of women seem prudish and superfluous, giving them privilege in the name of "liberty" and "equal rights" to make public furnaces of their lungs, public gin-vats of their bellies, public peep-shows of their thighs, and wallowing-troughs of their beds. There seemed no sane middle-ground, where men could be God-loving, yet not venomously bigoted; where men could be sport-loving, without becoming gin-corroded satyrs.

Never before in all history did the town's mattresses take such a beating. Love, once the finest of all fine arts, became carnal license. Professional Aphrodites went the way of horse-drawn carriages. The competition of charitable amours did to them what the chain stores did to Mr. Liederkranz's corner grocery. Amid yowls of "Health," women began their public undressing—meanwhile starving themselves into the boneyard to

become "boyish." Grandmas bared their battered Chippendale
and Sheraton gams, and koochied along Broadway for the edifi-
cation of motormen. Many a lorn sailor followed a re-vamped
stern down the street, only to find—on facing the prey—that
it was pre-General Grant stuff. It was, perhaps, the most blatant,
ugly, and vulgar decade in American annals—not alone on
Broadway, but in Terre Haute as well. The dames captured the
barber-shops, and men quit singing bass.

The new-rich descended like locusts on the town, a modern
Coxey's Army. Apple-knockers, on maiden orgies, brought their
souls to the city and gave Broadway first mortgage. They were
foreclosed in a flash. They returned to their pastures, walking
on their heels. Good taste beat a hurried retreat, lest her nipples
be bitten off. The muggy spendthrifts undertook the defloration
of art. They debauched music under the guise of modernism.
Yokels gawked at canvases of charlatans and were told that
Rembrandt was a bum. Mushroom millionaires purchased pictures by the square foot and sculpture by the pound. Most of
these portraits and landscapes seemed to be the result of backing
a bran-stuffed Holstein against a wall and after a clyster. Nar-
row-shouldered buffoons kicked the gong in opium-dens and then
sat down to pianos, beating the black keys with the frenzy of
jungle-phallicists, ministering to sex-vibrations, while dancers
engaged in abdominal massages and drooled with the idiocy of
the hour. The vandals sacking Rome were ten times as kindly
as the spendthrift horde on Broadway.

The Wall Street delirium was reaching the pink-elephant stage.
There was one financial depression, but so strong was the
gambling lust that "prosperity" was re-won. Chambermaids and
counter-hoppers had J. P. Morgan complexes. America had the
swelled head, and the brand of tourists that went to Europe
became ambassadors of ill-will. One grand gesture, and one
only, entered this gauche decade of pandemonium and vulgarity,
—and that was the Lindbergh flight. Broadway mumbled about
the decency of youth and then lapsed into a Sisyphean culture.

It took the recent, rock-bottom panic to shake the tin-horn bangles from the Christmas tree.

If only the religious fanatics and the political hypocrites footed the bill!

During this ugly cycle, architecture reared its head above a banal, stupid scene. A few gems, exquisitely cut, were set against the sky, forming a fine cod-piece for Manhattan. Although letters were at low-ebb, a few minds insisted on having their say. Ben Hecht, Sherwood Anderson, Eugene O'Neill, John Dos Passos, and Theodore Dreiser gallantly opened the battle, with Sinclair Lewis and Mencken taking the trenches of bigots and nit-wits. These and their disciples were damned and starved in that day, but now are reported to be feeding well and often.

The World War killed nearly everything that was the old Broadway. Prohibition, the mock-turtle soup of purists, provided the *coup de grâce*. Before the war, one might walk Broadway and meet friends. There were men and women worth being pointed out. It was Cohan's Broadway, not the street of today—not the Broadway of Goldfogle, Chin Low, the Flea Circus, one-arm lunchrooms and bargain sales. One might have a drink, openly arrived at and decently toped. When Wilson Mizner came back for a visit, he had to carry twenty-four candles in his pockets for fear the lights might go out on him, leaving him alone on Broadway and among stupid strangers.

Broadway is dead. Dare we add: Long live Broadway? It was such a friendly street, in the days when Paul Whiteman had but one chin. At sunset the counter-hoppers got off the thoroughfare, and the grand old stem began to wake up. The cream of the town came thither. But Prohibition shot the heart out of Broadway and its people. The delicatessen dealers moved in and made a picnic-ground of the famous promenade.

Broadway's immediate fall was caused by profiteering, followed by racketeering. A commercial chill came over the thoroughfare. The street began to fill up with nickel-creeps, taxi-dance joints and chop-suey parlors. Auction stalls put up banners; the gyp-brotherhood moving into Broadway stores only to sell out. Then the big picture houses came. And now it was just an Allentown Fair. Juice-joints pre-empted corners with their pineapples and oranges. Hot-dog stands, barkers, kootchie-ladies and give-away huts, that would not be permitted in a small-town carnival company, were allowed on the new Broadway. And from this witchpot rose the modern criminal, with his gun and his automobile, his financial backers and his high-priced lawyer—his mouthpiece. The old gangster was supplanted by the modern torpedo.

Broadway's mice grew up to be rats.

Fallon caught the old Broadway going out and the new coming in. He was in the middle of the jam. Murder once had been considered a crime of violence; it was becoming commonplace. Million-dollar hauls in bucket-shop operations or in other forms of robbery were growing less rare. Mr. Fallon was the first and greatest of the criminal lawyers to benefit by the subsidizing of criminals by men who had huge budgets for legal defense. Fallon became so successful; he lent such polish and sagacity to counsel tables of the "Big Shots", that it was regarded as two strikes on the prosecution when Mr. Fallon was retained for the defense.

Fallon made articulate a crime-organization that was born of a nation's disorganization. He became the Great Mouthpiece for the grand dukes of Racketland. He, himself, later longed to escape the web in which he was entangled. He sometimes voiced this hope. "There's still time to get out."

Time. . . .

I wonder what would happen to the ladies and gentlemen of the radio audience if, some fine night, the announcer were to say: "When you hear the musical note, don't bother to set your clocks at all, for it will be the Angel Gabriel's trumpet. (Courtesy of the C. G. Conn Band Instrument Company.)"

Chapter Eleven

*

MR. COSTELLO CLAIMS THE HORNS OF CUCKOLDOM

T HE personages of this chapter are posed under fictitious
names for reasons that are absurd and strange. First of all,
the chief character left prison recently and is now on his second
honeymoon. Is any book—barring the Bible and the Sears-Roe-
buck Catalogue—important enough to warrant interference with
love? Then, too, the lady depicted hereafter is dead. Let us not
hesitate to boot the coffins of the gentlemen, but let us at least
withhold the name of a lady who was beautiful, desirable, and
full of the devil.

Sid Costello ostensibly was in the business of buying and selling
curb stocks at No. 20 Broad Street, New York. Although an
ex-waiter, he had the dapper ways and the turfy legs of a retired
and prosperous jockey. Indeed, he loved the race-track more
than he loved women—establishing thereby a new record in the
realms of passion.

Almost any night, Mr. Costello could be seen here and there
on Broadway. Occasionally he frequented the Waldorf-Astoria
in Fifth Avenue, to peer at the legs of ladies that swanked in
Peacock Alley. Because of these libidinous appraisals, Nifty Sid
Costello was a charter member of that group of oglers known
as weight-guessers.

Although he followed the horses with the persistence of a
guilty conscience, Mr. Costello was singularly ill-starred as a

plunger. He was a born genius for selecting the thoroughbred that was destined to run last on any given day. Perhaps his outstanding effort in this respect was the afternoon he bet on Man o' War, and in the only race which that magnificent stallion lost. Mr. Costello had but to smell a horse while strolling Broadway, and he would look automatically for a bookmaker.

I regret to report that Mr. Costello was entered in the note-books of the New York police as a badger-man. That is to say, he was credited with framing lonely gentlemen of the hinterland, with the aid of a fair accomplice. Mr. Costello's lady would entice the victim to an apartment of compromise; then Mr. Costello, burbling with "grief" and "rage," would break in on the couple, claiming betrayal and collecting damages on the spot.

Mr. Costello's badger-money enabled him to select more losers at the race-course next day.

Mr. Costello's wife used an assortment of names, principally Maude, Edna, and Daisy. She appeared at tea-room dansants and in cabaret circles as Miss Nifty Costello. She was twenty-five and of a comeliness that would raise Casanova from the dead. Through the haste of journalists, who have to rush matters into print, Miss Nifty's nickname was confused with the tag of her husband. Mr. Costello thenceforth was labeled "Nifty Sid."

In January, 1918, and according to subsequent testimony, Nifty Sid resided with his library of form-charts at No. 170 West Seventy-fourth Street. His wife, however, lived at No. 200 West Fifty-eighth Street. This maintenance of separate homes puzzled the police, inasmuch as the Fannie Hurst plan of A-House-Divided-Against-Itself-Cannot-Flop was not then in vogue, and Judge Ben B. Lindsey had not gone companionate.

Mrs. Costello kept a beaded eye-lash raised for badger-victims. On one January evening (a meatless day, too, it was) and with the war beginning to bore everyone except Pershing, Mrs. Costello spied a lonely patron in her uptown cabaret. It was against her principles to see anyone, especially a gentleman, lonely. She sat down beside the gentleman, a Mr. Spangler, and poured out her heart!

Mr. Spangler looked at the floor-show, sipped a drink or two, tipped everyone handsomely, and went home to Jersey. On his next visit to town—and the next and the next—he called at the cabaret. Maude, Edna, and Daisy learned that Mr. Spangler was wealthy; that he was a partner in a steel company. When she told Nifty Sid of her prospect, he acted as though one of his horses was in the homestretch, a length to the good.

"He sounds like pay day, sweetheart," said Mr. Costello. "Don't let your chisel slip."

Mr. Costello was sure of his wife's skill. He went ahead with arrangements pending the next call of Mr. Spangler. He enlisted the aid of a steam-fitter named Dill to act as friend and witness to the anticipated compromise. Mr. Dill received a down-payment. Sid promised him a handsome cut of the proceeds as the trio went into rehearsal.

"He's here," the lady telephoned Sid one evening. "I'm going to concentrate."

"Get him to the apartment if you have to bring him in an ambulance," directed General Costello. "And if you can't get him cockeyed, do what I told you to. See?"

"Oke, lover," said the lady.

Mrs. Costello was in a particularly dramatic mood tonight. Mr. Spangler lent a gentlemanly ear to her litany of woe. "It's tough on a single woman, this sort of thing."

"Then why don't you get out of it?"

Maude, Edna, and Daisy lifted a neatly-penciled brow. "What can a girl do? There's the show business, of course, but I ain't the kind that would let just any old manager maul over me. And that's what they like to do to a nice girl."

Mr. Spangler toyed with his cocktail. "I suppose so."

"Just because I'm divorced don't mean . . . don't mean . . . well, anyway, I wouldn't."

"I suppose not."

"Oh well, I wish't men was diff'rent. There was my husband. What a fool I was, and him all the time crossin' me up like I was just dirt!"

"What happened?"

When the orchestra died down so that the lady could speak in a tragic undertone, she said: "The same old trouble. You know? Women! It busted me up complete."

The early evening passed pleasantly enough for Mr. Spangler. He drank sparingly. The lady made another telephone call to her husband. He was impatient. "What round is it?" he asked.

"He ain't a lush," she reported. "Should I slip him the business?"

"You might as well sweeten his coffee. Ain't he even held your hand?"

"No. All he does is listen to my record."

"Well, if *you* can't make a fanny-feeler out of him, even Ziegfeld couldn't, so I guess you should give him the Mickey Finn."

The Mickey Finn contains ingredients that produce immediate nausea, and when a man is served with a drink thus spiked, the bathroom is trumps.

"Is it a strong one, Sid?"

"Just enough to make his stomach play both ways from the deuce. Don't worry, sweetheart. Just a nice run-out powder."

"I'll do it right off."

"Shake a leg, baby. And when you get him home, signal us with the flash-lamp. We'll be acrost the street."

The lady returned to the table, and in taking her chair upset Mr. Spangler's old-fashioned cocktail. "Oh, wasn't that the dumb thing!" she said.

"It was my fault," said Mr. Spangler, who was a gentleman.

"No, I was just plain dumb to do that." She signaled a waiter. "Hey, Trommer, get the gentl'm'n another old-fashioned."

"I don't want any more," said Mr. Spangler. "I just drink to be sociable."

"Aw, now, Mr. Spangler! We'll have just one more between

we two. We'll make a loving cup out of it. All right, Trommer, just bring one."

Mr. Spangler kept looking at his watch. "I should be at my hotel. I've got business in the morning."

"I wasn't built for this kind of a life, neither," said Maude, Edna & Co., fumbling in her vanity for a mirror. She palmed the Mickey Finn capsule as the waiter set the cocktail on the table. "Did you bring the good stuff, Trommer?"

"It's what you been havin' all night."

"The last one tasted like an old shoe," she said. "Here, let me smell it first."

She pretended to smell and taste the liquor. "I'll drink your health, Mr. Spangler. Then you finish the rest." She took a swallow. "Here's to us. Skald." She put the capsule in the small glass. She held the glass for a while to allow the Mickey Finn to dissolve. "Yes," she said, "I wouldn't go in show business and let just any old manager make love to me. You don't think I'm that kind, do you, Mr. Spangler?"

"I'm sure you're not."

"Well, here's your half of the lovin' cup. Are you good at toasts? Let's hear you make a toast."

"I can't remember any."

"Well, just make one up. Something about love."

"I can't think of any. I'll just drink your health and go home to my hotel."

"You ain't like the rest of the lawn-weeders that comes in here and make pretty speeches," she said. "A girl feels more safer with somebody like you that is on the level. I get so fed up with the weisenheimers that park here and make a big flash and knock their wives and. . . . My Gawd! Mr. Spangler! Is somethin' wrong with you?"

"I . . . I . . . " Mr. Spangler was making futile gestures, as though flagging an imaginary train. "I . . . I . . . "

"You better go to the Johnny," advised Maude, Edna, etc., "as it looks like you was about ready to heave."

Mr. Spangler raced to the washroom, beating Nature by a whisker. He was gone a long time. The lady did some telephoning during his absence. "Good Gawd, Sid!" she said. "You must of got that one from the Du Ponts."

"Is he taking the count?"

"It gouled him," she said, "I thought you only made a mild one?"

"When he comes 'round a little, pretend that you want to take him to his hotel. Then have him stop at the apartment for a rest, like I told you."

"I'll bring what's left of him. He looked awful second-handed."

"Flash the light four times out the window. Two long, and two short flashes."

Mr. Spangler returned to the table and sat down weakly. "I'm afraid it's ptomaine."

"Could I order you some bicarbonate?"

"No, I'll go to my hotel and call the house doctor. Would you mind calling a cab right away?"

She summoned Trommer. "Get a cab right away for the gentl'm'n," she said. Then she put her hand on Mr. Spangler's icy hand. "Now you just looka here, Mr. Spangler. You been white with me, and I ain't goin' to see you go home alone."

"I'll be all right. It must have been the crab-meat."

"You're just a great big boy," she said. "You overgrowed kids don't know how to take care of yourselfs. I'm goin' to see that you get to your hotel. You need mother'n. Yes you *do*, now."

Mr. Spangler was too deflated to object to anything. Maude, Edna and Daisy, Inc., and Trommer warped him into the cab. On the way uptown, Mr. Spangler gagged like a miser on alimony day. "I usually have a fine digestion."

"It's li'ble to happen to anybody, Mr. Spangler. Them attacks is just a warnin' that you should ought to be careful and watch your diet."

"I thought the fresh air would straighten me out," he said.

"You ain't no better, are you?"

"Not much. I'll be all right when I get to my hotel."

"Now you just looka here, Mr. Spangler, they's no use of you goin' there all alone, when somethin' might happen."

"Nothing can happen. I'll call the house doctor."

"Don't be bull-headed. My apartment is a coupla blocks from here. Suppose you stop off? I'll make some tea. You can barge out when you're rested up."

"It's late. I'd better go to my hotel, thanks."

"Well, then, if you don't know what's good for you, I'll just take charge. Hey, you, taxi! Turn off here. Number 200 West Fifty-eighth. I said '*West* Fifty-eight,' not '*East.*' These taxi-cowboys is just plain dumb, Mr. Spangler."

"I'd better go on. I'll drop you off."

"You'll come in and rest. I ain't a-goin' to be kep' awake all night worryin'."

Mr. Spangler was trying gallantly to repress another attack of nausea. He was in no shape to argue. They got out of the cab, and the lady steered him to her apartment. Mr. Spangler thought he should dab his face with cold water. His hostess pointed. "It's in there. You'll find clean towels on the rack."

As he went inside the bathroom, Mr. Spangler noticed vaguely that the lady was toying with a flash-lamp. He had other matters to attend to; not until later did he recall the flash-lamp and the woman's position near the window.

Mr. Spangler stayed quite a while in the lavatory, giving Nifty Sid and Steamfitter Dill opportunity to respond to the lady's signal. The conspirators mounted the stairs and waited outside the apartment door. Mr. Spangler came from the bathroom at the moment when fists began to flail the door-panels. The portal itself gave way when Steamfitter Dill applied his sewer-wading brogans.

Mr. Spangler stared at the incredulous drama. Mr. Costello, screaming, was to be seen in the grip of Steamfitter Dill. The latter was restraining his friend. Mr. Costello had a dagger in his right hand.

"Get ready to die!" Mr. Costello announced. "This is my wife, and I'm takin' the law into my own hands."

Mr. Spangler was speechless. Steamfitter Dill's was the next voice heard, unless we except the swooning moan of Maude, Edna and Daisy. Mr. Dill was clenching the sword-hand of his employer. "Let's keep our head, pal," he said. "Should I 'phone for a cop?"

"Let me at him!" roared Mr. Costello. "He's ruint my home."

"Will you let me explain?" asked Mr. Spangler.

"You love-thief!" Mr. Costello yelled. "You're goin' outta here feet first and with a stick-pin in your belly. God! this busts me up proper."

"If you'd let me explain——"

Steamfitter Dill assumed the duties of *arbiter elegantiarum*. "I wouldn't give him no lip, Mister What's-yer-name. You done enough as it is——"

Mr. Spangler was angry. "I've not done a solitary thing."

Mr. Dill sniggered sarcastically. "Yeah? Well, we caught you wid your pants down, didn't we?"

"Listen here, whoever you are, I was sick. I went to the——"

"I know all about that," said Mr. Costello's Petronius. "You heard us comin' and you ducked into the can, pretendin' that——"

"Look here, you," said Mr. Spangler. "I didn't pretend anything."

"I think it's a lotta banana erl," said Steamfitter Dill. "And if I was you, I'd do sumpun to square it wid my pal."

Maude, Edna and Daisy roused from her coma. She was sprawled on the floor, clinging to a casement curtain as though about to ring up a fare. She moaned in a manner that today would bring her a fortune as a broadcaster of blues songs.

"We been comp'mised!" she said. "We been comp'mised!"

Nifty Sid glared at his wife. "You tart, you!" he said. "You cheap alley-tart! I'll croak you, too."

Mr. Spangler gnawed at his leash. "You damned fools! Get out of my way. You're crazy. You're *all* crazy!"

Steamfitter Dill still held to his buddy's lethal hand. "Easy there, pal. Let me handle this." Then to Mr. Spangler. "Mister, I really should ought to let my pal loose, only they'd be no pernt in a murder. I got half a mind to put the lug on you myself, you muzzler!"

"You lie," said Mr. Spangler.

"I wouldn't get gabby, if I was you," said Steamfitter Dill. "You're liable to get rear-end trouble. It makes my blood berl just to look atcha."

"I repeat," said Mr. Spangler, "that nothing has occurred to hurt your friend or his home. Anyway, the woman told me she was divorced."

"Then you *admit* it!" shouted Mr. Costello, renewing his struggle to escape Steamfitter Dill's grip

"I admit nothing," said Mr. Spangler.

"I suppose," suggested Mr. Dill, "that you went to the terlet to look at some movin' pitchers. Now listen, mope. You gotta do sumpun quick."

"Do what?"

"You gotta come true wid some damages."

"Oh," said Mr. Spangler, "it's blackmail, is it?"

"You shet up and come true. You sperled my pal's home. Now you come acrost wid twenty gran'. Hear me? You're goin' to give up twenty gran', and I don't mean ginger-snaps."

"I'll see you in hell!" said Mr. Spangler, moving toward the door.

At this moment, Mr. Costello broke loose. He slugged Mr. Spangler, and was abetted by Steamfitter Dill. Mr. Spangler was no match for both assailants. He began to run. He got downstairs and through the front door, and with the two men and the now very much alive Maude, Edna and Daisy, Ltd. at his heels. At this moment the resourceful Mr. Costello improvised a marvelous plan for bringing back a victim. He began to call lustily:

"Stop, thief! Stop, thief!"

Heads popped from apartment windows. Mr. Spangler elected to escape a most embarrassing time of it. He did the sensible thing. He returned to the presence of his tormentors.

"I kinda thunk you would see the light," said Steamfitter Dill.

The exercise had dispelled all signs of illness from Mr. Spangler. "Now look," he said. "I'm going to my hotel. You'll hear from me later."

"You don't get away that easy," said Mr. Costello. "You're going to pay. Now you listen to me. I'm going to let you go. I know who you are—all about you. And if you don't come through with twenty grand in forty-eight hours, I'm going to sue my wife for divorce. And I'm naming you, and suing you for alienation of affections. Won't *that* look nice in Jersey.

"You crook!" said Mr. Spangler.

"You better be on the up-an'-up wid us," advised Steamfitter Dill. "The finger is on you."

"You're all crooks!"

"We'll be waitin' to hear," said the steamfitter.

Mr. Costello put aside his property-dagger and went to law. He sued his missus, asking $100,000 heart-balm of Mr. Spangler. Broadway buzzed with the news:

"Nifty Sid is busy among his sugar-cane."

Mr. Spangler had a clear conscience and was no coward. He engaged a detective agency. An operative began work on Steamfitter Dill. Mr. Spangler then took his case to the District Attorney's office. The three alleged badgerites were indicted on a conspiracy charge. An assistant district attorney brought them before a magistrate in West Side court for arraignment.

On the day of arraignment, Eugene F. McGee hunted frantically for his partner. He found the auburn-haired Fallon visiting the Forty-second annual show of the Westminster Kennel Club at Madison Square Garden. Some St. Bernards were in the show-ring as Mr. McGee arrived.

"Come away from those dogs," said McGee. "We have some important business."

"I never saw such beautiful animals," Fallon said. "Colonel Ruppert's Oh Boy just lost the open class."

"You can see 'em some other time, Bill. We've been called in on a tough case."

"We like them tough, don't we?"

"It's our first big case, and we can't afford to lose."

McGee told Fallon about the Costellos and the badger-game. Mr. Fallon listened and then said: "The jails are too crowded, Gene. We must help the tax-payers cut down the overhead."

District Attorney Edward Swann, a stately and conservative gentleman, was flabbergasted when he learned that his files had been ransacked.

"The Costello records have disappeared, Judge," he was told.

Judge Swann's white hair seemed to stand. "Unthinkable!" he said. "Unthinkable!"

That was the first sensation of the Costello case. The attention of the press was drawn to the affair, despite the weight of war news—with the Germans advancing on a 400-mile front after the Kaiser's separate peace with Russia. It was the first of many cases defended by Fallon in which valuable documents disappeared. No one can prove that Fallon took these or other records, but it is certain that he always seemed conversant with the secrets and war-plans of his adversaries.

Mr. Fallon kept his clients out of jail pending the trial, which was placed on the calendar for February 21. Although McGee urged him to work hard, Mr. Fallon spent his evenings at the theater or at the Café des Beaux Arts in West Fortieth Street, where there were supper dances presided over by Madame Samya.

"Did you do any work at all last night?" McGee asked.

"What's the hurry, Gene? Say, I was on the Ziegfeld roof last night, and saw Frisco. What a dancer!"

"This is a big case, Bill."

"Frisco is the best dancer I ever saw. They say he was introduced to Jack Barrymore the other day. Barrymore was wearing a flowing Windsor tie. Frisco looked at the tie as he shook hands and said: 'Mr. Barrymore, are you drying your socks?' "

McGee was worried. "This case is no set-up, Bill."

"Gene, you always look so darned serious; as though somebody had just died."

The Costello trial was had before Judge Mulqueen in General Sessions. The Assistant District Attorney spoke of Nifty Sid's "shameless lust for money." Mr. Fallon appeared to be asleep at the counsel table.

A reporter talked with Fallon during morning recess. "Mr. Fallon, how can you sleep when things look so tough for your clients?"

"Was I really asleep?" asked Mr. Fallon.

"If you weren't, you're a good actor."

"Well, perhaps I *did* get a few winks," said Mr. Fallon. "I had a long night last night. I've got to have my rest, and when I sleep in court it upsets the prosecutor. It is an inference that I am sure of my client's innocence and that the prosecutor's speeches bore me. As a matter of fact, the prosecutor *does* bore me."

When the evidence for the People was in, the case looked hopeless for Mr. Fallon. The detective-agency operative testified to pool games played with Steamfitter Dill. The latter, according to the detective, confided the whole plot. He did not, of course, know that a detectaphone had been installed beneath the pool-table, and that stenographers had taken down the incriminating babble. Mr. Fallon slept on and on. Mr. Costello began wondering if, after all, he had not erred in retaining a Rip Van Winkle for counsel.

When Mr. Fallon rose, there was no trace of weariness or boredom in his mien. What a figure he made as he got to his feet! The jurors roused from slumped attitudes. They heard a captivating voice. They saw the most confident man possible standing before them. A new and cock-sure personality had come to the Big League.

Mr. Fallon called Mr. Spangler in cross-examination. Fireworks began to explode. The prosecution hurled numerous objections. The Court ruled out many of Fallon's questions, but not before the jury got their full import. Mr. Spangler repeated again and again the facts attendant on his visit to the cabaret washroom and his subsequent call at the bathroom of Mrs. Costello. Mr. Fallon nodded and yessed the witness. And then came the cunning thrust that was perfectly timed and adroitly worded to overthrow with laughter the entire case of the People.

Mr. Fallon, suavely and with mock-dignity, walked toward the witness. "In short, Mr. Spangler," he said, "you attribute all your worldly troubles to two trips to the toilet!"

The court-room was convulsed. The bailiff rose and shouted for order. The Judge rapped his gavel and threatened to clear the room. The Prosecutor was furious. Mr. Fallon seemed innocently surprised that his question had caused such furor. He ran his fingers through his thick hair, then folded his arms across his chest.

"Answer 'Yes' or 'No,' Mr. Spangler."

"I object," howled the Assistant District Attorney. "I move to strike out the question."

Mr. Fallon looked appealingly at the jury, which was having trouble keeping in countenance. "But Your Honor," he said, turning to the bench, "this witness has been testifying all afternoon that he went twice to——"

The court intervened. "Mr. Fallon, you will not make a travesty of this court. The objection is sustained. The witness will not answer, and the question is to be stricken."

Mr. Fallon bowed elaborately. "In that case, Your Honor, I save an exception, and the witness may stand down."

The jury retired after the summations and went into an immediate deadlock. Mr. Fallon's disconcerting question had made six of the jurors forget completely the testimony of the detective-agency witnesses, as well as other damaging statements. The trial ended in a disagreement, and to all intents and purposes the Fallon clients went free.

Chapter Twelve

A RHAPSODY IN ANKLES

BROADWAY accredited Mr. Fallon within the year as its ambassador without portfolio. An underworld, dazzled by his successive legal victories, enthroned him as The Great Mouthpiece. So colorful was the man, and so widespread the publicity heralding his accomplishments, that he began to receive mash notes. Broadway had been accustomed to employing caribou-faced counselors, whose very homeliness was the hall-mark of learning. It was a relief when a good-looking Daniel came to judgment.

A Fallon client seldom spent a day in jail pending trial. If he were not acquitted, he was reasonably sure of incredible delays or a jury disagreement. Donald Henderson Clarke, novelist and former journalist, called Fallon "The Jail Robber."

In the face of overwhelming evidence, Fallon's specialty was hanging a jury. His device was to address the entire summation to one juror—the one he judged susceptible to that form of flattery. It seems incredible how many times Fallon accomplished a hung jury by the count of 1 to 11. Hints of jury-bribing began to travel the court-corridors. Such rumors became a refuge for assistant district attorneys, as they emerged punch-drunk from the Fallon boxing-lessons.

Occasionally there was an opponent who offered competition —Ferdinand Pecora, for example. As a whole, however, the Criminal Courts armada seemed a fleet of swanboats trying to ram the battleship *Texas*. The District Attorney—an able lawyer of the old school, and an exceedingly fine gentleman—chewed holes in his brief-bag whenever Fallon came to the bar. A bare mention of Fallon made prosecutors so dizzy that their silk hats did balloon ascensions. Broadway's Cicero laughed all the while, and behaved like three thousand imps of Satan.

Mr. Fallon was an enemy of boredom. Beneath his gay bravado and lust for mischief-making lay a serious desire to expose the ponderous pugging of the courts. There seemed no limit to the number of ancient technicalities and obscure loop-holes that he invoked. Many lawyers admired Fallon's ability, envied his audacity, but frowned on his ethics. That is usually the case when a member of any profession departs from the rut. It is conceivable that the scientist who eventually discovers a specific for cancer will be termed an empiricist, smeared with tar, and rump-booted from the medical societies.

An addle-pated censor is Civilization, standing forever close by, blue pencil in hand, punctuating the lives of the zestful ones; placing commas for their laughter and semi-colons after their tears. And if you want a period, you must await the black pencil, which is death.

With Fallon fronting for the go-as-you-please brigade, Broadway paraphrased Mr. Browning, and sang: "God's in His heaven; all's well with the underworld."

Certified checks and currency came in sheaves to the Fallon office. Mr. Fallon was a careless business man and kept no accounts. He refused to be bothered with such things. Consequently, he was apt to appropriate the firm's income without thinking of McGee's share. This led to a hilarious, daily race between the partners, each endeavoring to be first at the mail-box for the pay envelopes. The unwritten rule was, winner-take-all. Most amazingly, there were no quarrels over the spoils.

Fallon never was known to count his money. He took a fee and put it in his pocket, accepting the client's word that it was the correct amount. That he often was short-changed is probable; but if he were, he never knew it; and if he had known, he would have been the last person to complain.

Fallon would not countenance a lying client in the counsel room. A notorious smuggler and diamond thief once solicited his services. Aware of Fallon's generosity toward poor criminals, the gem thief tried to capitalize that trait.

"I'm broke, Bill," the man said. "You're the only one that can save me a long stretch in the sneezer."

"But you stole $100,000 in diamonds," Fallon countered.

"You're all wet. I didn't pull that job."

"The diamonds are missing; it looks like your work."

"I didn't do it, Bill. Honest to God."

"Look here," Fallon said. "I happen to *know* that you stole the diamonds. Why don't you tell the truth?"

"I didn't do it, Bill, and I'm flat. You're the only one I can turn to."

"How about the diamonds? You can raise plenty on them."

"Bill, I haven't got no sparklers."

Mr. Fallon smiled. "My friend, you don't need a lawyer."

"What do you mean?"

"I mean that anybody as innocent as you doesn't need counsel. So don't worry."

The man was frantic. He offered a retainer of $10,000. To this Fallon answered: "I wouldn't defend you if you gave me fifty thousand, and all the diamonds besides. I advise you to go on a cheese diet; it agrees with rats. Now get out."

Two classes of clients always were sure of free services at the Fallon clinic—the beautiful and the poor. He said he "simply couldn't charge for defending a good-looking woman." When Peggy Joyce paid him a fee, he turned it in on an automobile. He added a thousand dollars from his own pocket and presented the car to Miss Joyce the same day she gave him the fee.

"My God!" said McGee. "We're not poverty-stricken, Bill, but we shouldn't try to be Sir Galahads too often."

"Tut!" said Fallon. "Do you want me to go about town feeling *commercial?*"

Broadway was unable to reconcile Fallon's spendthrift habits with certain grotesque economies. The fact that he cut his own hair puzzled the patrons of John the Barber. One of the first things a super-gangster, pimp, or gambler does, on coming into money, is to loll in beauty-chairs, getting curried, scented, and massaged until fit to be placed in the Metropolitan Museum of Art. I expect any day to hear of Otto Kahn purchasing Torpedo Tim, mistaking him for a Franz Hals.

"I guess Bill Fallon's just eccentric," said Spooner, head-waiter at Billy La Hiff's Tavern. "But it's *his* hair."

Nor would Mr. Fallon patronize the laundry. Whenever his linen became soiled, he threw it away, purchasing a new supply as needed. He wore expensive neckties, but seldom paid more than a dollar and a half for a shirt. His shirts had attached collars and sewed-on cuff-buttons, Mr. Fallon being too impatient to bother with cuff-links or collar-buttons. On coming to New York he had but one article of jewelry, a scarf pin. He soon dispensed with that.

He wore his clothes well, and, as prosperity continued, patronized exclusive tailors. Yet he seldom owned more than one pair of shoes at a time, and never allowed them to be shined. He had shapely hands, but chose to bite his nails rather than go to the manicurist. He retained a valet, who robbed him nightly, and by the clock. Instead of dismissing the man, Fallon thought the pants-raids hugely amusing. He placed a counterfeit hundred-dollar banknote in his pocket one evening, thinking it a fine trick to play on the predatory valet. Mr. Fallon's man, however, refused to nibble at the spurious lettuce. Next day Mr. Fallon absent-mindedly tendered the counterfeit bill at the florist's. It led to all manner of trouble. Mr. Fallon roared with merriment, regarding this turn of events an even better joke than he had planned. He was one practical joker who didn't resent the jest being tossed back.

On certain days, Mr. Fallon would smoke many cigarettes.

Again he would go for weeks without a puff. But he seldom bought his own smokes, depending on companions to keep him supplied. Nor did he care what brand was offered. Against this, no one at his table could pay the dinner-check. His tips were enormous.

Although he often purchased imported motor cars for lady friends, Fallon was notorious for making women companions walk to and from the theater or café. If distances were great, he took them—evening wraps and all—on the subway. "I like to walk," he said, "but if we really *must* ride, the subway is fast."

The precise time when Mr. Fallon began to sample the flesh of the city is not certain. Circumstantial evidence points to January, 1919, as the period of his first extra-marital exploit. Up to now he had been an untarnished—although thoughtless— husband and father.

Mr. Fallon's presumable initiator to antics eulogized by the kings of France was a widow. Her husband had been killed in an automobile accident. Fallon and the lady frequented the Ferncroft Inn at New Rochelle. There were roulette wheels and card tables, at which Fallon's companion nightly challenged her fortune. Eventually Mr. Fallon tired of watching the lady's play. Gambling in conventional form never appealed to him. He was wretched at cards—although he fancied himself unusually good. Furthermore, he was unable to sit still for long at a time.

Fallon's well-known aversion to sitting was summed up by Mr. Tammany Young, actor and celebrated gate-crasher. "They say he's got a glass backside, and is afraid it will bust if he sits down."

Mr. Fallon was not yet a hard drinker. He usually sang "When Irish Eyes Are Smiling" after the third one, or recited from Tennyson, Byron, or Kipling. When in romantic mood, he liked to sing "Where My Caravan Has Rested." When he reached the verse "You will understand their message," it was not uncommon to see mascara dripping from the lashes of Broadway ladies. There was a deal of the poet, Tom Moore, in Fallon. He seemed happy when two or three women wept over him; still happier if they quarreled—which was not an infrequent occurrence. Once, when a certain actress threatened to horsewhip another claimant of Fallon's affections, he was simply bloated with joy.

After successfully defending a group of men uncovered by Assistant District Attorney Jim Smith in vice raids and John Doe proceedings, Fallon received a comely visitor one afternoon in January, 1919. She was the wife of a Francis T. Inch. Mrs. Inch, a genteel-appearing woman, had been on the stage out west under the name of Betty Brewster. She told Fallon that she was in deep trouble.

"Then you came to the right place," said Fallon. "Now tell me everything."

"I'm charged with attempted blackmail, and I'm innocent."

Mr. Fallon nodded. "My clients always are. I'd be helpless if they weren't."

Mrs. Inch said she had been framed with marked banknotes. Her accuser was Eugene P. Herrman, President of the Herrman Motor Truck Company. Subsequent testimony purported that Mrs. Inch sought to extort monies from Herrman under threat of involving his name with that of a certain Mae Hayes.

According to the evidence, Herrman was having dinner one evening with his wife and three children. The telephone rang.

"I'll get it," Herrman said. "You've been on your feet all day, Anna."

"Hello," said Herrman.

A woman's voice came over the telephone. "Is Mrs. Herrman there?"

"Who is it?"

"I have a message for Mrs. Herrman. Would you please call her?"

Herrman turned from the instrument. "It's for you, Anna. I don't know who."

"Hello. Mrs. Herrman speaking."

"Oh, is this you, Mrs. Herrman?"

"Yes. Who is this?"

"This is Mae Hayes."

"Who?"

"Mae Hayes. Perhaps you haven't heard of me."

"What did you want, Miss Hayes?"

There was a pause. Then: "I just wanted to tell you, that while you were in Atlantic City last March, your husband and a friend met me and a friend, and took us to your apartment, where we spent the night."

Mrs. Herrman called her husband: "Gene! Come, quick!"

"What's wrong?"

She gave him the receiver. He called: "Hello. What do you want?"

The mysterious caller laughed, said a few unintelligible words and hung up. Mr. Herrman went to his office next day. He testified that the same woman's voice again came over the telephone.

"Well, old man, how did you like the message your wife received last night?"

Herrman was furious. "Who are you? What do you want?"

"I am Mae Hayes, and I have to undergo an operation."

"What's that got to do with me?"

"I need some money for hospital expenses. I think you should help out."

"You say this is Mae Hayes?"

"No, it really isn't Mae Hayes; but she's in trouble. I'm a friend of hers. And I am asking you, for her."

"All right," Herrman said. "Meet me at the Hotel Woodruff tomorrow. How much do you want?"

"I'll have to ask Mae. I'll let you know. Will you wait for a ring?"

"Yes."

After a time the telephone rang again. The voice said: "Mae says she'll leave the amount to your generosity. Otherwise, she'll have to visit your wife."

"Be at the Hotel Woodruff."

Mr. Herrman retained detectives. He placed them behind a screen after they had prepared $215 in marked bills. According to the operatives' testimony, Mrs. Inch appeared and told Herrman that if he paid her, Mae Hayes wouldn't bother him again. The detectives alleged they saw the transfer of currency. They arrested Mrs. Inch.

"Where *is* this Mae Hayes?" Fallon asked in consultation.

"Somewhere in Cincinnati."

"There *really is* a Mae Hayes?"

"Absolutely."

"Have you any money?"

"Very little."

"It may be expensive to find Mae Hayes."

"That's why I came to you."

"What do you mean?"

"I haven't much money. Another lawyer *couldn't* win, without getting Mae Hayes to New York. *You* can win regardless."

"Thanks," said Fallon. "Who told you I could?"

"Your whole manner tells me."

"In that event," said The Great Mouthpiece, "we'll go to dinner. I have an idea. It's about your ankles."

Mrs. Inch was astonished. "My ankles?"

"I've been studying your ankles. They are very handsome. They are more eloquent than any lawyer."

"I'm afraid I don't understand."

"When I put you on the stand——"

"*Must* I go on the stand?"

"It's a long shot. When you go on the stand, you're to wear a snug dress, one that comes to your knees when you sit. You will act aloof; at no time seeming conscious that your ankles are showing. You will display your calves constantly to the jury. It will take their minds off the case. I'm sure of it. Men are that way—jurors in particular. Furthermore, you look too refined to be at all bad."

Mr. Fallon permitted newspaper reporters to talk freely with Mrs. Inch. He whispered to her: "Try out the ankles on the newspaper boys."

The Park Row connoisseurs confirmed Mr. Fallon's opinion of the Inch charms.

"Powerful interests are trying to get this innocent girl out of the way," Mr. Fallon told the reporters. "It's up to you to see that she gets a fair deal."

Mr. Fallon spent $2,500 of his own money in vain, trying to locate Mae Hayes. The Inch defense seemed as fragile as an author's credit. The Great Mouthpiece, however, refused to worry. He allowed McGee that privilege.

"You've got that worried look, anyway," he said to his partner. "You may as well have the game as the name."

"You've got to be on your toes, Bill," said McGee. "The D.A.'s office is gunning for us, and this looks like their best bet."

Mrs. Inch came to trial in January, 1919, in Criminal Courts Building, where sits the criminal term of the Supreme Court. Many noted defendants had come and gone from this same room, passing over the "Bridge of Sighs" that connects the building with the Tombs. Among them were Roland B. Molineux, Harry K. Thaw, Police-Lieutenant Charles Becker, Michael Rofrano, and Dr. Warren C. Waite.

Mr. Fallon made sure that Mrs. Inch had an ample supply

of sheer silk stockings. It must be remembered that in 1919, a man—juror or otherwise—was in rare luck to see a lady's leg as high as the knee. The Inch jurors were given something more stimulating than Blackstone to think about on dark nights.

When Mrs. Inch took the stand, the jurors seemed like arbiters of a Miss America contest. Mr. Fallon led her gently through direct examination, asking (as usual) many leading questions that were ruled out. He held his witness as long as possible, so that her ankles might accomplish the work assigned them. The newspapers carried glowing accounts of the Inch underpinnings.

In cross-examination, the prosecutor kept thundering: "Yes, but *where* is this supposed Mae Hayes? Why hasn't she been produced in court?"

Mr. Fallon made notes on flaps of match-books, an annoying habit he had when he wanted to fluster an opponent. He had found a dictionary on his way to court. He presented it to one of the prosecutors, saying:

"On hearing you address the court today, I am sure this book *can't* belong to you. However, take it. I can think of no one who needs it more."

During court-proceedings Mr. Fallon amused himself with surreptitious gambling games. At the start, and during the examination of talesmen, Fallon bet McGee he could remember the name of each tentative juror, and that he would address each man by his full name, referring to his age and occupation. There were about sixty men so examined before the jury was selected. Mr. Fallon staked a thousand dollars on his terrific memory and won, hands down. As the trial progressed, Mr. Fallon discovered that the judge's seat was squeaky. He wagered hundred-dollar bills on the number of squeaks per minute.

Spectators imagined that the whispered conferences of the partners had to do with the cross-examination. The actual conversations were something like this:

"Seven squeaks, Gene. That's four hundred I'm in the piece."

"You lie like hell, Bill. There were only *five* squeaks."

"There's something stopping up your ears."

"It's the District Attorney's voice."

"I'll bet you a hundred it isn't his voice. It's his pronunciation. I just gave him a dictionary. I'll bring a grammar to-morrow."

"Try not to cheat. I'm almost out of cash."

"You can give me I.O.U.'s."

"Let's bet on the number of spectators with big noses, Bill. It's safer, and you couldn't cheat so much."

"I never cheat. Say, Gene, do you think it's the bench that squeaks?"

"What else *could* it be?"

"Maybe His Honor has mice, and doesn't know it."

"Nix! He's looking at us!"

"Then he's seeing two of the finest young men at the bar. Say, Gene, do you remember Brother Hooley?"

"And how! You led him a dog's life, Bill."

The Assistant District Attorney's voice was raised. "The People rest."

"They should," Fallon said, half-aloud, to McGee. "They must be pretty tired of the men they elect to office."

The case seemed hopeless, but when Fallon faced the jury he acted as though it were already won. Before rising for summation, he confided to his Fordham classmate, William J. Murray, then a reporter for the *Herald*: "I've picked the right juror. Watch me make a pal of him."

Fallon directed his entire address to that juror. After the judge's charge, which Fallon wrangled over to a point where he faced contempt proceedings, the jury retired. Eleven men wanted to convict. One stood for acquittal. Whether it was the one Fallon had singled out, I cannot say.

Mrs. Inch waited for the verdict in the sheriff's office. She played solitaire. During the deliberations, an amusing incident occurred. Mr. Johnny O'Connor arrived with Little Billy, the famous Lilliputian actor.

Mr. O'Connor introduced Little Billy to Fallon. "Did you ever hear of Admiral Dot?" Fallon asked. "He was a great pal of mine."

"I heard of him, but he never interested me much," said Little Billy.

Mr. O'Connor explained that Billy had an underworld complex, and was anxious to meet a few criminals. "I took him to see some gorillas," Mr. O'Connor added, "but he wouldn't believe they were the real McCoy."

"You been kidding me," said Little Billy. "I want to see *killers*, like you read about in the papers."

"Perhaps I can help you," Mr. Fallon said. "There's a fellow due in another part of court right now. He's up for the death-sentence."

"You mean the electric chair?" asked Little Billy.

"Right."

"Gee, that's swell!" said Little Billy. "Could I get a knock-down to him?"

"I'll see," Fallon said. "It will be difficult. This man tried to escape from the Tombs a month ago. He climbed the wall, slipped, and then fell inside, breaking both ankles."

"O'Connor," said Little Billy, "you been holding out on me I can't hardly wait."

"Since his attempted escape," Fallon said, "this man's been under heavy guard. The public has been excluded from the court-room during the trial. Here come the sheriff's men now."

"Which is the killer?" asked Billy.

"The one in the middle, with the handcuff on his left wrist."

"Oh, boy!" said Little Billy. "This is *life!* I wonder if I could shake hands with him?"

"I'll do my best," said Fallon. He induced the sheriff's deputies to permit Little Billy to talk with the killer.

"How does it feel to be like you?" Billy asked.

The killer looked down at the questioner. "Well, little pal," said he, "it feels swell. Yes, pal, it feels swell."

"Could I go with you and hear what the judge says?"

The killer turned to one of the guards. "Hey, cap, could the little mug train wid us?"

O'Connor, Fallon, and Little Billy were permitted to hear the death-sentence. As the Judge droned his words, the killer kept looking at Little Billy. The Lilliputian shivered. When he heard the court pronounce "death in the electric chair," Billy broke out in goose pimples. As they led the doomed man away, Billy followed.

"Gee, but you're some man!" Billy said.

"Glad you liked the show, pal," said the killer.

Billy stammered: "I'd like to have something to remember you by, pal."

"The hell you would! Well, I'll fix you up."

To the amazement of custodians, who daily searched the killer, the latter produced from his trouser-leg a long butcher knife. Before anyone recovered from the shock, he handed the knife solemnly to Little Billy.

"Keep this for me, pal. But don't never use it, excep' in self-defense."

The startled guards hurried the man to his cell, stripped him, and searched his clothes and cot.

At 11:15 o'clock the evening of January 30, 1919, the foreman of the Inch jury sent word to the bench that the twelve men could not reach an agreement. The jury stood eleven for conviction and one for acquittal. Mrs. Inch was released on bail, pending a second trial.

"We'll bring her to trial at the earliest possible time," the District Attorney told the newspaper men. "Fallon can't get away with this sort of thing forever."

Mr. Alfred J. Talley, first assistant to District Attorney Edward Swann (and later a judge in General Sessions), took command of the second Inch prosecution. He was an able man, learned in the law, but seemed to lack a sense of humor. In appearance and manner, he resembled Mr. Herbert Hoover.

"It's about *time* they gave me a run for the money," Fallon said. "The People shouldn't send boys on men's errands."

Mr. Fallon said to his client: "We've *got* to find Mae Hayes this time. With her, and with a new idea of mine, we'll get the brass ring and ride on."

Mrs. Inch wondered if her attorney had another plan similar to the ankle-display.

"Not exactly," he said. "I am going to have a high fence built about the witness chair, making a sort of pen. Nobody is to know that I am the instigator of the fence. In fact, I shall scream about the injustice of it. Furthermore, I *don't want to put you on the stand this time.*"

"But why a fence?"

"Ah! I shall charge that the prosecution built it expressly to hide your ankles and humiliate you. In interviews, you will describe it as a 'spite-fence,' and yourself a martyr."

"You have amazing ideas, Mr. Fallon."

"I'm getting to believe so, myself."

Mrs. Inch came to trial before Judge Vernon M. Davis. Everyone was astounded, on arriving in court, to find a fence about four feet high, extending from the left end of the bench to the end of the jury-box. A hitherto hidden fact is that Fallon had consulted his friend, David Belasco (and may roses never wither on his grave!), and together they chuckled over the arrangements. When Mr. Fallon directed that a saloon's old swinging-door be placed on the contraption, Mr. Belasco uplifted both hands:

"I couldn't do better myself," said the dean of the drama.

"I wanted your approval," Fallon said. "You have an eye for these things."

"Some day, William," said Mr. Belasco, "I'm going to have a drama in which you are to be the star. You are an actor. The stage is your real calling."

Throughout the years, Fallon harbored the thought of deserting the law for the stage. It was one of his last dreams. And Belasco was one of his firmest friends. The late dramatist and producer often consoled Fallon in the dark hours. Belasco, too, loved life and lived it to the full—and in one of his last conversations he spoke of Fallon.

"What happened to him," said Belasco, "might have happened to anybody's boy. He never grew up. I believe he would have been one of the greatest geniuses of the stage. He had everything that goes to make the intelligent, artistic star. I think he failed more through success than anything else. His environment overwhelmed him. He was fundamentally good, no matter what appeared on the surface. There is no question as to his artistic ability. He had soul."

Prosecutor Talley and Chief Clerk William Penny were at a loss to account for the "spite-fence." The court-attendants knew nothing about it. Mr. Fallon appeared almost apoplectic with rage and disgust.

"This hurts!" he screamed. "The insult of it! The shame! That civilization permits men to treat a beautiful, frail woman in this manner shows to what depths we have sunk since the age of chivalry. I have half a mind not to go on with the case!"

A Mrs. Mae Hayes Benjamin suddenly appeared in court. Mr. Fallon smiled knowingly at the press. He nodded as he saw the pencils of newspaper toilers racing over sheets of paper-pulp.

"The newspapers ought to put me on their payrolls," he whispered to McGee. "The editors should thank God for me, like the Jews in Russia did for William Sulzer."

"Look out that the newspapers don't attack us some day," replied McGee.

Fallon was momentarily serious. "He who lives by the press must die by the press. We're all Doctor Cooks at the North Pole. Kissed today; kicked tomorrow."

Mrs. Benjamin explained that she recently had been married. She stood before Eugene P. Herrman. He denied that he ever had seen or heard of her. Mr. Fallon called her to the stand for the defense. She was a small and decidedly pretty woman, and seemed constantly on the verge of tears. She said she knew the plaintiff.

"What were your relations with him?" asked Fallon.

"I object," Mr. Talley said.

For a quarter of an hour Mr. Fallon kept re-wording this question. Mr. Talley kept objecting. The objections were sustained almost without exception. Judge Davis would not permit the witness to describe her alleged friendship with Herrman, aside from her claim of having known him. Mr. Fallon brought from the witness an alleged telephone conversation, said to have been had between her and Herrman three weeks before the second trial of Mrs. Inch. Under secret instructions by Fallon, the telephone charges had been *reversed*, from Cincinnati to New York. This enabled Fallon to get the record of the call before the jury. Mr. Herrman later admitted he had had a conversation with a woman who called herself Mae Hayes.

"What was your exact conversation?" Mr. Fallon asked the woman.

Mrs. Benjamin replied: "I said: 'This is Mae,' and told him I was married, and that my husband and I were happy. I told him that Betty was in trouble, and that something ought to be done to help her. He said: 'You get into communication with the District Attorney's office.' I said: 'Must I come to New York to testify?' He said: 'Do as you like.' "

Mrs. Anna Herrman went on the stand to corroborate her husband's testimony. Fallon undertook a severe cross-examination—a procedure he thoroughly disliked in the case of a woman. Mrs. Herrman testified to a telephone call from a person claiming to be Mae Hayes. That was on June 12, 1918, she said. On June 14, she added, the same woman telephoned her *again*, and on the same subject.

"The voice was that of Mrs. Inch," she said.

"Now, now," said Mr. Fallon. "You say you are able to identify a voice you heard only *twice*, and over the telephone? And then, after a *lapse of months*, you are positive it was the voice of the defendant, as *heard in court*?"

Mrs. Herrman suddenly leaned against the "spite-fence" and fainted. A recess was declared.

Fallon confided to McGee: "I hated to do that. But it will weigh with the jury."

Fallon tore into anyone that went on the stand for the People. He grilled Herrman. He showed him two photographs, and asked if he recognized them. The question was objected to and ruled out. Efforts to put the question in different form were unavailing. The inference was that the pictures were snapshots of a man and a woman.

On March 13, the second day of the trial, Mrs. Inch was committed to the Tombs for the first time since she was released on bail shortly after her initial trial. This is a customary procedure in criminal cases, the defendant's bail being extended only until the hearing begins. Mrs. Inch had been permitted to go home the first day. She was surprised at the commitment and burst into tears.

"I have a sick husband," she said, "and my mother is dying from the shame of this thing. What are they trying to do to me?"

"Don't worry," Fallon said. "You won't be in jail long."

His words were prophetic. In summing up, he cast insolent aspersions on the Assistant District Attorney.

"My friend, Talley, here," he said, "has political aspirations."

"That is not so," Mr. Talley interrupted.

"Oh," said Fallon, "then you haven't any ambition?"

The court intervened. Mr. Fallon continued: "I was once an Assistant District Attorney. I had ambitions. I longed to become District Attorney. I sought to gain as many convictions as humanly possible. It would help me to realize my ambitions. Talley, here——"

Mr. Talley interjected: " '*Mr.* Talley,' if you please!"

Fallon bowed. "As I was saying: Mr. Talley-if-you-please, has ambitions——"

"That is not so," said Mr. Talley.

"Mr. Talley-if-you-please, says it is not so. Maybe not, but I repeat: I was once in the same position as Mr. Talley-if-you-please——"

"Mr. Fallon," the court said, "please keep within bounds.'

After many more sly references to "Mr. Talley-if-you-please," Fallon suddenly made the "spite-fence" an object for attack.

"Look at that monstrosity there!" he cried, pointing at the fence. "They tried to fix it so that this poor girl would have to sit there and peer over the top of a fence at her counsel." Then, in an effort to spike any suspicion by the jury as to the defense's motive for *not putting Mrs. Inch on the stand*, Mr. Fallon thundered: "You may ask *why* I did not permit my client to go on the stand. She *wanted* to go on the stand, but I would not allow it. Why?" He again pointed toward the spite-fence. "That is *why*, gentlemen. Would you allow a mother or a daughter of yours to be humiliated in that fashion? To be put behind a fence like an animal? No, gentlemen! Nor would I allow my client to be so humiliated and insulted. That's why I didn't put her on the stand at all."

At eleven o'clock next morning, Judge Davis began his charge to the jury. Mr. Fallon noted fourteen exceptions to the charge as read. The case was submitted to the jury at a quarter after twelve o'clock. Judge Davis admonished the jurors that their first problem was to determine to what extent the testimony of various witnesses was to be believed.

Mr. Fallon yawned and said he was "going somewhere less mentally deadening than a court-room." He did not come back at all. In the evening he took a lady to see Fay Bainter in "East is West." He received news of the Inch jury between acts. McGee represented Mrs. Inch during Fallon's absence.

After ten hours of deliberation, and on the evening of March 18, 1919, the jury announced it was unable to arrive at a verdict.

The jury was discharged by Clerk Penny, under instructions from Judge Davis.

"My client," said McGee, "has consented to the discharge of this jury only at my special request. We shall demand a new trial and vindication at the hands of a jury."

Mrs. Inch chatted with reporters. "I'm not so anxious for a new trial," she confided. "The first trial interested me. The second was only mildly amusing. I am, on the whole, becoming bored with court proceedings."

The jurors in the second trial stood 6 for acquittal and 6 for conviction. "We lined up that way on the first ballot," said Henry Mayper, the foreman, "and that's the way the vote stood at the end."

Though still under indictment, Mrs. Inch never again came to trial.

Chapter Thirteen

FUN IN GRANT'S TOMB

EDDIE WESTON, the singing waiter at Tobey's tenderloin joint, moved with his beer-tray among the cellar tables. Some twenty customers, including half a dozen commercial Venuses, grew sentimental over their schooners as Eddie warbled:

"Down-n-n-n-nn by th' ole mill-l-l-ll stream-m-m,

Wear I firs' met choo. . . . "

In April of the year 1905, Tobey's was one of the bawdiest resorts of New York's sporting fiefs. It was a rathskeller at No. 51 West Thirty-first street, and recently had been sold by a Mr. Tobin to Walter Joyce. Primarily it was a drinking establishment, but ladies of the district found Tobey's an ideal bazaar for the disposal of love *à la carte*. It would have been a most suitable place for Dr. Wassermann to have conducted his research work concerning the blood-stream habitat of corkscrews.

Fights of all sorts occurred nightly at Tobey's. The bouncer was kept busy. His name was Doyle. He had a middle as big as a Billy Sunday tabernacle. He used that part to ram recalcitrant patrons—first crushing them against wall or bar, then propelling them to the stone stairs leading up to the street. He was known as "Belly" Doyle. His midriff was the finest ram since the Roman trireme. Mr. Joyce kept a bung-starter in reserve, but usually relied on Doyle, the bouncer, calling out:

"Give 'em the belly, Doyle!"

Mr. Doyle usually stayed at the door, as lookout. When a

fight started, it was his business to keep out the police, as well as to master-mind the fray.

Eddie was slinging beer and warbling in throaty tones:

"Wid yer eyez-z-z-z s'bloo-oo-oo-oo,
An' yer heart s'troo-oo-oo-oo. . . . "

The consumptive piano-player's Duke's Mixture cigarette bobbled on his moist lower lip as he pounded the keys. He nodded as Eddie put a short beer beside the derby on the piano-top.

"An' it wuz dere I knoo-oo-oo-oo,
Dat I furst love jew. . . . "

Half a dozen young toughs pushed past the protuberant stomach of Belly Doyle and chose a table. Their leader was a nineteen-year-old chap. He was sharp-eyed and not more than a hundred and twenty pounds. He appeared very cocky. His name was Peter Regan. He was called "Kid" Regan and "Petey." He was the black sheep of a good family. His brother was a detective-sergeant on the New York police force; an upright, brave officer.

There was one woman in Petey's party. "Red" Gray, "English Harry" Anderson, Harry Davis and Jack McGee were his male companions. They began casting torrid remarks at the singing waiter.

"Pipe de canary!" said Mr. "Red" Gray.

"Youse will have to soft-pedal," warned Belly Doyle.

"When does the balloon go up?" asked the Kid, sneering.

"I don't want no trouble from youse, see?" said Mr. Doyle "I know what youse is here for."

"A wise guy," said English Harry. "Should we start somethin', Kid?"

The Kid studied his beer. "Not yet. Wait till the dame shows up."

The "dame" was a person named Flossie Sterling. The Kid had been told that Flossie was going about "knocking" him; saying, among other things, that he was a mediocre gallant. The Kid promised to humiliate Flossie before the eyes of his pals.

Eddie kept slinging beer and singing:

"You was sixtee-ee-ee-eenn. My village quee-ee-ee-nnn. . . . "

During a lull in table-talk and clashing of glassware, high-heeled shoes pattered on the basement steps. Mr. Doyle opened the door. Flossie came in. Mr. Doyle locked the door. Flossie sounded a ripe raspberry as she swished past the Regan table.

"She's givin' yah the bird," said English Harry to the Kid.

Mr. Regan rose. "I gotta present for yah, Flossie."

He picked up his half-emptied glass of beer. He threw the beer in Flossie's face. Then he hurled the glass at her. She screamed like a third alarm. Belly Doyle closed in. The Kid's partners rallied to their leader's side. Glasses began to fly. Fists were used; then blackjacks and brass knuckles. The whole place swirled with the battle. All the patrons joined the fight. Proprietor Joyce sought to grasp Regan's arm. He got a knife-wound in the chest. Eddie, the singing-waiter, ran to his room to get a pistol. He couldn't find one. He returned in time to receive a blackjack on the skull. He woke up singing: "You wuz sixtee-ee-ee-eennn." There were knife-rips in Eddie's arms and chest. Joyce rose and was knocked down again by one of Petey's ruffians. He lay very still. Splotches of blood were on the floor and walls of the dive.

"The cops!" English Harry warned.

The Regan party fled. Patrolmen Brueck and Boyle arrived. They called an ambulance. Dr. Farr, the ambulance surgeon, took Joyce and Eddie Weston to the hospital. Joyce died on the way. A knife-blade had pierced his left lung.

Petey the Kid left the City. The police said they were unable to locate him. The newspapers, particularly The New York *World*, kept harping on the inactivity of the police in apprehending Regan.

An indictment charging manslaughter was returned. The Kid kept hop-scotching about the country. Early in 1908 Detective Peabody located Regan at New Orleans, but he escaped before word arrived from New York to hold him. In 1908 he was arrested in Los Angeles on a swindling charge. In January of 1909, nearly four years after the indictment for manslaughter,

Regan was captured in Los Angeles. Detectives Fogarty and Kear of Central Office brought him to New York on requisition papers issued by Governor Charles E. Hughes. Governor Hughes' warrant charged Regan with felonious assault. He was tried and sentenced to a year in Sing Sing prison. After his release, he was not heard of officially until July of 1919, when he chose to operate a swindle inside the gray walls of General Grant's Tomb on Riverside Drive.

If Sigmund Freud were on the level, he would get busy and tell us *why* Grant's Tomb exerts such powerful influence on two classes of citizens—the love-lorn and the sucker. Insofar as I know, the General didn't give women a tumble, but devoted his leisure to bad cigars and good liquor. Yet, when a sailor from the fleet stands with a girl before the sepulchral well that holds the bronze sarcophagi of General and wife, he grows dithery with love.

A perusal of the Grant record indicates that he was a set-up for designing business men, but *that* can hardly explain the bargain-counter influence of the Tomb on visitors from far away. One glance at the General's place of sepulture, and a tourist is seized with a desire to purchase Brooklyn Bridge, City Hall, Central Park, or any other landmark offered for sale by metropolitan slickers.

Petey the Kid was one of the first to pre-empt the sucker-concession at Grant's Tomb. He returned from the provinces with a pair of post-graduate dice and a yearning to exist without toil. He had a confederate, whose name may have been Jordan. Together they trimmed gullible ones who came within the spell of Grant's Tomb. The Kid did a side-business at race-tracks, where he made book, but his soul was with General Grant.

In July of 1919, Robert G. Hamilton, Jr., came to New York from San Francisco. He had several points of interest on his itinerary, places about which the folk back home would be certain to inquire. Grant's Tomb was prominent on the list.

While gazing at the twin-beds of death, Mr. Hamilton got friendly with Kid Regan's confederate. They whispered of this and that. They went outside and continued their talk.

"Yeah," said Mr. Jordan, "I got lotsa pals in Frisco. Good ol' Golden Gate! I used to have lotsa fun South of the Slot."

Mr. Hamilton warmed to such deserved praise of his home city. Mr. Jordan went on: "These New Yorkers give me an ache—you know where. They know it all. For instance, I know a fella who's allus braggin' about the dough he carries around. That's the New Yorker for yah."

"There *is* a lot of money here," observed Mr. Hamilton.

"I ain't sayin' they ain't, Mr. Hamilton. Money's O.K., but it shouldn't ought to be a man's God. To hear this bozo tell it, you'd think he was the only guy with jack. Do you call that refined, Mr. Hamilton?"

"I guess not."

"What he needs is a good lesson. Him and his bankroll! I been plannin' to put him in his place."

"Yes?"

"A friend of mine learned me a trick. It's a darb. Wait till I pull it on that loud-mouthed guy with the noisy bankroll!"

Kid Regan's confederate then described the three-cornered coin-matching game. "It takes two to play the joke," he said. "Supposin' me and you was goin' to pull it on the fellow I was talkin' of. Well, we would all match coins, and the odd man, havin' heads or tails, whichever it happened to be, would win."

"What's tricky about that?"

"Nothin', except me and you would agree beforehand never to lay heads at the same time, or tails at the same time. You'd just lay heads, say, and I'd always lay tails. Then one of us would be a cinch to cop, because the other of us would lay the same as the fellow who is being kidded. See?"

"It sounds like a good joke."

"Of course, we would give him back his sugar, after we had put the bee on him."

"Naturally."

Mr. Jordan beamed. He happened to see a smallish man climbing the granite steps. "Holy mackarel!" he said. "Here comes the very gink I was talkin' of! What do you know?" He called to Petey the Kid, who was whistling happily as he mounted the steps: "Hey, you, Peter. Hello!"

Petey the Kid was convincingly surprised at the meeting. "Howdy, yourself. How's tricks?"

"Speak of the devil," said Mr. Jordan. "I was just talkin' about yah. Here, meet Mr. Hamilton of Frisco. Mr. Hamilton, Mr. Regan."

"Hope youse didn't tell Mr. Hamilton everything yah know?"

"I was just this minute sayin' that you have it pretty soft with all *your* roll."

"Well," said Petey. "I guess the wolf won't never have pups at *my* door."

"How'd you like to match coins, Peter? I want to get some of that easy money."

"I don't want to pick on guys like youse," said Mr. Regan.

Mr. Jordan turned to Mr. Hamilton. "He ain't so sure of hisself after all."

Peter was offended. "Would it look respectful, if we wuz to gamble in such a historic spot, wid a great Gen'ral stretched stiff in front of us?"

Mr. Jordan's face went red, white and blue, in patriotic succession. "I never thunk of that. I wuz just clownin', anyway."

"Look here, Jordan, youse might of been clownin'; and then again, youse mightn't. Underneath, youse might be sore because I got a big roll, and youse have to crab along."

Mr. Hamilton was sorry to see two New Yorkers quarreling over class distinction. Mr. Jordan spoke up: "I told you, Mr. Hamilton, that money wuz *some* men's God."

"Well," said Petey the Kid, "just for that crack, I'm goin' to match coins wid youse, Gen'ral or no Gen'ral."

Mr. Jordan winked at Mr. Hamilton. He whispered: "You lay heads, and I'll lay tails. We gotta learn him a lesson."

The stakes were small at first. Mr. Regan didn't win a single joust. Soon he was ten dollars in the hole. Then twenty, thirty, sixty. "I guess I better go find a nigger, and change my luck."

"Suppose you put up the dough, instead of keepin' track in your head," suggested Mr. Jordan.

"Oh, so youse don't truss me, is that it?" growled Petey.

"I truss you, but Mr. Hamilton here is a stranger. Maybe he won't want to write it on the cuff no more."

"Oh, it's all right," said Mr. Hamilton.

"It ain't business," said Mr. Jordan. "I think we should ought to put up real dough."

"If youse think I ain't got real dough," said Mr. Regan, "peg this!" He flashed a sheaf of bills (stage money, with a twenty-dollar bill wrapper).

"Pay the sixty you owe, before we match anymore. Or, now, maybe you don't want no more of our game?"

Mr. Regan sneered. "The hell I don't! Only we been matchin' for chicken-feed. Tell youse what! Let's play onct more; only it must be for *real* dough."

Mr. Jordan conferred with Mr. Hamilton. "How much you got on you?"

"I haven't any cash at all."

Mr. Jordan was mortified. "But we got to show him *somethin*'. I'm a little short myself. You ain't got *no* dough?"

"Only some traveler's checks."

Mr. Jordan brightened. "That's O.K. We can't lose. How much you got?"

"I have five checks for fifty dollars each."

"Then put it in my hands as stake-holder," Mr. Jordan whispered, "and we'll take him like our friend, Mr. Grant here, took Richmond."

Mr. Hamilton placed the $250 in traveler's checks in Mr. Jordan's hands. The latter then announced to Petey: "All right, greaseball. You ast for it, and now you're goin' to get it. We'll match just onct for the sixty you owe us plus this here $250 besides."

"Ready?" asked Mr. Regan, palming his coin.

"Shoot," said Mr. Jordan. When the coins were upturned, Mr. Hamilton had heads. Mr. Jordan, too, had heads! There was but one chance for the two "educators." If Mr. Regan had heads, it would be a dead-heat and would call for another match. But Mr. Regan had *tails*, and was odd man.

"Come acrost wid the dough," said Mr. Regan.

Mr. Hamilton was a most unhappy man. Mr. Jordan tried his utmost to appear melancholy. Mr. Regan repeated his request. "Hand over that jack, or I'll call a cop." The traveler's checks were given him. He swanked down the steps of the tomb. Let it be said to his credit that he sought to atone for any lack of respect shown the illustrious dead, by whistling: "Hang Jeff Davis to a Sour Apple Tree."

"One of us must of slopped over," said Mr. Jordan, slinking away. Mr. Hamilton found himself alone with memory and the purple serenity of the sepulchre. He went out and told his troubles to a policeman. The policeman referred him to the District Attorney. A big vice campaign was in progress. The Citizen's Union was interested. Mr. Leonard Wallstein, counsel for the Union, brought the Regan case to the attention of The New York *World*. The *World* assigned its premier reporter, Donald Henderson Clarke, to the case.

For a long time there had been hints that a "Master Mind" was ruling a criminal empire in New York. The *World* inferred that this "Master Mind" was in cahoots with the police. The fact that Kid Regan's brother now was a lieutenant of police was regarded as significant. The fact that Lieutenant Regan had had twenty-three years of meritorious service, had won medals for bravery, and citations for conspicuous duty, did not weigh with the *World*.

"There's a Master Mind," was the journalistic cry.

We soon shall come to this "Master Mind." Right now we must go on a shopping tour with Petey the Kid. He went to Brill Brothers haberdashery at Forty-seventh street and Broadway on Saturday, July 19. It was one of those humid, lazy days that made Mr. Babcock, the credit manager, think of the country club; and Mr. Lazarus, the clerk, dream of the surf at Coney Island.

Mr. Regan paused at a counter, where Mr. Lazarus was flicking dust from a rack of scarves. "I want some unnerwear," Mr. Regan said. "The best youse have got."

"What size?" inquired Mr. Lazarus.

"About a twenny-seb'n waiss, I guess."

"We have a fine assortment of linen shorts."

"I want silk."

Mr. Regan purchased $18 worth of intimate wear. He then offered a fifty-dollar traveler's check in payment. Mr. Lazarus called the credit manager. Mr. Babcock responded. He asked Mr. Regan to sign the traveler's check. Mr. Regan signed it *twice*.

"You are Mr. Hamilton, of course?" said Mr. Babcock.

"Surest t'ing," replied Mr. Regan.

"I'll get your change," said Mr. Babcock, retiring to a telephone. He called the National City Bank, on whom the check was drawn. He was told that a Mr. Hamilton had been flimflammed out of this and four other checks. Mr. Babcock reported to the police. He came back to Mr. Regan, who was growing restless.

As the Kid left the store, he was arrested by James F. Fairman, a police reservist. The Kid had a pen-knife in his hand. A small, sharp blade was pointed at the arresting agent. Patrolman Gill arrived on the scene.

"Where'd yah get that money?" asked Patrolman Gill.

"I won it at craps in my hotel," said the Kid.

"What hotel?"

"The Longacre."

"Come with me," said Gill, "and tell it to the judge."

Broadway awoke one morning to find that the government expected to share in its income, in the form of a tax. Here was a fine howdy-do. Imagine anyone—even Uncle Sam—trying to *take anything* from a street that lived on the *take!* Broadway turned to Bill Fallon in its distress.

"I tell you," said the proprietor of a girl-show, "Bill Fallon is tops. The damned income-tax people claim I owe $56,000. Bill's got it down to $380 already, and he says by the time we get through, the United States will be *owin' me!*"

Word went 'round that Mr. Fallon was adept at defending persons sued for income taxes. He couldn't handle all such business, but he did what he could, and at handsome fees. Not only Broadway, but the fur trade and garment barons sought his advice. Mr. Fallon went into the Federal Courts and loomed as brilliantly there as he had elsewhere. His bag of tricks was bigger than the gift-sack of Santa Claus.

While Mr. Fallon was immersed in income taxes, his firm was retained by Kid Regan. Of itself, it was not a big case—just a small-time confidence game. But somehow, anything that Fallon touched took on importance. The "Master Mind" cry was sounded. Kid Regan suddenly became part of a huge and mysterious crime-syndicate governed by the suave, mild-mannered Arnold Rothstein, so-called King of Gamblers.

Mr. Fallon not only was busy with his income-tax cases, but was enjoying intense play on Broadway. More and more, he was seen in company of the street's gorgeous women. Even *his* robust constitution was unable to stand the pace without recourse to artificial stimulus. His drinking increased perceptibly. Not yet a confirmed alcoholic, Fallon became a steady drinker. He was throwing money right and left, feeding the Broadway ravens in the manner of a tourist in Venice, flinging corn to the pigeons of St. Mark's.

When the District Attorney learned that Fallon was retained for the defense of Petey the Kid, the silk hat did its customary balloon ascension. The New York *World* bellowed for action. The Citizen's Union brayed for summary justice, Mr. Donald Henderson Clarke—than whom no better reporter ever blew the collar from a mug of beer—wrote powerful pieces for his paper. Clarke liked Fallon, and Fallon liked Clarke. As honest as a village blacksmith, and as jovial as a tavern-keeper, Clarke made things warm for Fallon. But Fallon was broad, and admired a sincere foe. He relished Clarke's personality and ability. Clarke was all man, open and above-board.

Said Fallon: "The authorities are trying to hurry me, are they? We'll see."

Judge John F. McIntyre, an excellent, though brittle-tempered jurist, sat on the Regan case in Part II of the Court of General Sessions. "There will be no delay," he said. He entered the case for trial on August 12, 1919.

"The only way I can win this case," Fallon very frankly announced to Clarke, "is to ride the judge. Just watch me do it. I'll have him talking to himself and cutting out paper dolls before a week passes."

Mr. Regan was charged with forgery and grand larceny. Under the New York law, a defendant, after pleading not guilty, is entitled to forty-eight hours in which to get ready for trial. Judge McIntyre endeavored to force the trial immediately.

When the trial was about to begin, there was no Fallon in court. Mr. McGee appeared and announced: "If the court please, we are ready, subject to our engagement in the United States District Court."

There was a long argument, the Judge sensing that Fallon was trying to engineer a delay. "This trial," said the court, "will not be impeded. You may have another day, and then we shall proceed regardless."

McGee appeared the next morning and very mournfully said: "Your Honor, we are ready, subject to engagement in the United States District Court."

The Assistant District Attorney whispered something to the Judge. The latter raised the defendant's bail from $7,500 to $12,000, and without explanation. McGee went to the telephone and conferred with Fallon.

"Move at once to dismiss the panel of jurors," said Fallon.

Mr. McGee almost knocked the judge from the bench with this motion. "If the court please," he said, "the court has raised the defendant's bail in front of the panel from which will come the jury that is to try the case. I move to dismiss the panel."

Judge McIntyre was furious. "The court, in raising the bail of the defendant, did not disclose the reason. The motion is denied."

"I move to dismiss," said McGee, "on account of Your Honor's further remark."

The court reluctantly ordered a new panel. "You will be ready without fail tomorrow," said the Judge, enraged at this automatic delay. Next day the court was in an uproar. Fallon and McGee had done what was believed to have been an unprecedented thing. They had slipped before Supreme Court Justice Lydon and obtained a writ of prohibition, preventing the trial until the income-tax cases in Federal court were concluded.

The Judge was grim when he glanced at the counsel table and saw no Fallon. When Mr. McGee rose, the Judge glared.

"Your Honor," said McGee, "I have here a writ of prohibition from the Supreme Court to prevent bringing this case to trial at this time."

The amazed Judge called on the District Attorney's staff. "I want this action reported to the Appellate Division," he said. "I never heard of such an astounding situation."

The Prosecutors argued, asking that the court dismiss the writ on the ground that Fallon had remedy by appeal. The Judge ordered that immediate efforts be made to have the writ vacated. He then said to the prosecutor: "You will take this to higher authorities, and see if it is not contumacious conduct." The court addressed McGee: "You will remain in court, pending word from the Supreme Court."

"If Your Honor please," said McGee, "I am compelled to decline. I am engaged in a trial in Federal Court." Mr. McGee walked out. Everyone gasped at the effrontery of the Fallon partner.

Fallon dined at Hahn's Restaurant at noon. He glanced up from his *filet mignon* (with truffles). "Well, Mr. McGee, are you getting His Honor properly baited for the arrival of the matador?"

"God help us, Bill," said McGee, "if your foot slips!"

"McGee," said Fallon, "I saw the finest-looking girl in the world last night!"

"You'd better not think of any *girl* while we've got McIntyre so upset."

"She is a soubrette in 'Listen Lester'," Fallon said. "Her name is Gertrude Vanderbilt."

"What are we to do next?"

"There must be *more* delays. . . . What a charming young woman Miss Vanderbilt is!"

The afternoon of the Supreme Court order, Assistant District Attorney Waugh had the writ vacated. Judge McIntyre ordered the trial for next morning.

"Bill," said McGee, "the judge is plenty sore."

"I'm not so sure he's sufficiently hot."

"Then you ought to hear him for yourself."

"We must be sure. Was there any steam spurting from His Honor's ears?"

"I don't believe we ought to risk further mischief-making."

"I haven't had so much fun since Fordham. Let's get McIntyre completely crazy by exhausting the panel."

"I hope we don't go to jail for contempt."

It was Saturday. McGee appeared in court when the case was called first on the calendar. He approached the bench.

"If Your Honor please," said McGee, "I have here an affidavit stating reasons why Mr. Fallon cannot try the case today."

Mr. Waugh had expected such a move. He, too, submitted an affidavit for the prosecution, giving reasons for immediate trial.

"The trial will proceed forthwith," said the court. "I assign you, Mr. McGee, to defend."

"If the court please," said Mr. McGee, "I must decline the appointment. I have prepared the case that Mr. Fallon is now trying in the Federal Court. My presence there is imperative."

The court thereupon assigned Franklin Greer as counsel for the defendant, and gave him until noon to confer with his new client. Mr. Regan got to his feet and objected.

"I hired my own counsel," said Petey.

"Sit down!" said the court.

Mr. McGee talked a moment with Regan. Then he addressed the court. "I respectfully suggest, that because of statements made in this court yesterday, the case be transferred to another court."

"What does counsel mean?" demanded Judge McIntyre.

"I refer to a statement made by Your Honor yesterday, in which, and while talking with me, you said Lieutenant Regan, the brother of the defendant, was involved in this matter."

The court was in a screaming mood. "Counsel is making a statement that is absolutely untrue!" There was a silence. Then: "And if a statement of that character is made *again*, the court will take summary action."

There was a pause. The court continued: "This is the first time since I have been on the bench that I have had any trouble of this sort. I have always been courteous, fair, and impartial to counsel. To insure a fair trial of this case, I direct the clerk to call a jury from some other part of the court—men who have not heard the remarks of the court and of counsel for the defendant."

Mr. McGee retired and reported to Fallon. "Well, we have the court sufficiently steamed," Fallon said. "I shall wind up my business in Federal Court immediately. You go back and say I shall be on deck Monday to take charge."

Mr. Greer was examining talesmen at noon, when Mr. McGee reappeared. He told the court that Mr. Fallon would be ready Monday.

"Nevertheless," said the court, "the examination of talesmen will be continued until the panel is exhausted."

It looked as though a jury would be selected before night, and the trial begun. McGee talked with Fallon over the telephone. He came back and surveyed the scene. There was a tentative jury in the box. There were only four additional men left in the panel. Mr. McGee immediately excused (on peremptory challenge) *five* of the prospective jurors. When others were called to fill the five places, it was found that only *four* men were available. That made but eleven in the jury box. There was nothing the court *could* do but continue the trial until Monday.

And on Monday, the gay, confident Mr. Fallon swept like a flame into court and began at once to heckle everyone.

At the outset, the District Attorney sought to show that Petey was a man of bad record. Fallon objected again and again to these slurs on his client's past. His objections were overruled. The prosecutor was elated. In order to upset the District Attorney, Fallon engineered the removal from the D.A.'s files of some important papers bearing on an *entirely different* case. This acted as an irritant.

"Where were you in February of 1908?" the prosecution asked Regan.

"I object," said Mr. Fallon. "What has *that* to do with the present trial?"

"Objection overruled," said the court.

"I was in New Orleans," said Mr. Regan.

"Where were you in January, 1909?"

Mr. Fallon again objected and was overruled. And so on for a long list of questions, tending to show that the Kid was a fly-by-night and involved in various crimes.

"If the court please," said Mr. Fallon, in excepting, "I wish to state that the admission of such questions makes a travesty of the trial of my client."

"Counsel will sit down," said the court.

Then came questions concerning the Kid's acquaintance with a host of underworld characters.

"Did you ever know 'English' Harry?" asked the prosecution.

"Object," said Mr. Fallon. "What difference in the world

does it make *whom* this boy knew? It is all highly prejudicial, as well as being wholly incompetent, immaterial, and irrelevant."

"Objection overruled."

Mr. Fallon began a re-direct examination of Petey. It seemed that no jury *could* have sympathy for one that had fled so many authorities and had been in such bad company.

"Petey," Mr. Fallon began, "did you ever know any of the following persons: President Wilson? King George? Lillian Russell? Sir Oliver Lodge? . . ."

"I object!" shouted three assistant district attorneys in unison.

The court was astounded. "Mr. Fallon, you will not make a farce of this trial. It is unthinkable that such a manifestly foolish question be put by an attorney."

Mr. Fallon bowed. "Your Honor, that is the position I myself take. It is the position, if you will recall, I took a few minutes ago when the prosecution asked *similar* questions——"

The court interrupted: "Mr. Fallon, I warn you."

Mr. Fallon then said: "Petey, the prosecution has gone into exhaustive investigation of your alleged travels. Will you not tell me if you ever *climbed the pyramids or slid down the Alps?*"

The prosecutors rose again. The laughter in the court was stilled only after threats to clear the room. Mr. Fallon was roundly rebuked by the bench. He sat down. It was apparent that his daring, ludicrous sally had made a deep impression on the jury. The best minds of the District Attorney's office hastened to the fore, but it was too late.

When Judge McIntyre charged the jury, Mr. Fallon took vigorous exception to several points. In his speech of exception, he said: "The court's charge is an *animated summation for the prosecution.*"

There was a gasp from veteran court-attachés, who realized the dangerous implication of such a remark by counsel to court. His Honor was thoroughly enraged. He half rose from the bench. His face flushed. "Please repeat what you have just said, Mr. Fallon."

"I regard the charge as read," Mr. Fallon said, "as an animated summation for the prosecution."

The court hesitated for a moment. Then: "The jury will retire. Mr. Stenographer, you will read from the record what has just been said."

When the reading was concluded, the court addressed Mr. Fallon: "What have you to say to *that?*"

With contempt-of-court staring him in the eyes, Mr. Fallon folded his arms and replied: "I have nothing to say, except I believe that, consciously or unconsciously, the court has been unfair to the defendant in part of the charge. I mean no disrespect to the court. I asked for an exception in the only manner I thought it might be sought. I ask Your Honor to read your own charge, and see, in your calmer moments, if you did not, consciously or unconsciously, do as I said."

It cannot be put into words the eloquence and drama that entered the foregoing. The judge's pen had been poised over a paper as though ready to commit Fallon to jail for contempt. The court was deeply moved. He said:

"I shall read the record and will be guided in my action by the result."

Judge McIntyre was a man of undoubted force of character and of sterling intellectual qualities. He had been baited and wilfully bearded by Fallon. That the Fallon appeal deterred him seemed a miracle.

The next day found Fallon waiting in court to learn if, after all, he was to go to jail for contempt. Almost the entire staff of the District Attorney's office trooped in. Alfred J. Talley, first assistant, passed Fallon. The latter nodded sweetly. He noticed that Mr. Talley was laden with law-books.

"Ah, Talley," said Fallon, "you have some books, eh? If there is any point of law, I'd be glad to save you the trouble of hunting it up in a book."

The Judge completed his instructions to the jury. As the jury went out, reporters talked with Fallon.

"Well," they asked, "what do you think?"

"I think," he said, "it was a shame I had to miss that double-header yesterday at the Polo Grounds. The Reds beat the Giants twice, and we need those games."

The jury reported a hopeless deadlock and were discharged. The prosecution gagged. The court-room was crowded. There was a cheer. That cheer was not for Regan, one might be sure. It was for Fallon. He was a legal Babe Ruth, and he had knocked another home run.

Mr. Talley was looking at a book. Mr. Fallon said: "You've got the wrong book. It isn't in that one. It's in another one."

Four days later, Petey again faced a jury. Assistant District Attorney Jim Smith took charge, saying he would beat Fallon to a frazzle. Broadway said: "Oh, yeah?"

There was more talk of a "Master Mind" working behind the scenes.

During cross-examination of Hamilton, in which Fallon racked him as though *he* had been the real offender, Judge McIntyre interrupted to say:

"Mr. Fallon, if there is a re-occurrence of the trouble we encountered in the last trial, I shall take summary action."

Fallon seemed suave and innocent. He seized on an opportunity to have the bench make further comment. Such comment might weigh with a jury in favor of the defendant; or, it might provide grounds for an appeal.

"To *what trouble* does Your Honor refer?" he asked.

"I must state frankly, Mr. Fallon," the court said, "that I admire your ingenuity."

The second trial also ended in a disagreement. It seemed impossible to beat Fallon.

Donald Henderson Clarke disclosed an interesting bit of by-play in the Regan trials. It was noticed that the Brill Brothers' clerk was grilled unmercifully by Fallon in the first trial. The witness emerged without a scar from the second. In fact, he made a very good witness for the State on his next appearance.

Mr. Clarke revealed that the clerk came to Fallon before the second trial, saying:

"I'm a great admirer of yours, Mr. Fallon. Will you do me a favor? Last time you cross-examined me, you made me look terrible. I never got through being kidded at the store. They all said the manager was a good witness, but I was a bad one."

"Glad to do anybody a favor," Fallon said.

In the second trial, Fallon went after the manager with uncalled-for savagery. He permitted the clerk to be what is called a "very smart witness." That was Fallon's way.

Chapter Fourteen

THE MAN WHO LIVED IN DOORWAYS

F ALLON became acquainted with Arnold Rothstein, the most publicized of underworld financiers, in January, 1919. Off and on thereafter, Fallon was Rothstein's mouthpiece, and represented various Rothstein serfs.

Mr. Rothstein was bulleted not many months ago. He died in Polyclinic Hospital, refusing to name his executioner. Whether his passing was a loss to mankind and a gain to either branch of the Hereafter, or vice versa, is a problem too weighty to handle in hot weather and hard times.

The man appeared constantly in newspaper banners and body-type as "The Master-Mind of the Criminal Empire." The fixing of the Black Sox baseball scandal was attributed to him. He was said to have engineered sinister race-track coups. Mysterious and far-reaching dope plots were laid at his door. His critics presumed him to be at the bottom of strikes, gold-brick schemes, fake prize fights, and to be a fence for gem and bond thieves. The press posed Mr. Rothstein as the "brains" of nearly all the skullduggery brewed by the sonny-boys of modern crime.

Somehow, I gag at the portrait of Arnold Rothstein as Master-Mind. I tried to swallow it, but was forced to regurgitate, and eventually to expel.

Mr. Rothstein, weighted down with lethal lead and clipping-bureau offal, proclaiming him a Master-Mind, died an exalted pawn-broker. His pocketbook was the skull; his bankroll the

201

brains. He was an excellent executive, as we Americans judge such things.

A. R. was a tremendous gambler, with a joss-house pallor and an arterial system that, instead of blood, held a solution of arsenic in ice-water. He would write you a bail piece of $50,000 on the cuff—but if you owed him a $10 premium on a similar bond, Mr. Rothstein would hound you to death to get it. Few men have been so scrupulous as he in collecting debts, or so lax about meeting obligations. Indeed, the metal suppositories that goosed him into the grave were etched with I.O.U.'s.

Mr. Rothstein *did* have a hold on the underworld. But that hold, and his grip on the popular imagination, were two entirely different things. His usurer's soul and the availability of his bankroll placed him automatically in the king-row of the criminal checker-board.

Aside from money matters, and a vanity that would have cracked a Versailles mirror, Mr. Rothstein was a pleasant enough companion. He didn't eat with his knife, and his conversation was not half as dull as that heard at authors' teas (which accounts for his not having been shot sooner). He detested liquor, and usually refused to traffic with anyone that drank to excess. He contributed to charities, lent his limousine to gentlemen of the cloth, and made self-conscious gestures in the direction of art. He fancied himself a connoisseur of oriental rugs and of certain achievements in oil.

Mr. Rothstein was ready to gamble on anything except the weather. There was no way of fixing that. A.R. was particularly fond of dice. There are stories of how he staked $100,000 on a single cast; but let us not overlook the fact that his bankroll and his credit were tremendous; that he could play for many losing hours, awaiting the arrival of a parade of sevens.

Inspired by the knowledge that A.R. carried huge sums and gambled for mighty stakes, gunmen occasionally raided Mr. Rothstein's traveling crap-games. Authenticated gamblers arranged the soirées at various places where police or criminal invasions were least likely to interfere.

Having lost quite a bit of money to hold-up artists, Mr. Rothstein felt imposed upon. He dealt coolly with immediate situations, but in retrospect boiled when he thought upon the rapes by plug uglies.

In January, 1919, Mr. Rothstein was flinging dice with nineteen others in an apartment on the fourth floor of No. 301 West Fifty-seventh street. The dice were in his pale, slim hand, and were clicking like a great-grandma's false teeth at her golden-wedding anniversary.

"Four is my point," announced Mr. Rothstein in a mild, pleasing voice.

Four is a somewhat abominable point in the game of craps. Mr. Abe Attell, ex-featherweight pugilistic champion, nodded as he listened to the rataplan of the dice. There was a world of eloquence as he echoed: "Little Joe!"

The cubes scarcely had leaped from Rothstein's hand when a heavy rapping shook the door. "Open up, there!"

Another invasion by gunmen? Mr. Rothstein's hand found a pistol. He aimed at the upper door-panel. There were three shots, and three neat punctures in the door. Then came a confusion of voices, and solid blows against the door. The wood cracked, then splintered. A large hand groped through the breach. Thick fingers manipulated the lock and the chain-check. Warnings sounded. Eight city detectives, led by Inspector Dominick Henry, entered the room. Two of the detectives, Walsh and McLaughlin, bore superficial wounds. The coat-sleeve of a third had been pinked. The gamblers stood dumbly. No one moved toward the pile of currency on the floor. During the storming of the door, Mr. Rothstein had vanished.

"Where's Rothstein?" asked a detective.

"He ain't been here," said one of the gamblers.

"He's been here, all right," said the detective.

The wounded McLaughlin went to an opened window. There was a fire-escape platform abutting it. He looked out and down through the steel ribs of the platform. He saw in the dawn a man crouching on a ledge at the second story. It was Mr. Rothstein. He had been stopped by the lack of a ladder from platform to ground. Mr. Rothstein not only returned to the scene of what he called: "which-shooting-do-you-mean?" but volunteered the use of his limousine to carry the wounded officers to the hospital.

The authorities held twenty men for the grand jury on suspicion of felonious assault. Bail was set at $1,000 each. Mr. Rothstein—who was as handy as a bottle for the train—provided the bail. Magistrate Francis X. McQuade dismissed nineteen of the gamblers. The court held Rothstein for a hearing on the assault charge. District Attorney Swann ordered a big gambling inquiry. He assigned his assistant, Jim Smith, to handle it. Everyone involved suffered amazing lapses of memory. No one had seen Rothstein with a gun. No one had heard shots. The boys, as it is said, didn't know nothing.

Mr. Rothstein, to be sure, had counsel. It began to look as though the shooting of police officers *might* be serious. A.R. retained Fallon "in case of a trial." Mr. Fallon, however, remained under cover. Judge McIntyre dismissed two indictments handed up by the grand jury, one for felonious assault in the first degree, the other in the second degree. Lack of evidence.

Fallon now was Rothstein's mouthpiece, and all Broadway knew it.

The Rothstein mask failed from the first to awe Fallon. He played smart-alec jokes on Rothstein, defied him and quarreled with him frequently concerning drink. Rothstein strove with a curious, child-like zest to outdistance Fallon intellectually. Repeated defeats seemed to teach the gambler no lesson. It cannot be said that either man loved the other. Yet they worked efficiently together.

Both were overflowing with little vanities. Each was aware of the other's pet conceits. It was a great blow to Rothstein when he heard that Fallon had said:

"A.R. has mouse's eyes."

Rothstein retaliated by spreading the report that Fallon not only cut his own hair, but touched it up with henna. In these childish battles, Fallon won because he could laugh. Rothstein lost because he could not laugh. When Fallon heard of the Rothstein charge concerning dyed hair, he said:

"Did you ever see a mouse that had false teeth?"

This was a crusher. Mr. Rothstein had shopped painstakingly for his set of false teeth. The Rothstein gumware was so excellent that few of his acquaintances along Broadway knew that the teeth were from the hand of the potter.

Mr. Fallon sensed that Rothstein had an almost neurotic fear of ill health. He called one day at Rothstein's insurance offices. During the conversation, Fallon leaned forward suddenly. "Good Lord! A.R." He then sat back as though he had spoken out of turn.

"What's wrong?"

Fallon manufactured a guilty look. "I was just thinking out loud."

"Thinking what?"

Fallon fumbled. "Are you feeling well?"

"Certainly. Why not?"

"Aren't you eating too many sandwiches?"

Rothstein looked steadily at Fallon. "What are you getting at?"

"Don't you think you should go to Atlantic City?"

"I never felt better in my life."

"That just goes to show how appearances can deceive. Are you *sure* your stomach isn't upset?"

"I know it isn't."

"Then it must be your gall bladder."

"There's nothing wrong with me."

"Is that what the doctor told you?"

"Hell no!" said Rothstein. "I haven't been to the doctor. There's nothing wrong."

"I hope you're right," said Fallon, rising to leave.

"What's your hurry?"

"No hurry, only I'm not going to tax the strength of a sick man."

Rothstein was mad. "Who says I'm sick?"

"You say you're not," said Fallon. "Certainly *you* should know."

After Fallon left, Rothstein went immediately to a doctor's office. The doctor found nothing wrong. Rothstein went to another doctor, and still another. Finally, and after a fourth going-over, he was convinced that nothing was seriously the matter with him. When he heard how Fallon was broadcasting the joke, the Great Pawn-Broker was furious. With all his press-built reputation as a Master-Mind, and his pose as the inscrutable czar of the underworld, we find Rothstein asking this question of Fallon's partner:

"Between us, do you think Fallon is smarter than I am?"

Mr. Rothstein often stood in Broadway doorways, looking at passers-by, and conferring in whispers with mysterious persons. Mr. Fallon said of him:

"Rothstein is a man who dwells in doorways. A mouse standing in a doorway, waiting for his cheese."

Chapter Fifteen

LOVE IN A TAXICAB

ERNEST FRITZ, Tuckahoe taxi chauffeur, had two things on his mind as he arrived in New York City the afternoon of March 22, 1919. One was the purchase of a Ford taxicab. The other was an appointment with Florence Coyne, a stenographer in a Manhattan office.

It was a Saturday half-holiday. Spring was displaying its symptoms in the three customary places—the throats of birds, the buds of trees, and the glands of men. The lion-breath of March had dwindled to a purr no less soothing and rhythmic than the hum of Fritz's new motor.

Fritz and Florence Coyne had been more than friendly. They both were married and resided in Tuckahoe. Fritz had a wife and one child. Mrs. Coyne was living apart from her husband. Fritz was twenty-eight years old. Mrs. Coyne was twenty-four and very pretty. She was a woman of insatiate physical demands, and whenever Fritz held her in his arms, imperative urges flamed inside him.

These two young persons conjured forbidden dreams that whirled them away from a world of social discipline.

Fritz met Florence by appointment. They went to buy some spring clothes. They drove about town, and then dined at the Cosmopolitan Hotel in Chambers Street. They drove some more, having several drinks at speakeasies. Towards midnight they started for Tuckahoe, pausing occasionally along the way to light fresh emotional fires, or to fan old ones. Their last stop—a protracted one—was at Newhall and Rosedale Avenues, a short distance from the Bronx River. Alcohol and desire caused them to behave like mice dancing in the oxygenic atmosphere of a bell-jar. They found the front seat too uncomfortable, too restraining. Fritz and the girl decided to visit in the rear of the cab. They engaged in a petting party that out-distanced the imagination.

During months studded with adulteries, this pair had met clandestinely, hurled themselves without preliminaries into squirming contact. Tonight they yearned for untried libidinous thrills as they huddled in the cab. During violent pawing explorations by Fritz, he tore the young woman internally, and by manual miscalculation. She shrieked with horror and pain.

"What's the matter?" he asked, rousing for a moment from his amative delirium.

The young woman's torso was convulsed. A warm, moist presence was manifest, together with the gushes of pain. "Something terrible has happened!"

The hysteria that follows the accidents of illicit love gripped the man and the woman, with the same force, but with widely divergent effects. The woman, fainting from the loss of blood, was in a ghastly condition. She behaved like a drowning person. The man, pitched to earth from his high-flying spasm, was gruff, random-minded and futile. They fell together to the floor of the cab. The woman's cries became more faint, her breathing less labored. In a baffled, half-awake manner, Fritz kept plucking at the woman's clothes and body, as though trying to restore her with sham-battle gestures of love. She made no response. There was a strange sound in her throat, like the tearing of an old cloth.

Motorcycle Patrolman Leis was chugging up Rosedale Avenue, his searchlight thrusting a yellow fang ahead of him as he thought of a big, hot breakfast.

"Hey, in there!" called Patrolman Leis, throttling down and dangling his sturdy legs either side of his motorcycle. "Hey, in there! Hello!"

There was no reply. The officer pointed his pocket torch toward the cab, but the batteries had gone dead. He kicked loose his parking-stand. It dropped to the ground with a metallic jar. He gripped his handle-bar and the seat, jerking his heavy cycle to its steel rack. Then he went to the steering-post of his machine, unslotted his roadlight and used it as a lantern. He saw no one in the front of the cab. He kept calling: "Hello, you," as he explored the back of the parked car. He held the light in his left hand. He rubbed his holster with his free hand, making sure the flap was undone. He saw two figures huddled on the floor of the cab, a man bending above a woman.

"Hey, you," he called sharply, "what's all this about?"

The man blinked against the glare of the patrolman's torch. "It's nothing, officer. This woman fainted."

Patrolman Leis was not unaccustomed to the grotesque attitudes of romance. "Fainted, eh? Well, it's a funny way to bring her to. Let's have a look."

Fritz rose from his crouch. "She's had a few drinks. She often gets this way."

Patrolman Leis shook the woman. He maneuvered his light and saw a little lake of blood. "Just fainted, hey? Turn this bus around, neighbor, and drive to Fordham Hospital."

"Look here, officer——"

"Get up at that wheel, you."

"Have a heart, officer. I got a kid. I'm a married man."

"Didn't you know you had a wife and kid when you started out this evening? Move over, I'll drive. Want to tell me what happened?"

"We were on our way home when she got to feeling bad. She begun to bleed."

"I'll say she did. I guess you know she's in a bad way?"

"She often faints and bleeds."

"Uhuh! Then this ain't the first time you two stayed together?"

"I wish you'd not take me with you."

"You should have thought of your wife and kid sooner. They always think of 'em after the funny business is over. What about that blood?"

"I don't know."

"Maybe you stabbed her. Where did you throw the knife?"

"What do you think I am? A fool?"

"A guy with hot pants is always a fool. How about that knife?"

"You know I didn't use a knife. Why would I stab her?"

"That's what I'm asking you? Why did you?"

"She often bleeds. You know damned well I didn't stab anybody. And she'll be all right."

"You're in a tough spot, partner, if I know my onions; and I think I do. Better come clean."

"Give me a match."

"Smoke up and think it over. This dame is in a bad way."

At Fordham Hospital orderlies put the woman on an ambulatory stretcher and rolled it hurriedly to the operating-room. Dr. Barrow listened for heart-action. He removed the stethoscope tubes from his ears.

"She's dead."

Patrolman Leis brought out his note-book. "Would you give me the facts, Doc, for my report?"

The doctor whispered to the patrolman. The latter puckered his lips against a pencil-stub. "How do you spell 'hemorrhage,' Doc?"

The doctor spelled it. The patrolman then asked: "But how could it happen, if he didn't use a knife?"

"It appears that the whole inside was ripped out by a hand. It's uncommon, but not unheard of."

The patrolman was bewildered. "Did he mean to do it?"

"Ask your prisoner. There are types known to psychiatrists

who get their pleasure in this manner. Whether he is of that type, or it was an accident, is a matter for the authorities to thresh out. Is there anything else I can tell you?"

"I thought I'd been up against everything and seen everything," said the patrolman. "Thanks, Doc. . . . Say, how do you spell 'prolapsus,' or whatever it was you said about that hemorrhage?"

The authorities arraigned Fritz on a short affidavit before Magistrate Tobias in West Farms Court. The judge held him for examination and without bail. Dr. K. Sellers Kennard, Medical Examiner of Bronx County, prepared for the autopsy on Mrs. Coyne. District Attorney Francis Martin of the Bronx told Dr. Kennard he wanted a most exhaustive *post mortem* procedure.

"Just to be sure," said Mr. Martin, "I'll ask Dr. Schultze if he'll help."

Dr. Otto H. Schultze was Medical Assistant to District Attorney Swann of New York. With the possible exception of Medical Examiner Norris, Dr. Schultze had no equal in the autopsy chamber.

The two experts worked for three hours at the slab. Several other physicians and surgeons attended. Mr. Martin asked: "Well, gentlemen, what are your findings?"

Dr. Kennard said: "It looks like the work of a pervert, a ripper. In addition to the internal, abdominal tearing, the woman's face and breast show bruises. Her jaw and nose are fractured. There are lacerations on her shoulders and head, perhaps caused by finger-nails."

"The cause of death?" asked Mr. Martin.

"The immediate cause," said Dr. Kennard, "was hemorrhage."

The grand jury indicted Fritz on a charge of first degree murder. He went to the Bronx County Jail to await trial. He appealed to his former employer, the Hon. Charles A. Perkins, one-time District Attorney of New York. Mr. Perkins turned the case over to the firm of Fallon & McGee.

The press meowed, as usual, for hasty trial of the alleged ripper. Mr. Fallon sought to delay the trial as long as possible.

"The public must have an opportunity to forget the worst features of the case," Mr. Fallon confided. "A trial now would carry Fritz post-haste to the electric chair. A year from now will see him a free man. The public is as forgetful as a lover."

It was not until February, 1920, nearly eleven months after the death of Florence Coyne, that the Fritz case came to the Bronx Supreme Court. The trial caught Fallon at a time when he was as busy as a moth in a lighthouse. He was scheduled to defend a political extremist before Judge Bartow S. Weeks on the date of the opening of the Fritz case.

Said McGee: "How are you going to be in both places at the same time?"

"You stall Judge Weeks, while I knock over the Fritz case."

Judge Weeks told McGee: "I shall expect counsel to be ready a week from today. If Mr. Fallon is unable to be here at that time, court will assign other counsel."

The Great Mouthpiece came to the Bronx court with a record that well might impress anyone. He had defended *one hundred and twenty-six* homicide actions of various degree, and *without a single conviction!* Twenty-two of these had been capital cases. That is not the whole story. Fallon had advised numerous other lawyer-friends, gratis—among them the highly successful Leonard A. Snitkin—in the handling of murder defenses. It is estimated that, directly or indirectly, Fallon saved more than fifty persons from the death-penalty. With a few more Fallons before the bar, the electric chair would have become a playground for spiders.

Could he have saved Gerald Chapman from the rope? Or Ruth Snyder and Judd Gray from the chair?

We have seen how Fallon played and dallied during other cases. We have encountered him in assorted moods—a mischief-lover, whose sarcasms brought scarlet to the faces of prosecutor and judge; a smart-alec, whose brilliance alone saved him from contempt-of-court commitment; a heckler and a bluffer, a bully-ragger, who could make a witness falter, hesitate, and backtrack, no matter how sterling of purpose the witness might be. Now we find a different Fallon—at the height of his powers, mentally dominant, physically blessed, and with a case which so absorbed his interest that he put aside his bottles and shut his doors against courtesans. It is one of the finest portraits we have of this man in his maturity.

It is true that he did not give the Fritz case much thought until the week before a trial that no longer could be delayed. But once started on this task, he plunged into it with a competence that was prodigious and masterful. In the light of his habits, we cannot expect to see him turning the profound pages of court-decisions or books of law. But he read day and night. His books were those of psychologists and physiologists. Of these, he compiled a list of 482, rejecting more than 300 after cursory perusal, and carefully studying the contents of the others.

When he learned that the prosecution was bringing a professor of gynecology from Harvard, and summoning other specialists on female matters, Mr. Fallon sent hurriedly to New York for text-books. He had only one night in which to familiarize himself with this intricate subject. During that night—and relying on black coffee to keep himself awake—he practically memorized four standard works. Perhaps no better compliment could have been paid him than that of an expert medical witness, whom he figuratively throttled next day:

"Mr. Fallon, I did not know you were an M.D. When did you get your degree?"

Mr. Fallon replied: "I received my degree last night. I began practice this morning."

When Fritz came to trial before Justice Vernon M. Davis (who had presided at the Inch trials), he faced great odds. He had signed three statements purporting to point to his guilt, and all were offered in evidence. Not only did Fallon meet numerous obstacles in the Bronx court, but Judge Weeks in New York was clamoring for Fallon's appearance there in connection with the communist's case. Worst of all, Fallon's mother was hopelessly ill. She had suffered a paralytic stroke and was confined to her bed.

The seating of a jury for the Fritz case was difficult. Nearly everyone had read the grewsome details and had formed an opinion. There was another element, too, that handicapped Mr. Fallon. A majority of the talesmen were not friendly to taxi-cab chauffeurs. For instance, there was Talesman Austin Carr.

Mr. Fallon: You have said that you dislike taxi drivers. Do you mean any particular taxi driver?

Talesman Carr: No. I mean *all of them*.

Mr. Fallon: Excused.

District Attorney Martin, a dignified and scholarly man, outlined the case to the jury. The details were unthinkable. During the opening address, one spectator fainted. Fallon interrupted again and again with objections, charging the prosecutor with prejudicing the jury.

It was Fallon's scheme to admit freely that his client had caused the death of the woman. (The three signed statements were too big a hurdle for him to do otherwise.) He took the position that the whole affair was an accident. But how to prove it!

Fallon sought to implant the accident theory in the minds of the jury. He did this by mouthing the word "accident" at every opportunity. Many of his objections were made solely to allow him to say:

"If the court please, I object to the prosecution's method of screaming the word 'guilt' in connection with my client. It casts an unfair shadow over this *accident*."

Patrolman Leis told his story, saying among other things: "And on the way to the hospital, the prisoner was cool."

Mr. Fallon (in cross-examination): And how, pray, did you come to such a positive conclusion?

Officer: Why, he chatted all the time, and kept smoking cigarettes like nothing had happened.

Mr. Fallon: Have you ever heard of men lying on the battle-field, or in field-hospitals, smoking cigarettes to divert their minds?

The Prosecutor: We object, Your Honor.

Mr. Fallon: A cigarette would be a most natural pacifier for anyone, particularly after such an *accident*. Furthermore——

The Court: Objection sustained.

Other evidence for the People showed that a progressive saloon party had preceded the slaying. Then came the expert witnesses. Fallon was eminently prepared for the avalanche. When Dr. Kennard testified to the autopsy findings, Fallon hurled himself upon the learned doctor with such whirlwind force that the whole court rocked. The structure of the female body was gone into exhaustively. Intimate measurements concerning the particular cadaver were argued. Mr. Fallon developed from this and other witnesses that Mrs. Coyne was so built that her vital organs lacked proper support. He threw a bombshell into the case by developing the fact that the woman had been a mother; that there had been evidence of inadequate suturings—or perhaps none at all—in the post-natal procedure by the attending obstetrician.

Finally, and after propounding a lengthy hypothetical question, Fallon assumed his characteristic "charge-upon-the-witness" pose, his finger pointed like a pistol.

"And now, Doctor, is it not possible that the injury you testified to could have been caused by a *coughing fit?*"

"It wasn't so caused," said the witness.

Fallon thundered: "I am not asking you if it was or wasn't
caused by a coughing fit. I am asking: *could* it not have been
caused by a violent cough?"

The witness hesitated for a moment. "Yes, it *could* have been
possible."

Mr. Fallon folded his arms across his big chest. He turned to
the jury with a beatific expression, as though to say: "Now,
gentlemen, let's enjoy this admission together, you and I."

The State rested on February 20, but so daring was a subsequent coup launched by Fallon that the People sought another
innings in rebuttal.

Mr. Fallon received word shortly before the State rested that
his mother was gravely ill. He hastened to Mamaroneck, put his
flaming golden head beside the snow-white head on the pillow.
He trembled with grief. The woman on the bed was the one
real thing he had—and soon, he felt, she would be gone.

When he returned to court and rose to begin his spectacular
defense of Ernest Fritz, the jury seemed to find in Fallon a new
and compelling personality. The memory of his hours in Mamaroneck was yet with him.

Soon, however, the battle monopolized Fallon's every energy.
The melancholy lustre left his eyes as he opened fire. Daringly
and unexpectedly, he presented Dr. Schultze as the *first witness
for the defense!*

District Attorney Martin, it will be recalled, had asked Dr.
Schultze to take charge of the autopsy on the Coyne cadaver.
The District Attorney had invited the celebrated post-mortem
operator as *insurance* against possible slips. And now the audacious
Fallon was presenting him as a *defense witness!*

A crowd overflowed the courtroom. Here was drama. Here
was the most colorful court-actor of the decade gracing the
stage. Twenty girls from Morris High School were denied ad-

mittance to the court room. Attorneys were describing life's most
intimate performances. Nowhere else is the analysis of love so
ghastly, so obscene, and so lacking in taste as in courts of law.

When Dr. Schultze took the stand, District Attorney Martin
rose to object. "I challenge the right of this witness to testify
for the defense."

Mr. Martin pointed out that Dr. Schultze was Medical Assistant to District Attorney Swann of New York, and, as such,
was ineligible as a defense witness. The court ruled that Dr.
Schultze might testify.

Mr. Fallon: It has been testified that Mrs. Coyne's jaw was
broken. Was it broken?

Dr. Schultze: It was not.

Q: Was it dislocated? A: No.

Q: Were there bruises on her body? A: Yes.

Q: Would any or all such bruises have caused death? A: No.

Q: The defense maintains that Fritz and Mrs. Coyne were
in the back seat of the car, embracing ********** and that such
manipulation by the defendant inadvertently caused the hemorrhage. In your opinion, could such an accident be possible? A:
It would be entirely possible.

This answer was as welcome to the prosecution as an attack
of mustard-gas. A violent bickering arose between Messrs. Martin
and Fallon. The court warned both sides.

Fallon welcomed court-recess on Washington's Birthday. He
visited his mother. Later in the day he went to New York
to confer with McGee. Judge Weeks was impatient over Fallon's
defiance of the order to put in an appearance at the communist's
trial or give way to other counsel.

Fallon and McGee were "hiding out" in the Braddock Hotel,
uptown. McGee was happy over his partner's sustained industry.
He sought to safeguard Fallon as much as possible, keeping him
away from Broadway temptations during the Fritz trial. The
partners were talking over their sandwiches when the telephone
rang.

McGee looked at Fallon. "You didn't tell anyone where we were, did you?"

"Of course not," Fallon said. "Not even my wife."

"I think you *did* tell somebody you were here," McGee said.

"I did not," Fallon said. He spoke into the transmitter. "Hello."

"Is this Mr. Fallon?"

"Yes."

"This is the switch-board operator. There's a long distance call from Cleveland. The party won't give his name."

A voice unrecognizable to Fallon spoke: "Never mind who this is, Mr. Fallon. Will you take a case involving plenty of money?"

"I'm pretty busy right now."

"You won't be too busy for this one. Can you leave right away for the middle west?"

"I'm defending a case. Besides, I have no time for mysteries. What's it about?"

"You'll get another long distance call at 6 o'clock tonight. We think you'll deal with us."

"Who's 'we'?"

"Never mind. Will you be there at six o'clock?"

"Maybe."

"It'll be worth your while."

The caller hung up. Fallon told McGee: "Somebody's kidding us."

"I don't know about that. I have a hunch."

"What is it?"

"I think it has something to do with the stock certificate robbery."

Fallon raised his brows. "Nicky Arnstein?"

"I wouldn't be surprised."

"Funny about that call."

"His people would have to be careful."

Mr. Arnstein was charged with having engineered the theft

of between $4,000,000 and $5,000,000 in securities from Wall Street messenger boys. He now was a fugitive.

It was February 24, 1920. Dr. Schultze was on the stand. Mr. Martin was cross-examining.

Q: Now, Doctor, did you know that the defendant once worked for Charles A. Perkins? A: I was aware of it.

Q: And of course you know that Mr. Perkins was once District Attorney of New York? A: Yes.

Q: As a matter of fact, you served Mr. Perkins in the same capacity that you now serve District Attorney Swann? A: That is correct.

Q: That is, you were Medical Assistant? A: Correct.

Q: Is it not a fact that Mr. Perkins is a friend of yours? A: I suppose so.

Q: And is it not a fact that Mr. Perkins, as your former chief, induced you to appear here as a witness for the defense? A: That is entirely incorrect.

Q: But you do know, do you not, that Mr. Perkins is an advisory counsel in this case? A: I don't know.

Q: Did I not tell you in my office that Perkins was advisory counsel? A: I don't remember.

Q: Then you don't know?

Mr. Fallon (objecting): The witness has testified to that. The Court: He says he does not remember.

Q: Did you not tell me just after you performed the autopsy that this was a most atrocious crime? A typical ripper case? A: I deny having made such a statement at any time.

Q: Did you not at one time express an opinion about this case, different from that in your written report? A: I never have expressed any other opinion.

(A protracted argument arose between Mr. Fallon and Mr. Martin.)

Mr. Fallon: If the court please, I object to the manner of

the prosecutor. His insinuations and his charges of guilt are highly prejudicial. I ask that a juror be withdrawn.

(The juror was not withdrawn. This would have meant a mistrial.)

Q: Then your report coincides with your present opinion? A: There were certain other factors not necessary to include in the report. I should like to bring them out now.

Q: You will get a chance to bring everything out. Did the fact that Mr. Perkins appointed you to your present position affect your testimony, after you learned Mr. Perkins was interested in this case? A: No.

Mr. Martin emphasized that whenever he had talked with Dr. Schultze he always had had a witness present.

Q: Well, then, Doctor, how did Mr. Fallon come to know what your testimony would be, so that he could summon you here as a witness for the defense?

(Mr. Fallon whispered hoarsely, as though to a neighbor at the counsel table: "I'm clairvoyant." There was a return of his old-time mischievous look as he gazed at the jury.)

The Witness: Mr. Fallon told me that you told him I was not going to be called as a witness.

(Mr. Fallon was again whispering hoarsely: "That's how I win all my cases. I let the prosecution hang itself.")

Mr. Martin: Did you know that I went to District Attorney Swann and made charges against you, and told him you gave me the cause of death as murder in the first degree, and then went over to the other side and prepared their case?

Dr. Schultze: Yes, and he told you how ridiculous it was!

Mr. Fallon by now had gained such comfort from expert witnesses—whether his own, or those for the State—that he decided he could risk his client on the stand. He chose, however, to do something dramatic, something that would serve as a literal focal point for the jury.

When court convened next morning, the death-car itself was standing before the bar!

"Ernest Fritz," called Mr. Fallon. The jurymen kept gazing morbidly at the death-car. "Take the stand."

Fallon had not told Fritz of his plan to produce the taxicab in court. The defendant had entered the room with a debonair manner. He had seemed in complete control of himself. When he first saw the car, he drew his hands across his eyes, as though dumbfounded and doubtful. There were blood-stains on the machine. Fritz's mother and wife had attended all the sessions. They now withdrew from the court-room, gasping when they saw the car. They remained in the corridor outside while Fritz was testifying.

By Mr. Fallon: Under what name did you know the woman who was killed in this *accident?* A: As Florence Glennon.

Q: Did you love her? A: I loved her.

Q: Had you ever seen her before the day of the accident? A: Yes.

Q: Under what circumstances, and how often? A: As often as we had a chance. We had lots of social drinks together.

Mr. Fallon's gaze swept the crowded courtroom. Many women were in the throng. Fallon worked best before large crowds. He half-started as he recognized an attractive woman sitting in the third row. He often had seen her on the stage, but so far had not met her. She was Miss Fannie Brice, the wife of Nicky Arnstein. Mr. Fallon began to perform with added zest. He had overmuch of the actor in him.

The witness testified to a long list of hotels and roadhouses as trysting places for him and his beloved. He freely admitted all intimacies as portrayed by the prosecution. Fallon, with inimitable daring, not only encouraged his witness in these admissions, but saw to it that Fritz actually *added* to the list of adulteries!

Q: Then, will you tell the jury why you indulged in these affairs with the woman who was *accidentally* killed? A: Because I loved her.

Q: Did it ever enter your mind to injure her in any way? A: Why, I wouldn't have harmed a hair of that girl's head! I loved her dearly.

Mr. Fallon sighed. "That is all. Take the witness."

Mr. Martin rose for cross-examination. Q: You signed three statements, as testified to by the police, did you not? A: I am not sure.

(Mr. Martin offered as exhibits the three alleged confessions.)

Q: Is this your signature on these three documents? A: It may be.

Q: Would you say that you didn't sign these confessions of guilt?

Mr. Fallon: I object, Your Honor, to the continuous and unwarranted declarations of guilt by the prosecutor.

The Court ruled that the witness might testify to the authenticity of the documents, but directed the jury to disregard remarks of counsel on either side as to guilt or innocence of the defendant.

Q: Are these documents the ones you signed? Or are they not? A: I said at the time I was arrested that I was not guilty. (The witness began to shout.) And I say now that I am not guilty! I signed something or other, yes. But I was too dead to the world at that time to know what I was doing.

Q: But you were not so dead to the world but that you were able to make *corrections* to what had been dictated, were you?

Mr. Fallon: I object! I object to such unfair tactics.

Q: You have testified that you were in love with Mrs. Coyne. What was your attitude toward your wife? A: *I loved them both.*

Mr. Fallon had not asked Fritz to sit in the death-auto. Believing it would be better psychology to have the District Attorney request the witness to do so, and forecasting that such a demand would be made, Fallon now smiled knowingly. The prosecutor asked Fritz to re-enact the affair. Fritz hesitated and looked appealingly at his counsel.

Mr. Fallon waved and said: "Go ahead, Ernest. Show how the *accident* occurred."

As the dignified Mr. Martin accompanied the defendant to the door of the cab, Mr. Fallon also rose and stood beside the prosecutor. To the latter's disgust, Mr. Fallon assumed an exaggerated courtesy. "Won't you step inside with him, Mr. Martin?"

"No," said Mr. Martin. "I'll remain here."

Mr. Fallon kept edging Mr. Martin toward the running-board, palpably trying to upset his dignity and endeavoring to make the situation seem comic.

On his way from court that afternoon, Fallon was delighted to have Miss Brice introduce herself. "You're the man to defend my husband," she said. "I'm sure you can establish his innocence."

"Miss Brice," said Fallon, "any man that refused you a favor would be lacking in appreciation of art and womanhood."

Fallon now believed he had broken the back of the Fritz case. "They're bringing in so many experts that I know they are conceding defeat. The more experts they bring, the more muddled the whole thing will be for the jury. But just for fun, I'll have some more experts of my own. It will be the battle of experts."

Mr. Fallon almost laughed aloud when the prosecution produced District Attorney Swann as a witness to deny he had characterized Mr. Martin's murder-and-ripper-charges as "ridiculous."

Mr. Martin: Then, Judge, just what were your words? A: I said that the Medical Adviser was under civil service, and could not be removed except after trial on charges.

Dr. Otto A. Pozdena of the Bronx Health Board swore that Dr. Schultze had said: "It's a most atrocious crime. A real ripper murder." Dr. George Hohmann testified he had heard Dr. Schultze direct Dr. Kennard to insert the word "homicidal" in the death certificate. Dr. George Burgess McGrath of Boston was an expert witness for the State. The jury was dizzy. It was far easier for them to remember the word "accident" than the Latin of the learned ones.

Mr. Fallon called Dr. Justin Herold for the defense. Dr. Herold was professor of jurisprudence in medicine at Fordham

University. He was author of several books on legal medicine. He had been coroner's physician in New York City before the consolidation of the boroughs and the creation of the post of medical examiner. Mr. Fallon propounded the theory of the prosecution in the form of a question, including all the vivid and horrible details. Then he asked:

"And now, Doctor, what is your opinion as to that?"

"My opinion is that death in nowise was caused as charged."

Mr. Fallon also produced Mr. Perkins. Q: What was your motive in seeking to assist in this case? A: As Fritz's former employer, I thought it my duty to do all I properly could to help him.

Mr. Fallon added another daring and surprising stroke. He called Mrs. Coyne's husband, Herbert Coyne, *for the defense!* Mr. Coyne had been a prisoner in the Tombs. Mr. Fallon procured a writ of *habeas corpus* before Justice Tierney so that Coyne could testify. The man upheld—as best a layman might—Fallon's contentions as to the woman's physical peculiarities, her tendency towards hemorrhages.

Meanwhile, in New York, Judge Weeks was fuming and fretting over Fallon's exceedingly long delay in arriving for the trial of the communist. Mr. McGee entered appearances in that court and bore the brunt of the judge's threats.

On March 9, almost a year after he had been arrested and charged with murder in the first degree, Ernest Fritz was found not guilty! The jury deliberated only three hours and thirty minutes.

Instead of being overjoyed, Mr. Fallon left the court-room in a rage. That mood persisted until he met McGee in a New York hotel.

"What on earth is the matter, Bill?"

"It's my last homicide case. I'm through."

"What are you talking about?"

"I never was so mad in my life. We sat there and heard the

verdict. The man went scot-free. Do you think he thanked me? Not on your life! Can you guess what he said?"

"What?"

"He turned to me, and in the most matter-of-fact way asked: *Do you think I can get that cab back?*"

Mr. Fallon, having abstained from liquor for nearly a month, began to drink up. Before nightfall he was swackoed. He sang and recited for McGee. He spoke extemporaneously on the subject of Judge Bartow S. Weeks, whose anger now was at white heat.

"You'd better be in court tomorrow, Bill. Weeks is almost crazy."

In the morning, and after keeping an irate court waiting a full hour, Mr. Fallon braced himself with black coffee and appeared. "Mr. Fallon," said the court, "I well understand that you were occupied elsewhere, but that does not mean you could not have yielded to other counsel. There will be no further delay. Proceed with the case."

Mr. Fallon raised his hand, shook his head, clutched at his throat with his other hand, gargled, spewed and gasped.

The court was astounded. "What is counsel trying to do?"

Mr. Fallon endeavored to speak, but it was apparent his larynx was not functioning. He made several further efforts to raise his voice above a croaking whisper. He finally went to the bench and scribbled: "I cannot talk. I wore out my voice defending my client in a murder trial. I ask the court's indulgence, and pray for a postponement."

The Judge twisted and fidgeted as though he had eczema of the hips. "It seems that this trial is beset by calamities. Very reluctantly the court consents to postponement until Monday morning. But I warn counsel, that if there is further delay or any late-coming, there will be consequences more serious than a mere rebuke or removal of counsel from the case."

That evening, with Mr. Fallon again in his cups, a court-officer shadowed him on his Broadway rounds. At eleven o'clock the officer went to a telephone atop the New Amsterdam Theater roof. Whether he called Judge Weeks or not, no can say authoritatively. His conversation, however, was overheard.

"Yes, sir. Mr. Fallon is here. He's setting at a table with three dames. Potted to the eyes. His voice is plenty strong. I'll say! He got up and sung 'Mother Machree' in the loudest kind of voice. Everyone cheered and yelled: 'Hooray for Bill Fallon!' Yes, sir. His pipes is O.K. I'll put it in writing. You said it, Judge!"

On Monday, and with the alleged communist wondering what it was all about, court opened. There was no Fallon. He was very much rummed-up, and was sleeping in an uptown hotel. Not even his wife—who was used to his thoughtless behavior—knew where he was. She had been waiting for him at their apartment in the Penwick.

The court mounted the bench. McGee stood before the bar. The Judge was as glum as an unpaid landlord. Mr. McGee had brought Miss Rosenberg, Fallon's nimble secretary, to court. Fallon had instructed her that he was "desperately ill."

"Your Honor," said McGee, "Mr. Fallon is a very sick man."

"Where is he?"

"I cannot say. I have his secretary here. She may be able to tell Your Honor."

Miss Rosenberg reported: "Mr. Fallon is too ill to come to court."

The Judge leered. "Well! You will call up his home from my chambers. We'll find out *just how ill* he is."

Miss Rosenberg sensed that she had been misinformed. She called up the Fallon apartment. Mrs. Fallon answered the ring. That troubled woman knew that something was wrong. She did not know, of course, that a court representative was listening in as Miss Rosenberg asked: "Mrs. Fallon, *didn't* you call up this morning and say that Mr. Fallon was ill in bed with a cold?"

Mrs. Fallon replied: "Of course he is. Why do you ask?"

Chapter Sixteen

✳

THE BIG PUNCH AND JUDY SHOW

J ULES W. ARNDT STEIN was one of the most gracious persons that relieved the Broadway baroque. Faultless in manner and striking in appearance, he carried with him the atmosphere of an English club. He would have resided in London instead of New York, had it not been for the fogs that break down creases in one's trouser-legs. Also, the American bathroom is infinitely superior to the European lavatory.

Plumbing is America's contribution to art. When we recall that Leonardo was something of a plumber, we feel entitled to demand that the trustees of the Metropolitan place a few Stilson wrenches, some wiped joints, and half a dozen throne-chairs next door to the Morgan collection.

Herr Jules spent an hour or more in his bathroom each morn. His ablutionary rituals were perfectly amazing. That he had any skin left was the wonder of dermatologists.

An early riser, Herr Jules (called "Nicky") nevertheless was affable and polite. Seldom did he fail to distribute morning kisses and formal inquiries as to how his wife and guests had slumbered the night. He would give his breakfast order in a kindly, modulated tone, thereupon retiring to his bathroom. By the time Nicky had completed his Roger-Gallet marathon, his cutlets would be cold and his coffee a tepid drug. This condition of viands exercised a manifold influence on the temperament of the eminent tub-and-bowl addict. A pained expression crept to the lately scoured lineaments. Never did he shout, scream, or resort to epithet. He merely put aside his serviette, lifted his polished chin with disdain, rose from table, called for hat and morning stick, and went for a walk, hungry and unwilling to confide in anyone less than God.

Nicky's father was a German Jew; his mother Holland Dutch. He was born in Scandinavia and came to America when one year old. He was well educated, generous, finicky, hospitable, temperamental, self-sufficient.

Journalists somehow contracted Nicky's name, making it "Arnstein," instead of Arndt Stein. He was not a person to argue. He let it go as Arnstein. Had it been a matter concerning the bathroom, Nicky would have roared like a seal. The bathroom, as may be imagined, was something sacred to him. It was his study, his den. Let no one claim he erred in this attitude—it's the only place where a man may have privacy.

Mr. Arnstein had tried his immaculate hand at several undertakings. He was a contractor for a time. He played a severe game of cards on transatlantic liners. He was resourceful, a man of great dreams, and he wanted to be concerned with legitimate business. Two things prevented. One was his reputation, which unfortunately dogged him. The other was an unstable nature. When Nicky entered a business, no one was more enthusiastic than he. Mediocre equipment would not do. He must have the best. He ordered expensive carpets and period furniture. But when Monday was like Tuesday, and Tuesday like Wednesday, Mr. Arnstein wouldn't show up Thursday. On Friday, he dreamed anew.

In 1918, and when Nicky was thirty-eight years old, he gained the love of a most remarkable woman—Miss Fannie Brice. She was twenty-one. It is redundant to say of her that she was a true artist. First of all, she was entirely a woman. She rose from the Ghetto to a foremost place on the comedy stage, and by her genius alone. She knew her way about town, and yet was far removed from the worldly world and the fleshy flesh. Love meant, to her, loyalty and faith. When she married

Nicky, she took him at face value. She was one of the great souls that don't demand questionnaires of mates. Despite all the well-meant, but inaccurate writings concerning her, Miss Brice never contributed a dime to Arnstein's support, nor for his legal defense. Nor did she ever receive from him any moneys, bonds, jewelry, or other valuables. Let us consider that Miss Brice was a star with Ziegfeld at the time she married Arnstein; that she was getting $2,500 a week as early as 1918.

Fannie had one baby, Frances, at the time of the big robberies. Nicky was fond of the child, but was the sort that never lets an emotion grow, lest it mount beyond control. Nicky sometimes slipped into the nursery to fondle Baby Frances, but if caught in the act, would put on an indifferent air, humming or whistling to show how independent he was of paternal softness.

Although the newspapers called the $5,000,000 theft "The Big Bond Robbery," there were no bonds concerned; they were stock certificates.

Mr. Arnstein, emerging from his bathroom one crisp morning, deduced that his mutton chops had been warmed over. His epicurean soul was affronted. Miss Brice was yet abed, having worked late for Mr. Ziegfeld on the Amsterdam Roof. Nicky flicked the meat-platter with burnished nails, rose, and called for his hat, coat, and stick. After half an hour's stroll, during which he pondered the advantages of the French breakfast of rolls and coffee over the meaty dishes of Anglo-Americans, he returned to his huge apartment at No. 1 West Eighty-third street.

After he had passed the morning reading, Mr. Arnstein received a telephone call. It was from a former employee in various close-to-the-law ventures, a Mr. Nicholas Cohn. "Could you come to Washauer's for a cocktail? I got something to ask you."

Mr. Arnstein said he could not make it before five or six o'clock in the evening. Mr. Cohn said he guessed he could wait, if he had to. Mr. Arnstein resumed reading the poems of Robert Service.

Mr. Cohn, it seems, had been an active force in the so-called bond robberies. The proposition had grown too big for him to handle. Once obtained, the securities were not so easily disposed of. Cohn told his colleagues he knew a big banker, who would take the loot off their hands.

"Who's this here banker?" the boys wanted to know.

"I'm mentioning no names. He's going to act under cover."

"How do you know he will?"

"I'm going to let you see him."

"Oh, we'll meet him, then?"

"Not exactly. He's too classy a fellow. He won't want to meet no mugs. But I'll tell you what. I'll arrange to meet him and talk to him. You can see us together, and when you get a flash of him, you'll know he's the real McCoy."

Cohn and Arnstein had a cocktail at 5 o'clock. They talked for some time. The Cohn mob stayed in the background, sizing up the tall, distinguished "banker." All this was most unfortunate for Mr. Arnstein. Better for him had he remained with Mr. Service in a poetic Yukon. It became necessary to kiss Fannie Brice good-by.

"I'm in a little trouble," he said. "I've got to go away for a while. It's best you don't know where."

Fannie Brice was upset. She was not a woman of secrets. "Have you done something you shouldn't?"

"I've done a lot of things I shouldn't," said Nicky, "but this time I want you to know I'm innocent. Please believe me, and stick it out."

There was nothing craven about Miss Brice. "I'll take your word for it, Nick," she said. "Good luck."

Mr. Arnstein already was marked by the authorities. Not only did the State want him, but the Department of Justice was getting ready for a pounce. The securities, it was alleged, had been transported for disposal to the District of Columbia.

Nicky didn't go to Grand Central or to Pennsylvania Station. He took a chance that officers had not yet gathered at the One Hundred and Twenty-fifth Street Station. He went there in a cab. He was slightly disguised. It was the beginning of a two-year fight to keep out of prison.

On Washington's Birthday anniversary, 1920, the mysterious telephone call came to Fallon and McGee as they were resting the holiday in the Braddock Hotel in One Hundred and Twenty-sixth Street. As sketched heretofore, Fallon told the unidentified Cleveland caller he was busy with the Fritz case. Fallon and McGee, highly puzzled, waited for the second telephone call. It came at 6 o'clock.

Another voice, also that of a stranger, was on the wire. The second call was not from Cleveland, *but from St. Louis!*

"We want you to come by the next train, Mr. Fallon."

"I can't."

"Could you send McGee?"

"Send him where?"

"Hang up, and don't let anyone use your wire for the next hour. You'll get another call."

Fallon hung up. He told McGee of the conversation. McGee laughed uneasily. "Something big is happening. It's the Arnstein case, as sure as Brother Hooley loved baseball."

"Yes," Fallon said, "I believe it is. They're calling us from various cities to keep tracers off the trail."

At about 7 o'clock a third long-distance call came from *Chicago.* The conversation was brief, noncommittal.

"Have the party you named go to Cleveland. Go to the Blank Hotel and register. Somebody will come see you. Good-by."

"Very well," said Fallon.

McGee packed his bag and went to Cleveland. He arrived at the specified hotel to find a convention of school teachers in session, and all rooms taken. The room-clerk could do nothing. McGee roused the manager.

"It's important I register here. I've come all the way from New York to see a man."

"You'll have to wait," said the manager. "I'll let you register, though. You can use my room until there's a vacancy."

"O.K.," said McGee.

He hardly had begun to wash-up when there was a knock. McGee went to the door, opened it and saw a stout stranger. The man asked if he were talking to Mr. McGee.

"You are."

The stranger closed the door. "Will you show me your driver's license. I got to be sure."

Mr. McGee identified himself to the satisfaction of the stranger. "I recognized you by your picture, but I wanted to be doubly sure," the caller said. "We're going to take a ride."

"Will I have time to wash up, and change my linen?"

"No. Our car is waiting."

They went out to a parked car. The stout stranger looked at his watch and said to the chauffeur: "Step lively. We only got an hour."

They drove without speaking. They drew up at a railroad station west of Cleveland, barely in time to make a train. The stranger parted from McGee. "When you get to Blank town, get off the train. Walk east on Blank Street."

McGee got off as directed. As he walked up the street, he was hailed by the driver of an automobile.

"Here's your car, Mr. Sellers."

McGee went to the car. "My name is not Sellers."

"I know it ain't," the driver whispered. "Get in anyhow, Mr. McGee."

There was another ride for an hour, and to another small town. When they reached the main street, the driver said:

"Here's where you get out at, Mr. McGee. Take a walk up the first side-street to the left. You'll meet a certain party there."

"What party?" asked McGee.

The driver smiled. "I ain't the least idea. You can call him Mr. Arnold, though."

McGee began his walk. He turned into a sort of lane. He

saw a slender, self-assured man. The stranger approached him, "Delighted to meet you, Mr. McGee. My name is Arnold."

McGee shook hands. "Arnold? Or Arnstein?"

The slim stranger gestured politely. "It's Arnold for the time being. I'm sorry Mr. Fallon couldn't come. I wanted very much to talk to him."

"You may talk to me."

"Yes, I know."

McGee and Arnstein walked along the country road. Nicky seemed impressed by McGee's description of Fallon. At the close of the conversation, Arnstein said:

"Here it is in a nutshell: with my arrest, the police and federal authorities can point with pride to solving the theft of the securities. I'm confident I can prove my innocence, despite any of my—er—former entanglements. That is, I think Fallon can establish my innocence. I know, however, that bail will be prohibitive. As a matter of fact, I'm low in funds. This proposition has been expensive. I want it understood that my wife is not financing me; that she doesn't know where I am, or how I'm getting along. I shan't call on her to stand any more trouble. I want you to go back and report to Fallon. Tell him I'm willing to surrender if bail can be obtained. We must first see what bail they want."

They said good-by. As McGee started to go, Arnstein said: "Just one thing more: Will you please call my wife, and tell her I'm all right?"

McGee reported to Fallon: "Arnstein tells me the authorities are trying to mix Rothstein in this business."

"Rothstein's not in it," Fallon said. "He's blamed for everything. I wonder what the police would do for alibis, if it weren't for Mouse-Eyes?"

Miss Brice met Fallon at the Fritz trial. She believed in the innocence of "her man." She worked herself into a critical condition because of the furor.

Fallon finished the Fritz case, as well as the communist trial, and had conversations with the offices of District Attorney Swann. First Assistant District Attorney Dooling was handling the Arnstein matter.

"I won't hear to any arrangement of bail," Mr. Dooling told Fallon.

"If we agree to $50,000 will you listen?"

"I don't think so."

Arnstein had been missing for nearly six months. A nation-wide search had failed to locate him. Government agents were reinforced by local authorities of many states. Nicky made trips to Canada, and otherwise kept on the jump whenever his underworld connections warned him that officers were closing in. New York authorities began to despair of capturing Arnstein.

Fallon twitted Arnold Rothstein: "They're calling Nicky 'The Master-Mind' now. Your throne is in danger."

"I'm waiting to see how smart you are in handling *this* mess," Rothstein said.

"If you stick around me, my boy, you'll learn a lot."

Mr. Dooling finally asked Fallon point-blank: "Do you *know* where Arnstein is?"

"Naturally not," said Mr. Fallon, "but he can be *produced*."

"When?"

"Whenever we receive a guarantee of bail within reason."

"What do you want?"

"Fifty thousand dollars is to be the bail. Also a letter addressed to all authorities that Arnstein is not to be arrested; that he is on his way to surrender to you."

Assistant District Attorney Unger advised Mr. Dooling: "You can't give such a letter."

"Very well," said Fallon, "I can't risk having my client arrested on his way here. Your letter can read that Arnstein is in the custody of this office. You can send detectives with my partner, McGee, to bring him here."

"Send them *where?*"

"They'll not have to go far out of town. But they are not *actually* to arrest my client."

Detectives Mayer and Brown of the Wall Street squad and Lieutenant Geghan were assigned. They accompanied McGee to the Astor Hotel, to await a telephone call advising McGee where to go. It was agreed that after the telephone call, the detectives were not to follow McGee if he left to purchase railroad tickets. This was to prevent a "leak" as to the city where McGee was to take them.

The party had dinner and discussed various sports events. The call came. McGee slipped out to purchase the tickets. Twenty minutes before train time, he escorted the officers to Grand Central Station. All got out of their cab. They walked *through* the station. McGee called another cab. They drove across town to Pennsylvania Station. They barely made a train for Pittsburgh. Despite these precautions, the whole world learned that the authorities were "on their way to Pittsburgh to get Nicky Arnstein."

When the party arrived at the Fort Pitt Hotel, McGee checked into a double room. He left the detectives and—according to instructions—went to the William Penn Hotel and registered. There he received a telephone call from an unidentified person.

"You're not alone," the caller said.

"No," McGee replied, "we had to do it this way."

"I don't like the idea of the three dicks with you."

"They happen to be square-shooters."

"I never heard of such a thing as square dicks."

"Well, these men are square. They won't pull any funny business."

"Is the bail settled?"

"Not quite. We're working on that angle."

"Well, you go back to the other hotel. Better move the dicks to the William Penn just before twelve."

Shortly before midnight, McGee interrupted a card-game. "Come on, boys. We're going to check out."

Arnstein's friends were taking no chances on tapped wires or other surveillance tending to reveal prematurely Nicky's whereabouts.

"Could we just play out this hand?" asked one dick.

"We've got to move, boys," said McGee. "It's part of the bargain."

The party checked in at the William Penn. Half an hour later the telephone rang for McGee.

The voice (this time over a long-distance wire) said: "Jump to Rochester and register there."

"What in hell is this anyway?" one of the officers asked McGee. "It looks like the run-around."

"I don't know any more about it than you do," McGee said.

The party entrained for Rochester. The night of their arrival, McGee received a long-distance telephone instruction. "Wait in your room for forty-eight hours."

"This is murder!" said a detective. "You'd think *we* was the prisoners."

"It's over my head," said McGee.

At the expiration of forty-eight hours, another long-distance call came to McGee. "Go to Utica."

The detectives were getting sour with touring. From Utica they went to Niagara Falls. It was winter, and the falls were frozen. The travelers got alpine-stocks and shoes with ice-cleats, and took ice-climbing exercise.

"I never did think these winter sports was on the up-and-up," said one of the officers. "Everything's gettin' to be a lot of boloney."

Another mysterious command sent the party back to Utica, and then to Syracuse. The calls were being relayed from city to city to prevent tracers. One man in Chicago would call another in St. Louis. The latter would call a third party in Cincinnati; the third would pass word to a fourth, who would call McGee.

Finally, and after nearly two weeks of leap-frog, an anonymous caller said to McGee:

"We're not satisfied about the bail. It looks like a double-cross Go back to Pittsburgh. If you don't hear from us, you may as well go home."

Arrived in Pittsburgh, McGee tried to get in touch with Fallon. He couldn't locate his partner. He telephoned the Opera Café, Fortieth Street and Seventh Avenue, a bonny spot frequented by newspaper men, actors, and Broadway lawyers. The bartender at the Opera Café answered the telephone.

"I don't know where Mr. Fallon is," he said. "I hear he is busy with some murder case. A guy named Fritz or something. I ain't seen him around here for a coupla days. If he floats in I'll tell him."

"Have him call me at Pittsburgh," McGee said.

Next day, a New York newspaper carried the headline:

M'GEE IN PITTSBURGH TELEPHONES BARTENDER

The Opera Café telephone had been tapped.

The McGee caravan of dicks went to Syracuse again. McGee announced that he was "fed up." The detectives didn't have to announce that they were fed up. It was self-evident that they were. The party started for home.

Newspaper men had been besieging McGee for interviews. He had evaded reporters so far. As he stepped from the train at Albany, he heard himself being paged.

"It must be news from Bill," he said to a detective. He called to a red cap, who was shouting his name: "Here, boy! Here you are."

An Albany newspaper man stepped between the red cap and McGee. "Where's Arnstein?" asked the reporter.

"Oh, damn it!" said McGee, giving his old-time football muscles their first workout in years, as he sprinted back to the train.

Publication of the news that McGee had talked with the bartender at the Opera Café frightened Arnstein. Had it not been for that and the bail-delay—which made Nicky fear a double-cross—he would have surrendered sooner than he did.

Fallon now was playing Broadway with reckless zeal. His

health seemed unimpaired by late hours or by increased drink, but his dissipation eventually was bound to exact its price. He required frequent bracers during court-recess. Still, his recuperative powers were remarkable. After a hard night, he rallied on black coffee. He swallowed liberal quantities of olive oil, regarding it as a cure-all.

In Federal Court one morning, Fallon was submitting affidavits. A strictly prohibitionist Judge sniffed and then fixed his eyes on Fallon:

"Is it *possible* that the court smells *liquor* on counsel?"

Mr. Fallon bowed. "If Your Honor's sense of justice is as keen as your sense of smell," said he, "then my client need have no fear in this court."

This reply so amused the teetotaler Judge that he treated the Fallon client with great consideration.

It need not be presumed that Fallon's every relationship with handsome women resulted in erotic response. It so happened that he enjoyed a non-physical friendship with a friend of Miss Brice, a young woman of charm and refinement. He called this woman "Blondy." It is fair enough if we refer to her as Hannah Pearce.

Fallon at first gave Hannah his usually effective speeches on moonlight and the glories of womanhood. But somehow she understood his flair for romance, laughed good-humoredly at his Don Juan gestures, and finally captivated his imagination by refusing to succumb to flatteries. Fallon might as well have been a winsome child, in so far as Hannah was concerned. And that's the way she handled him. The Fallon type demands of its women early surrender—or none at all. It was unspoken, but understood by Fallon and Hannah, that when he called, Cupid was required to check his bow and quiver at the door.

I have finally decided to set down two examples of strange behavior that have kept my skin steaming for the last month.

On one side is the danger of alienating the reader's interest in this impulsive, vain, brilliant, reckless, gay, tragic fellow, William J. Fallon. On the other side is the need for portraying him as he was.

Example No. 1: Fallon undoubtedly was pious beneath a thick veneer of Broadway foolhardiness. Yet, on a Good Friday in 1920, and while dining with Hannah at the Knickerbocker Grill, the following incident occurred:

"I was going to order steak," Hannah said, "but I just happened to remember."

"Remember what?" Fallon asked.

"It's Good Friday."

Mr. Fallon put down his menu card and said to the waiter: "In that case, bring me a big, thick steak."

Example No. 2: It is sure that Fallon worshipped his mother, who by this time was extremely ill. Yet in some of his romantic forays, and when capitulation seemed slow or uncertain, he drew on his stock of "property" wedding rings. He would take a ring from his pocket and say: "I don't think you can doubt me now. Take this and wear it for me. . . . My mother's wedding ring!"

Fallon was completely the actor; the dramatic effect of the moment was all-important to him, dominating his cerebral centers and shutting off his functions for reflection and balanced conduct. I do not believe that, up to now, alcoholic short-circuits had enfeebled his monitors. It was this characteristic—which I choose to call the Ajax Gesture—that led Fallon to step on the toes of powerful personages, and eventually to make ruinous motions that even his native brilliance and compelling personality could not survive. In youth all things are forgiven by them that envy youth its bloom. But when autumn comes, let the play-boy beware. The wolves lope down to tear the flesh of him who dares laugh in the wilderness.

Despite the general excellence of New York's police officers, there were some that missed their calling. Of the minority that should have been bowling over steers in abattoirs were the troglodytes who brow-beat and persecuted Fannie Brice.

During Nicky Arnstein's long absence, Miss Brice continued to work in the Ziegfeld Frolic. Occasionally she received mysterious telegrams, but instead of reassuring her, such messages served to increase her worries and her doubts. She got little sleep, sometimes lying awake until 10 o'clock in the morning. She kept smiling, and when Hannah came to live with her, Fannie said:

"I'm getting tired of being so drowsy at show-time that I have to put on my hat in bed."

Whenever she went for a stroll, detectives followed Fannie. They seemed sure she knew where the missing securities had been hidden. They tapped her telephone wires and watched her mail box.

"It's lucky I had more privacy on my honeymoon," she said.

One afternoon there was a rehearsal on the Ziegfeld roof. Fannie—always a conscientious worker—felt too ill to attend. Mr. Ziegfeld excused her. She spent the time with Baby Frances, who then was seven months old. Hannah had gone on a shopping tour.

When Hannah returned to the apartment house, the elevator man said:

"There's three ginks upstairs. They look like flat-feet."

Hannah was concerned. She listened for a while at the door. She heard growling voices. When she let herself in, a thick-skulled detective shouted:

"Who are you?"

"Just a little chorus girl from the Follies," said Hannah.

"Ah," said the dick, "a wise gal, hey? Come here, you!"

Fannie Brice was hysterical. She kept moving from Baby Frances' buggy to this chair and that, clasping her hands and begging the official lunks to let her alone. When one of the intruders grabbed Hannah by the wrist and flung her to a divan, Fannie seemed fascinated by the scene. She sat and stared.

One of the detectives leaned above Fannie, plying her with third-degree questions. Her lips moved, but her voice seemed dead.

"So you won't come across, eh?" the cross-examiner said. "All right, then we'll turn this joint upside down until we find the stuff."

Hannah kept thinking of Fannie's jewelry—some $50,000 worth of diamonds that she had earned as a theatrical star. At the threat of search, Hannah wasn't so sure the men were above seizing the jewelry. She rose from the divan.

"Hey, you cutie," said a detective. "Don't you leave the room. You ain't going to use no telephone, see?"

"I wasn't thinking of a telephone," Hannah said.

"Maybe not, but you looked like you was."

"If you must know," Hannah said, "I was going to the bathroom."

"Do Follies dames go to such places? Well, go ahead, then; but trot right back, see!"

Hannah went through Fannie's bedroom on her way to the bathroom. She picked up a necklace and other valuables. She didn't know just what to do. She believed the detectives might search her and Fannie. She had a sudden idea. She came from the bathroom and pretended to be pacifying Baby Frances. While fondling the child, Hannah tucked the jewels in a diaper and shoved the garment beneath the buggy-seat. The detectives began a rough search of the apartment. They never thought of mussing up the baby carriage, although Hannah said: "Why don't you frisk the baby?"

Fannie got a grip on herself. She asked Hannah to call up Fallon.

"Oh, no you don't!" said one of the men.

"Very well, then," Fannie said. "I'll ask you to take me to the District Attorney's office. I have *some* rights."

The detectives went into a football huddle. When they came out of it, their spokesman said: "Awright. Come ahead to the D.A.'s. You got a car?"

"Yes," said Fannie. The five persons got into Miss Brice's Baker Electric. During the drive downtown, Fannie simulated a gaiety she did not feel. She kidded the detectives. They were not what might be termed intellectual giants. They resented her flippancies.

Arrived at the District Attorney's office, Fannie received some courtesy. "Won't you sit down, Miss Brice?"

"No, thanks," she said, "I always stand up when I have an audience."

"Would you rather stand while talking to these gentlemen?"

"I'd rather sing a song."

The authorities questioned her for some time. It was plain that she knew nothing about any robbery or any fugitive from justice. The District Attorney permitted her to go home. The shadowing was continued.

Fannie was heartbroken about the front-page news that daily screamed at her. She lost weight. She finally was down from 136 to 80 pounds. She had a temperature of 103 degrees, but never missed a performance. Instead of quitting, she introduced the famous song: "My Man." After the nights of forced laughter and comedy, she almost staggered home to cry as Hannah sat beside her bed. A physician advised her to drink wine, but she was a teetotaler. She refused to eat, subsisting on a pint of milk a day. The funny thing about life is that most of the medals are given to men.

Fallon often called at the Brice apartment. He admired Fannie tremendously—and, of course, he liked to visit with Hannah.

"Tell me," Fannie said, "and don't think it will go out of this room: *Where* is Nicky?"

"As God is my judge," Fallon said, "I don't know. Every communication that comes to me is from anonymous sources and by a roundabout route. I honestly don't know, Fannie."

"Don't you think he should come in, regardless of anything?"

"It's the question of bail," Fallon said. "I've racked my brains. They'll want $100,000. It's a lot of money. If I hadn't been so careless, I could have mustered it myself. But you know me."

"Yes, I know. You spend it as fast as you make it."

Fallon corrected her. "Faster."

"I thought I had a lot of multi-millionaire friends," she said. "Where are they now?"

Fallon shrugged. "The fair-weather friends are where they always are, and where they always will be—out where the sun is shining, and the weather calm."

He was silent for a while. Then he said: "Fannie, there's one place, and only one place, where we could raise the bail."

"Where?"

"A.R."

"Rothstein!" She was silent for a time. Then she said: "My instincts are against it, Bill."

"Your instincts are right, and they are the same as mine. The authorities think Rothstein had a finger in the robbery, and is acting as a fence for the securities."

"*Did* Rothstein have anything to do with it?"

"I'm sure he didn't, but the minute he goes Nicky's bail, it will seem proof positive of the connection."

"What makes you so sure Rothstein would go bail?"

"Simply because you are a celebrity. He's a champion-chaser. He loves to be a 'big shot'."

"For God's sake, do something before we all go crazy!"

One evening on the Amsterdam Roof, and after Fannie had sung "My Man," she sat at a table with Fallon. Arnold Rothstein was in the audience. He sent a note to the Fallon table: "Will you introduce me?"

Fallon looked at Rothstein and nodded. Rothstein came over and sat for a while, gazing at Fannie. He suddenly said in a pleasant, matter-of-fact way:

"I'd be glad to take care of that matter for you, Miss Brice."

Fallon interrupted: "You needn't put yourself out, A.R. It's all taken care of."

Rothstein was miffed. He said to Fallon: "I happen to know it isn't. What do you think of that?"

"I could be arrested for what I think," said Fallon.

"That might be possible, too," Rothstein said.

"But it isn't probable," said Fallon.

"You'd better think it over," Rothstein said. "I'll expect a decision in twenty-four hours." He cleared his throat and added casually: "By the way, Bill, I'd make it sooner than the twenty-four hours, if I were you."

Fallon sniffed. "Oh, you would, eh?"

"Yes, I would. I have it straight that your man has been spotted, and may be brought in any time."

Fannie was frightened. "I think we should accept, Bill."

Fallon gestured. "All right. What'll it be?"

Rothstein settled himself comfortably. "I'll put up $100,000 in Liberty Bonds."

"But you'll cut the coupons yourself, I suppose," Fallon said.

Rothstein seemed unperturbed. "Yes," he said, "inasmuch as the bonds belong to me, I suppose I'll tend to little things like the coupons."

Fallon notified the mysterious telephone caller next day that bail had been arranged to the full satisfaction of the authorities. Within twenty-four hours Nicky Arnstein was with Fallon in Mamaroneck. Fallon and his client stayed the night of May 15 at a little hotel in Mamaroneck. The proprietor had known Fallon since the latter's boyhood. He had a keen interest in the career of The Great Mouthpiece. The owner of the hotel, of course, had no inkling as to the identity of Nicky. He outdid himself to see that Willie Fallon and his friend were given privacy and metropolitan attention.

"My friend is very sick," Fallon said. "The slightest noise or shock might be fatal. We leave tomorrow morning for New York, for an operation on his stomach."

"Nobody will bother you, Willie," said the proprietor.

At breakfast next morning, the proprietor himself served Fallon and "Mr. Arnold" in their room.

"Nobody would ever think that you was going to be operated on today," said the proprietor.

Mr. Arnold smiled. "After today I'll not be able to eat ham and eggs, or any greasy food. I'm having a last fling."

The proprietor nodded. "I hear it makes a fellow sick to eat before he is operated on. Something about the ether."

Mr. Arnold smiled again. "You won't tell on me, will you?"

"I sure wouldn't. A friend of Willie Fallon's is a friend of mine."

Mr. Fallon was hunting in his grip for a quart. "Will you have a shot, Mr. Arnold?"

Mr. Arnold inclined his head. "I'd be glad to join you, Mr. Fallon. But of course I'll have to ask our good friend here to keep this a secret, also. My surgeons must never know."

The proprietor was effusive. "Now nobody's goin' to hear a thing from me. I'm close-mouthed, like nobody's business. I was just telling my wife yesterday. We was talking about a certain party here in Mamaroneck. You know, Amy, I says, you know, gossip don't never get a fellow a thing. And I ain't kidding when I say that I know it's a fact that——"

Mr. Fallon interrupted: "Do you suppose there is any ice downstairs?"

"Surest thing, Willie. For you, anything! Why, I've knowed Willie since he was knee-high to a duck. If you don't believe it, Mr. Arnold, ask Willie. Ask his old man. How long is it, Willie, since I've knowed Joe? Eighteen years? Let's see. I was married in '81. The Fosters rented us our first place in '83. Maybe it was '84. No, it was '83, because that's the year——"

Mr. Arnold was tapping the tip-top table. "Suppose we drink it without ice, Bill?"

The proprietor shifted from one foot to another. "I'll go get it right away. I guess they ain't no better lawyer than Willie in the country, Mr. Arnold. I ain't sayin' that just because Willie's standin' right there with a glass in his hand. I'd say the same thing if I never seen him again, or even if he was stuck up or had the swell-head, which he never could have. I guess you got a big case now with that Goldstein fellow. Have they caught him yet, Willie?"

Mr. Fallon couldn't wait any longer. He took his drink at bottle temperature. The proprietor was abashed. "Aw, now, Willie! I'll go get your ice."

Mr. Arnold, too, was weary. "Needn't mind. I want my drink *before* the operation. Not after it."

"Gee, but I'm sorry, Mr. Arnold. Well, Willie, I'll get some ice anyhow. I'm curious to know, though, what kind of a critter this fellow Silverstein is. What's he like, Willie? Do you happen to know him, Mr. Arnold?"

"I've met him socially once or twice," said Mr. Arnold. "You mean Mr. Finklestein, though, don't you?"

"That may be it," said the proprietor. "I'm so lousy on names."

"You might bring some ice at that," Fallon said. "I'm going to have another eye-opener."

"I seen the picture of this Something-Stein in the papers," said the proprietor. "There's a man, I said to my wife, who might of amounted to something big, if he had of shot square."

Mr. Arnold sighed. "I'm told he is no good at all."

The proprietor screwed up his mouth. "Oh, I think there is some good in everybody, Mr. Arnold. I know that this Steiner is a crook, but maybe he just got started wrong."

Mr. Arnold was thinking of the ice. "At least," he said with emphasis, "he got *started*."

Mr. Fallon had taken another neat one from his bottle. "We'd like to talk over some things in private. You won't mind?"

The proprietor went to the door. "I hope the doctors don't find nothing much wrong, Mr. Arnold. Should I bring the ice?"

"Never mind the ice," said Fallon. "It's bad for the stomach.

Arnold ought to have known better than ask for it; the fix *he* is in."

The proprietor came back. "But he *didn't* ask for it. You did. It was you, Willie, who asked for the ice. Wasn't it, Mr. Arnold?"

"No," said Mr. Arnold, "I asked for it. It was a mistake. I apologize."

"I was sure it was Willie that asked. I was standing over here by the dresser. No, I was a little to the right. More toward the window. Like this. You was setting there by the tip-top table, Mr. Arnold. I remember you was tapping like on a piano. Willie was at his grip, looking for his bottle. Then I said: 'Nobody would think you was going to be operated on today.' Then you said: 'This is my last ham and eggs.'"

"And I meant just what I said," Mr. Arnold put in.

"Of course you meant it," said the proprietor. "Did I even act or hint like you didn't mean it, Mr. Arnold?"

Mr. Arnold had a mournful look. "Maybe you didn't doubt me about the operation, but you surely acted funny about the Epstein matter?"

"How do you mean?"

"Well, when I said that Bernstein was a crook, you stuck up for him."

The proprietor was dismayed. "You got me plumb wrong, Mr. Jerold. Why, I don't give a damn if they hang this Einstein! In fact they ought to. He's the lowest down sort of a heel! Sure you don't want any ice, Willie?"

"All we want is privacy."

After the proprietor had gone, Fallon remembered he had an appointment with a reporter for The New York *World*. Donald Henderson Clarke had arranged an exclusive story of the surrender of Nicky. He had turned over the assignment to George Boothby, another excellent reporter, who was to meet and ride into town with Miss Brice, Fallon, and Arnstein. It was to be a noteworthy newspaper beat. Herbert Bayard Swope, the dynamic editor of The *World*, was so excited over the prospective scoop that he put a bet on the wrong horse. The whole town was on its ear with excitement.

"And here we are," said Fallon, "in my home town, and they won't even give us ice."

There was a knock. Fallon opened the door cautiously. The proprietor was standing at the threshold. He looked so worried that Fallon was afraid the police were in the offing.

"Willie," said the proprietor, "something terrible has happened!"

"What is it?"

"We ain't got no ice! And I told the missus last night to be sure and——"

Mr. Fallon closed the door.

The entry of Nicky Arnstein to the City of New York was somewhat dramatic. As they swung into Fifth Avenue, with Mr. Fallon at the wheel of Mr. Arnstein's blue Cadillac landaulet, the metropolitan police were having their annual parade.

Much has been written concerning this entry. It has been claimed that Fallon deliberately chose this pageant and this hour for riding past the long line of marchers—a gesture of contempt for the men, anyone of whom would have given a year's pay to have arrested Nicky.

This makes a tremendously effective anecdote, but the facts do not substantiate the legend. Fallon did not know that the parade was on until he bumped into it, quite by accident. Once in the Avenue, he refused to turn aside. Arnstein was fearful of an arrest.

"Don't worry," Fallon said. "Your bond is up, anyway."

At Criminal Courts Building, Fallon and Fannie Brice got out of the car and waited, while Nicky went alone to surrender. No one molested the tall, distinguished man with the little black moustache. It is written that he met a policeman in the corridor; that Nicky was forced to identify himself, and begged to be arrested. This, too, is an apocryphal version. Assistant District

Attorney Dooling had been notified and was waiting. The reception of Arnstein was quiet, business-like, and brief.

It is true, as related by Donald Henderson Clarke, that while Nicky was inside, and Fallon was strolling with Fannie, that the Arnstein automobile was *stolen*. It is also true that Fallon called Arnold Rothstein, and that Rothstein notified the gangster, Monk Eastman, to return the car at once. The car was back, with *apologies*, inside the hour.

Meanwhile Mr. McGee was in Philadelphia on another wild-goose chase. When he read newspaper accounts of the Arnstein surrender, he felt in the mood that was his years ago, and on the day he administered a lacing to Fallon and Finch in the Fordham pool room.

The metropolitan press soon credited Arnold Rothstein with having had much to do with the so-called bond robberies. Mr. Sol Meyers was holding examinations before United States Commissioner Gilchrist in Federal Court concerning the gigantic theft. Mr. Meyers represented the National Surety Company, a concern that had insured the stolen stock certificates.

When Arnstein returned to the city, he was examined before the United States Commissioner under the Bankruptcy Law. He answered a few questions. It began to look as though he were going to sink deeper in the mire, merely by replying to inquiries concerning his former habits and connections. It was here that Mr. Fallon invoked a then little-used device to shield clients. It since has become so prevalent that the notebooks of court-stenographers are bristling with the familiar reply by a witness:

"I refuse to answer, on the ground that to do so might tend to incriminate or degrade me."

This is known as objecting on "constitutional grounds." Mr. Arnstein gave this answer. The court, however, maintained that Arnstein must answer all questions. The Judge committed him to Ludlow Street Jail for contempt. Fallon obtained a writ of *habeas corpus* to test out the commitment. He presented this writ to each Federal Judge then sitting in the Southern District. Each and every Judge refused to sign the writ.

"There's only one course left," Fallon said to McGee. "We must enter an order delaying the issuance of the writ."

This was done, and an appeal was taken from that order directly to the United States Supreme Court. Mr. Fallon then went to Washington and to added fame, and to a love-affair that became the wonder of Broadway.

Chapter Seventeen

✳

EROS DANCES TO TRUMPET AND DRUM

FALLON was ill with neuritis an entire week before his departure for Washington. His wife found it difficult to keep him abed at their Belleclaire Hotel apartment. Unused to ill-health, Fallon construed his bed-ridden outlook as a change of moral intent. He smothered his pain with grandiose phrases of reform.

It was his habit to return home when surfeited with Broadway pleasures, there to re-discover that his wife was patient, forgiving, self-sacrificing. On the occasion of his present illness, he was more contrite than usual; more appreciative of his wife's almost maternal love. Agnes Fallon listened forbearingly to his indictment of Broadway's jazz-tempo, and to his fluent resolutions.

He said he was fed up with foolishness; that at last he had come to his senses. He sang the traditional anthem of hamstrung, giddy husbands: There's no place like home. All else was empty and a sham. He wanted to rise from bed, scurry to Washington on the Arnstein writ; sway the United States Supreme Court with arguments . . . then return home, a saner, more dependable husband and father. He owed it to Agnes and the children to give them something of himself. Of what was a man thinking, to let business, or anything else, interfere with wholesome, domestic love?

"We'll quit New York, and get a little place in the country; away from the noise and the struggle. We'll go to the Adirondacks, to Canada, the South Seas . . . anywhere but this lunatic's playground, where the dancers perform before distorted mirrors."

Mrs. Fallon placed a hot-water bottle at his affected left arm and smoothed his frown. The sick man began a gusty arraignment of himself. He was unworthy of faith and of continued forgiveness. From this tirade, he switched to an execration of civilization's pitfalls. Before long he was excusing his faults, extenuating the circumstances of his domestic misdemeanors.

"An unwholesome environment is bound to react on a man —any man. I don't care who. The pace is killing. A man of consequence must drain all his resources, mental and moral, to meet the requirements of modern criminal law. I hate it! I detest the whole business. The Broadway parties and the make-believe of it all! They're false, the people and their play. Everything is false. Even I am false. You are not. Just myself and the people I have allowed to come into my life. I am unreal, and the others are charlatans. Everyone is artificial except you and the children."

Mr. Fallon characterized the world as a trap, and Life a pelt-snatcher. "We are skinned at our traps," he said, "even before our hearts quit beating. It's all wrong. What was God thinking of when he breathed into the first man? We'll go away. A small place in the mountains. The air will be clean and laden with spruce-smells. We'll begin over. All over again."

Mr. Fallon was unable to sustain any mood overlong. He finally wearied of embalming his past with explanations and burying it with hymns of reform. He fell into mystic silence, staring at the wall, as though marveling at the glibness of his moral guarantees. He frowned, as if his brain were struggling to catch what his lips had been saying. He cocked his head on his pillow. Were far-away voices echoing in his sub-conscious?

Then, after all the bellowings of guilt, of mitigating circumstance and of the world's sink-holes, he half sat up in bed, his rather short nose wrinkling, as though smelling a mischievous truth:

"Neuritis and Conscience are first cousins."

Mr. McGee called and urged the sick man to get all the rest possible before going to Washington. Mr. Fallon was in great pain, but the thunder of his moral sophistries seemed to have released a weight from his spirit.

"I've had enough of this bed," he announced. "We're leaving on the night train."

Fallon sued out a writ of *habeas corpus* in the United States Supreme Court, bringing Arnstein from Ludlow Street Jail to the District's jurisdiction. Nicky, in custody of United States marshals, accompanied Fallon to Washington. They retained a suite at the Willard.

The Supreme Court of the United States listened to Fallon's arguments as attentively as had any of his juries. The highest tribunal of the land recognized in Fallon a man of logic as well as eloquence. Few counselors had behaved so confidently in maiden appearances before the court of last resort. When the black-robed arbiters learned that Fallon was ill on his feet, one of their number extended him an unusual courtesy, saying:

"Mr. Fallon, you may take as much time as you think necessary to present your argument."

Nicky Arnstein held gay parties at his suite. He produced teatables pyramided with enviable wines. Women came in the evenings and remained, until dawn unveiled with impartial light the city's few good sculptures and its many bad ones. They downed fabulous quantities of wine and pampered the vanity of the men. Fallon forgot his neuritis in orgiastic rites. The Washington dryads babied him, surfeited him with amorous gifts. His recent babble of reform soon was forgot. He plunged headlong into the Dionysian festival, and his extreme dissipations may be said to have begun at this period.

Every airplane and every man has a "ceiling," says my learned friend, L.H., the bio-psychologist. Beneath that limit, the man or the plane functions rationally and without undue fluctuation. Above it, there is uncertainty, erratic behavior, inability to perform with precision. Fallon now was perilously close to his "ceiling."

He had recurrences of remorse and a desire to escape. These periods brought on fresh attacks of the bottle. He stuck to his glass like a clingfish to its stone. His eye-lids grew puffy and tired. His skin felt thick and tender. His liver began to backfire. He dosed himself with bicarbonate of soda and olive oil. A man of lesser vitality and spirit would have cracked with the force of a bursting fly-wheel.

Suddenly rebelling against the gaiety at the Arnstein apartment, Fallon one night announced he was going to the theater. Arnstein allowed the party to continue of its own momentum, and strolled out with Fallon. They dropped into the foyer of Keith's vaudeville house. They talked little as they looked at the pictures and the billing of the performers. Mr. Fallon stood before an easel, on which was a frame holding several photographs of a young woman.

"That's funny," he said. "I saw this girl a long time ago in 'Listen Lester.' I meant to make her acquaintance, but somehow I never did."

Mr. Arnstein adjusted his nose-glasses, peered over Fallon's shoulder and said: "Gertrude Vanderbilt, eh? I met her through Fannie."

"Let's catch her act and go backstage after the show."

"Why not invite her to the apartment?"

"Do you know her that well?"

"I think she'd come. I'll tell her you want to meet her."

"Anything you say. What do you know about her?"

"No more than I've been told. She could have her pick of several backers, but she seems rather serious about a career. She's been on the stage since girlhood. She was a child-protegée of George M. Cohan in one of his musical shows."

"Not married, is she?"

"She was fifteen when she married a comedian, old enough to be her father. It didn't take. She's quite some girl. Smart, as well as good-looking."

They bought tickets and went inside. Fallon didn't understand precisely why he was impatient, but he found the opening numbers of the program uninteresting. He was glad when the proscenium sign changed, and the name, "Gertrude Vanderbilt," appeared. He experienced a sudden anxiety, an absurd fear that the woman either would fail to materialize, or, coming on, would not make an impression. When she danced nimbly from the long, shimmering stage-hangings, Fallon didn't applaud. He felt self-conscious, although he couldn't find explanation for his weird mood. The dancing girl looked small against the draperies. There was a virility in her swiftly moving legs, and her eyes were alert.

The drums were rolling and trumpets crackling. The dance that followed the final song was imbued by the spirit of war. Fallon watched the supple, slender woman swirling while the music seemed to be holding her free of the stage-floor, as a column of water from a fountain upholds a ball. Strange he had not sought her out the night he saw "Listen Lester." Random measures of "Ships That Pass in the Night" sailed through his brain. Well, he would see her tonight. Would she surely come to the apartment? Would he hold her hand and tell her fine things? He felt vaguely anxious and uncertain.

The roll of the drums died away and the trumpeters rested the brass bells of their horns against their knees. "Are we going backstage?"

"I'll send a note by an usher," Nicky said.

He wrote on a card: "Please come over to the Willard tonight. William J. Fallon will be there.

(Signed) "Nicky Arnstein."

Miss Vanderbilt's maid placed the card on the dressing-room table, and against a vase of roses near the mirror. The young woman came from her bows with a desire to go at once to her hotel, take a nap, read, and then dine in her room and rest until the night-show. She glanced at the card as her maid unhooked her costume. She threw the note aside. She picked it up again while removing her makeup. She did not readily place the name, William J. Fallon. Then she recalled she had worked one time as a chorus girl in a production entitled "Fifty-Fifty." A Mr. Fallon had had something to do with backing that enterprise. She believed this was the Fallon referred to in Arnstein's note. She remembered Arnstein principally as the husband of Fannie Brice.

After her act that night, Miss Vanderbilt felt too tired to go out. She was a woman of excellent habits. She didn't drink, and she preferred normal sleep to the artificial antics of male flesh-pinchers. She telephoned Arnstein's suite, making excuses.

Nicky was effusive. "Oh, come on over, Gertie. We've planned on you. Fallon is sulking in a corner."

"A lot that means to me," she said. "I only know Fallon slightly. I'm tired."

"I can't begin to tell you how disappointed I am. Wouldn't you drop in for just a few minutes?"

"Well, I'll come over, but I'm not going to dress."

"Of course not. Come as you are."

Still thinking that it was Fallon, the theatrical man, Miss Vanderbilt put on a simple sweater and skirt. She threw a fur coat over her plain outfit and strolled from the Hotel Washington to the Willard.

When Nicky introduced her to Fallon, she was plainly surprised. Her surprised expression mystified Fallon as he shook hands. His neuritis was bothering him somewhat, but he managed to offset the pain by concentrating on champagne, romantic fluencies, and the medium-blonde guest. He struck his usual theatrical attitudes, kept on his feet almost the whole evening, dancing with Miss Vanderbilt, then leaning over her as she sat (slightly bored by it all), and spouting quotations from durable lyricists. All this attention was lost on the tired ingenue. She wished she had not come.

Fallon believed he was progressing splendidly. He judged Miss Vanderbilt's monosyllabic replies as indicative of interest in him.

She rocked him to his heels when she said, at the close of one of his romantic speeches: "Before I go home, I'd like to tell you that you're the most conceited man I've met in a long time."

He looked as bewildered as a boy that has been kicked in the rear while peeking through the key-hole of Aunt Sadie's bathroom.

"That's very unkind," he said finally.

She kept looking at him steadily. "No, I don't think so."

"What makes you say I'm conceited?"

"Don't you know that you are?"

He shrugged. The movement of his shoulders didn't comfort his neuritis. "I'm sorry you don't like me. Really I am."

"I didn't say I don't like you."

"Then you do like me, even if I am conceited?"

"I didn't say I liked you, either. I think you've been terribly spoiled."

Nicky Arnstein had caught the latter part of the conversation. He was secretly delighted when he heard Miss Vanderbilt pan the usually irresistible Fallon. He interrupted by offering a fresh supply of wine to the attorney—Miss Vanderbilt remaining unwined in the group of bibbers.

"Will you get my wrap?" she asked Arnstein.

Fallon was pouting. When Nicky left, he asked: "You aren't going to run away in bad humor are you?"

"I'm not in a bad humor," she said. "And I'm not running away."

He took her hand and pressed it. "We were just getting acquainted. Don't go yet."

"I have to be rested to work," she said. "You see, I'm not a lawyer."

He looked deflated. "I don't believe you like me, Gertrude."

"What difference would it make, one way or another?"

Nicky was approaching with her coat. She moved as though to cut short further conversation. Fallon came closer. He was trembling. He gave Nicky such a pleading look that the former delayed delivery of the Vanderbilt coat, pausing to speak to one of the guests while Fallon belabored the young woman with emotional phrases.

"I've been thinking of you ever since I saw you a long time ago in 'Listen Lester.' This afternoon I could have kicked myself for not having sought you out sooner."

"It's getting late," she said, "I'll have to say good-night."

"Don't say it in such a cold, formal way."

Her tone was ironical. "What do you think I should do? Kiss you?"

He seized her hand again. "Don't make a joke of it."

"Make a joke of what?"

"Don't you believe it possible for a man to fall terribly in love, and without warning?"

"I've heard of it, but right now I'm more interested in a good night's sleep. Let's not bore each other."

"Good God!" he said. "What kind of woman are you?"

"That's another stock phrase, isn't it? Why don't men think up something new to say? Always the same questions, the same gestures, the same sighs. . . . I don't like to hurt anyone's feelings, Mr. Fallon, but really. . . . Oh well, let's say good-night and forget it."

He seemed dejected, then half-angered. "Won't you give me a chance? I must see you again. Tomorrow. Let me call tomorrow."

"I'm very busy. Give me a ring sometime in New York."

"Please let me see you tomorrow."

"No. I can't be annoyed."

"Please don't put it that way. You can't know how important it is that I see you again."

"Important to whom?"

"To me."

"Oh! Well, it's important to me to be left alone."

"Will you do me a favor?"

She caught Arnstein's eye and motioned him to bring her wrap. "I think you've had too much to drink tonight."

He was still close to her, his lips at her hair. He almost

groaned. "Gertrude. Come to court tomorrow. The Supreme Court of the District. Come there and hear my arguments. Won't you come? That's the favor I ask."

"I'm not interested in courts."

"Please come. You will see me as I really am. Honestly, I'm not so conceited. You'll see." He paused, then reversed himself. "Yes, you're right. I am conceited. I'm a fool. But I want you to come to court. It will help me. I've been ill. You make me forget illness, pain, the world . . . everything. . . . "

"Here, now. That's enough of that. When you sober up, call me at my hotel. Good-night. . . ."

"Please believe me, Gertrude. I never before met any woman that stirred me as you have stirred me. When I saw you so long ago, I felt strangely——"

"That's why you waited two years——"

"Don't torture me, Gertrude——"

"You'll feel better in the morning."

"I'll never feel better until we are friends."

"If I were you, I'd go right to bed, Mr. Fallon."

"If you were I, you'd jump into the Potomac River."

She half-smiled. "Well, that mightn't be a bad idea, either."

Nicky was at her side, holding her coat. "Sorry you're hurrying off. What's wrong with Bill?"

Fallon mumbled. "Nothing's wrong with me."

Nicky lifted his brow. "Maybe not, but you have the look of a boy that has just lied to his mother."

"He's been working hard over his court-case," said Miss Vanderbilt. She extended her hand to Nicky. "See you in New York sometime." Then she gave a hand to Fallon. "You'd better get some sleep."

A sudden petulance gripped Fallon. "When I need advice, I'll ask for it."

This did not anger the woman. She looked at him sweetly. "You're feeling better already. Keep up the good work."

"I'm sorry," he said.

"Don't spoil everything by apologies," she said.

After Gertrude had gone, Arnstein went to a chair, where Fallon was slumped. "What the hell happened? Didn't you hit it off with Gertrude?"

"Oh, shut up," said Fallon.

Arnstein looked at his attorney with mild amusement. "Well, well! The handsome barrister is in love again."

"Open some Scotch."

"I wouldn't mix wine with Scotch, Bill."

"Well, I would."

"You've got to be in court in the morning."

Fallon was enraged. "Everybody is trying to tell me my business tonight."

Mr. Arnstein crooked his finger and his servant came. "Will you bring a bottle of Scotch and a tall glass with cracked ice for Mr. Fallon?"

"I don't want a tall glass, and I don't want any ice."

"Yes," said Mr. Arnstein, "Cupid has pierced little Willie's rear with an arrow. Are you sure it's an arrow? Maybe it's only a splinter."

"Let me alone," said Fallon. The servant came with the Scotch. Fallon sulked in a corner. Several women, brazen with wine, sought to enliven his mood. He brushed them aside as though they were June bugs. He was in love. The glory of the court-room now seemed an empty thing. He felt dizzy and terribly alone. He dozed. Mr. Arnstein's man put Fallon to bed. He dreamed of bats and a sky that had a huge, livid crevice, zigzagging from moon to earth. He awakened in the dim light, wondering where he was. Then he remembered vaguely the woman and the night of frustration. He reached for the telephone, got the Hotel Washington on the wire. Another defeat. Miss Vanderbilt had left word she was not to be disturbed. A smart woman. She knew the telephonic habits of drunken men and of their disregard for awkward hours.

Miss Vanderbilt never knew exactly why she rose early and

told her chauffeur to drive her to the District's Supreme Court. Yet she found herself there, and she saw the look of amazing gratitude on the handsome face of the impulsive Fallon. When he went into action, Miss Vanderbilt found it hard to believe it was the same man she had seen in the first hours of the morning. His court-room behavior stirred her deeply, undeniably. She knew little of law or of its requirements, but she felt intuitively that here was a true champion. He was confident, alert, daring.

Fallon watched her from the tail of his eye. He put added pressure in every boiler. There was no trace of post-alcoholic evidence in his clear, ringing voice, nor in his graceful movements. Here was an artist in his own right; an actor, too; intelligent in interpretation, sure of his lines. Miss Vanderbilt left her card with a court-attendant. On it was written the word: "Delighted."

It was late night. The show was over. Bags were packed. The vaudeville troupers were at the railroad station, some of them nodding on the benches, others wandering between newsstand, water-taps and wash-rooms—the aimless pacings of animals in captivity. Fallon and Gertrude strolled outside the terminal building, watching the lights of the city flick out in twinkling series.

"I'm glad I'm going away," she said.

"Why do you say that?"

"Don't ask me why. I'm just glad, that's all."

He was silent a long time, then: "I want to go with you. I'll buy a ticket, and send a wire to McGee."

"Don't be completely insane."

"I am insane. Insane over you. Why not? Who am I to fight off love? Why should I fight it off?"

"I wish you wouldn't put your arm about me. Don't you understand?"

"Understand what? For God's sake! All I understand is that

I love you, madly, desperately. All else is an ash-heap beside a dirty road. I'm going with you."

"No, you're not. You'd better call a cab and go to your hotel. Forget me. Go back to your parties."

He began to storm and rant. "Parties! How tawdry they all are! A cage of monkeys picking fleas off each other. A chattering bunch of ring-tails. Here and there a muddled baboon, grimacing into a looking-glass, mistaking the shiny surface for the depths of eternity, and calling the image of self Beauty and Importance. Life! Yesterday an empty dream. Today. . . . Oh, Gertrude, you have made Today possible. Yet you would make it impossible. Don't go away. Don't go. I'll be so empty. Don't go! Or, let me go with you."

"Please call a cab. Please go. Now."

"Why do you keep saying that?"

"I'm afraid."

"Afraid of what? Of me?"

She hesitated. "I wish you'd go."

"Why are you afraid? Tell me."

"I'm afraid of us. It can't be. It mustn't."

He suddenly placed his arms about her and kissed her.

When he accompanied her to the train, Fallon seemed buoyant, weirdly happy. Gertrude was bewildered and sad. She felt that she had lost a battle. She had little to say. He tried to exact promises from her; letters, long-distance telephone calls, a return to Washington as soon as the Arnstein trial materialized and her booking was done.

She half pushed him from her compartment. She drew the blinds and wept as her maid undressed her. Fallon stood on the platform, vainly trying to get her to lift the blind. Then he returned into the train and pounded at her door. She finally opened it and kissed him good-night.

The conductor began halloing, the bell tapped softly. Fallon swung from the steps as the engine began straining like a great, windy ox in a yoke.

That night Arnstein said: "Little Willie knows where the jam closet is."

Fallon and Arnstein were present when the Supreme Court of the United States handed down its decisions. The proceedings were solemn but dramatic. The writer of each judicial pronouncement stood up to read a synopsis of his work. Mr. Justice McReynolds, black-robed and grave, read the findings on the Arnstein *habeas corpus* appeal. Arnstein thought it curious to hear himself referred to as the "relator now confined in Ludlow Jail," inasmuch as he was that moment within the sound of the jurist's voice.

The decision ordered the United States District Court of the Southern District to issue the writ of *habeas corpus*.

Once again the Arnstein case came before the Supreme Court, this time on the contempt-of-court angle—wherein Arnstein had refused to answer questions, claiming constitutional privilege. The second decision also favored Fallon's client, and was a far-reaching one. The highest court held that a man has the right to assert his constitutional position at any stage; that although Arnstein had answered a few questions before having recourse to his constitutional claim, the fact was not material. The witness, according to the decision, was the best judge of whether or not an answer might tend to incriminate or degrade him.

The Fallon forces returned to New York to map out a campaign. Two major courses were open. Fallon could defend Arnstein in New York courts, but the risks were enormous. There was an official animosity towards Arnstein, as well as an overwhelming urge by district attorneys to bring Fallon low. The press crooned for justice like the droning of a bag-pipe. Furthermore, under the New York law, a man could be convicted of a felony on the uncorroborated testimony of an accomplice. Such testimony was assured when a man named Glick turned State's witness.

The other course, and the one selected by Fallon, was to defend his man in the Supreme Court of the District of Columbia. Arnstein and his aides, it was alleged, had disposed of the stolen securities in Washington and in Boston. A Washington court could not convict a person of a felony on uncorroborated evidence. Furthermore, the penalty in the District of Columbia was two years in prison, as against a possible twenty-five years in New York.

Arnstein now had three bails; one for $50,000 in New York's Court of General Sessions; one for $10,000 in the Bankruptcy Division of the United States Court, Southern District, and $5,000 in the Supreme Court of the District of Columbia.

During Gertrude Vanderbilt's absence on her vaudeville tour, Fallon longed for her madly. He called often on the long-distance telephone, and only her entreaties and the importance of the Arnstein case kept him from dropping his work and going to her. He composed few letters, having a definite but unexplained antipathy toward writing to women. Such letters as he did send were curiously lacking in the burning phrases that came to his tongue when he spoke his love. He was a master of the oral medium, in love as well as in court. But when the Meistersinger tried to translate his notes to written words, the rhythms were blurred, and the harmonies a barnyard serenade.

Still, he could and did write: "I love you," and many poets have failed to top that signal of distress.

Gertrude remembered him with a variety of emotions. She had balked at his first postures and attempted flatteries. But always she kept thinking of the nameless thrill of that morning in court; of the later walks and conversations. Once stripped of his cavalier's mask, he had shown the face and heart of impulsive youth. She had found him unusually charming, quite aside from his physical attractiveness. He teemed with charity and tolerance.

There was in him neither suspicion nor bigotry. He thought every woman good. For those that were bad in the world's eyes, he had excuses. He had caught fast to her heart in that one good-by kiss at the railroad station. He had revealed his physical self, but with a decency, an honesty of approach, that appealed to her. She saw in Fallon a man who was clean-limbed and competent. And she knew then, as she knows today, that Death could ride away with him, but Age would forever pass him by.

In answer to Fallon's earnest appeals, Gertrude consented to be in Washington when the Arnstein trial came before a jury in the Supreme Court of the District of Columbia.

Mr. Justice Gould presided at the first Arnstein trial. Fallon pronounced him the greatest judge ever to sit in any of his cases. He was learned in the law, a renowned professor at Georgetown University, a man of wit, humanity, and courage.

"Two Presidents offered Judge Gould a place on the United States Supreme Court bench," Fallon once said. "He declined that great honor, partly because he was opposed to the Prohibition Law, and partly because he felt himself better fitted for other tasks. I loved him as I did my own father. There was no greater legal brain in America."

The trial, coming after long-drawn moves and counter-moves, attracted wide attention. Contrary to his usual custom, Fallon did not bicker with this learned court. He was polished, suave, resourceful, although alert. He was in sound health again and fired by love and ambition. He was by now, however, a steady drinker—and sometimes not so steady, in the complete sense of the word. He virtually had broken his domestic ties, although he refused to let the world learn the exact truth. He made but one known comment in regard to a legal separation.

"She [his wife] has suffered enough. The least I can do for her is to keep my unfortunate conduct out of court."

Judge Gould took extraordinary pleasure in trying the Arnstein case. Nice questions were involved. Fallon's brilliant moves,

his startling grasp of technicalities, his almost instinctive ability
to scent openings in an opponent's guard found ready applause
in the mind of the eminent court. Judge Gould welcomed Fallon
to his chambers, treating the defender with a cordiality that
might have elicited adverse comment concerning any jurist less
ruggedly honest and able.

During an informal chat, the Judge went so far as to express
himself as sorry that Fallon didn't have keener competition.

There were only two persons available at this time to testify
in corroboration of Witness Glick. One was a Pullman porter.
The Negro said he remembered Cohn and Arnstein boarding
a sleeping-car many months before the trial.

Mr. Fallon: And how can you recall Mr. Arnstein so vividly?

Porter: Because he ain't the kind that travels in a plain Pullman berth.

Q: What do you mean by that? A: Why, he's a *drawing-room
man.* Not no berth-man. No, sir!

Q: Has Mr. Arnstein ever been pointed out to you *since* this
trial started? A: Yes, sir.

Q: By whom? A: By a Government man. [A Department
of Justice operative].

The last question deflated the porter's testimony by implanting
in the jurors' minds an inference of manufactured circumstance.

The second corroborating witness was a hotel clerk. He testified that Arnstein had registered as a "Mr. Arnold" at the
Hotel Washington on a certain date. Fallon succeeded in damaging this testimony by proving that a traveling salesman from
the west, a man named Arnold, had registered there that day,
and that but one Arnold appeared on the hotel record.

Fallon then elected to keep Arnstein off the witness stand.
He felt that the jury *might* acquit his client if he testified in his
own behalf; but the danger was that such testimony could be
used subsequently in a New York action. Fallon expected a disagreement, and that is what he got. The jury could not break
its deadlock, and Arnstein faced a second trial in that court.

Mr. Justice Gould was not satisfied with the sort of opposition given Fallon. He hoped there would be stiffer competition in the second Arnstein trial. He said as much to Fallon.

"There's only one man in the District that can extend you to the limit," he said, half banteringly.

Fallon laughed. "Maybe you can dig him out."

"I'll see what I can do."

"Who is this man?"

"His name is William Lahey. A whirlwind. You'll have no walk-over with him, please believe me."

"I'm anxious to meet Mr. Lahey."

The underworld, from coast-to-coast, was toasting Fallon as the greatest mouthpiece of modern times. He was on his way— so it seemed—to greater fame and fortune. Arnstein, however, was not entirely satisfied with the result of the trial. True, he was still out of jail, and Fallon had shown tremendous ability in staving off the combined attacks of the authorities and the press. But the long-drawn threat of prison was getting on Nicky's nerves. He became irritable. He was critical of Fallon's private life. He declared that a love-sick attorney was worse than none at all. This led to acrimonious debates. The name of Gertrude Vanderbilt came up constantly.

Another child was born to Fannie Brice, a boy. She named him for William J. Fallon. In a moment of good humor, Nicky forgot his disputes over Miss Vanderbilt and presented Fallon with a large ruby ring, set in platinum. Fallon gave the ring to Gertrude. She lost it in a taxicab. This incident brought matters to a head. Nicky began to fling one insult after another at Miss Vanderbilt. He described her in terms far from flattering.

"You'll go plumb to hell over her," he told Fallon. "You ought to have a guardian."

"Most of the people I've defended," Fallon said, "needed my services because they failed to mind their own business."

"So that's the way you feel about it, eh?"

"That's exactly the way I feel. And you can take it or leave it."

"Well, I don't propose to take it. How do you like that?"

"I like it fine. How do you like it?"

Arnstein glared. "This is no time for you to carry on an affair."

"It's the best possible time."

"A slip-up would mean prison for me. Doesn't that influence you at all?"

"Have there been any slip-ups?"

"I should have got an acquittal."

Fallon bristled. "Look here. You don't know a thing about law, and less about morals. You were lucky to get off as well as you did. If you don't like it, you can get another attorney."

"Oh, so you'd run out on me, eh?"

"I'll run out on anyone that tries to chaperon me."

"Well, you might lay off that God-damned——"

Fallon got up. "You'd better keep shut before you say something you'll be sorry for."

"To hell with you and her! If you want to bitch up your life, go ahead. But I'm damned if you'll bitch mine up. I don't mind how much you drink or chase around, but when you go off your nut about this woman, how in hell——"

Fallon stormed out of the room, screaming: "I'm through! Do you hear me? I'm through! I wouldn't defend you if you were dying."

When McGee learned of this scene, he tried to prevail on Fallon to reconsider. "You couldn't walk out on a client," he said. "Let's try to patch it up."

"You seem to like him," Fallon said. "Well, go ahead and defend him. I make you a present of him."

"You're upset, Bill. Sleep it off and come to your senses."

"Well, well! You're a moralist, too. Is that it?"

"There was nothing said about morals. But you surely can't throw down a client."

"I came near slugging him. I think I'll go back and swing on his jaw."

"Good God, Bill! Get hold of yourself. I don't care what else you do. Your private life is your own affair. But don't quit this case. Think of me."

"You're all right."

"If you run out it will break us. You know how many people would be glad to see us thrown. Come on, Bill. Cool off."

Mr. Fallon began packing. "I'm leaving for New York. I'm not coming back."

McGee took Fallon's hand. "Bill, you've had too much to drink. Sober up and then we'll talk."

"I'm through. What do I have to do to make it plainer?"

"All right then. If you're through with this case, you're through with me. Is *that* clear?"

"You're the one that's drunk."

"No, I let you do the heavy drinking for the firm. I hate to see the partnership broken, but it's up to you."

"I'll be able to get along without you."

"Then so long, Bill."

"Aw, go to bed, Gene."

"You just said you'd get along without me. Well, go ahead and see how you like it."

"I believe you're in earnest."

"What have I got to do? Submit an affidavit?"

"Well, then, quit the firm. I'm beginning to get bored."

"I'll never bore you again."

Fallon shut his grip. "I hope I can depend on that."

McGee went to his room. It was the first serious rift between the partners.

Mr. Justice Gould chuckled when the authorities named Bill Lahey as Special Prosecutor in the second Arnstein trial. Judge Gould anticipated some fine fireworks. When the case opened, however, he learned with dismay that Fallon was not at the counsel table. McGee and a Washington attorney named Wampler defended Arnstein. McGee's heart was heavy. Able though he was, he knew he was not in a class with his former partner as a trial lawyer. Indeed, who of all the bar was the equal of The Great Mouthpiece?

The talented Bill Lahey, hand-picked for the promised bout with Fallon, lived up to expectations. For two weeks he conducted the prosecution with fiery skill. Meanwhile Nicholas Cohn had decided to surrender to the authorities, after a period of retreat. Three others of the supposed securities-ring were in custody. There were five men in all now appearing on trial in Washington as co-defendants.

McGee realized the supreme need of Fallon at this moment. Arnstein sulked and affected to minimize the loss of the colorful counselor. McGee thought matters over, then put in a long-distance call to Fallon's New York apartment.

"I hesitated calling you," McGee said, "because I don't want to have anything further to do with you. Still, I've got to think of my client."

Fallon's voice was gay and friendly. "Oh, come on, you big mutton-head! We *couldn't* stay mad at each other."

"That's not what I called you for. I want some advice."

"Then you may have it, Gene, and I won't charge you a nickel. Shoot."

"Should I place Arnstein on the stand, or shouldn't I?"

"I'd keep him off the stand."

"Yes, but we've got to go the limit this time."

"Well, then, if you want to put him on the stand, why do you ask me for advice?"

"I really don't know what to do. Glick has testified there is no arrangement between him and the D.A. in New York as to immunity. But there must be. His testimony is plenty strong."

"Well, if Arnstein goes on the stand, his testimony will be used against him in New York. If he doesn't go on the stand, they'll have very little here to use against him."

"I'll keep him off the stand then. Thanks."

"Don't mention it, Gene. When are you resuming the partnership?"

There was a pause. Then: "I won't work with a quitter."

Instead of growing angry, Fallon laughed heartily. "Just for that, I think I'll bill you for my advice."

After a long and wearing second trial, Arnstein waited for the jury to come to a verdict. He was nervous. The four others were rather bewildered by it all. Finally the jury returned its pronouncement.

"Guilty as charged in the indictment."

Arnstein sat forward in his chair, a pallor spreading across his face. There was a half-angered smile on his lips. He almost hissed: "Fallon did this to me. Fallon sent me into this. God damn that woman!"

Justice Gould pursed his lips and said he would pronounce sentence next day. He went home feeling rather ill. Word was brought to him that Witness Glick—who had testified there was no promise of immunity involved in his turning State's witness —was being released by the New York authorities. It was hoped that the Judge would take this alleged development into consideration in passing sentence on Arnstein.

On the morning of sentence, one of the strangest and most dramatic happenings in recent legal history occurred; a situation that would be ruled out of fiction on account of its improbability.

Justice Gould dropped dead.

There was much scurrying about. The Presiding Justice of the Supreme Court of the District took over the duties of the late Judge Gould. He called the five convicted men before the bar and sentenced them to servitude in Leavenworth Prison.

McGee and Wampler appealed the case immediately to test the right of a judge, other than the one that had heard the testimony, to sentence. They lost the appeal. Nicky went to Federal Prison. He held Fallon accountable. He believed that Fallon's advice to McGee, keeping Arnstein from the witness stand, to be a deliberate piece of revenge. This feeling was heightened when someone informed Nicky that the jury would have acquitted him had he testified in his own behalf.

Mr. Arnstein served his term. On returning to freedom, he cut up domestically to a point where the loyal, self-sacrificing Fannie Brice no longer could stand the strain. She obtained a divorce.

Chapter Eighteen

A PANIC IN IVORY

THERE was a ring-battle in St. Louis in 1912, wherein a dramatic episode occurred. Abe Attell, for fifteen years the cleverest fighter of his ounces and inches, answered the bell against a third-rate local boy. Attell feinted his raw rival into knots during the early rounds; side-stepping, slipping, and blocking blows like a master. It was a great exhibition.

In the fourth and fifth rounds the former world's champion featherweight became slower of leg and arm, less baffling. His opponent landed with a churlish right; blinked with astonishment, and scored again. He grinned and began to flail earnestly. When the bell sounded for the seventh round, the sleek Attell walked slowly from his corner. Instead of squaring off, his face toward his antagonist, Attell breasted the ropes. He raised his soggy gloves while the fight-fans stared. He said:

"Gentlemen, I'm all through. I've given you the best I could, and I'm all in. I retire now."

Mr. Attell's pugilistic record was too impressive for any man to view this as the act of a craven. It was the gesture of a sensible artist. Less imaginative maulers continue far past their peak, becoming shock-absorbers, and ending as stumble-bums. Mr. Attell knew he had fought out his string. He had earned between $225,000 and $250,000 as a boxer. Unfortunately, he was a spender and a gambler. He found it necessary to enlist his wits in assembling another bankroll.

In 1919, when the World Series baseball scandal gnawed the livers of loyal fans, two men were foremost on the list of supposed "fixers." They were Arnold Rothstein and his alleged "front," Abe Attell.

The post-season series found the Chicago American League Club—the White Sox—opposed to the Cincinnati National League Club—the Reds. The defeat of the Chicago contingent was a staggering reversal of form. Charles A. Comiskey, "The Old Roman," saw his magnificent athletic machine crack, then crumble, before the bats of the Reds. It was most mystifying.

This sports swindle—bigger than any coup of the once-famed Maybury Gang—bloated the wallets of gamblers. The fixers promised to divide $100,000 among eight players of the White Sox (later called "Black Sox"). There were hitches in the pay-off, Mr. Attell coming to taw with little more than one-tenth the promised bribe.

A telescoped version of the swindle is that "pioneers" approached Rothstein in the Hotel Astor lobby, urging him to master-mind the situation. He refused. Armed with inside information, Mr. Rothstein hastened with characteristic zeal to capitalize his knowledge. He put down large bets on the Reds, and let nature take its course. According to subsequent testimony, Attell traded without sanction on Rothstein's name and influence to engineer the sable enterprise.

The former featherweight champion was on the ground early. He quartered in a large suite at the Hotel Sinton in Cincinnati. A coterie of twenty-five New York gamblers were in his retinue. These sharp-shooters let it appear that they were on the Rothstein staff. Once the series was fixed, the metropolitan layers infested hotel lobbies, button-holing anyone that might possess a Chicago dollar.

Attell & Co. wagered heavily on Cincinnati the first day. They won. A representative of the corrupt players called to collect the promised moneys—$20,000 being the fee stipulated for each losing game.

The caller saw stacks of bills on every horizontal plane of the suite, excepting the ceiling. Dresser-tops, tables, and chair-seats held yellow-backs. Mr. Attell, buried in currency, was perspiring with prosperity and behaving like a farm-hand making love in a hay-stack.

"Don't bother me now," Mr. Attell said. "I need all the dough I can lay my hands on. We got to make a clean-up to-morrow. It takes capital, partner. It takes capital."

The collector teetered on his heels. "The players are gettin' worried."

"What *they* got to worry about?"

"They was promised twenty grand at the end of each game."

"You go back," said the former champion, "and tell them not to burn."

"But when does the ghost walk?"

"Tomorrow."

Mr. Attell repeated this scene next day, and after the Black Sox had thrown the second game. Owner Comiskey was chewing holes in his score-card, baffled by the ivory-brand of baseball presented by his stars. The players dreamed of illicit wages and instructed their nuncio either to *collect* or to announce that they were through with the deal.

Mr. Attell again stalled off the ambassador. "Like hell they'll double-cross us! I'm acting on orders. You know *whose!* Ain't the Big Fellow's word no good?"

"How do we know the Big Fellow really is backing this?"

Mr. Attell displayed a telegram as an earnest of good faith. The telegram—later pronounced a fake—read:

HAVE WIRED YOU TWENTY AND WAIVED IDENTIFICATION

A R

The collector said the Black Sox were palpitating for stealthy backsheesh. Attell placed $10,000 on a table. "Give this to the mugs."

"They're restless," said the nuncio.

"They got nothing on me," said Mr. Attell. "I was born restless. The odds is shortening. Everyone is hep that the series is in the bag, and we need all our capital."

The Black Sox grumbled. They formed a counter-plot. They *won* the third game. The gamblers grew neurotic and called a meeting of the board of directors. They formulated a new deal. St. Louis and Boston gamblers entered the depraved pool. To soothe the befuddled players, some nefarious Kris Kringle placed currency under the pillows of certain of the athletes.

The Black Sox tossed off the world's championship. A scandal broke. The Cook County grand jury began sitting in Chicago. Mr. Attell retreated to New York. The grand jury indicted eight players and four alleged gamblers. There was a trial in June, 1921, before Judge Hugo Friend, himself a once-noted athlete. The indicted players were: Eddie Cicotte, Shoeless Joe Jackson, Buck Weaver, Claude Williams, Swede Risberg, Freddie McMullin, Chick Gandil, and Happy Felsch.

The widely publicized proceedings of the Chicago grand jury annoyed Mr. Rothstein. He consulted his mouthpiece, Mr. Fallon.

"I want you to stop this noise," Rothstein said.

"I want you to get on a train and walk right into the lion's den," said Fallon.

"You mean go to Chicago?"

"Right."

"Are you crazy?"

"Only in the earlier stages of insanity. Go to Chicago. You can stop an indictment with your Svengali pan."

"Of all the dopey advice I ever had! And I'm paying you for it, too."

"Listen. Go to Chicago and begin brow-beating everyone. Find fault with everything. Be temperamental. . . . I've got a great scheme."

"You'd better have."

"It's about photographers. Listen. . . ."

Mr. Fallon outlined his plan. He would notify Chicago papers that Rothstein was due before the grand jury. They would be certain to assign photographers. Rothstein was to scream before the grand jury, claiming he was being treated like a criminal.

"I don't want any photographs," said Rothstein.

"Hold your hat over your face, then. It's the best bet I can think of."

"You'd better take a night off and do some more thinking."

Reluctantly, Rothstein followed Fallon's advice. He went to Chicago. As predicted by Fallon, enough news photographers were present to have covered the World War. They leaped in front of Rothstein, jerked their gadgets, and flash-lighted him with booming salvo.

The first thing Rothstein did on entering the grand jury room was to make a red-hot speech. "Gentlemen, what kind of courtesy is *this?* What kind of a city is this? I came here voluntarily, and what happens? A gang of thugs bars my path, with cameras, as though I was a notorious person—a criminal even! I'm entitled to an apology. I demand one! Such a thing *couldn't* happen in New York. I'm surprised at you!"

This was a challenge to civic pride. So eager were the jurors to match Chicago hospitality with that of New York that they failed to indict the Master-Mind. For some years later, at least two of the courteous jurors called regularly on Rothstein in New York, receiving from him dinners, baseball and theater tickets.

Mr. Fallon next represented Mr. Abe Attell. The Chicago grand jury *did* indict that gentleman, and on a charge of conspiracy. New York officers arrested him on behalf of Chicago authorities. Mr. Fallon obtained his client's temporary release in $1,000 bail. Fallon's procedure was bold and effective. He swore out a writ of *habeas corpus*, and made the extraordinary statement:

"The man sought by the Chicago authorities, the man indicated by the Cook County grand jury, *is not the same man as my client, Abe Attell!*"

This astounding position made Broadway wonder if Mr. Fallon were not going daffy. Then, in May, and before Magistrate Corrigan in West Side Court, Mr. Fallon surpassed his earlier bids in the Attell matter. He *produced* the man who had made the original complaint against Abe Attell, a citizen named Sam Paas. Mr. Paas had lodged an accusation before the Chicago grand jury that Attell and others had taken $500 from him.

Mr. Fallon worked briefly and effectively. Q: Are you the witness that complained and then testified before the Cook County grand jury against a certain Abe Attell? A: I am.

Q: Did you ever see the Abe Attell who now is here in court? A: No; I never saw this man before.

Q: Had you ever seen him until he was pointed out to you in this courtroom an hour ago? A: No

The District Attorney's office was unprepared for this testimony. The Court upheld the writ of *habeas corpus,* and also dismissed a short affidavit charging Attell with being a fugitive from justice.

Officers rearrested Attell that same afternoon on a warrant calling for his extradition to Chicago. Fallon smiled.

"I must leap on my bicycle at once," he said. He obtained an immediate adjournment from Justice Tierney in Supreme Court. No matter how rapidly District Attorney Swann's men moved, Fallon was too nimble and elusive for them.

Judge Swann was as disgusted as a lady with a run in her stocking. He said he would "see about this Attell funny-business, Fallon or no Fallon."

Judge Swann sought to connect Attell's New York maneuvers with the World Series machinations. Meanwhile, Mr. Attell had vanished from Broadway's hustings.

"I'll not produce my client," said Fallon, "unless there is a specific charge made, or my client is indicted. This is merely a dodge to reach someone else (Rothstein) through Attell."

After a mouthy hubbub, Mr. Attell escaped with a whole skin. He opened a shoe-store, which he called the Ming Toy Bootery, at No. 1656 Broadway. It was beneath Roseland Dancing Academy. Some months later, the fire marshal found a five-gallon can of gasoline and some oil-soaked newspapers in the bootery. Mr. Attell disclaimed any intention to stimulate commerce by imitating Prometheus.

"Somebody is trying to frame me," said Mr. Attell.

A panic in ivory followed the series debacle. Baseball hitherto had stood as the one sport invulnerably honest. Now the fans were threatening a boycott. Something herculean had to be done. The worried baseball magnates cried for monkey-glands. Comiskey wrecked his superb team, and the guilty players were banished from organized baseball. The owners drafted United States Judge Kenesaw Mountain Landis at a salary of $50,000 a year to become baseball's Czar.

The lean and white-haired judge performed Voronoff rejuvenations and Steinach ligatures, but the vital influence that restored baseball to something of its former prestige was a pot-bellied, delightful person named Babe Ruth. He began busting home-runs with great swirls of muscle and blows of bat. The magnates seized on the home-run interest of fans and quietly introduced a lively baseball to the game. With this puck, ordinary hitters broke out in an epidemic of home-runs. The magnates denied they were using a sensitive type of ball. Only recently have they admitted it in a left-handed manner, by putting another, less lively sphere into play.

As for Mr. Ruth, he already is a legend, yet a man of rare reality. On one tour he was cautioned about plain talk in the presence of fair admirers. He promised to pipe down. During an informal party one evening, a lady asked him concerning his health.

"It's just fine, miss," he said. "Just fine."

"But the papers say you get indigestion once in a while."

"The papers know a lot, don't they?"

"Isn't anything *ever* the matter with you?"

"Nothing," he said, "except I have to get up once in a while at night to urinate."

When confronted with this remark, and reminded of his

promise to display more conversational culture, Mr. Ruth was as surprised as though he had struck out.

"What's wrong now?" he asked. "I said 'urinate', didn't I?"

Fallon mingled with baseball men. He loved the game and he had many good friends on various clubs, particularly the Giants. Mr. John J. McGraw, manager and part-owner of The New York Giants, was Fallon's favorite. McGraw was as pleasant a companion as anyone might select. That is, if you didn't try to insult him. Stoutly knit, as game as a pit-bird, he was very much in earnest when socking time was declared.

On a night in August, 1920, Mr. McGraw was at a theatrical club, preparing to shove off for home after the drinking of a toast or two. It was scrub-woman hour when Mr. McGraw fancied he saw an ancient enemy sitting in the grill. There was some third-baseman's language, and then Mr. McGraw and William H. Boyd, an actor, came to grips.

During the impromptu demonstration of the manly art, a water carafe lost its further usefulness when plopped against the McGraw skull. Then, according to ringside commentators, Mr. McGraw left the club with a peace-maker, John C. Slavin, a retired actor and one-time leading man for Ethel Barrymore. A third member of the departing group was Winfield Liggett, former naval officer. The three took a cab to the McGraw home, No. 301 West One Hundred and Ninth Street. According to the cab driver, Thomas Meagan, McGraw was first out of the cab. The two other men followed.

Mr. McGraw is known in baseball circles as "The Little Napoleon." As such, he wants to be let alone. When his escorts sought to lend their good offices as far as the door, another argument ensued.

Who hit whom, and why, is problematical. When the encore was concluded, Mr. Slavin lay unconscious on the walk, his skull fractured. The incident aroused wide publicity. Much that was unfair was said of Mr. McGraw. There was talk of Demon

Rum having had something to do with the pugilistic evening. Dry agents sought to interview "The Little Napoleon." The District Attorney's office busybodied until Mr. McGraw shut the front door and stayed in bed.

During his retreat, Mr. McGraw received solicitous telephone inquiries from Mr. Wilton Lackaye, the dramatic star. Mr. Lackaye later called in person. Whatever was said—and neither Mr. Lackaye nor Mr. McGraw is slow of wit or word—Mr. Lackaye's jaw suddenly received a consignment of knuckles. It must have been a money-blow, for it broke Mr. Lackaye's leg, giving him what is painfully known as a Potts' fracture. More publicity followed.

Mr. McGraw consulted his friend, Fallon.

Fallon immediately got busy to stem the tide of insinuations, liquor-talk, and general abuse directed at one of baseball's most interesting figures. He made the unusual demand that his client *be indicted!*

Mr. Fallon conferred with Albert B. Unger, Assistant District Attorney. Then he issued a statement to District Attorney Swann. It read in part:

"My client is entitled to have an indictment brought against him, so that he can meet and refute certain intangible accusations. The injury that befell Mr. Slavin was absolutely accidental, and involves neither moral nor legal guilt on the part of anyone. Further than that, Mr. McGraw in no way participated in this happening, nor in any way contributed to it.

"In view of the suggestions that have been made without any foundation whatever, it seems only just and fair that the matter be proceeded with at once, lest the people be led to believe that an absolutely accidental occurrence involves some criminal or reprehensible act. . . . *Mr. McGraw has a right to be indicted. . . .*"

Fallon also worked for an indictment on the liquor charge in United States District Court. Such an indictment was returned.

On Oct. 29, 1920, Mr. McGraw entered a plea of not guilty before Federal Judge Julius M. Mayer. The indictment charged that "The Little Napoleon" possessed a bottle of whiskey on August 8, the date of the bout. Mr. McGraw was completely cleared of the charge. The jury was out five minutes. The hoorah in the press came to an abrupt end.

Mr. McGraw's fame probably will rest more securely on his decision to change "Big Six" Christy Mathewson from a first baseman to a pitcher, than on his purported indulgence in the bellicose with artists of the stage.

When Fallon chose love in preference to duty, and after the first Arnstein trial, he found himself without a partner. There no longer was a genial, self-effacing McGee to dress the stage, shift the scenery, and stand in the wings with prompter's script. Without his Warwick, Mr. Fallon did not function in as kingly fashion as before. He seemed a kite without a tail.

With his passion for dramatizing life—visualizing himself always as Thespis—Fallon was not a man for solitude. He soon acquired another partner. For less than a year he was associated with John H. Gilbert, an exceedingly able young attorney, and a man of moral worth. They established offices in the Knickerbocker Building.

This edifice formerly was the Hotel Knickerbocker. It had housed a famous bar, where, in pre-dromedary days, the price of beer was raised from five to ten cents a glass. This boost in tariff was intended to discourage newspaper men and actors as guests. (It did, like the devil!) When the complexion of Broadway began to pustulate with *acne vulgaris*, the Regan family closed the Knickerbocker Hotel, surrendering the structure to offices.

Mr. Fallon chose for his quarters none other than the former suite of Signor Enrico Caruso. This office overlooked Broadway and Forty-second Street. Signor Caruso took his voice, his piano, his wife, baby daughter, and accompanist to the Hotel Vanderbilt. Mr. Fallon's first gesture, on entering his new and elaborate offices, was an imitation of the celebrated tenor singing an aria from *Pagliacci*.

The Great Mouthpiece's manner of living was so economically erratic that he went from wealth to insolvency and back again, as though driven by a battledore. Miss Vanderbilt sought to teach him the advisability of keeping a reserve supply of money, but on Broadway Mr. Fallon did much of his thinking with his spinal cord.

On occasion he did not know whether or not he had any ready money. He would say to Miss Vanderbilt:

"Well, Baby, what'll it be tonight? Do we eat, or do we *dine?*"

Quite oblivious to temporary insolvency, The Great Mouthpiece equipped his new suite with the best of everything. Wanamaker's provided a specially woven carpet, a thick-pile classic in green. A huge leather couch and four built-to-order leather chairs were set against the walnut panelings. A great desk, costing $1200, was installed. The desk soon was stacked high with all manner of papers—Mr. Fallon being the most careless man alive. Mr. Oscar Hammerstein, III. presented Fallon with an ornate cellarette. It had a sliding panel and a trick lock. Mr. Fallon not only utilized this cubby for his Scotch, but found it an ideal place to store documents, jewelry (when he had any on hand), or pawn tickets (when there was no jewelry).

As will be recalled, Mr. Fallon eschewed personal gew-gaws. Oddly enough, he entertained a late passion for watches. Perhaps he developed a fondness for time-pieces because of Miss Vanderbilt's gift of a thin, platinum watch. He kept her picture in the back of it. He gave her a photograph of himself, taken on his arrival in New York. Miss Vanderbilt had this portrait engraved on copper-plate. She placed it on her piano. It is still there.

Mr. Gilbert contributed to his partner a massive chair. It resembled a Napoleonic throne, and had on its back-rest the initials: "W.J.F." embossed in gilt. When asked concerning the chair, Fallon said:

"No, I don't think I'm Napoleon. I'm too tall for that."

Mr. Fallon bought for himself and family a white-stone mansion in West Seventy-seventh Street. In a financially flush moment, he paid $40,000 for this house. He purchased a similar one for Miss Vanderbilt. He lived, however, here and there, like a gypsy, not caring where he spent the nights.

He purchased many oriental rugs, contracting to pay much more than they were worth. It appears he went in for such luxuries to bait Arnold Rothstein, the underworld's leading connoisseur of Oriental floor-coverings. When Rothstein asked how much such-and-such rug cost, Fallon made it appear he had paid little or nothing for the article. This excited Rothstein's envy of Fallon's "bargains."

To Miss Vanderbilt's lectures on extravagance, Fallon would reply: "What's the difference? I'm going to die young and die broke. My wife's people have money. My father is well fixed. I have only my own life to waste."

Mr. Gilbert found it unwise to continue for long with such a moon-wandering partner, no matter how brilliant. Perhaps the Peggy Joyce case was the immediate cause of severing the connection.

Miss Joyce arrived from one of her European jaunts, laden with diamonds. The customs men thought she should pay a huge tax. Miss Joyce is the least dumb of beautiful women. She objected to the tax. Also, she had a fear that New York mobsters might decide to rob her as she came off the pier.

Aboard the *Mauretania* was Mr. William Halligan, noted comedian, globe-trotter and everybody's friend (except Volstead's).

"You've got to be protected physically and spiritually," said Mr. Halligan.

Before I proceed, I must cite the time when Mr. Halligan attended the Dempsey-Firpo fight. In the excitement, Mr. Halligan stood up at the ringside, obscuring the view of a rough citizen, who yelled:

"Set down, yah heel, or I'll bust yah in the puss!"

Mr. Halligan retorted: "Was your father a married man?"

The rough neighbor replied that he was desirous of meeting Mr. Halligan on the field of honor. "And," he said, "youse can name the spot and the kind of a fight youse want."

"You mean I shall have the choice of weapons?"

"Youse can choose bed-slats. It don't make no diff'rence to me. See?"

"In that event," said Mr. Halligan, "I choose *grammar*."

On advice of Mr. Halligan, Miss Joyce sent a wireless to Val O'Farrell. You will recall how Mr. O'Farrell worked in the Osborne case, so many pages ago, and how his assistant pounded off a finger-joint while stringing a detectaphone wire on a zero-roof.

Mr. O'Farrell met the big boat. "I feel safe with you," said Miss Joyce. "But what about the customs men?"

"Have you a lawyer?" asked Val.

"Yes, but I don't trust him."

"Why not?"

Miss Joyce was toying with a rope of pearls. "Well, he's always asking me to *pay him*."

Mr. O'Farrell nodded. "That *is* serious. Tell you what. Get Bill Fallon. He'll straighten out this customs thing like nobody's business."

Mr. Fallon hastened to the pier. In less than ten minutes after his arrival, Miss Joyce, gems, O'Farrell, and Halligan were on their way home. (Not until a few months ago was Miss Joyce asked to pay some $20,000 on those very gems.)

It seems that Mr. Gilbert had had something to do with arranging for Fallon to go to the Joyce rescue. When Mr. Fallon got one close-up of Miss Joyce, all commercial matters fled his skull. He simply couldn't charge *her!* It would have been too unromantic. He showered Peggy with expensive attention. He neglected his office work. Bills were overdue. Mr. Gilbert moved out.

On the day Mr. Gilbert departed, the sheriff decided to take

Mr. Fallon's furniture. Fallon came whistling to his office to find little there except the ghost of Caruso's voice. He was greatly perturbed—not on account of personal loss, to be sure, but because Miss Joyce was due any moment to call at his offices.

"I wouldn't have her see me in this bare office for anything in the world," said Mr. Fallon to his secretary. He stooped to pick up a stray tack. "Mail this tack to the sheriff. He must have overlooked it."

Mr. Fallon sent messengers scurrying to head off Miss Joyce. Meanwhile he received word that his home had been foreclosed. Several other matters (including a battle between two women concerning his affections) came up during the day. But all that seemed to worry him was the fact that Miss Joyce might catch him in such bleak and unlovely setting. The Actor needed his scenery, his stage-thunder, and his properties. Why had he let McGee leave?

He rescued the cellarette by dint of great strategy, moving it from room to room, then into the hall; then wheeling it back again when the sheriff's men were glutted with the joys of dispossess. Mr. Fallon now went to the trick lock, opened the compartment and took his bottle from its nest of pawn-tickets.

He was downing a man's drink when the telephone company called in the person of a lank young fellow with as many pliers, forceps, and pull-me-quicks as any dentist. Mr. Fallon watched the workman remove the unpaid-for instruments, and offered philosophical comments. He found a cigarette on a window-sill.

There was a frown on Mr. Fallon's pink forehead. "It seems," he said, "that the telephone company is of itself a plain refutation of the adage: 'Talk is cheap.'"

"I don't getcha, boss," the bent-over man said.

"It is an age of mutual distrust." Mr. Fallon inspected the cigarette. "May I smoke?"

The workman looked up wonderingly. "What did you say, boss?"

Mr. Fallon displayed the cigarette. "Do you care if I smoke?"

The workman was disgusted. "Hell, no!"

"I just wanted to be sure."

"I don't give a damn what you do."

Mr. Fallon lighted his cigarette. "Thanks, my friend. You're the most broad-minded man in the city of New York."

The workman straightened to his knees and waved his pliers. "Say, what's the angle? Do you think you're kiddin' somebody? *Can you smoke!* Hell's bells!"

A special messenger now arrived at the office. He handed Mr. Fallon an envelope and departed. In the envelope, Mr. Fallon found a note signed "A.R." and ten bills, each of $100 denomination. He addressed the workman:

"Did you know that the Lord provides?"

"Say, mister, I'm paid to jerk 'phones, and not to answer no riddles."

"Yet your employers *live* on talk."

"It's none of my funeral what they do. I got my orders. See?"

Mr. Fallon selected one of the ten bills. He extended it to the workman. "Take this and buy out your boss."

The workman was suspicious. "I don't want no tips. Thanks just the same."

"Then give it to your wife."

"I'll not be seeing her."

"Separated?"

"Kind of. She's up at Saranac."

"Tuberculosis?"

"Yep."

"How bad?"

"Worse than that."

Mr. Fallon returned the bill to the envelope. He looked out the window and down on Broadway. Finally he got his black fedora hat and put it on. Then he walked over to the workman.

He held out the envelope. "Don't ask any questions. Take it. I don't need it. Open it when you get home. So long."

"So long. Sorry I spoke short."

"Forget it."

Mr. Fallon went to the Knickerbocker Grill, where he had

unlimited credit. His scouts had headed off Miss Joyce. It was a great victory.

Fallon hurried to his mother's bedside on several occasions, always with a terrible feeling that she was about to die. One night he received word that the end was expected. He had been singing to a group of fair-weather pals. He ran from a speakeasy telephone to the street. The rain was beating down. He had trouble getting a cab.

"Go to Mamaroneck," he said, "and step on it!"

"Hey, there," the cabby said, "I don't like going away to hell-and-gone. I'm supposed to be off in an hour."

"There's a fifty-dollar tip in it, if you make time."

"It's bum weather for speedin'."

"Never mind. I'll get you out if they hand you a ticket."

The mother barely recognized her son as he bent above the bed. She passed through that night, but not long thereafter she died. Fallon never seemed quite so buoyant again. He drank harder than before. He grew careless about appointments with clients. He told lies.

One day a message arrived from Arnold Rothstein. A.R. asked Fallon to come to his Eighty-fourth Street home. When Fallon got there, he found Gene McGee in Rothstein's "den" on the top floor. Each was astonished at seeing the other. They shook hands and talked about trivialities, as though unable to shake off a feeling that they should be enemies but could not be such. They warmed up and each told the other of recent activities. McGee had been plodding along. Fallon was hanging his hat in the offices of various Broadway attorneys.

Mr. Rothstein appeared ten minutes after the former partners had been shown to the den. He sat in silence for a while, looking at one of his rugs. Finally he said:

"You fellows have been fools. Together, you were the great-

est team that ever hit town. Apart, you're not so forty. Let's
have a new deal. I want you to go back together. I'll finance
you."

"Fine!" Fallon said. "I certainly need some ready cash."

Mr. Rothstein leered. "Not so fast. First I want to know if
you're both willing to resume the partnership?"

"Certainly," Fallon said. "How about you, Gene?"

"I guess it's O.K," McGee said.

Mr. Rothstein leaned forward. "There are three conditions."

"I *knew* there would be *conditions*," Fallon said.

"You need money," Rothstein said. "The conditions are:
first, none of us is to tell lies to either of the others; second,
neither of you is to take a single drink; third, any money that
the firm gets has got to be deposited in a bank. I'll supervise all
moneys. We won't have any more of that loose book-keeping.
You can take these conditions or leave them. What do you say,
Fallon?"

"I'm on."

"Remember what I said about drinking."

"I'll go on the wagon."

"O.K. Then how about it, Gene?"

"Whatever's right."

Mr. Fallon was elated. "There's only one thing, A.R. How
much are you going to put up?"

"I'm coming to that. I have a lot of business, legitimate business. I'll turn over all my legal work, mortgages and loans. I'll
put in an expert in the mortgage line, so you won't have to
bother about it except to clear it through your office. I'll back
you for $50,000. This agreement will be off the minute one
lie is told, one drink is taken, or one fee is kept out of the
bank."

"Do we get the $50,000 now?" asked Fallon.

"Not by a hell of a sight! I *know* you too well."

"Then what *do* we get?

"You'll get along on a drawing account of $100 a week each,
and like it."

McGee spoke up. "Say, A.R., is this agreement on the level, or are we kidding each other at the start?"

"If you think I'm kidding, you're crazy," said Rothstein.

"I couldn't live on any $100 a week," Fallon said. "And if you think I can, *you're* crazy."

"It isn't a question of money," said Rothstein. "I just want to keep you boys within bounds."

"Make it $250 a week each," Fallon said. "I dare you."

"Two fifty it is, then. I'll fix up your office, defray all expenses, hire stenographers and other help. Wouldn't it be much nicer if I needed $100,000, and could come to you fellows and *borrow from you,* instead of you being broke all the time and having to come to *me?*"

Mr. Fallon got up and bowed. "It would be lovely."

"You were born a wise guy," Rothstein said, "and I guess you'll die that way. You're so smart you're broke. Now I'm going *with* you, to see you both sign the pledge."

"He should hire out as a chaperon," Fallon said.

The three sought a priest. Rothstein watched the reunited partners put ink to the pledge. Before the afternoon was over, Fallon tapped the Great Pawn-Broker for a thousand dollars. By nightfall he had a longshoreman's bun.

Once together again, the partners enjoyed brisk business. Journalists christened the firm "The Broadway and Forty-second Street Bar Association." Fallon got his Seventy-seventh Street home out of hock, and appeared prosperous. But his old habit of spending more than came in was unbreakable.

Mr. Fallon decided that the $250 a week drawing-account could be outwitted. He began levying on *future* weeks. He joked about his cleverness in finding a loop-hole in Rothstein's plan. The second week, he anounced to McGee:

"I'm spending next June's drawing account today. Tomorrow we should be well into July. How Arnold hates to give up!"

About three weeks after the tri-party pact, Rothstein rushed into the Knickerbocker offices. McGee was alone, going over some contracts. He looked up. "What's wrong, A.R.?"

Mr. Rothstein was excited. "Fallon is drinking!"

"You don't *mean* it?"

"You know damned well he's been soused ever since he signed the pledge. He's not to be trusted."

"You must make allowances."

"He can't make a sap out of *me*. All he thinks about is dames and booze. He can't get away with it."

"He may have had a cocktail or two."

"Don't make it any worse, McGee. You ought to know better than pull that line."

"Don't squawk to me. I'm not Bill's nurse."

"I had a hunch he was hitting it up. I been calling here all day. Why didn't you answer?"

"Was it *you* that called?"

"You know damned well it was me! You're as bad as he is. A couple of two-timers. I called his house and they said he was *sick*. Well, I wasn't going to let Pretty Boy get away with that. I went to see him."

"Was he sick?"

Mr. Rothstein chattered with rage. "I found him in *bed*. The stew-bum! But he tumbled to what I was going to do. He knew I was coming. He called up one of my best friends, a man I wouldn't want to be made a sucker in front of for anything. When I got there, I found my friend sitting beside Fallon's bed. What could I do? I couldn't say anything. But I'm through! Do you hear me?"

"Hear you? Even the traffic cops can hear you."

Rothstein was not a man to permit anything to peter out, once he had planned it. He called at the Fallon offices a few days after the "sick spell." He began to lecture Fallon, who appeared contrite, and who promised to let his right arm wither before touching another drink.

"All right," Rothstein said, "I'll forget your slip-up this time."

"But don't forget some dough," Fallon prompted.

Mr. Rothstein offered $1,500. Fallon argued him into advancing $2,500. "We need some petty cash, Arnold."

"There's nothing petty about $2,500," said Mr. Rothstein. "It takes a laborer a whole year to make that much."

"That's why they're laborers," said Fallon.

"Well, don't drink. Get hep to yourself."

That evening Mr. Rothstein walked into Dinty Moore's. He saw Mr. Fallon hobnobbing with several other gentlemen of Broadway. Rothstein's camera eye took in four tall glasses. One of them was in Fallon's hand. Rothstein affected cordiality. He went over to Fallon, stood there a moment, then deliberately relieved Fallon of the glass. He smelled it and tasted the fluid. Mr. Fallon beamed. He had beaten Rothstein to the punch. Fallon's office-man, Ernest Eidlitz, had been drinking ginger ale. Mr. Fallon had switched glasses with the fat Mr. Eidlitz. When Rothstein had finished a sandwich and departed, Mr. Eidlitz resumed his ginger-ale round, and Mr. Fallon his highball.

The next day Rothstein visited Fallon. "All bets are off, Bill. You're hopeless. Don't bother to pay back any money I've advanced. Just call it a day. I'll take my loss."

"I'm surprised," Fallon said.

"Uh huh! You went to the Palais Royal after you left Dinty's, didn't you?"

"You're not having me tailed, are you?"

"A friend of mine happened to have a table near you."

"Yes. I saw your wife there. I spoke to her."

"Never mind *who* told me. You were as stiff as a board. You talked kind of loud."

"I had to. My girl was deaf. She's too proud to wear an ear-trumpet, and——"

Rothstein spoke in a restrained fashion. "Save your wisecracks for the tarts. Just *why* did you yell out that 'Arnold Rothstein ought to join Billy Sunday?'"

"So you could master-mind the collection plate! How do you like that? You poor faker!"

Rothstein rose quietly and left the office. In ten days he came back again, offering to patch up differences.

"What are your *conditions* this time, A.R.?" Fallon asked. He was half-seas over. He seemed spoiling for an argument.

"Don't be so nasty."

Mr. Fallon rose, steadying himself against his desk. "What is to be this time—a prayer-book or a pound of flesh?"

"What's eating on you, Bill? You know how I feel about liquor. I can't risk having souses tend to my business. Give me a real promise, once and for all, not to drink. I'll see that you make at least $15,000 a year from my account alone. What say?"

"What do I say? Listen. Your olive branches are made of poison-ivy. I can't be bothered."

Although Fallon indirectly served Rothstein interests thereafter, a definite break was at hand. Oddly enough, Mr. Fallon went on the water wagon for two weeks. He ate enormous quantities of chocolate bon-bons whenever he felt the need of a drink.

The Vanderbilt romance seemed to have been the top-flight of Fallon's emotional career. Nevertheless, he was subject to occasional heart-wanderings. Peggy Joyce for a time dazzled him. So much so that he asked Val O'Farrell, the detective, if he would not cancel a bill that O'Farrell was anxious to collect from Miss Joyce.

"Who's she?" asked O'Farrell. "Where does she get off at?"

"You *surely* wouldn't press a small item like $250 against such a charming woman?"

"The hell!" said Mr. O'Farrell. "I charge pretty people the same as ugly ones. I want my dough."

Mr. Fallon shrugged. "The whole world has gone commercial."

"You can't buy food with beer-caps."

"You are persecuting my client."

"I want my fee. I've been stalled long enough."

O'Farrell went to the Earl Carroll Theater, where Miss Joyce was star in the "Vanities." Someone tipped off the beautiful Peggy that the town's foremost Sherlock was descending on the place. The entire cast got ready to receive O'Farrell with Broadway apothegms.

As the sleuth broad-shouldered his way toward Miss Joyce's dressing-room, he heard a hidden actor shout: "Lend me your nose; I want to putty a window!"

O'Farrell rapped. His ears burned as a group of chorus-boys delivered a plainly pre-arranged raspberry. He called out: "I know you're in there, Peggy! I want my money."

There was no sound from Miss Joyce's room; but from other cubicles came groaning slogans:

"Get out, yah big dog!"

"Look at him. I bet he's got a gun on."

"A pay-toilet is too good for him."

Mr. O'Farrell grinned. He rapped good-by on the Joyce portal. "O.K., Peggy. Stay in there if you want to, but you won't do any acting for a long time when I get through with you."

Next day Mr. O'Farrell received through the mail, special delivery, a check from Miss Joyce. It was for $500. Inasmuch as his bill was but $250, he claimed a world's record for having been *overpaid* by the most astute of beautiful women.

Pretty Peggy's maritime adviser, William Halligan, and her attorney, Mr. Fallon, had become pals since the day Miss Joyce came down the gangplank of the *Mauretania* with her jewels. They trained together a great deal in night resorts. Mr. Halligan had opened his famous "Indoor Yacht Club."

They called on Miss Joyce occasionally in her apartment above the Rosary Florist Shop, East Fifty-sixth Street and Park Avenue.

"Peggy's a mighty good fellow," Mr. Fallon said as they mounted the stairs.

"She reminds me of Rockefeller, if he was good-looking."

"I hope you've got some Scotch in that package."

"It's wine."

"That's great. Wine will go great on a cloudy day like this."

"I like wine with my rain. This is good wine."

"The best is barely good enough for Peggy."

"I'll say."

The maid admitted the two pals. Miss Joyce was telephoning her mother, long-distance. Her voice was dreamily stimulating. "Yes, dear mother." She frowned when Mr. Halligan broke an ash-tray. Then her face grew pleasant again. "Of course, dear mother."

Mr. Halligan was examining some burglar-proof bars at Miss Joyce's door. Miss Joyce terminated her conversation in time to hear Mr. Halligan remark: "These bars are not to keep burglars out—they're to keep the suckers in."

"I'll ask you to leave," Peggy said to Halligan.

Rain now began to beat against the windows. Mr. Fallon entered a plea for his friend. "He was only joking, Peggy."

"You may go home, too," she said.

Fallon was dejected. "It's raining."

"That's just fine," said Miss Joyce. "You both may go. Right now!"

Fallon made other entreaties. "Please, teacher——"

"Don't be kittenish," said Miss Joyce. "Get out."

They left the apartment and stood on the walk, the rain drenching their skins through summer suitings. All the cabs suddenly seemed to have found fares.

Mr. Halligan grimaced. "I forgot my wine, too. My error."

"The next time you try to hang a picture," said Mr. Fallon, "I hope you mash your thumb."

When Fallon presented Peggy with an automobile, one of his lady friends heard about the gift. She was fit to be tied. She announced to a few close friends that she was going to look up Miss Joyce and tell her *whose* property Fallon was. As for Fallon, well, she'd just. . . .

One afternoon Mr. Fallon was striding romantically about the Joyce drawing-room. "There is something about you, Peggy, that suggests moonlight and dreams. It's not your face, your lips—not any one of those things separately, or even the whole of them together. It's something that is indefinable, mystic, and——"

Miss Joyce's maid came in. "That same lady is on the telephone."

Mr. Fallon compressed his lips, as though to hold back a flood of poetry until a more propitious time. Miss Joyce flounced pertly. "I'm not in."

The maid retreated. Miss Joyce changed her mind. "I may as well tell her myself. Wait. I'll answer."

"Who is it?" asked Fallon.

"Some woman, a magazine writer. She's been asking all week for an interview. Telegrams, telephone calls, notes. It's a dreadful bore."

"The right kind of publicity is always good, Peggy."

She went to the telephone. Fallon heard her say: "Yes, Miss Holloway. I know. Yes. But I am very, very busy. I appreciate that. Yes. And thank you very much. No, I really can't see you now. No, I can't do that. I'm in conference this minute with my attorney. What? Well, that's an odd way to get an interview, isn't it? Very well, I'll let him answer a few questions for me. I'll see."

Miss Joyce left the wire and returned to the drawing-room. "I said you'd speak for me. Get rid of her."

Mr. Fallon, still bubbling with ecstatic thoughts of moonlight and dreams, went to the telephone. "This is Mr. Fallon, Miss Joyce's attorney. May I be of service to you?"

An extraordinary familiar voice singed his ear. "You're God-damned right there's something you can do! You double-crossing liar! Come right down, and come quick! I'll be waiting in a cab in front of the florist's."

Miss Joyce noticed Fallon's serious expression. "What's wrong?"

He got his hat and mumbled apologies. He went to a window abutting a fire escape. "You'll pardon my leaving so soon, and by such an unconventional stair."

Chapter Nineteen

THE COLOSSUS OF ROGUES

Bobby Tourbillon came from Atlanta, Georgia, in 1901, at the fat-cheeked age of sixteen, to ride in what the circus program described as "The Circle of Death." Bobby mounted a bicycle twice daily, dashed down a chute and into a den of rather wistful lions. He soon tired of passing in front of growling beasts, and resigned when the circus left Newark, N. J. He came to New York, the biggest and best lion's den of all.

Bobby frequented the poolroom of "Curly" Bennett in Broadway. There he eventually became acquainted with leaders of the metropolitan underworld. He also tarried betimes at Danny Clancy's saloon in Seventh Avenue. Soon he was regarded as a promising young man of Shady Lane. He experienced the first of his fifteen arrests in 1908, at the age of twenty-three.

His full name was Robert Arthur Tourbillon. The Underworld took the initials of the three names and called him "Rat." Sometimes they tagged him "Ratsy." He assumed many aliases in his astounding career of crime, but became best known under the label of Dapper Don Collins.

A Fifth Avenue tailor employed Ratsy, and it was there that he acquired a knowledge of fine clothes. It was during his sartorial studies in the Fifth Avenue establishment that the police first recognized Ratsy as a Raffles.

On the night of June 15, 1911, Ratsy and two others entered the Hotel Roy, in West Thirty-fifth Street. They robbed the clerk of $160. Judge Edward Swann (later District Attorney) said, in pronouncing sentence on Ratsy:

"He is as smooth a rascal as ever came before me. He is a real Raffles. I consider this man a very dangerous character, for he is such a smooth talker and such a fine dresser."

In 1916, the New York Telephone Company sustained heavy losses through coin-box robberies in the upper west side. The Police Commissioner planted detectives in almost every large pay-station of the thief-infested territory. They rounded up a gang. Tourbillon, now known as Collins, was of this gang.

When Federal authorities heard that Dapper Don was in the toils, they petitioned for his release so that he might be re-arrested as the head of a syndicate of white-slave blackmailers. The Government held him in $50,000 bail. A Federal Judge sentenced him to two years' imprisonment in Atlanta.

On Collins' release from Atlanta, he heard that a frugal-minded German of upstate New York had saved $20,000, and had stored it in a trunk. Collins looked up a former partner, and together they planned to relieve the German of his wealth. The proposed victim was a Julius Scholtz.

Obtaining a trick-badge, Dapper Don arrived at Mr. Scholtz's orchard and farm. It was a warm day. Mr. Scholtz's apples were taut with sap; the cider-mill was giving off fragrant juice.

Mr. Scholtz came from his cider-mill to greet his callers with the rugged and laconic frankness that comes of living remotely. "Vell, vot?"

Dapper Don displayed his purported Government badge. "We're United States officers," he said, "from the Department of Internal Revenue."

"Vell, vot?"

"What is your name?"

"Scholtz."

"Mr. Scholtz, we are obliged to search your place."

"I gat nuddings."

Dapper Don was suavely polite. "It is merely a matter of

form, Mr. Scholtz. We are searching all farm-houses for articles such as liquor."

"I only gat cider. Vant some?"

Dapper Don bowed. "We shall be delighted to drink a glass or two with you, Mr. Scholtz."

"Come inside. I gat nuddings."

They sat for a while at a plain table, sipping the new, tepid cider. "Got any hard cider?" Dapper Don asked.

"Only dat you drink. Vant some more?"

"I think not." Mr. Collins yawned. "Sorry, Mr. Scholtz, but we'll have to look through your things."

"I gat nuddings. I show you."

The men affected to search the house. Then Collins came on the trunk. "What's inside this?"

Mr. Scholtz pointed to his battered trunk. "You mean inside him?"

Dapper Don nodded. "Yes. Inside 'him.'"

"I gat only few ol' dings. Papers. I open him."

When the two men saw only bundles of German newspapers, they knew they had been misinformed. They exchanged winks and then had a parting drink of cider. When they started to go, Dapper Don held out his hand.

"Good-by, Julius."

Mr. Scholtz stared woodenly. He watched them get into their roadster, and as the noise of their engine died away, he kept standing there and repeating: "He said 'Goo'by, *Julius.*' How he know I gat name Julius?"

Mr. Scholtz kept wondering how these men knew his given name. His wonderment grew as he watched his plump apples go into the press. Finally he knocked off for the day, walked half a mile to a telephone and conferred with the police of the nearest town. Twelve hours later Dapper Don was arrested on a charge of impersonating a federal officer.

The firm of Fallon & McGee defended the "Good-by, Julius" case. It was their first trial in Federal Court. Fallon represented his client successfully—as he subsequently did in the case of Curley Bennett on a white-slave charge. From that time on, Fallon found Dapper Don a most amusing companion. They appeared often together on Broadway.

When asked why he chummed with such a notorious character, Fallon replied:

"Because he is a philosopher as well as the Chesterfield of crime. He performs in a gentlemanly manner. The first bit of philosophy he ever dropped in my company made me laugh and made me like him. We were discussing whether any man is normal, precisely sane; and what sanity consists of. Collins said: 'Between the ages of sixteen and sixty, no man is entirely sane. The only time any man between those ages is sane is during the first ten minutes after he has concluded the supreme love-gesture. Fifteen minutes after, and the old insanity creeps back again!' "

Official records cite ten aliases for Dapper Don. The police files describe him as a bootlegger, thief, and confidence man. His depredations were enormous; his versatility amazing. He robbed railway-express messengers, kidnaping one from a train near Harrisburg, with the same ease and skill as shown in the direction of one of the first huge rum-syndicates. He administered drug-rings, showing a genius for plotting his enterprises and a daring in executing his deals.

Dapper Don was beloved by many women. It was in the rooms of Mrs. Hazel Davis Warner that John H. Reid was shot mysteriously on the morning of May 15, 1921. Physicians at Fordham Hospital attended Reid. They believed him to be dying. Reid said he had shot himself, but when it was pointed out to him that the position of his wounds were such that he could not possibly have inflicted them, he refused to accuse anyone. Detectives said that Collins was more than interested in Mrs. Warner and that he had shot Reid.

In importing dope, Collins was regarded by Dr. Carleton Simon, head of the New York narcotic bureau, as the king-pin of drug-smugglers.

Prohibition brought Collins to the peak of his career. He was affable, good-natured. His polished manners and classy garb concealed a most desperate character.

In June of 1921, Collins acquired an exceedingly fast yacht, the "Nomad." It was a former submarine chaser. In purchasing the craft, Collins posed as Charles A. Cromwall, prominent Philadelphia banker. He put a crew aboard and allowed a lady friend to take turns at the wheel. He set out from Philadelphia for southern waters.

The Philadelphia members of the crew believed they were making for Palm Beach. A few miles east of that resort, their fellow seamen from New York appeared on deck, leveled pistols at their heads and ordered them to steer for the Bahamas.

On Sunday evening, December 11, the "Nomad" returned to Philadelphia. Cromwall (Dapper Don) had his good Captain make for the Mathis Yacht Building Plant at Camden. No sooner had the boat pulled into the wharf than a watchman hailed it.

"You can't dock here," the watchman shouted.

Dapper Don strode to the starboard rail. "Don't be foolish, my good fellow."

"You can't dock. See?"

"Listen, my man. We're merely putting her on the marine railway for repairs in the morning. Do you want us to sink here?"

"Well, that's different." The watchman strode off.

Two hours later, the same watchman saw a motor truck drive up to the dock. He became suspicious again. This time, bubbling with authority, he rushed to the wharf. "Now what's comin' off?"

Dapper Don burst into good-natured laughter. "You certainly are stupid. How do you hold your job? I've told you, old man, that she's going on the marine railway in the morning. We want to take off the furniture first."

The watchman rubbed his chin. "Oh."

That night, Collins' confederates unloaded half the "Nomad's" cargo of 1,800 cases of liquor. The same night he slipped down the river. When the watchman made his morning rounds, he found no trace of the vessel that was to have "gone on the marine railway."

Collins unloaded the remainder of the cargo at Chester, Pa. The truck to which the liquor was transferred broke down at Leiperville. The crew concealed the liquor hurriedly in a saloon, where customs agents seized it. Dapper Don and his lady-love of the moment were indicted, together with three of their New York "seamen."

Collins knew Arnstein and Rothstein intimately. He admired Rothstein for the latter's peculiar sense of humor and his ability to mimic various Broadway characters. He was present the night when Lilian Lorraine, Ziegfeld star, had her famous run-in with Reuben, the delicatessen dealer.

Reuben's, across from the Ansonia, was Rothstein's favorite hang-out (later he took up at Lindy's). He would sit there for hours, sipping six or seven orange juices, thinking of his money, and holding long telephone conversations.

Miss Lorraine had an apartment above Reuben's, and on hot nights sent down for supper-snacks. One night Miss Lorraine felt in the mood for a bit of food. She called Reuben's. Rothstein answered the telephone, imitating Reuben's voice.

"Send up a chicken sandwich and a pint of milk," said Miss Lorraine.

Rothstein didn't register the order. He went to a corner cigar store and called up Reuben. He imitated Miss Lorraine's voice.

"This is Lilian Lorraine," said Rothstein in falsetto. "I'm having a party. Send up six dozen club sandwiches, some caviar, a lot of pickles and twelve quarts of milk. Hurry."

Reuben was anxious to please. "I'll do my best, Miss Lorraine. This is the after-theater rush-hour, you know."

"I can't help it. We're hungry."

"I'll do my best."

Reuben bustled about. In half an hour the real Miss Lorraine called and Reuben answered. "Did you have to kill the chicken?" asked Miss Lorraine.

"Just a few minutes, Miss Lorraine. It's a big order at this hour."

Miss Lorraine thought Reuben was getting sarcastic. "Are you trying to kid somebody?"

"It'll be right up."

"It better be."

Rothstein had returned and was sitting quietly at his customary table. Miss Lorraine called once more. This time Rothstein answered the telephone, again imitating Reuben.

"I'm so sorry, Miss Lorraine. It will be right up."

Two waiters, each carrying a large hamper, finally went to Miss Lorraine's apartment with sandwiches and milk. Soon there was a report that Miss Lorraine was storming and kicking at the hampers. Reuben himself went to the rescue.

He was mystified. "Isn't everything O.K.?"

"What are you trying to do?" asked the lady. "You know I didn't order all these things."

"But I answered the telephone myself," said Reuben.

"I asked for a chicken sandwich and a pint of milk."

"I'm sorry, but I distinctly heard you say you had a party and wanted six dozen club sandwiches and a dozen quarts of milk. I heard you——"

Miss Lorraine's temper was something to marvel at. The waiters and their employer made for the stairs. Reuben passed Rothstein, who was sipping coffee serenely.

"What's wrong?" Rothstein asked.

Reuben was muttering: "Actors are all crazy. Don't know their own minds."

Collins once said to Fallon: "Everyone hates Rothstein because he makes them pay back what they borrow."

"He wants to be known as the greatest fixer in the world," Fallon said. "He likes to help everyone with bail, rescuing the boys from tough raps, shining in the eyes of tough fellows as being their friend."

"Yes," said Collins, "and in that way he can protect the money he loans. But he gets everyone sore if they borrow his money; that's so he will be the first person they'll pay back when they get flush."

In 1924, Dapper Don was in Paris, a fugitive from New York jurisdiction, and doing this and that thing to get along. He was also enjoying the adoration of the ladies. One woman, Mrs. Helen Petterson, former wife of Otto Young Heyworth, interested herself in Collins. He was posing as Harry Hussey in Paris flim-flams.

In Paris, Dapper Don resided at the fashionable Hotel Majestic in the Etoile quarter. He had had a fairly successful season in Berlin and was in funds. During a New Year's party at the Majestic, Mrs. Petterson "fell" from a third-floor window. The circumstances of that leap or fall remained a mystery.

When Dapper Don failed to protect his hotel bill, he found himself in a French prison. Mrs. Petterson, limping daily from her room in a hospital at Neuilly, visited him. "We are going to be married," she said to inquirers.

Early in 1924, Lieutenant James F. McCoy of New York Police Headquarters and Lieutenant Charles F. Kane of the District Attorney's office were in Paris, in connection with the extradition of Mourey, the author of the Shattuck burglary exploit. They went for a visit to Sante Prison. The head of the prison invited the visiting officers to attend the morning line-up.

As the prisoners stood in line, McCoy nudged his partner. "I'm damned if that isn't Ratsy Tourbillon!"

Lieutenant Kane nodded. "It's Dapper Don, all right. What a coincidence!"

"Hello, Rats!" shouted McCoy.

Collins looked up, startled. Then he composed himself. "Were you addressing me?"

"Come on, Rats. Don't you remember us?"

"I haven't had the pleasure."

The superintendent of Sante Prison was startled to learn that he was host to a crook of international repute. When confronted with his record, Collins admitted his identity.

"It is my misfortune," he said.

The officers cabled America. They arranged for extradition on the specific charge of grand larceny, Collins having been convicted in 1920 before Judge Mulqueen of relieving Frederick C. Robb, an American Express Company employee, of $5,000, some jewelry and a watch. His attorney, Fallon, had obtained an appeal. It was while under $5,000 bail, pending decision, that Collins had fled abroad.

Dapper Don came home in grand style aboard the steamship *Paris*. A first-cabin passenger, he shared a fine stateroom with Detective Daley of New York. He referred with splendid irony to Mr. Daley as "my secretary." Passengers were aware that one of the two was under arrest as a noted crook, but were unable to learn which was which. They generally presumed that Daley, and not the immaculately dressed Collins, was the criminal.

The two men endeavored to hide from reporters that met the *Paris*. The news men found them in the smoking-salon. Dapper Don evaded most of the questions and kept repeating: "You'll have to ask my secretary."

The reporters showed him a clipping and a picture of Mrs. Petterson. Collins remarked softly: "She's a beautiful woman."

"But aren't you going to get married to her?"

"Ask my secretary. You might let me keep this clipping and picture, however."

One of the reporters asked: "Say, did you shoot John Reid?"

Dapper Don, turning to his "secretary," said: "I wonder if any door mats or milk bottles have been stolen since I went away? I presume it will be laid to me."

Dapper Don went to police headquarters to have his pedigree taken. He said his name was Arthur Collins, and that he was thirty-five years old.

The registering lieutenant asked: "Residence?"

"Hanley's Hotel, No. 101 Center Street."

The lieutenant was dubious. "Why, that's the Tombs Prison, and Hanley is Warden."

"If you want to know my right address," said Collins, "it is the Hotel Majestic, Paris."

"What's the charge?" the lieutenant asked Detective Daley. Before the latter could reply, Collins shouted: "Moprey!"

The crime of "moprey" is a classic jest among criminals. It is supposed to consist of exhibiting oneself in the nude to a blind woman.

The last heard of Collins was something over a year ago. He was then in the New Jersey State Prison at Trenton. Judge William B. Harley in Quarter Sessions sentenced Don on April 26, 1929, to a three-year term. He was convicted for conspiracy to swindle Thomas Weber, an apple farmer of Egg Harbor, N. J., of $30,000.

Collins occupied a single cell at the prison until August, 1930, reading newspapers, magazines and otherwise improving his mind. In August there was a shake-up in prison management. It was charged that certain prisoners at Trenton, including Don, were receiving preferred attention. Collins and other "renters" were put to work. Don went into the automobile plate-pressing department. He was credited with thirty cents a day and permitted to spend a dollar a week on luxuries.

"A pleasant vacation," he said, "has been spoiled for me in this exquisite American prison. When I get out, I'm going to Paris."

Chapter Twenty

THE BROADWAY AND FORTY-SECOND STREET
BAR ASSOCIATION

Two Christmases ago, a New York department store set up an athletic pavilion for demonstration of gymnasium fixtures. Reducing-machines for the ladies, electric horses for the gentlemen, and other appurtenances for physical well-being were on display. A trim-muscled fellow, clad in trunks and discreet flannels, worked at the various gym-traps, showing Christmas shoppers what a Godsend it was to have a punching-bag or a rowing-machine in the home.

One afternoon the trim-muscled fellow put on his mittens and began plopping a pear-shaped bag. He stood on a slightly elevated platform. He delivered snappy, accurate blows, and smiled in approval of his own grace and rhythm. The shoppers, mostly women, crowded the pavilion and wondered if the trim-muscled fellow were married.

Above the clop-clop of the oscillating bag rose a strong, assertive voice:

"You're lousy!"

The trim-muscled fellow missed the third beat of his four-four time—the moment when the bag should glance from fist to elbow in orthodox ricochet. This error is known as muffing a Tommy Ryan.

The man restrained a temper that properly didn't belong among ladies. He smiled hypocritically, making a mental reservation to the gospel of metropolitan bazaars: The customer is always right.

He changed his tempo and barely had entered the Kid McCoy, fist-elbow-forehead technique, when the same assertive voice rose, even more emphatically:

"You stink!"

The trim-muscled fellow gagged, lowered his hands and peered at the audience in a bewildered way. He assumed that the jarring voice had come from none other than a powerfully-knit woman, who now was leering at him. She wore rather mannish attire and had a belligerent stance. If there were any doubt as to who the heckler was, it cleared when the woman said:

"You're so rotten you ought to brain yourself with a toy balloon!"

There was a sort of death-rattle in the demonstrator's perspiring throat. "Maybe you could do better than me, Madam."

The woman grunted. "If I couldn't, I'd give myself up to the nearest T.B. hospital."

"Suppose *you* show us how to do it."

The lady peeled off a tailored jacket and leaped to the platform. She drew on the mittens, pounded them, one against the other, to settle them to her knuckles. She then began an exhibition that any pugilist would envy. She whaled into the bag, the rapid blows sounding like machine-gun trills. The manager of the sports department was on his way from the hockey-counter to the buyer's office when he saw the strange spectacle. He stood open-mouthed as the audience cheered. The manager saw the demonstrator standing in a deflated manner, leaning against a set of pulley-weights and chewing his lip. The manager stared hard at the woman's sizable bust. "Who's the dame with the big water-wings?"

"Go ast her. I'm quittin'."

"You wouldn't quit in the busy season?"

"You heard me, pal. I'm tossin' in the towel right now. See?"

The manager waited until the woman had whammed the air-apple a good five minutes. Then he introduced himself. The woman, not at all winded, shouted: "If you want a real salesman for this sort of thing, why don't you hire me? That bum you've got should be in the Flit department."

"Come in my office, Miss," said the manager.

Inside the office, the manager said: "I'm going to put you on. Will you be able to report at once?"

"This minute, if you'll not divulge my name."

They had a long talk. The woman was Charlotte Poillon. She and her sister, Katherine, were the much-publicized Poillon sisters. She got the job, and more than made good.

The joint career of the Poillon sisters began in 1903, when Katherine sued William Gould Brokaw for $250,000, charging breach of promise. The defendant settled out of court for $17,500. In that same year the sisters were evicted from their hotel.

A judge fined them $10 in 1907 for disorderly conduct. In 1908 they were arrested on a charge of defrauding the Hotel Bristol of $135. In defense, they said that Magistrate Barlow had agreed to pay their hotel bills. They got a three-months' sentence and their pictures in the Rogues' Gallery.

In 1909, Charlotte busied herself with her fists. She was arrested, accused of beating a Negro bellboy. Also in that year the manager of the Hotel Willard asked for a summons to oust the sisters from that place. He said they would not pay their bill.

In 1912 Charlotte sued Rector's Café for $25,000, asserting the management had ejected her from that refectory. The defendant said Charlotte had appeared there in man's attire. In 1915 a former boarder sued Charlotte to recover $75 he said he had lent her.

In 1923, Charles H. Dusenbury accused the sisters of defrauding him of $3,000 in securities, and other valuables. When arraigned before Judge McIntyre in General Sessions, the sisters cut up didoes. They not only refused to plead to the indictment, but resented it being done for them. Judge McIntyre ordered that a plea of not guilty be entered in the record, and fixed bail at $15,000 each. The sisters rejected counsel appointed by the court.

"We want an Irish counselor," said Charlotte, pounding the table. They didn't believe that Samuel Feldman, the appointee, was Irish. They objected also to Judge McIntyre as the presiding officer in their case. The judge several years before had been attorney for William Gould Brokaw.

Charlotte's voice could be heard in the corridor outside the courtroom: "We'll not be forced to plead, and we refuse counsel you assign us." She again banged her fist on the table. "You can't railroad us, Judge McIntyre!"

The judge leaned forward. "Please remember that you are women, or I may forget that you are."

Sister Katherine shouted: "I remember only too well that I am a woman. I have been reminded of *that* by some of your club members, Judge McIntyre."

"I don't understand that," said the bench.

"There's a whole lot you don't understand."

The complainant in this case, Charles H. Dusenbury, was seventy-three years old. He was an agent for the *Churchman* and the *Evangelist*, religious publications. He was once the proprietor of a string of laundries. He admitted he had promised to marry Katherine, but insisted she swindled him of $1,500 in stock, a deed to property in New Jersey, numerous amounts of cash, and some jewelry.

The elderly wooer affected clothes of clerical cut. His faith in humanity was vast—until he met Katherine. She weighed 200 pounds, and was fifty-one years old. They first met in front of a Piggly Wiggly store on upper Broadway. They spoke concerning the new store, and then Mr. Dusenbury said: "I'm going your way."

They walked several blocks discussing religion. Then Mr. Dusenbury said: "What do you think of the murder of the Reverend Hall?"

"It was terrible," said Katherine.

"That's what I think."

They were as unanimous on other subjects, and Mr. Dusenbury suggested another meeting. Soon, Mr. Dusenbury alleged, Katherine began to tap him for funds; first $100 to go to Albany "to tell her wealthy brother of her engagement." "My dead wife's jewels and other money followed," said Mr. Dusenbury. "I want to warn my fellow men."

"Bosh!" said the sisters, Charlotte and Katherine. "We do not intend to stand for another railroading. The Poillon sisters are strong for fair play. Mr. Dusenbury wants to get revenge on the marriage-business."

After a stormy series of charges and counter-charges, a note professing Mr. Dusenbury's love of Katherine cropped up. The District Attorney recommended that the case be dismissed. The Poillon sisters went free.

Fallon & McGee represented the sisters in the bankruptcy proceedings of W. Nelson Edelsten, General Agent for the Equitable Life Assurance Society. Edelsten filed a petition of voluntary bankruptcy, saying he had liabilities of $37,395 and assets of $43,510.28. Certain of the assets, he maintained, were uncollectible. Among the latter were claims against Katherine Poillon, amounting to $23,338.

The sisters appeared with their usual self-certain poise. Charlotte—who once had boxed with Gentleman Jim Corbett— glared at the court.

"What is your occupation?" the court asked Katherine.

She spoke up. "What would you characterize a woman who stays home and attends to her business?"

"I would say such a one would be a wise woman," said the court.

"Then I'm a wise woman," said Katherine. "That's my occupation."

It was made known that Charlotte was capable of earning $50 a day as a detective for the Burns Agency. In October of 1920, she trapped a man suspected of stealing Mrs. Enrico

Caruso's jewels, valued at $45,000, from the tenor's home at Easthampton, Long Island.

The sisters attended most of Fallon's cases and haunted his offices in the Knickerbocker Building. One day, when the partners needed some ready money—a chronic condition—McGee telephoned Charlotte and asked for a thousand dollars. She was furious. "Where do you think we'd get that much money, you big loafer? I have half a mind to clean you up. You're making my sister cry. Don't do it again. Ever!"

Fallon said: "I wouldn't solicit Charlotte for money. She's liable to connect with your chin."

"I believe she would, at that," said McGee.

"They tell me," said Fallon, "that the sisters have kicked the devil out of several wayward husbands. The gag is that a neglected wife hires them to entice a flirting husband into a cab. They go for a short, sweet drive; then bingo! The black-sheep spouse catches some knuckles and is tossed out. On arriving home he is about cured of his desire to wander in foreign pastures."

So successful was the firm of Fallon & McGee, riding over courts and hynotizing juries, that the press referred to the partners as "The Broadway and Forty-second Street Bar Association."

In January, 1921, District Attorney Charles B. Andrus of Saratoga County, New York, went to trial for alleged neglect of duty. It was testified that he had received protection money from Jules Formel, a gambler, for the privilege of operating a gaming house at No. 210 South Broadway, Saratoga Springs. The privileges were purported to have been bought in the summer of 1919. The earnings of Formel's place ranged from $7,000 to $38,000 a night. Formel was indicted and tried three times. Fallon represented him in the first two trials.

Arnold Rothstein lurked in the background of this situation. Rothstein was eager to have Fallon clear the Saratoga atmosphere so that he could open an establishment, "The Brook." He offered $60,000 to certain politicians for that privilege.

Arrested with Formel was Charles White, known as "Gold Tooth Moore." The trial was set for Ballston Spa, eight or nine miles from Saratoga. The action was politically important. State Senator Brackett, a Republican, and an extremely able lawyer, took charge as special prosecutor. The general idea was to show that Democrats were no good at all. Virtue makes her home with minorities.

Lawyers in this case, as well as an Albany Supreme Court Judge, had headquarters at the United States Hotel in Saratoga. Mr. Fallon presided at parties every night, and was late to Court each morning. The Judge remonstrated with him.

"What makes you late every day?"

Mr. Fallon replied: "The hotel is a long way from this court, Your Honor."

The judge snorted. "It appears that I have rooms at the same hotel where counsel for the defense resides. The court will instruct the bellboy to awaken both court and counsel at the same hour from now on."

The next day Fallon bribed the bellboy to call the judge half an hour later than usual. The judge was tardy getting to court. When he saw Fallon sitting there "impatiently," he raised his brows.

Senator Brackett announced that he was "going to clean up Saratoga." [May we all live that long.] Was the Senator responsible for an unusual display in a local paper, at the beginning of the Formel trial? There was a large headline:

FALLON & McGEE'S RECORD OF DISAGREEMENTS

Under this banner was a long list—a very long one—of all Fallon trials that had ended in hung juries. The fact that these juries disagreed by the score of 11 for conviction and 1 for acquittal was emblazoned in big type. The headline of another article was: "11 to 1!" And then some question marks.

Fallon invited his Broadway cronies to Saratoga. Senator

Brackett, frowning and alone, saw new faces at the Fallon table day after day. Ostensibly they were attorneys for the defense. Senator Brackett sought to impress the jury that he was alone, and that the defense was having an *army* of talent. To emphasize his aloneness, Senator Brackett edged his chair near the jury box, as though to say: "Look at all the expensive men the defense has hired. Look at me—all alone!"

When time came for the presentation of testimony, Fallon rose.

"Your Honor, I move a mistrial."

The court was puzzled. "On what ground?"

"My client is not receiving a constitutional trial."

"Counsel will amplify his statement."

Fallon pointed to the lone figure of Senator Brackett, who by now was sitting at the very corner of the jury-box. "In all my cases, if the court please, I have had but twelve men on a jury. Now, it seems there are *thirteen* men!" He shook his finger at Brackett. "Who is this extra juror? Who is this Juror Number 13?"

All through the case, Fallon kept referring to Senator Brackett as "Juror Number 13." At the close of the testimony for the prosecution, Fallon amazed everyone by rising to say:

"Your Honor, *there will be no defense.*"

Fallon summed up, ridiculing the evidence of the prosecution, and referring to "Juror Number 13." The jury disagreed, standing eleven for acquittal and one for conviction. Fallon waved a copy of the newspaper article that read "11 to 1," and said to Senator Brackett:

"There you go, Senator. Eleven to one, once again! Your figures are right, but you got the teams mixed. We scored the eleven this time."

At a second trial before Justice Van Kirk, a jury again disagreed after four hours' deliberation.

Fallon was unable to take charge of Formel's third trial, McGee representing the gambler. The principal witness, Mrs.

Formel, fractured a leg and couldn't appear. The jury found Formel guilty on a charge of conducting a gambling house.

One of Fallon's largest fees (quoted at $125,000) and his most flagrant neglect of duty came in the much-discussed Donegan case. Edward J. Donegan was a Brooklyn kindling-wood dealer, who became a liquor wizard. He stood trial in 1922. The Government alleged that Donegan drew profits of $30,000 a day as a bootlegger. He obtained liquor permits from the Prohibition Director's office and had them forged. His warehouse withdrawals were colossal. He lived in showy fashion and had a bodyguard of expert guns.

When Federal officers ran Donegan to cover, he retained Fallon. He gave The Great Mouthpiece twenty-five one-thousand dollar bills as an ante. Fallon is said to have squandered it in one Broadway whirl. He then drew on Donegan for other large amounts, meanwhile doing nothing to stave off conviction. With astounding celerity, a Federal jury convicted Donegan. A judge sentenced him to ten years in Atlanta and to pay a fine of $65,000. The Government also set about collecting $1,653,797 in undeclared income taxes from Fallon's client.

Donegan went to prison declaring: "That God-damned drunken Fallon did this to me! If it takes until I die, I'll get square! He took my dough. He did nothing."

Fallon said he did the best he could for Donegan. "The trouble is, all these fellows expect miracles. Well, sometimes the rabbit doesn't come out of the magician's hat."

Chapter Twenty-One

THE BUCKET BRIGADE

FALLON's introduction to Wall Street charlatans was through Dandy Phil Kastel, a small, alert manipulator of bucket-shops. The Arnstein case may be said to have marked Fallon's moral collapse; and now his advent to shady financial circles laid a foundation for ethical dry rot and professional ruin. It was the spectacle of a man failing through success.

Kastel was the brains of several off-color financial houses. One and all went on the rocks after numerous investors had poured stupendous sums into the funnels of the bucketeers. Kastel was active in the affairs of Dillon & Co., one of the brokerage houses which failed in 1921. He then formed Wilk & Co. He also was said to have been the directing genius of J. C. Rabiner & Co., and of Culver & Co. and others.

The firm of Wilk & Co. was born in a New Street barroom. Dandy Phil Kastel and Harold Sonking met there one day for a few drinks.

"I'm looking for a connection," Sonking said.

"Let's open a brokerage house," said Kastel.

"I thought you had been expelled by the Consolidated Exchange?"

"Only suspended," Kastel lied. "Anyway, we can organize a firm and go into the exchange and make money. I won't appear, but I'll handle the business."

"I got a deferred dowry coming from Jake Wilk, my father-in-law," Sonking said. "I'll see what he is going to do about it."

Wilk gave his son-in-law the dowry. Sonking then put up $7,000 and Kastel put up another $7,000. Neither figured openly in the formation of the firm. Old man Wilk and a man named Blume appeared as the founders of the concern. Wilk delivered a lecture to his men:

"The customer is wrong nine times out of every ten. For that reason, we must trade against them if we are going to make any money."

The bucketing began. When an order was given to the firm, it was executed; but immediately, in a dummy account, a trade was made against the sale; or a sale against the purchase, thus balancing and washing the transaction.

Edwin J. Chapman, gifted financial writer of the *Commercial*, described how, on one occasion, a large trader with Wilk & Co. decided to visit the offices of his brokers, to look things over. He had been accustomed to conduct all his transactions from his home, either by telephone or wire. He had the misfortune to telephone the bucketeers that he planned visiting them next day.

When this gentleman descended on the offices, the bucketeers had retained a gang of unemployed book-makers, touts and pimps. This mob thronged the Wilk offices. The visitor saw a horde of seemingly feverish investors gazing at tickers or gathered before a blackboard where quotations were placed with great speed.

At intervals some voice would call: "Buy me 100 shares of Steel," or would give an order for sale or purchase of some equally well-known and prosperous stock. The visitor was completely confident that his house was an important one. Incidentally, he left behind him $10,000 in cash for "investment."

Dillon & Co. was formed in a startlingly similar fashion to the founding of Wilk & Co. The New Street barroom also was the meeting place for Kastel and Daniel Dillon. Kastel had just passed through the failure of Dunn & Co. When Dillon asked concerning that defunct firm, Kastel said:

"The company was going all right, and things were moving

nicely; but a swell-headed Jew in the firm got funny, and we were thrown out of the Consolidated."

Referee Peter B. Olney, Jr. experienced difficulty in connecting Kastel with Dillon & Co. when that firm blew up. But finally it developed that Kastel was the real head of the concern. He had withdrawn, under the names of many non-existent men, thousands of dollars.

Once again Kastel was revealed as backer and principal profit-taker of another bankrupt bucket-shop, Goldberg & Heim.

Mr. Kastel was smooth and garrulous. Some of the Broadway crowd believed him to be of Japanese descent. He was small, slim of build, had a rather flat nose, slanting eyes and tight mouth.

Kastel decided that Fallon could be of immeasurable service to the bucket brigade. He put Fallon on the payroll, but entered his name in obscure, complicated, and code-hidden books.

"We're all crooks down here in the Street," Kastel said, "but some of us belong to an exclusive financial club."

Gertrude Vanderbilt succeeded Ina Claire as leading lady of David Belasco's "Gold Diggers." She and Fallon visited frequently with Mr. Belasco. The latter suggested that Fallon go on the stage. The dean of the drama said he would have Willard Mack collaborate on a vehicle suited to the Fallon temperament.

Belasco liked to recall old triumphs, but essentially he was not of the past. He was forever looking toward new stars, new successes. Fallon sounded out Belasco concerning his youthful association with famous women. Belasco refused to "give up" information concerning long-ago romances, but once he said to Fallon:

"When I was a youngster in Paris, I took flowers to the great Bernhardt."

"Then what?"

Mr. Belasco smiled. "She ran her beautiful fingers through my hair."

"Then what?"

"We were life-long friends."

Concerning his celebrated collar, Belasco said: "It is really not a clerical affair. I actually wear an Ascot tie. Black, yes, but not ecclesiastical."

"Certain critics charge you with insincerity of gesture," Fallon said.

"Certain of my critics should be digging their graves. They'll need them soon."

"Do you regard yourself as sincere in everything?"

"My dear William Fallon, you and I are much the same. We both believe implicitly in the thing we are planning, or the thing we are doing *at the moment*. Tomorrow brings other plans and other beliefs. That is as it should be with the artist, with the man who is not in a rut. However, the one thing we do believe in, always and unchanging, is beauty. Well, come over to the theater. I want you to see some tiles from the Alhambra and some fine armor I just got."

Above the Belasco Theater in West Forty-fourth Street, Mr. Belasco kept one of the finest private collections of jades, amber, rare glass, and antiques. In one portion of his "work-shop" was an array of Napoleoniana; books, letters, furniture, a campaign hat of the Emperor, and numerous rosaries that had belonged to Josephine. He asked Fallon to sit at a desk that had belonged to Alexandre Dumas, the better to view a suit of fourteenth-century armor.

"Dumas wrote *The Count of Monte Cristo* at this desk, and——" Mr. Belasco's eyes bulged. "Well, I'll be damned!" He walked over to the armor, examined it and then exploded. "The God-damned focl!"

"What's wrong, D.B.?"

"Ruined! By God! Raped!"

"What on earth?"

"This armor! It was a priceless piece. Somebody has *shined it with stove-polish*."

By now Broadway agreed that Fallon cared for Miss Vanderbilt more than he had for any other woman. He was a constant visitor at her home, No. 309 West Eighty-fourth Street. Of the money he accepted from Dillon & Co. (Kastel), much was received when the firm was actually insolvent. Two checks, one for $1,000 and another for $3,000, went to Miss Vanderbilt (according to testimony before Referee Olney), and were used to pay Halstead & Gresser for plumbing at the Eighty-fourth Street house.

Nearly all the Dillon firm's customers were out-of-town innocents, some of them on the edge of poverty. These persons contributed from their savings, their money being spent by Kastel in Broadway profligacies and at the race tracks.

Trustee Keyes Winter said that when Daniel Dillon opened his office in March, 1921, his capital consisted of no cash, an earning capacity of $100 a week and a life insurance policy for $3,000. Dillon was in control of the firm for only a week. Then Kastel took it over and a contract was drawn with Kastel, Harold Sonking, and Frank B. Taylor. Kastel was to provide cash capital of $50,000 and was to manage the business, transferring to Dillon & Co. the business of Dunn & Co. (which was Kastel's concern).

Dillon's contribution was his name and his respectability, for which he was to receive $200 a week and 5 per cent of the profits. Kastel was to get 65 per cent of the profits; Sonking and Taylor 15 per cent each.

Actually Kastel put only $20,000 into the firm. The business was that of a regular stock brokerage house, but had no connections with any firm owning membership in any exchange. The only way business could be done by the company was through regular channels and by paying the regular commissions.

Within a week, Kastel's original $20,000 had been checked out, and from that time on, all funds came from customers' cash advances for the purchase of stock.

"It is possible to report," Trustee Winter said, "that during six months' existence, the bankrupt firm dealt with 264 bona fide customers, whose names appear on the books. A great volume of the orders of these customers was obtained by solicitors talking over the telephone from New York City or Albany. The bankrupt's telephone expenses were relatively enormous—$7,667.71 for the six months."

From these customers, Dillon & Co. collected $321,351.68 in cash, and securities representing $253,509.72. They took the savings of women and boys. Nothing appeared too insignificant to be accepted by Kastel's firm.

Trustee Winter found that Kastel had paid $8,630 to Fallon in the first two months. He learned that Kastel had purchased for Doris Sheerin, a motion-picture actress, a Hudson seal coat. Kastel handed the furrier a Dillon & Co. check for $910, and said: "I'm the whole works in that firm."

Mr. Winter examined Sam Goldberg, a former Dillon bookkeeper, endeavoring to follow the intricate trail of the Fallon account. He found that it led to an account under the name of Ernest Eidlitz. It also bore the title of "Account No. 2,000."

Eidlitz was Fallon's general handy-man. A short, hugely built fellow of middle age, Eidlitz accompanied Fallon as a mascot on Broadway sorties. He affected to know everything about Fallon and blinked mysteriously whenever his chief's name was mentioned. Eidlitz kept his eyes and ears open, and later permitted his mouth to follow suit. Right now he was Fallon's devoted servant and pal. He called his master "Pill." He lived on the fat of the land—and on some of the lean, too.

Although urged to represent actions for divorce, and for large fees, Fallon refused that type of practice.

"I am fundamentally opposed to divorce," he said, "because of religious grounds and my own personal taste. I want none of it."

There is but one instance where Fallon consented to represent a divorce plaintiff. He brought the husband and wife into conference, then lectured them and effected a reconciliation.

Fallon appeared in the case of Colonel Samuel L. James and Mildred Adams. The Colonel was a speculator and a horse-racing handicapper. Mildred Adams claimed to be the turfman's wife. She sued him in 1923 for $250,000, alleging that the Colonel had engineered a fake wedding and subsequently had married another woman in New Orleans. She said the Colonel thus had broken his pledge to support her for life.

Miss Adams entered legal proceedings against the Colonel. In settlement, Colonel James released $7,500 of American Telephone & Telegraph Company stock, an $11,000 balance in the brokerage house of J. S. Bache, and otherwise paid Miss Adams substantially.

When Miss Adams retained Fallon & McGee, she placed in their hands as evidence a bundle of the Colonel's letters, certain stock, and a certificate purporting to be the marriage paper that had sealed her to the Colonel. Mr. Fallon, with his usual carelessness, put these things in the ornate cellarette given him by the younger Oscar Hammerstein.

One day Fallon received a tip that the certificate was a forgery. Shortly thereafter Miss Adams' belongings disappeared from the cellarette. Fallon had promised to produce the certificate and other evidence in court. When commanded to do so, he said his office had been burglarized. Miss Adams was panicky. She demanded that Fallon return the evidence. Fallon faced contempt when he claimed he could not do so. Fortunately, he was able to fall back on a photostatic copy of the certificate, which McGee had had made. Otherwise the existence of such a document would have been moot. Even so, Fallon was in bad odor, both with client and court.

Supreme Court Justice Lydon substituted Attorney J. Gainsburg as counsel at the request of Miss Adams. Three attorneys appeared one morning, each representing a separate issue involving an order to show cause why the certificate, stock, and letters should not be returned to Colonel James instead of to Miss Adams' new attorney, Gainsburg. Justice Lydon signed an order commanding Fallon to surrender all documents and property he was holding for Miss Adams.

J. H. Gilbert represented Colonel James. In his argument, he alleged that Miss Adams had "burglariously entered" the James apartment at No. 200 West Fifty-fourth Street and had taken $51,000 in securities. Mr. Gilbert intimated black-mail.

Attorney Gainsburg rose. "This southern gentleman, whom I may refer to as a common gambler, married my client. When Mildred James came back from the hospital, Colonel James threw her out. She refused to live with him when she found he had another wife in New Orleans."

Mr. Gainsburg then wanted a referee appointed to decide if Fallon's cellarette burglary claim was authentic. Mr. Fallon rose to say:

"Fallon & McGee need no apologists, and we offer no excuses."

It was Fallon's habit, when in court, to refer to himself in the third person. He added:

"Fallon offers no excuses. Fallon & McGee join you in asking for a referee."

The court reserved decision. Miss Adams claimed that her marriage ceremony had been performed by Magistrate Peter Barlow. He since had died.

There was considerable talk about Miss Adams bringing a bigamy charge against the Colonel. Word leaked out that Arnold Rothstein had approached Colonel James, saying: "If this charge is made, you'd better take advantage of my bonding company." This made it appear that Fallon, although representing Miss Adams, had staged the robbery of the cellarette to destroy evidence.

"Well," said Fallon, "I'm not going to worry. I think I'll pull out of this mess pretty soon."

Terence Farley was appointed referee in a proceeding started to determine whether Fallon & McGee should be adjudged in contempt of court for their failure to turn over the evidence to Miss Adams when she retained new counsel.

Fallon's journalistic associate at Fordham, Congressman Loring M. Black, was counsel for Colonel James. Congressman Black put Fallon on the stand before Referee Farley. He began to rake The Great Mouthpiece without stint.

Then came an unexpected event. Colonel James received the alleged marriage certificate *through the mails*. It was a very mysterious happening. Then, when matters still looked cloudy for Fallon, he prevailed on the Colonel and Miss Adams to take an automobile ride.

"Just go out together and look over Riverside Drive. See if you can't talk things through."

At the office of Terence Farley an announcement suddenly came that Colonel James had agreed to pay and forget.

Mr. Fallon retreated to the Knickerbocker Grill, ordered a fine steak and said to his platonic friend, Hannah Pearce:

"I was born lucky. May I cut your steak for you?"

Fallon represented twenty-three defendants of the firm of Durrell-Gregory in October and November of 1922. They were charged with fraudulent use of the mails in selling American Tire Company stock. On the jury was one Charles W. Rendigs. He was Juror No. 3. He held out steadfastly for acquittal.

About this Juror No. 3, a storm gathered, later to break with devastating force, bringing together in battle some of the most powerful influences of press and politics.

Although seven persons, in addition to the twenty-three who were tried, had pleaded guilty to using the mails to defraud, and six of the twenty-three had declined to put in any defense, the jury brought in a verdict of not guilty. They had been deliberating four hours. United States District Judge Rufus E. Foster discharged the defendants.

Chapter Twenty-Two

THE PRETZEL-BENDERS' CONVENTION

EDWARD MARKLE FULLER and William Frank McGee, operators of E. M. Fuller & Co., bucket-shop, failed on the Consolidated Exchange for more than $4,000,000. They were tried three times without a conviction. William J. Fallon was their attorney. The names of many persons prominent in New York affairs entered this case.

Foremost among the official figures involved was Thomas F. Foley, Alfred E. Smith's political sponsor. "Big Tom" was an old-fashioned boss, picturesque, good-hearted, loyal to his friends. He was a native of Williamsburg, now a part of the Eastern District of Brooklyn. He was born in a tenement house, February 3, 1852. He quit public school at thirteen to become a butcher's errand boy, being unusually large and strong for his age.

At fifteen he was helper and apprentice in a blacksmith shop. He became acquainted with numerous truck drivers and listened to them talk politics. While still in his teens he frequented a saloon in Bedford Avenue. It was a font of political wisdom. In 1870 he acquired a proprietary interest in the place. When the saloon was raided, Foley moved to Manhattan, where he joined Tammany Hall. That was in 1873, and after the collapse of the Tweed Ring.

He worked in a saloon and was useful to his party. In 1876 he became owner of a bar in Walker and Oliver Streets. He acquired other drinking-places, and in 1877 was captain of an election zone of the old 3rd Assembly District, of which William P. Kirk was "boss."

Foley's principal saloon was for years in Center and Franklin Streets, across from Criminal Courts Building and The Tombs. Politicians found it a convenient rendezvous. Lawyers and friends of prisoners at The Tombs gathered there. Foley maintained an office adjoining the saloon, where he conducted a real-estate business. He also was active in the placing of bail-bonds.

Foley was for some years a friend and lieutenant of Patrick J. Divver, known as "Paddy" Divver, boss of the old 2nd District. Divver provided a five-story clubhouse in Madison Street, his organization being known as the Divver Club. A few years later, Foley quarreled with Divver and set out to wrest from him the district leadership. Together with Daniel Riordan— later Congressman—Eugene Driscoll, and others, Foley opened the Downtown Tammany Club. It was across the street from Divver's. In a short time Foley won patronage for Democratic voters of the district. He supplanted Divver as leader.

The feud continued for eleven years, lasting after Divver's death and being maintained by Divver's son. In the autumn of 1912, young Divver joined the Foley forces after Driscoll had bolted Big Tom.

Meantime, in 1897, Foley had become a member of the old City Council for one term. Later he served on the Board of Aldermen. In the fall of 1907, Tammany Hall elected Foley as Sheriff. He served two years, then retired, but his leadership continued.

In 1915, Mike Rofrano—backed by Mayor John Puroy Mitchell—made a desperate bid to oust Foley. The rivalry was violent. Gunmen participated. It was claimed there was a plot to assassinate Foley. One of his lieutenants, Michael Camara, was slain. Rofrano was tried for the murder, but was acquitted. Foley won the contest for leadership.

One of Foley's most bitter feuds was with William Randolph Hearst, and on account of the Driscoll bolt. Foley vigorously opposed the publicist's efforts to dominate the New York Democracy.

After the Driscoll affair, Foley said: "I am Hearst's enemy for life, and I'll do everything in my power to beat him for any office." Foley threatened to withdraw from Tammany Hall if it allied itself with Hearst. When the publicist ran for office, ballot boxes full of Hearst votes were dumped in the Hudson. The vote-counters could not swim.

Foley, by himself, was enough to make Hearst and his editors gag, but the publicist's pet hate was Alfred Emanuel Smith. As Smith's political godfather, Foley drew added fire from the Hearst cannon. Smith stood the attacks without undue comment until a day in 1919, when his mother opened a Hearst newspaper and read a charge that her son, Al, was responsible for a scandalous milk situation that affected the babies of the lower East Side. There was a milk-war, the farmers withholding their milk from January 1 to January 18. Smith's mother wept and otherwise was upset. The then Governor Smith's brown derby bounced with rage. The Hearst papers might attack him; it was all in the game. But when pictures of starving babies were shown, with a caption charging Smith with the condition, and when Smith's mother was hurt by the implication, it was too much. He went after Hearst in Smithsonian earnest. He claimed that the baby-pictures were photographs taken in Armenia, and not portraits of New York infants.

After the three Fuller & McGee hung juries, and in the spring of 1923, Nat J. Ferber, a reporter for The New York *American*, was assigned at the request of Mr. Hearst to find out "who was protecting the bucket-shops." Mr. Ferber was asked to discover why persons such as Fuller & McGee came again and again into court and never suffered conviction. Mr. Hearst was convinced that some powerful influence was protecting these men. He thought—and hoped—that Foley and Tammany Boss Charlie Murphy were the "influence."

Mr. Ferber now is a distinguished novelist. He then was a distinguished journalist, a digger, and an extraordinary reporter in an era of top-notch news gatherers. He had been places and seen things. Born in a tenement near Brooklyn Bridge in 1889, he became successively a messenger boy for the A.D.T., an errand boy on a newspaper, a grocer's boy, a rubber in a Turkish Bath, a watchman in the same bath on "ladies' day," a super in a stock company, a candy butcher, an all-star athlete, a contributor to The New York *Evening Mail*, a prize-fight trainer, a copy boy, a "ringer" on the football team of a private school, a rustler of cans of beer for beauty-parlor clients and care-taker of his mother's babies. Then, after he had lost a water-race from Brooklyn Bridge to Coney Island—a one-legged swimmer beating him by half a mile—he turned accountant. Later he became a star reporter.

In newspaper work, Ferber studied the State's method of retiring bonds. His subsequent articles on the subject led the State of New York to make drastic changes in its financial system. His exposition of bond-steals of $31,000,000 resulted in the resignation of several public men. The Ferber articles led the late Supreme Court Justice William Howard Taft to call into council, in Philadelphia, all the District Court Judges of the nation with a view toward reorganizing the bankruptcy practice in Federal Courts.

On receiving the Hearst assignment to uncover the "higher-ups" in the bucket-shop ring, Ferber left the William Street building of the *American* and went to Childs' Bowery Restaurant. He amused himself for a time watching Bradford Merrill, Hearst's millionaire General Manager, nibble crackers and sip milk. He wondered about life in general; then got to thinking of particulars, such as a possible reason for Mr. Merrill wearing an ancient set of spectacles that were minus one temple.

Having been an accountant, Mr. Ferber decided he would like to peek at the books of Fuller & McGee. But how? They were in the custody of the United States District Court. Mr. Ferber ate butter-cakes, drank coffee, and cogitated. His office was positive that the "higher-up" in the bucket-shop ring was Big Tom Foley. And perhaps Charlie Murphy. Finally Mr. Ferber paid his check and put down a fifteen-cent tip. Mr. Merrill had laid a five-cent gratuity on the line.

"That's how he got rich," Mr. Ferber thought. Then the name "Foley" began to go through his large head. And then the name "Banton." Mr. Joab Banton was District Attorney of New York County. Mr. Foley had helped put him there.

The slim and immaculately dressed Mr. Merrill walked toward the offices of the *American*. Mr. Ferber hastened toward Criminal Courts Building and the offices of Mr. Banton. He was elevated to the third floor and went to the sanctum of Mr. Banton. The official and the journalist exchanged greetings.

Mr. Banton has a sort of Calvin Coolidge face. "What do you want today, Nat?"

Mr. Ferber came to the point at once. "We want Foley."

Mr. Banton smiled with a fidgety sort of humor. "Do you think I've got him hidden in my pocket?"

"No. You've got him in the accounts of Fuller & McGee."

"That's news to me."

"Is it?"

"It is."

"Might I have a look at the accounts."

"The Federal people have all the books."

"Will you give me a note?"

Mr. Banton wrote on the stationery of the District Attorney's office. He addressed the note to an accountant appointed by the Federal Court: "Please let bearer look at the books of Fuller & McGee."

Mr. Ferber went to No. 30 Church Street. He climbed two sets of stairs to the third floor. On his way he noticed the door of a photographer's office on the second floor. Somehow he was registering all sorts of details today, such as Mr. Merrill's missing spectacle-temple and the five-cent gratuity to the Childs' waiter.

On the third floor, in an enormous room where Fuller & McGee had milked four crops of suckers each year, Ferber saw the Federal man. He was a tall, young fellow, who smirked with a rather supercilious manner. He had a little goatee that wig-wagged like a boy scout's signal-flag. He took the note, read it, looked at Ferber and then waved his arms. He indicated the files. There were more than 100 files, most of them in a skelter on the floor. They were dusty and amazingly mixed up. But Mr. Ferber was an accountant.

With a reporter's divination, Ferber decided that any incriminating checks would be grouped somewhere in one nest. But where? He looked about until he found a file marked "District Attorney." He made up his mind to concentrate on that. So prevailing was his intuition that he decided to wait until the Federal man went to lunch. The latter already had expressed a polite annoyance at having been interrupted while thinking of food.

Ferber waited and waited. Finally, at 4 o'clock, he succeeded in starving the fellow out. Lucky for Ferber that he had gone to Childs' for butter-cakes.

Hardly had the man left the great room than Ferber leaped on the file marked "District Attorney." He opened it. His eye fell on a label: "Account 77." And there, smack on the top of a sheaf of checks, was one for Thomas Foley for ten thousand dollars! It was endorsed by Foley. Ferber's eyes stuck out like a bull's horns. He recalled having seen the photographer's office on the floor below. He seized the check and dashed down the stairs. The photographer was about to go into his dark-room to fix a hypo-bath.

"Can you make a photostat? Right away?"

"I could, but——"

"There's twenty-five smackers in it if you'll do it quick."

"What's it of?"

"A check. Here it is. Make it snappy."

"How big do you want it? Same size as this?"

"I want one as big as a window-blind."

"O. K."

Ferber waited until the check was photographed and the plate developed. Then he went back to the Fuller & McGee office, barely beating the Federal man returning from lunch. Ferber examined further Account 77. He came across checks made out to Arnold Rothstein.

Ferber left the finely-whiskered accountant, stopped at the photographic studio, picked up his photostatic copy, rolled it and put it under his arm. He then hastened to his office. His editor was elated. The latter wired Mr. Hearst that they had Mr. Foley on the hip—in fact, that they had him on both hips. Mr. Hearst replied with a few telegraphic hoorays from his San Simeon ranch in California, where he has a front-yard some thirty-five miles wide, and the Pacific Ocean for a duck-pond.

The presence of the Rothstein checks in the Fuller & McGee file was another, although lesser find, that gratified the *American's* editor. Not only would Foley be run to earth, but he would be linked with old Massa-Mind Rothstein, a bird of sinister plumage. Then there was Bill Fallon, The Great Mouthpiece. He had been altogether too cocky to suit certain members of the press. He was continually giving scoops to Herbert Bayard Swope of The *World*. When Nicky Arnstein surrendered, hadn't Fallon given The *World* an exclusive? And beyond all that, here was an opening wedge for a great crusade; for days of colorful, scandalous news, that might, as one editor suggested, "rock two continents." An editor on the trail of a story displays a passion greater than that of any ten boatswains, home after a year's cruise.

Daily, and for some days, Ferber visited District Attorney Banton. Always he carried beneath his arm a rolled-up photostatic copy of the Foley check. The original photostat had not been large enough to suit Ferber. He had an office photographer do one as big as a hotel blanket.

"What did you find?" Mr. Banton always asked politely. "Anything interesting?"

"Not much," Ferber would reply. "But we still want Foley. Will you deliver him?"

Ferber called on Mr. Banton one calm morning, said "hello," and unrolled his huge photostat on Mr. Banton's desk.

"How do you explain *this?*"

Mr. Banton examined it thoughtfully. He said he hadn't announced the existence of this check, for the reason that, if he had done so, it might interfere with a civil suit pending against the bankrupts.

Mr. Ferber said: "Uh huh!" and re-rolled his photostat.

The Hearst papers then broke the story. They began a bucket-shop crusade that was effective and amazing. Ferber uncovered gigantic swindles and acquitted himself with his usual skill. The Hearst columns attacked Foley savagely.

Ferber exposed 81 bucket-shops that were improperly charging their customers six per cent interest on five billion dollars worth of non-existent securities. He disclosed that these firms had been doing this sort of thing for three years. And almost everywhere the name of Fallon appeared. He was personal advisor to thirty per cent of the 81 concerns. The *American* decided to put the screws on Fallon.

It has been generally charged, and widely-believed, that William Randolph Hearst bore a personal grudge against Fallon; that he wanted him out of the way. The fact is that Hearst, up to the bucket-shop crusade, never had seen or known Fallon, and that the wild tales tending to explain the publicist's supposed hatred for Fallon are pure poppycock. As for subsequent attacks, Mr. Hearst didn't order them, either. He was interested, first, in settling an old score with Foley; second, in uncovering the real reason for jury disagreements in the trials of crooked financiers.

So far as Hearst himself was concerned, Fallon was a whisper that turned into a gale.

Getting the goods on Fallon was a man's size job. The *American* put reporter-sleuths to work. First they tried to cajole Gertrude Vanderbilt into peaching. This, it would seem, was a rather mystifying move, inasmuch as women usually don't "turn in" the men they love.

Next, the *American* got in touch with the huge Ernie Eidlitz,

Fallon's handy man, lobby-gow and 300-pound Broadway mascot. Mr. Eidlitz and his boss, "Pill," were not getting on so well together. Fallon charged that Ernie had been manipulating funds in a random manner. Ernie was pouting.

One day Fallon dined at Billy La Hiff's Tavern in West Forty-eighth Street. While there he saw his 300-pound Broadway mascot and lobby-gow, Ernie Eidlitz. Ernie was cashing a check. Fallon took him aside:

"I'm fed up with you," he said to Ernie.

"Why, what's wrong, Pill?"

"You're not going to 'Pill' me much longer! You're fired."

"What you mean, Pill? You couldn't do that!"

"You've been forging my name to checks, that's what."

"I never done it, 'Pill'."

"You just now 'done' it. Get out."

"When the *American* learned that 'Pill' had fired fat Ernie, they pounced on this development, using eloquence, food, and luxurious lodging to induce the bounced handy-man to talk concerning back-stage matters. Among other things, Ernie said that Fallon had robbed his own office in the Colonel James—Mildred Adams case. He told of many gay and immoral parties, but that wasn't news to the *American*, or to the world at large. Then Ernie opened up on Fallon's bucket-shop litigation. He was sure that Fallon was a giver of bribes.

Meanwhile all sorts of complicated inquiries and prosecutions were occurring. Whenever Fallon's bucket-shop clients came to court, it seemed impossible for the authorities to get their accounts. Books disappeared mysteriously.

Although attorney (under cover) for Kastel's firm of Dillon & Co., Fallon refused to inject himself into the case when it came before Referee in Bankruptcy Peter B. Olney, Jr. By now he was facing contempt-of-court proceedings in both State and Federal Courts. He was also, with Gene McGee, under indictment for destruction of bankruptcy records.

After Trustee Winter submitted his report to Referee Olney,

Fallon was called to the stand to explain various checks that had gone to him as Kastel's counsel. Fallon refused to answer questions on the ground they would tend to incriminate and degrade him.

Questions on which he pleaded constitutional privilege had to do with checks paid him by Dillon & Co., at a time when the firm was insolvent. Trustee Winter protested to Referee Olney that Fallon could not plead constitutional privilege. The Referee said he would permit the lawyer to enter the plea, but would give Mr. Winter a certificate to take the matter before a Federal Court. It was said to be most unusual for an attorney to prefer claiming his constitutional privilege to answering questions in court-proceedings of this character.

Fallon squirmed out of this difficulty and also was acquitted of the charge of destruction of records. Too, he evaded the contempt-of-court commitment with unusual eloquence and persuasiveness. The Hearst papers began thundering the slogan: "Get Fallon and Get Out." They referred to the "Broadway and Forty-second Street Bar Association" and dubbed Fallon the "King Kleagle of the Kriminal Klan."

The *American*, it seemed, was unable to hook Big Tom Foley for Mr. Hearst. It was necessary to land someone of sinister import, so Fallon became the principal game for journalistic sharkhunters. Instead of worrying about the situation (as a less cocksure man might have), Fallon thought up practical jokes. One of them was to get some of his underworld cronies to follow certain editors, popping from doorways like cuckoos from Swiss clocks. They scowled and behaved as though they were gunmen hired to do away with offending journalists.

The Arnold Rothstein checks, unearthed by Ferber, bore an amusing history. Messrs. Fuller and McGee were high-flying play-boys. Fuller liked to gamble. Rothstein accommodated him. The Great Pawn-Broker devised a simple but effective game— that of betting on automobile license numbers.

Rothstein and the bucket-shop big shots would stand at a busy corner and watch the motor traffic. They would choose the type of car they wished to wager on—a Cadillac, a Lincoln, or what have you?—then Fuller or McGee would elect whether they wished to bet on an odd or an even license number. If Fuller or McGee chose "odd," Rothstein would bet on the "even." Rothstein had amazing luck at this game. He should have, for it developed that he employed a fleet of assorted motor cars, an odd and an even number of each make, after the manner of Noah choosing animals for the ark. Rothstein's chauffeurs parked up the street and responded to his signals. When the pot was extraordinarily large and Rothstein needed an "odd" Cadillac, he would signal, and the "ringer" would dash into the breach. His crowning gesture in this respect was the day he suggested they bet on Mack trucks. At the crucial moment, and with Fuller wagering $10,000 on an "even" Mack, Rothstein's own "ringer" rumbled past with a load of bricks. . . . These were the checks that Fuller & McGee paid Rothstein. There were others, representing wagers on the crooked world's series, and some horse-races that may or may not have been fixed by The Great Pawn-Broker.

Fuller worked hard at his bucketing to make money, for the sheer joy of spending it. McGee was industrious at the illicit game, desiring wealth wherewith to build himself into prestige and power. He was the husband of Louise Groody, musical-comedy star.

Ferber's exposé resulted in William H. Silkworth, President of the Consolidated Exchange, going to jail. Silkworth once was a famous trap-shooter. He left his clay-pigeons to enter the Wall Street shooting-gallery, and was an up-and-coming man. When Silkworth went to jail, the Consolidated Building in Stone Street and Exchange Place, housing the second largest exchange in the country, was torn down. Financial bag-men skurried to cover. The skies were full of clouds.

In June, 1923, Big Tom Foley induced Charles A. Stoneham, principal owner of the New York Giants, to lend Fuller & McGee $147,500 in an effort to stave off the firm's bank-

ruptcy. Stoneham received back only $10,000. Foley himself
had lent McGee $15,000 before soliciting Stoneham. When
asked on the stand why he didn't take a note for the $15,000,
Big Tom replied:

"What the hell good is a note? If you pull out, all right.
If not, put it down as a bad bet."

The seventy-three-year-old Tiger, next in rank to Tammany
Boss Murphy, gave his testimony before Referee Harold P.
Coffin at No. 217 Broadway. He said he had endorsed none of
the checks from Stoneham, although each bore his name on the
back. He explained he had told McGee to endorse the first check.

"I assumed he did the same with all the others."

"How did you happen to intercede for these almost bankrupt
men?"

"I didn't know the partners very well," said Foley. "I am
a fool, and I've been a damned fool all my life. But I was
asked for help by McGee's wife (his first one, and not Miss
Groody). I have known her since girlhood."

"But didn't you know this was a bucket-shop?"

Big Tom grunted. "I don't know the difference between bucket-shop, the Curb or the Big Exchange. I only knew McGee's
wife, Nellie Sheehan, and that she needed help."

Big Tom turned down few calls for help during his long
life. This is indicated by his leaving a $15,000 estate out of
perhaps two millions of dollars that came his way. He was not
a spendthrift, in the accepted sense. He was a philanthropist, who
came from behind beer-taps and butcher-blocks to high political
influence.

It was Foley who got Fallon to defend Fuller & McGee. It
was only because of Foley that Fallon consented to represent
these men, for he never liked them.

The State Courts apparently could get nowhere with Fuller
& McGee. In Fuller's third trial, the jury again disagreed. It
was during this action that reporters Ferber and Carl Helm of
the *American* scanned the list of talesmen with great care. It

was they who noticed that one of the jurors was Charles W. Rendigs. They watched results carefully, and when Rendigs was one of four that held out for acquittal, they recalled that he had served as a juror in the Durrell-Gregory Federal case. In replying to questions qualifying him as a juror, Rendigs had sworn he never had known Fallon.

He now faced criminal action. Mr. Fallon defended him. The *American* began to work on Rendigs. The matter was laid before Colonel William Hayward, United States Attorney, with a view of establishing that Fallon had bribed Rendigs in the Durrell-Gregory case. A busy time was had by all.

On July 2, 1923, a Federal Grand Jury handed up four sealed indictments to Judge Fitzhenry. There were nine days of wonderment as to whom the findings related. On July 11, the judge opened the indictments. They named four principals: Edward Markle Fuller, William Frank McGee, William J. Fallon, and Charles W. Rendigs.

Fallon and his partner, Gene McGee, had frequented the corridors of the Federal Building daily, waiting for the opening of the indictments. On the day their contents became known, Fallon sat on a step at the head of the third-floor stairs.

"Why are you looking so solemn, Bill?" asked a reporter. "Don't you think you can beat this rap?"

"That's not what bothers me. It's this story in the *American.*"

"You mean the one about being the 'King Kleagle'?"

Fallon displayed a clipping. "This one. Somebody wrote that Fallon is looking seedy and down at the heels; that he is wearing shabby clothes. And after I've just spent $250 apiece for four suits, especially for the occasion! I'm going to sue my tailor."

The Fallon indictment charged him specifically with bribing Rendigs with $25,000 in the Durrell-Gregory case. Similar talk of bribery had followed the third Fuller trial the preceding May, but Rendigs at that time had said that the jury's failure to reach a decision had been due to doubt as to whether the testimony of J. Harold Braid, regarding Fuller's bucketing operations, had been corroborated by the account books.

The jurors had asked for these books, but Judge Nott ruled they were not entitled to have them in the jury-room. The bribery accusation in the Fuller case was made by J. Howard Beidleman. He charged that his secretary had been approached with a bribe of $1,000, offered by Edward J. McManus. McManus was indicted by the County Grand Jury.

In a fourth trial of Fuller for bucketing and grand larceny, Fuller and McGee began to get weak in the knees. Against Fallon's urgings, they decided to change their plea to guilty. The bucketeers had run afoul of the Federal courts. They had withdrawn certain papers from the receiver of the bankrupt firm of Fuller & McGee. Referee Harold P. Coffin ruled that the Trustee was entitled to everything belonging to the business. These papers were not forthcoming. Judge Mack upheld the Referee. Judge Goddard, after a reasonable wait, adjudged Fuller and McGee in contempt. He committed them to Ludlow Street Jail on May 18.

Fallon failed this time to keep his clients out of jail on the contempt charge. He argued a writ of *habeas corpus* before United States District Judge Learned Hand, but couldn't make an impression. The Judge characterized his argument as "preposterous." Still the most brazen of attorneys, Fallon began to quote decisions. The opposing attorneys were startled when he spouted glibly in support of his contentions. After a whispered consultation, one of the counselors rose and addressed the court.

"If Your Honor please, Mr. Fallon has been quoting two entirely different decisions, making them appear as *one and the same decision.*"

The court looked meaningly at Fallon, but refrained from comment.

Later that month, Fallon had a violent quarrel with Fuller & McGee. He charged them with lack of courage. They discharged Fallon as their counsel and retained Charles E. Griffiths, of Griffiths & Content, No. 12 Broadway.

The Federal indictment of Fuller & McGee charged them

with using the mails to defraud, through the operations of Charles H. Clarkson & Co., the Fuller & McGee installment-plan subsidiary. The partners of the Clarkson concern were Clarkson, Vernon B. Ingram, and Charles A. Gilham, whose wife was a cousin of William Frank McGee. The company began as a corporation, but when it was about to sink into bankruptcy, Gilham said they were advised that a corporation's books could be seized, but a partnership's could be protected under constitutional privilege. Clarkson & Company immediately ceased being a corporation and became a partnership. Fuller & Company contributed $100,000 to start Clarkson & Company. They handed it to Leo J. Bondy, best known as attorney for Charles A. Stoneham. Bondy deposited it. He then wrote out his own check instead. Then Fuller & Company withdrew $80,000 of the capital. Certain of the books were destroyed.

Colonel William Hayward, United States Attorney, investigated the Fallon-Rendigs bribery charge for six weeks. His assistant, Victor House, laid the evidence before the June grand jury. Fuller made two offers to "tell everything" if Colonel Hayward would grant immunity. This Colonel Hayward refused to do.

The Federal indictments charged that Fallon on November 6, 1922, gave Rendigs a check for $1,000; that he followed this with $1,500 on October 5, 1922, the day on which the juror was sworn in; that Fallon conspired to obstruct justice.

Fallon and Rendigs had met, according to the indictment, at Joseph R. Pani's Woodmansten Inn in the Bronx, on the day Rendigs became a Federal petit juror. Mr. Fallon, it was said, was accompanied by Countess Gosta Morner, otherwise Miss Peggy Joyce, when Rendigs came to the inn. It was asserted that the $1,000 check was drawn by Agnes R. Fallon and given by Fallon to Joseph R. Pani. The latter drew a Woodmansten Realty Corporation check for the same amount. This was given to Rendigs, according to the charge, and he deposited it on November 8.

Chapter Twenty-three

MR. FALLON CONSULTS THE STARS

HEARST's New York *American* added Fuller & McGee to their growing list of informants. The partners confessed their sins in a Park Row camp-meeting. There were too many eavesdropping Tammanyites; first at Ludlow Jail, and again at Governors Island, where the bucketeers now had lodging. The *American* represented itself as interested in justice, and persuaded the authorities to transfer Fuller and McGee to another place, which Julius Caesar might have described as a distant, fortified position. In the custody of United States marshals, and with great secrecy, Fuller and McGee became prisoners in the Hotel McAlpin.

Other newspapers learned of the hegira from the Island. But only the *American* had *entrée* to the hotel "cell-block."

To insure privacy, the *American* hired an entire wing of one floor; nineteen rooms in all, overlooking West Thirty-fourth Street. The reporters could view below them the sedentary statue of their pal, Horace Greeley, his bronze hair grayed by the carelessness of pigeons, and his wrinkled metal pants looking as though they once had belonged to Heywood Broun.

To keep the bucket-boys in good humor, McGee's wife, Louise Groody, visited him, as also did Fuller's girl. Then arrived a retinue of old friends of the former high-flying firm, to help them remember remote indiscretions in the stock racket. The partners could no more recall all their depredations than can a barber remember the individual hair-cuts of yesteryear.

One of these memory-prodders was an old chap. He was white-haired, red-cheeked, and saintly of countenance. He had a Cockney accent. Despite his seraphic expression, he had been one of the world's most famous card-sharps on transoceanic liners and de luxe trains. He reformed completely and abruptly one afternoon aboard the Congressional Limited, Washington-bound. He had engaged in a game of chance with a Congress-man, who not only turned out to have marked his deck, but trimmed the sharper worse than the legislator ever had hood-winked his constituency.

"It was a body-blow," the man said. "I never cared for cards after that—or for Congressmen. I was broken-'earted."

Reporters for several journals soon got wind of the new Fuller-McGee location. They stood on adjoining buildings with telescopes and binoculars, trying to penetrate the smug privacy of the curtained windows. Secret-service men cluttered the halls. It looked as though Mr. Hearst's men were starting a zoo.

It became necessary to sequester certain of the memory-prodders, to prevent leaks. They lived well. The former card-player was as irritable as the skipper of a becalmed clipper. When asked if anything was wrong with the food or the McAlpin mat-tresses, he sighed like a loose screen-door:

"I'm not used to such hinactivity. A man such as me must keep hoccupied."

"Why don't you play cards or something?"

The ex-card manipulator acted as though someone had slipped him an emetic. "Ever since that time on the Congressional Limited——"

"I know," said the *American* man. "We'll have to find you a job."

"For goodness sake, please do!"

The *American* man did some telephoning, then informed the former card-sharp that he was going to work.

"What doing?"

"Selling the *Encyclopaedia Britannica*. A swell job."

The guest raised his hands. "A very fine job, yes, as jobs

go. But how can I sell them when I am being detained here, a virtual prisoner?"

"Sell them to this mob right here."

For a day or two, the ex-card player kept walking about the nineteen rooms, interrupting important snitching by Fuller and McGee. The hotel-wing echoed with his wails: "I got a job, but no customers."

Finally, to keep the man from thinking on such matters as lack of trade and the Congressional Limited Affair, the other guests of the *American* began ordering encyclopaedias. The former card-player was elated. He became able to recall countless crooked things that Fallon had told Fuller and McGee to do.

Colonel Hayward placed the prosecution of Fallon and the questioning of Fuller and McGee in the hands of Assistant United States Attorney William Millard, an elderly, fine-mannered gentleman. Mr. Millard had no doubt but the time was propitious for knocking Fallon from off his high horse.

The *American* had a Brooklyn branch of their zoo in the person of fat Ernie Eidlitz. To keep Ernie out of the hands of Fallon's agents, the *American* sequestered him on the top floor of the Hotel Bossert. He was taken there the very night he had a date with his girl, Kitty. The boys kept priming Ernie with champagne and good food. For the time he forgot his tryst with Kitty, and talked volubly about "Pill" and what a terrible menace he was to society.

When Ernie's 300 pounds craved grouse, the boys got it for him. When he wanted roast duck, it appeared as though from Thurston's hat. Then, suddenly belching with grouse, champagne, and remorse, Ernie remembered his broken date. He did not realize that three days had passed in this gastronomic haven. He now wanted Kitty. And how!

When the boys tried to lift Ernie's mind from Kitty to Fallon, that part of him proved as heavy as his body. It was

Kitty he wanted. He insisted all night and next day that he wanted Kitty.

"I have a hunch he wants Kitty," said a reporter-custodian.

At the mention of that beloved name, Ernie rose to his feet and announced abruptly that he was going to "yump" from the hotel window. Fearful of such a splash, the boys went into a Nôtre Dame huddle. They proposed that Ernie risk going to the Bossert roof-garden, there to hear moaning brasses of musicians; there to sample further the delights of the chef's cook-book.

The *American* custodians formed a cordon about fat Ernie. He wobbled to the roof-garden, where Brooklyn's fastidious diners were grouped, the men in dinner-jackets, and the women in evening gowns. The bare shoulders of the women reminded Ernie of Kitty. He sighed, sat down and ordered five partridges. It looked for a time as though the chef would have to send out a party of sportsmen to bag them. Finally, however, they were produced. Veteran waiters marveled at Ernie's technique in wolfing the birds.

Suddenly, and during a pause in the music, and in the polite laughter and the subdued converse of the roof-garden patrons, there came a bellowing groan, then mighty sobs, and the rumble: "I want Kitty!"

Astounded by the sight of such a huge fellow slumping over the tiny bones of former partridges, the diners were numb. Then frightened. Men hurriedly put wraps about the shoulders of their lady-friends and scurried from the room. The place soon was deserted. In the cloak-room, nervous men could be heard saying: "A maniac!" "Who let him in?" And from the aching throat of Ernie: "I want my Kitty!"

With the spectacled Fuller and the round-faced McGee ratting it at high speed, Fallon faced a new disaster in the person of Juror Rendigs. They had been indicted together in State Courts for conspiracy to obstruct the administration of justice.

Rendigs now turned State's evidence and entered a plea of guilty.

The trial was before Fallon's ancient legal foe, former Assistant District Attorney Talley, now General Sessions Judge. Rendigs told how he had visited the Woodmansten Inn and had received Fallon's overtures to hang the jury. He testified he had met Fallon in the apartment of Fuller and McGee to "talk things over."

Referring to himself in the third person, as was his court-custom, Fallon shouted:

"It's a plot to get Fallon out of the way. The Hearst papers are looking for a goat. So they choose Fallon. It is a gigantic conspiracy."

Fallon claimed that Editor Watson was gunning for him because the *American* had been unable to horn in on the Arnstein surrender. He further alleged that efforts had been made to frame him at the Casino in Central Park, where preparations had been made to get his "confession." He intimated that Mr. Hearst had personal reasons for wishing him out of the way.

Mrs. Rendigs, wife of the indicted juror, testified that Fallon had endeavored to make love to her. It is possible that the prosecuting influences overstepped themselves a bit in this as well as other testimony. Fallon raised the cry of: "This is not prosecution. It is persecution." Possibly his mind went back to the time when he worked too vigorously to dethrone and disgrace Warden Thomas Mott Osborne through the lavender implication.

The scenes between Mr. Fallon (who conducted his own case), and Judge Talley were anything but peaceful. The court again and again reprimanded the stormy Fallon, and cautioned him against raising his voice. Mr. Fallon then began some of his old baby-face horse-play. He *tried out* his voice, in the manner of a singing student.

He said that a man facing jail might well be excused for not noticing how loud his voice was when raised in protest against a conspiracy. The jury must have believed Fallon, for they acquitted him.

Gene McGee sat at Fallon's elbow during this storm, and steadied his partner whenever the boat began to rock. The loyalty and friendship of McGee was an outstanding thing.

This case was prosecuted by Assistant District Attorney Hugo Winter, an able and cultured man, whose only fault was that he was too much of a gentleman to make a vicious prosecution effective.

After his acquittal, Fallon went to a speakeasy with a reporter-friend. He seemed disinclined to talk about his troubles. He spoke, rather, of old Fordham days, of baseball, and of Edgar Allan Poe.

"Many stories about Poe concern the Fordham country. Some biographers claim that he was mad. I don't know. Perhaps he was terribly sane, and the rest of the world mad. One of his letters sold recently for more than $400. The irony of it is that this letter carried a plea for a loan of $5. His wife was starving. Well, the high price of the letter shows one thing. It takes a couple of generations or so for the world to forgive a man for having been brilliant. If one wishes to be safe, one must remain mediocre. If a man happens to be a genius, let us say like Byron, humanity requires a century or more to condone that quality. Why, Byron was so gifted that they won't permit his bones to rest in Westminster Abbey. Well, drink up. Here's to Civilization! Here's to mankind that allows babies to starve, and permits rats to squeal."

"What do you consider your most clever trick in court?"

"I have no tricks. There is a great deal of bunk peddled about me. I merely know the law of evidence. In school, that's what I concentrated on most."

"What situation did you manufacture that stands out in your mind?"

"I never manufactured any more situations than did the prosecution. If you mean a psychological effect, I think, off-hand, of the time I was defending a dumb fellow on a murder-charge, first degree. I got him a rosary and told him to wear it in his

breast pocket, with a big handkerchief wrapped about it. He
kicked, saying he was a Methodist; that a rosary was bad luck.
I said: 'You do as I say, and when I lean over and point at you
while you're on the stand, you start bawling and crying. Then
pull out the handkerchief and let the rosary fall to the floor.'
We had to rehearse the thing at least twenty times. I saw to it
that several Catholics were on the jury. The day my client went
on the stand, I worked him into a rather genuine cry. I pointed
my finger, but he didn't go through with the plan. I had to
work on him some more, this time to *lessen* his grief to a point
where he might respond to cues. Then I leaned over, cocked the
old fore-finger and roared: 'Please don't cry. I know it is hard,
but I must ask these questions. Use your handkerchief.' This
roused the dumb cluck. He hauled out the kerchief and the
rosary fell to the floor. I noticed that some of the jurymen almost
jumped over the rail. Well, he was acquitted. I suppose the
rosary didn't do him any harm. . . . Let's go to my apartment,
and get some good stuff. Prohibition has caught me at the wrong
time in life."

After Rendigs had been convicted on May 21, 1924, and
had gone to The Tombs to await sentence, he made overtures
to District Attorney Banton. Within a few days he was telling
his whole story to the Federal authorities.

He revealed in detail and circumstance of having come in
contact with Fallon at a time when he, Rendigs, was in financial
difficulties. The alleged $25,000 bribe, according to Rendigs,
was an exaggeration. It was to be $5,000 for his vote to acquit
Fallon's clients.

"Half the money," said he, "never was paid."

When officers brought Rendigs into Criminal Court for
sentence on May 26, Fallon was in the building. The entire
place was buzzing with a rumor that Rendigs was "about to
come through." There was speculation as to Fallon's fate. When

interested parties combed the building, looking for Fallon, he had disappeared. Rendigs' sentence was postponed.

Fallon had received an inside tip ten minutes before Rendigs came across the Bridge of Sighs. His informant met him near the reporters' room.

"Rendigs has squealed. The whole works! He's on his way over now."

Fallon swallowed hard. He hurried down the broad stairs, not caring to risk the elevator. He went out a side exit, where a taxicab driver was parked. He drove to a friend's house, and there telephoned Gertrude Vanderbilt. Fearful that her telephone was tapped, he had prearranged five possible places for telephonic communication. She knew all the numbers, and all Fallon had to do was to give her the name of any of the five designated exchanges and she knew which number to call. He now said: "Call me at the Stuyvesant number."

Gertrude Vanderbilt had gone through humiliating experiences following her refusal to peach on Fallon. Always her name was linked with his in print. The unwholesome publicity interfered with her professional life, costing her practically all she had to tide the two of them through. Her house and furnishings were heavily mortgaged.

Clients lately had been fearful of retaining Fallon, no matter how brilliant he was. They preferred having an attorney over whom hung no cloud. Gertrude Vanderbilt stuck by Fallon in a manner new and strange to Broadway, advancing money and otherwise shielding him. She knew well enough that he was irresponsible, fickle, and morally unreliable, but she loved him. Her every action in regard to this man was a refutation of the left-handed insinuations that she was "on the make." She had talent, beauty and wealthy admirers. The latter never got as far as mid-field with her.

When she received Fallon's call, she didn't ask any questions. She went to an outside telephone and rang the Stuyvesant number. "I'm coming right away."

His voice sounded plaintive and weak. "They've got every place watched. Be careful."

Miss Vanderbilt didn't want to be seen in her own automobile. She took a cab. When she reached Fallon, she put her arms about him. "We'll see this thing through together."

"You've always been wonderful," he said. "You couldn't be any other way. I'm not well. I don't want to run away, but right now they'd railroad me sure. I've got to spar for time."

"I've got a place."

"Where?"

"Never mind. First I want to stop at Carnegie Hall."

"I don't think we should stop anywhere. Let's get off the streets."

"I want you to go to Evangeline Adams."

Fallon was surprised. "The astrologer?"

"Yes."

"The stars can't tell me much that I don't know."

"We'll see."

Fallon complained of being cold. He sat slumped in the cab-seat, his black fedora low over his brow, his coat-collar turned up.

Gertrude held his hand. "You are getting thin. You must rest."

"I need time. Time to think. Time to act."

"Did you weigh yourself lately?"

"I wish I could get a drink."

"You'd better lay off drinking for a while. Don't you think so?"

"I'd feel better if I had a shot. I've got to decide what to do. I've still got a brain. I've got a better brain than Hearst and all his men put together."

"You mustn't cloud your brain with alcohol."

"If I didn't have a better brain than Hearst, I'd have quit the law long ago."

"Don't worry about things now. Wait till you get your strength back."

Fallon was slightly hysterical. "If I didn't have a better brain than Hearst, I'd go shoot myself. I know why he wants me out of the way. And he knows, too. I'll be ready for him. You just wait."

"Let's talk of something else."

"I suppose you think I'm licked?"

"You'll never be licked."

"McGee gave me a good licking once. Back in Fordham."

"I don't mean that kind of licking."

"Gee, but Fordham is a great place! You haven't any idea how beautiful it was in the old days. So peaceful. So soul-satisfying. I never used to think much about yesterday. Now it seems as though yesterday was the only day there ever could have been."

"There will be a fine tomorrow."

"Yes, there will be a tomorrow. Today I'm hunted. Now I know how my clients felt when they were hunted. There's a sort of humorous phase to it. Hundreds of hawk-eyes looking up alleys for one man. I'm a criminal, the Hearst papers say. You know, whenever they write a story, they always say: 'Bill Fallon, criminal lawyer.' "

"What do you care what the papers say? What anyone says?"

"I mustn't go to jail. I mustn't."

"You won't. You have been clever in other cases, and for men that were no good. Now be clever for yourself. Only try to rest."

"It's so long since I've had rest. The word seems like the name of a stranger, someone I knew in my childhood. An old man whose name was 'Rest.' An old man who used to hold me on his knee when I was a child, and who went away never to return except in dreams. Yes, I'll rest some time. Right now I've got to think."

"You'll have plenty of time to think."

"I was a prosecutor once. I sent a man to prison for life, on a murder-charge. A year later, I found he was innocent. That's what cured me of wanting to prosecute. I got the Governor to pardon the man. But the damage already was done. His baby was the son of a criminal. Won't it be fine for my two girls to know that their father was in prison?"

"You're not going to prison."

"I went after the two that framed this man. I sent them up for perjury. I tried to square things. There was only one thing for me to do, and that was to quit being a prosecutor. I've kept a lot of people out of jail. It's the wrong system anyway. It gets humanity nowhere. It's a confession that civilization is a failure. Maybe everything is a failure."

When they reached Carnegie Hall, Gertrude said: "A lot of people laugh about astrology. But Miss Adams has told me wonderful things."

"You go on up and see her. I don't want to talk to anyone."

"Then you wait here."

Fallon sat back in the cab, his eyes closed. Miss Vanderbilt consulted Miss Adams for two hours. The astrologer studied the day and hour of Fallon's birth in relation to the position of the planets. The stars recommended that Fallon remain in hiding for at least a week.

Fallon's astrological chart, as prepared by Miss Adams' then secretary, Edith W. Kinkhead, showed that the most important testimony in the horoscope was the position of the malefic Saturn in the Ninth House, the House of Law, and its position and aspects to the moon, which ruled his House of Career and Public Standing. The moon was placed in the Twelfth—the most tragic—House of Undoing. Not only was the moon in that House at the hour of Fallon's birth, but it was afflicted by Saturn, Mars, and Uranus, all malefics. The Ruler of Fallon's horoscope was Venus, placed in the kindly, hospitable, and sympathetic, but rather weak sign, Pisces. Venus was in the fifth angle, or House, of the heavens.

Miss Vanderbilt returned to the cab. Fallon was half asleep.

She roused him. "Miss Adams says you have got to be careful, and to clear your mind. She says that you'll survive this trouble."

"I suppose."

"Even if you don't believe her, I do. Now I'll take you where you can get something to eat and a chance to sleep."

"I'm not hungry."

"But you will be."

"All I want is a drink."

"I'm afraid for you to drink. Your face is broken out with fever blisters. You take no care of yourself at all."

"I wonder what Rothstein is saying? He'll be glad to see me on this spot."

"Why should you care what Rothstein or any other person says?"

"Rothstein is peculiar. His whole aim in life is to school himself against fear. That's why he goes up to the toughest characters on Broadway and browbeats them. His system is to take the play away from people. Well, he never could get away with it when I was around."

"Let's not think about Rothstein. Let's think about you."

"He's a contradiction in terms. A lot of us are that way. He actually loves his wife, no matter how much he has neglected her. I have it figured out; he thinks he is not worthy to touch her."

"Oh, quit talking about him! I've got something more important than Rothstein to worry about."

"I have half a mind to drive into Broadway, get out and challenge the whole gang of back-biters. The heels! The squealers!"

"Keep your fighting strength until later. We're going to get you straightened out physically first, and then give your mind a rest."

"You never were critical of me, were you, Baby?"

"I don't know. I didn't preach to you, if that's what you

mean. But that's not saying I want you to drink yourself into the grave and do some of the things you've been doing."

"It's funny the things a man thinks of when he's a fugitive!"

"For instance?"

"We had a dumb fellow in my class at Fordham. Why do I keep thinking of Fordham today? His name was Rasmussen. Well, he's a big politician now. But wasn't he thick? And he still is thick. The public wants thick men at the helm. That's because the public is thick."

"What about Rasmussen?"

"I used to play jokes on him. One night I gave him a jar of iron pyrites and some acid. He was always trying to learn chemistry. I told him: 'Mix this. It's wonderful.' Well, he put the acid on the sulphide. Lord, what an odor! The prefect got up, opened all the windows, and we nearly froze to death while the smell was being banished."

"I guess you're not dying, mentally or physically, so long as you can think of such things."

"My ambition is to be able to laugh when I am on my death-bed. A lot of other people will laugh with me. The Hearst editors, for example."

He was silent for a time. Then he said: "Do you know, Baby, what would get my goat beyond any other thing?"

"No, dear. What?"

"If the judges, instead of getting up and thundering at me and squawking and pounding the gavel, if, I say, one of them were to yawn while I was speaking, it would ruin me for a whole week."

"Nobody ever yawned while you were in court. Or out of it, either."

"I hope I have taken a few years of boredom from the courts. How dull they are! But the public is impressed. They want judges with the faces of nineteenth-century bankers. What do you say we go to a night club? Let's be bold. We might as well."

"Now I *am* getting worried about your mind."

"Where are you taking me?"

"To the house of one of your old clients."

"We're pretty far up-town. Do you mean One Hundred and Ninth Street and Fifth Avenue?"

"Yes. You'll stay there until I'm able to get some money. I can't go to the bank, because I know I've been followed the last day or two. And I know my home, bank, and everywhere else are bound to be watched."

"I'm sorry I'm broke, Baby."

"Don't worry, dear. I've got my jewelry."

"I hate to have you pawn it."

"I'd do anything for you."

"How well I know that! We've had some good times, too, haven't we, Baby?"

"Yes, as good as possible under the circumstances."

"Why do you say it that way?"

"You know what I mean. So let's not go into that. We have a lot else to think about now."

"I never think much about anything but you, Baby."

Fallon stayed in hiding for three days at his former client's home. Gertrude had to raise money. She went to Billy La Hiff's Tavern and cashed a check. On her way out, she ran into Arnold Rothstein and another man named Nate. She endeavored to pass them without speaking.

Rothstein, smiling, stepped in front of her. "Why, Gertie, where are you going? And where have you been?"

"I've been cashing a check, if that means anything to you."

Mr. Rothstein was extra-courteous. "Well, now, Gertie, I would have cashed your check."

"Not my check."

"Now look here, Gertie, Bill was my pal. Of course he was careless, but nevertheless I know he needs money; and he can have it."

"He'll never come to you. So that's that."

Mr. Rothstein shook his head. Gertrude got into a cab and blew him a kiss. Old Massa-Mind stood at the curb a long while, pondering.

Back at the apartment, Gertrude said to Fallon: "I think I've been followed. We'll have to get out of here."

"I'd give myself up in a minute," Fallon said, "only the bail will be prohibitive. We've got to stall for time. Anyway, I'm not at all well. I want to be at my peak when I defend myself."

The Hearst papers gloated over the disappearance of Bill Fallon. It was an act tantamount to admission of guilt. Still, the editors felt that he must be captured to give the journalistic gesture its complete sweep. The *American* laid down a barrage of hoopla headlines.

In its June 3 issue of 1924, The *American* published a facsimile of a Governmental poster describing the fugitive:

"Wanted by the United States Government:

"William J. Fallon.

"Charged with giving a bribe to a petit juror in violation of Section 131 of the U. S. Criminal Code.

"Also for conspiracy to obstruct justice, violation of Section 37, U. S. Criminal Code.

"Also under indictment for concealment of assets from a trustee in bankruptcy and conspiracy so to do.

"Description—Grayish blue eyes, sandy pompadour hair, fair complexion, height five feet ten inches, weight about 165 pounds. Business, Attorney and Counselor-at-law.

"Communicate with United States Attorney, Southern District of New York, Old Post Office Building, Park Row, New York City, N. Y."

The *American* twinned this official bleat with rhetorical belches.

"When he failed to appear before Federal Judge English yesterday to stand trial for bribing Charles W. Rendigs, Fallon had his last chance. Yesterday he became a fugitive from justice.

But the arms of Justice are tireless. And the fingers of Justice are sure and they are strong. Sooner or later Fallon will be brought back to reap as he has sown."

The *American* recalled "that when he came before the Court of Judge Alfred Talley in General Sessions, he roared: 'I am indicted, but why haven't they (the Federal authorities) tried me? They don't dare try me!' "

Here are additional paragraphs from The *American*:

"That he will be disbarred is a foregone conclusion. Such a course, it is agreed by leaders of the bar, will only be a formality."

"Slippery Bill Fallon is through. His bail of $5,000 was forfeited when he did not appear."

When a copy of this newspaper was shown Fallon in his hiding place, he pointed to the disbarment forecast and said: "I guess they have been visiting Evangeline Adams, too."

Gertrude next moved Fallon to the home of George Moore, who had worked with her in vaudeville. They remained there for three days, while Gertrude looked for a furnished apartment. She was rehearsing in a show called "Marge." It was inconvenient for her to be with the fugitive except during the week-ends. She would have thrown over the theatrical work, but Fallon said: "If you do that, I'll go right out and give myself up. I've caused you enough trouble. You mustn't blast your career by throwing down your manager. I'll be all right."

Gertrude found a small apartment near Moore's. It was a homey place of three rooms. Fallon was restless. He paced the apartment at night and got what sleep he could in day-time. He awaited each dawn before retiring. He wanted to see the people come and go to the nearby shops. He welcomed the morning crash of ash-cans on the walks and the clatter of milk bottles. He stood at the window and envied the free people that went in and out the shop-doors.

Fallon's face felt sore. Fever blisters covered his upper lip.

He was unable to shave. He began to grow a scanty, blond moustache. He did not drink during the first days of his retreat. He kept a bottle in reserve, however, planning to swig the liquor in huge draughts whenever capture seemed imminent.

He had but one shirt. He laundered it himself at the apartment wash-basin. When Gertrude came to see him, he said:

"I'm not a very tidy housekeeper. And I'm a rotten cook. My coffee is impossible."

Two days after he had moved into the apartment, Gertrude said, "I don't know how much longer you are going to be safe. I have been followed. I tried all kinds of dodges, changing cabs, walking, and even taking street-cars. I have a hunch that they are closing in."

"All that worries me," Fallon said, "is the bail. It will be enormous. As for the case, I've got it figured out. The most I can get is a year in Atlanta or Leavenworth. But I have another plan, a desperate one."

"What is it?"

"I want to think it over some more. It involves several prominent persons. If they should catch me while you're not here, I'll leave a signal. I don't suppose they'd let me write a note."

"You could muss the house up."

"It's pretty well mussed up now. Tell you what: I'll stuff a pillow in the top dresser-drawer. If I am gone, and you find the pillow there, you'll know they got me."

"I'd probably know it by the newspapers."

"You can't tell. They might keep it quiet for a day or so while they put the works on me."

"Would they dare hurt you?"

"I don't know. I have Hearst and the Government against me. Still, as I said before, if I couldn't beat them, I ought to be sent away for life."

It's a big town and an easy town to hide in, say the fugitives who are known as lammisters. So, when the authorities are hunting a man, they first watch them who love the vanished person. Sometimes it is a mother or a wife that unwittingly betrays the hiding place. More often—and nearly always—it is the girl-friend.

The Government operatives, assisted by city sleuths and reporters for The *American*, followed Gertrude. They were at first unable to locate the apartment, but they were reasonably sure of the neighborhood. They began a house-to-house, and apartment-to-apartment, canvass.

Fallon stayed in his retreat and with the blinds drawn. He removed the lock from the door and substituted a Yale lock provided by Gertrude. He laboriously carved a new hole for the lock, using a rather dull pen-knife. It took him four hours to make the change. He could have used the place occupied by the other lock, but he wanted to have a peep-hole, through which he might inspect callers.

There had been several knocks at his door, but Fallon didn't answer. He had a feeling that capture was near. He began to drink now. He set his quart bottle on a table. He smoked cigarettes one after another. Finally he ran out of smokes. His liquor was two-thirds gone. He was extremely restless. He wanted to walk, to run about the apartment, but was fearful of making a noise. There were squeaky boards in the floor, and each time he took a step it sounded as though a ship's timbers were straining. He removed his shoes, so that his feet would not betray him. He stripped down to his underwear.

Fallon peeked through cracks in the front-blind. He made sure that the front-window was fastened. A fire-escape led from there. He wanted something to do. He sat down and recited poetry for hours, whispering the stanzas. His lip was so sore that it ached when he touched the scanty moustache. He looked in a mirror. His eyelids were puffy. He had pains in the region of the gall-bladder. He poured himself another drink. The bottle reminded him of an hour-glass, with the sands running low. The sands of his life were running low. Friends? Where were they now? Popularity? How ephemeral are the things of the world!

He got up, took his dirty shirt and went to the bathroom. He smiled in a grim sort of manner as he began to do his own laundry.

He was running the water gently when he fancied he heard a knock. He tip-toed to the living room. The knock was repeated. He heard voices, rather jovial ones. He listened. Someone was saying: "I'm getting fed up with peddling these damned things. If I don't sell one before night, I'm going to blow the job."

That *couldn't* be an officer. Fallon peeped through his door-hole. He saw two men with vacuum-cleaners. He opened the door. They greeted him with disarming eloquence as to the virtues of vacuum-cleaners.

"No, boys," said Fallon, "I couldn't use one of those things."

"But they're wonderful," said one salesman.

"You don't know the half of it," said the other.

"I haven't any use for one," said Fallon. "A broom is all I need."

The first man wagged his head sorrowfully. "A broom's awfully old-fashioned, mister."

"Brooms have gone the way of the livery stable horse," said the other. "You ought to have a vacuum."

The first man said: "Well, if he don't want one, Fred, he don't. So that's that. No use of punching the bag with a fellow. So long, mister."

"Sorry," said Fallon, "I wish you luck."

After the men had gone, Fallon began to worry. At first he argued that these men could not possibly have been spotters. If so, why hadn't they revealed their official identity and arrested him? Besides, they were making other calls. He had heard them knock at another door, and then another. And he had heard them give a woman on a floor below a loud sales-talk. He had heard her invite them inside, and then there had come to him the whirr of the vacuum. It reminded him of the prison dynamos and their hissing wail. No, these men were not officers. The devil they weren't! He sat up straight, as though the prison dynamos were sending a current through him; as though he were sitting in an electric chair. They *were* officers. They had been sent to find him. He was sure of it. He argued back and forth, through the night. His shirt, half-laundered, lay soaking in the wash-basin. He was still sitting there late into the morning. Then noon came. And 1 o'clock. Then he remembered his shirt. Odd that a man will suffer a vacation of mind, and then, in a time of trouble, recall a trivial thing such as a shirt soaking in a wash-basin. He was sick. He had been in such a stupid, unmoving posture all night and morning that he even had forgotten to finish his bottle. He now took a drink. He rummaged through a pile of cigarette butts, found one that was less crumpled than the others, and lighted it. It tasted like a piece of buggy-whip.

From the Old Post Office Building in New York City, Assistant United States Attorney Millard was sounding a police alarm. In the editorial offices of The New York *American* at No. 238 William Street, it was said that Reporter Carl Helm had been the man that ran Fallon to earth. A happy editor came down the circular iron steps from the composing-room, where he had been directing the setting of large type and the striking-off of banners on galley-proof sheets. He now directed the pasting up of these banners on office walls, on the big iron piers that supported the ceiling. The many banners bore one slogan:

HOORAY FOR CARL HELM!

So happy were the journalistic victors, that for a time they credited a rumor that Fallon had killed himself.

The big man-hunt was in its last stage. All were ready for the kill. Juror Rendigs was due again to be sentenced, this formality having been postponed. Now, at the suggestion of Assistant District Attorney Hugo Winter, the sentence again was deferred for a week by Judge Talley. Rendigs, perhaps, might be of further use in hamstringing Fallon before the Federal authorities.

It was the afternoon of June 14, 1924, when the hunters closed in on the apartment at No. 586 Academy Street. Fallon had been gone from the eyes of the law for three weeks.

Mr. Millard managed to be in the neighborhood as the last tiny springs of the trap were adjusted. Department of Justice Agents were in Academy Street. They watched the door of No. 586 Academy Street, and looked at the drawn blinds of the second floor hide-out. They behaved as though a most desperate man was waiting there to shoot it out. Although Fallon's life-long reputation would have indicated otherwise, the authorities appeared to think that he had an arsenal in his keeping. The air was full of hysteria and make-believe.

Daniel F. Dwyer, John Curtin, Herman Goldman and Charles A. Werner were the Department of Justice men assigned to get Fallon. At 2 o'clock they rang the bell of the apartment. There was no click of the door-latch in reply. As The *American* put it: "They rang again and again, but still the fugitive, run to earth, kept desperate silence."

"We'll go up the fire-escape," Dwyer said.

He and Curtin stepped to the escape from an adjoining apartment on the second floor. Dwyer tried to peer through the window. The crack made by blind and window-frame gave him a limited view of the room. Dwyer could see nothing but some clothing on a chair.

"He's still here," he whispered. "His clothing wouldn't be here if *he* wasn't."

They went to the ground and now got a key from the superintendent and opened the downstairs hall-way door. They mounted, the four operatives, to Fallon's floor. Dwyer began to pound heavily at the door.

"Open up, Fallon. We're officers."

The lock clicked. The knob moved. The door opened slowly. The officers saw a somewhat stooped, unkempt figure, a man in trousers and undershirt, and on his upper lip a scraggly blond mustache. His eyes were puffy.

"Oh," said Dwyer, looking at the mustache. "A disguise, eh?"

Fallon straightened his shoulders as though lifting a hod of bricks. "Come in. I'm not going to resist you."

The operatives kept their hands on the butts of their pistols. As they stepped inside, Fallon backed toward his liquor bottle. His hand trembled as he fumbled for the cork. His voice wavered as he strove for his old-time joviality.

"Will you gentlemen join me in a drink?"

"No," said Dwyer. "Come on, Fallon."

Fallon then poured himself a stiff drink. "I trust you gentlemen will excuse me for indulging alone."

The operatives did not answer. They began searching the apartment. "Not looking for weapons?" asked Fallon. Then he set down his glass. "Say, you fellows, will you let me finish fixing my clean shirt? I just laundered it. I do my own housework, you know. I'd like to shave."

The operatives recalled journalistic advice, both concerning Fallon's possible armament and about a probable attempt to kill himself.

"Sorry," said Dwyer, "but we haven't time for that."

"But look here," Fallon said. "Give me a chance to shave, will you? Just look at me! I must shave. Why, there's a whole bunch of you big huskies to prevent me from doing anything! I give you my word I won't try to hurt myself."

Dwyer was not a bad sort. "Take it easy, Bill. We'll have a barber shave you downtown. Get your clothes on."

"I never go to barbers." He seemed bewildered. "You said 'downtown.' Yes. You mean The Tombs. I've been there . . . lots of times."

"We're waiting, Bill."

"You fellows are good sports. I know how it is. But I dislike being seen like this. There'll be photographers."

"You look O.K."

"I know how I look. Terrible! I wasn't trying to get away. I've been a sick man ever since I got here. I've had a complete nervous breakdown. I would have given myself up a dozen times, only I couldn't get bail. I was turned down everywhere. I couldn't appear to plead my own case. Everyone ran out on me. That bonding company (Rothstein) turned me down. I have no money. No friends. I had to lie low until I could get my defense ready and figure a way of getting bail. I would have come in Monday anyhow. Please let me shave."

"We'll see that you're taken care of downtown."

Fallon sighed. He accepted a cigarette from Dwyer and puffed greedily. He drained the rest of his bottle. Dwyer got Fallon's shirt and held it for him. Fallon said nothing. He put his arms into the sleeves.

"Now come along, Bill."

And now The Great Mouthpiece shrank from a new and humiliating experience. An operative snapped a set of handcuffs on him. He winced, but said nothing. His back was to the wall.

Before submitting to the handcuffs, Fallon hastily put a pillow in the top dresser-drawer. It was his signal to Gertrude that he had been captured.

"Better take some clothes and toilet articles for your cell," Dwyer said.

"No," Fallon said. "I'll make out."

As they went to a taxicab, Fallon saw Mr. Millard. "Why, there's Mr. Millard. It's a fine day, isn't it? We had bad weather until today, and now the sun's out."

Mr. Millard said nothing. He had a personal interest in Fallon's capture, quite aside from the official recognition it might merit. He had been one of the prosecutors in the Durrell-Gregory case.

It was a Saturday, and the Federal Courts were closed early. Mr. Millard had arranged especially for United States Judge John C. Knox to sit in the Police Station of the 57th Precinct, Kingsbridge Terrace and Perot Street, The Bronx.

In the taxicab, Fallon borrowed so many cigarettes that the

available supply was exhausted. A halt was made to buy more. Fallon was searching his pockets, over and over again.

"I had some money some place. I'm sure I had a dollar bill."

"We'll buy the cigarettes," said Dwyer.

"I guess you don't believe me, but I surely had a dollar. Wait till I look once more."

He finally found his money. Instead of a dollar, it was a ten-dollar bill. He displayed it with child-like anxiety, as proof that he had not lied. "I knew I had it," he said. He behaved as if fascinated by this actual evidence of his claim of having money; as though he expected probable doubters to be fascinated, too. "I told you I had it! I didn't know it was a ten. A fellow should count his money. Let me buy cigarettes for everybody. We'll have a carton each. I *knew* I had the money somewhere."

As the taxicab went into Broadway, and downtown towards Park Row, Fallon kept referring to his triumph in having found his money.

"You must have spent a lot of money," Dwyer said.

Fallon looked out at Broadway. "Yes, I guess I have."

"Would you say you'd spent a quarter of a million around here?" asked Dwyer.

Fallon gazed at him with a mild sort of surprise. "A quarter of a million? Why, I once collected that much inside of two weeks." He spoke as though collecting and spending were one and the same thing—and for him the terms *were* synonymous.

"Are you sure it's all gone?" asked Dwyer.

Fallon sighed. "Yes. Thrown away on a lot of *good fellows.*"

"Then you're broke?"

"I'd say I was pretty nearly flat broke."

"And the good fellows—haven't they done anything to help you?"

"They left the ship to sink. One word and I would be free. But it would make trouble for a lot of big people. Nobody ever has hurt me except myself, though, and I'll never say that word."

They passed through the mid-town section and Fallon saw the fronts of places where he had laughed, drunk, sung, spent,

"I always hated to see people go to jail," he said. "When I was Assistant D.A. in Westchester, most of my money went to buy clothes for poor children."

"How are your own wife and children fixed?" asked Dwyer.

"They're provided for. My wife's father is wealthy, and my own people are well-fixed." He paused. "My mother is dead. It's fortunate she's not here to see me now. Still, if she had lived. . . . Oh, well. My family and my wife's family are decent people. I am not the kind to fit in with them."

Judge Knox fixed bail at $100,000. In default of this amount, Judge Knox remanded Fallon to The Tombs. Photographers snapped his picture as he walked, linked by handcuffs to the wrist of Dwyer.

Journalistic joys are as immense as they are brief. The *American* had made a clean sweep in its notable bucket-shop crusade. Too often there were crusades that started with fanfare of Park Row trumpets, but died down when culprits retained high-priced attorneys to bury their sins in the pigeon-holes of political desks, and then went unpunished. Too often an editor, fired with civic zeal (and perhaps the dream of increased circulation), started off bravely, and at the reins of a giddy band-wagon. Then, after driving a short way, he might discover that his snorting horses had become bone-spavined nags, and the gilded vehicle a dung-cart. Hence the hoorays at No. 238 William Street. There had been real results.

There were telegrams to the Hearst ranch at San Simeon. "Fallon is captured." Mr. Hearst breveted his soldiers on the field. The boys had started out with their artillery to level an ant-hill. They had knocked down a whole mountain.

The *American* lorded it over the other Park Row organs in the manner of Mrs. Blimpstead when she gets a new gown during a neighborhood feud.

The headlines throbbed: "SLIPPERY BILL FALLON CAPTURED."

Detail upon detail was repeated concerning the brave man-hunt. The blond mustache and the pillow in the dresser-drawer were not neglected. The interpretation of these matters was interesting:

"When found, Fallon had a well-started mustache as a *disguise*."

"In a search for *weapons*, and in one of the bureau drawers, was found a pillow, carefully tucked away. There was another on the bed. Slippery Bill had had a fair visitor perhaps, and had hidden his indiscretion in this manner."

Provided the latter statement were true, it was the first time in Fallon's career that he *hid* an indiscretion.

Other claims were made in print, such as:

"He began to whine." "The thought of suicide seemed to have come to mind." "Slippery Bill knew that he had come to the end of his rope and the end of his career."

There were interviews and near-interviews, pictures and all the typographical bric-a-brac beloved by triumphant journalists. One editor, excited by a belief that the celebration in his office was but a part of a nation-wide jubilation, exclaimed:

"It's bigger than the Armistice!"

In one article, The *American* said that Fallon had been taken past a cabaret closed by prohibition agents, and had said:

"I refused the Fuller & McGee case fifteen times."

"Then why didn't you refuse it the sixteenth time?"

"I was pulled into it. I don't like Tom Foley. He has the foulest mouth of any man in New York. I don't happen to like that sort of thing. Right over there, in that place, his tongue got me into a fight. . . . Many a better man than I has gone to jail. It won't worry me any. I've lived many lives in my thirty-seven years."

Concerning Miss Vanderbilt, The *American* quoted Fallon: "Gertie is a much maligned girl. She is splendid. Did she sell the house? What! For $35,000? It's worth $75,000. Peggy Joyce is a regular fellow. They don't make them any better. . . . Yes, there were many ladies. Perhaps they haven't all left me."

Day upon day the journalistic thunders continued.

"Fallon, the Lion of the Underworld, was caught unaware in his bathroom. The capture was expected to have turned into a pistol-fight. . . . The very thing that had so amused him in his meteoric career, and upon which he spent so many tens of thousands of dollars, betrayed him. That was love. Gertrude Vanderbilt, actress, his devoted friend, and perhaps his only friend, had been shadowed and had opened the trail to the fugitive."

When bail was arranged Fallon was feeling better. He promised McGee he would stay on the water wagon until after the trial. Ernie Eidlitz had been a fugitive following Fallon's Federal indictment. He now returned from Montreal on June 16 to testify against Fallon. He had been staying at the Hotel Windsor, incognito, as Herr Karl Albrecht.

On Fallon's arrest, McGee spent the rest of the day and Sunday trying to raise bail, which had been reduced to $35,000. Government authorities refused to permit McGee to see his partner in The Tombs.

Rendigs had turned on Fallon in less than a week after Fallon had defended him. He now was ready to aid the Government's prosecuting forces. Fallon believed himself virtually friendless, but to his astonishment letters began to come to him from members of the bar. Most of them declared a belief in Fallon's innocence. Many offered to defend him without cost.

Judge Knox set a date for trial after Fallon had spent a day and a night in The Tombs.

The capture of Fallon and his promised toboggan into a prison cell did not satisfy his ill-wishers. The *American* now began talking about disbarment proceedings. It was said there was a plan to induce the authorities to drop the prosecution if Fallon would consent to the disbarment and accept a term in Essex County Jail, or some nearby prison instead of Atlanta.

It was said Fallon didn't want to go to Atlanta because Donegan was there. Colonel Hayward was in attendance on a Cleveland Convention, and the purported dicker did not materialize.

When a detective-friend of Fallon's got wind of an alleged contemplated meeting between Fallon and an editor of The American, he summoned The Great Mouthpiece to his office.

"I hear you're going to squeal."

"No," Fallon said. "But they have a proposition to offer me."

"Yes, and to double-cross you."

"I don't think so."

The detective picked up the telephone. "All right, yellow! Then listen in on that extension to this conversation, and see what you think."

He called a man said to be a reporter. "Hello. Well, I see that you've got Bill by the short hair. It was a swell job, and he ought to go up. They tell me you're going to get him to sign up. Well, after he signs a confession, I suppose you'll put the rollers under him for keeps?"

The voice is alleged to have replied: "You said it. We'll put him where he belongs."

Fallon's face was white. He never had been heard to use foul language. But now he let loose a volley that almost made his companion faint.

"That settles it," he said. "The first axiom of law is: that an attorney defending himself has a fool for a client. Well, Fallon will defend himself from his own feet. They're framing me. I have one trump card. I must use it for my self-preservation. I'll make them wish they'd never heard of William J. Fallon."

Chapter Twenty-Four

BACK FROM ELBA

FALLON waited until the day before trial to "prepare" his case.
It was a Sunday. He spent *one hour* at the Public Library,
and scrawled a single page of notes on the back of a statement
to the press. He left the Library and walked to the home of
Gertrude Vanderbilt in West Eighty-fourth Street. His step was
quick; his strength had returned.

Gertrude sat beside him on a divan. "I can't get over how well
you look. You see, it didn't hurt you to go on the water wagon."

"I hardly think it's that. I'm in a fight. I thrive on trouble.
I sometimes believe I drink because of an urge for life; an
excessive zest for living."

"No one should try to drink life in one gulp."

"And why not? What has the length of life got to do with
the living of it?"

"Our ideas differ in that respect. We shouldn't even bring up
the subject."

He stretched his arms. "What a day! Everything *should* look
black, but it doesn't. How strange! I feel that Fallon is another,
remote person; some fellow that has come to my back door,
asking for bread and advice in the same breath. I'm out of
bread, but I'm full of advice. Gee, but the Library seemed de-
pressing, stuffy! I get a good laugh when I look at those stone
lions, though. They look like twin Rothsteins, after a losing night
at dice."

They talked for a time about the case. They discussed R. J. Shanahan and Dennis Nash, Syracuse attorneys, one of the many law-firms that volunteered to defend Fallon without cost.

"Shanahan is my chief counsel, but that doesn't mean a thing, Gertie. Bill Fallon will defend himself."

She looked out the window. "For a while, a week or so ago, I was afraid you were losing your grip. Now, it's the other way around. I'm almost afraid you're *too* confident."

"I've got the winning card. I hate to use it, but self-preservation is the main thing now." He wandered back to the subject of drink. "I promised McGee I'd lay off until this thing is over. McGee's getting to be a reformer."

"He's thinking of your good."

"He's been a real friend, Baby. . . . Funny, I don't like the taste or the smell of liquor. I suppose I make a face when I take the first one. I presume it's the effect that fellows like myself are after. Alcohol cancels reality, making truths of the lies that fantasy whispers. It's a constant tension, this life. I always said I drank to become relaxed. Perhaps I should have said 'released.' Tomorrow brings lowered vitality and a feeling of inferiority, with pious reflections and general depression, yet I and the other rummies long for anaesthesia."

"You're not a rummy. Quit talking that way."

Fallon laughed. "I told McGee that a lot of women and children were praying for me. They are, too. I'm getting letters, telegrams. Even cables. I told McGee I was receiving as many prayers as did Congressman William Sulzer."

He repeated the anecdote of how the Jews in Russia "knelt to pray for William Sulzer."

Gertrude was uplifted by Fallon's jovial mood. "You look ten years younger than you did a week ago."

"Fallon never will get old."

"Not to me, you won't."

"Nor to himself. Am I still youthful, Baby?"

"You're the handsomest thing that ever lived."

"Do you know, Baby, the tragedy of beauty is———"

"Oh, so you think you're *beautiful*, do you?"

"Didn't you just say so?"

"I said '*handsome*.'"

"You didn't say any such thing."

"I did."

"You didn't. You said 'handsomest.'"

"What's the difference?"

"Well, wouldn't 'handsomest' be beautiful?"

"I suppose."

"Answer 'Yes' or 'No.'"

"Yes."

"You're no good as a witness."

"Go ahead. What about this 'beauty,' and this 'tragedy?'"

"As I was saying, the tragedy is that beauty alone knows true degeneration. Ugliness has no hill to slide down. The horse-lipped youngster grows into '*distinguished*' old age. The malformed skulls become objects of veneration. But the graceful ones, the symmetrical and the beautiful—they fade, Baby. Promise me you'll never fade."

"I'm not beautiful. I'll be one of those 'distinguished' old women."

He looked at her for a while, then he put his arms about her and kissed her tenderly. "You're the most beautiful thing in all this world, inside and out, through and through. Why do you stick to such a worthless, irresponsible person as Fallon?"

"Because I love him."

"Promise never to leave me."

"I promise."

"But I'm going to die young."

"Why do you keep saying that? It's a terrible thing to say."

"What's terrible about death?"

"Would you say it was a *pleasant* subject?"

"Neither pleasant nor unpleasant. Why fool ourselves? The mistake men make is in trying to force meaningless lives to last beyond their span."

"Is your life meaningless? I never knew anyone to jump about so much mentally."

"I don't want to let my pride catch up to me."

"You have every reason to be proud."

"I detest reasons."

"Let's go for a walk."

"I'm for that. Up to Fordham. We'll jump up there, mind and body, and stroll through the old grounds."

Broadway packed the court-room of the Old Post Office Building when William J. Fallon went to trial before United States District Judge George W. McClintic of West Virginia. William J. Millard, Assistant United States Attorney, opened as Federal Prosecutor. There were two counts in the indictment, charging jury-bribing.

The city was a blast-furnace in this mid-summer of 1924. The atmosphere was humid. The crowded condition of the homely old court-room made it seem a jungle-pit. The perfumes of Broadway women, the tobacco-smells, the perspiration, the devitalizing odor that comes when hundreds of pairs of lungs exhaust the oxygen of a cramped chamber, made one feel like apologizing for being human. Still, to the expectant crowd that fought for uncomfortable seats, and to the mob held back at the door by blue-coated bailiffs, the drama of the moment obliterated thoughts of discomfort and quieted the protests of the nose.

Fallon appeared in court wearing his usual blue serge suit, his burgundy-colored neck-tie and his unshined Oxfords. His face was solemn, but the true Fallon fire was in his blue eyes. His bearing was erect. He moved with confidence. His apricot hair stood like flame on his large, finely modeled head. It was as though a great actor were re-visiting a stage well-known to him, in a theater that had witnessed his former triumphs.

The first shot was fired when Fallon moved for dismissal

of the indictment. The crowd scented sensational disclosures. Judge McClintic sealed the supporting affidavit as "too scandalous and improper to become public."

Broadway asked: "What's Fallon got up his sleeve?"

The Broadway observers nodded when Mr. Fallon took complete charge in cross-examination of the Government's witnesses. None of his old-time skill was lacking. His audacity was as great as ever; possibly greater. He was making a magnificent start. He confounded witnesses who had prepared to give damaging testimony. He became aggressive with the prosecutors and impudent with the court itself.

Ernie Eidlitz, Fallon's ex-handy man, was on deck. The happiness boys, Fuller & McGee, were there. So also were representatives of The New York *American*. Juror Rendigs came from The Tombs to spill his soul.

There were wranglings and clashes between Fallon and the court. Judging from his behavior, it was almost unbelievable that Fallon was a defendant, facing prison. The judge, in cautioning Fallon, said that the indicted attorney's "back was to the wall." Fallon seized on this phrase, turned it to his own advantage, and again and again shouted to the jury: "Fallon's back is not to the wall. He is in the front line. Fallon is the victim of a gigantic conspiracy."

This phraseology and this supposed conspiracy were used by Fallon to lay the ground-work for introduction of a most astounding and diabolically clever train of evidence. This evidence came with the attorney's own testimony on the witness stand. It was so shocking that it turned the interest of everyone from the case itself into other channels. The testimony involved the publicist, William Randolph Hearst, and his purported moral behavior. It was the trump-card referred to by Fallon in his earlier talks.

With characteristic bravado, Fallon in advance let it be known to the offices of The *American* that he was going on the stand to allege certain scandalous matters. He hinted at the nature of the charges broadly enough to cause excited huddles in the offices of the newspaper. There was a telephone call to the San Simeon ranch of Mr. Hearst.

Mr. Hearst often has been an object of attack. At times he has qualified for the position of All-American punching-bag. He never has boasted of having been a saint. Indeed, a halo would become him much less fittingly than does his black and battered Congressional hat. But one thing never can be said of him— that he ran from a fight. Nor did he run from this one.

A worried editor informed Mr. Hearst by long-distance telephone of the probable Fallon outburst. Mr. Hearst replied:

"Well, then, you won't be in doubt as to *what your headline will be for tomorrow's paper.*"

Mr. Hearst is entitled to a monument for *never having bored* anyone that worked for him.

Five character witnesses appeared for Fallon on the day of the big hoorah. Two of them were Charles C. Marrin, Assistant Corporation Counsel, and the Hon. Frederick Weeks, former District Attorney of Westchester County. There was testimony by Joseph Shalleck, a junior associate of the Fallon & McGee law firm. He corroborated the explanation of Miss Rosenberg, Fallon's secretary, concerning the $1,000 check made out by Agnes Fallon. That check was alleged to have figured in the bribing of Rendigs at Joe Pani's Woodmansten Inn.

Miss Rosenberg said she had received the check from Fallon on the morning of November 6, 1922, with instructions to get it cashed at the Knickerbocker Grill. Pani owned that grill as well as the Woodmansten Inn. The secretary said she went to the grill. Pani was not there. His head book-keeper cashed the check after she had had it certified.

She continued: "Then I turned over the money to Mr. Fallon. I saw him give $500 of it to Mr. Shalleck."

Fallon had discredited Pani's testimony, balling him up so completely that he got down from the stand, looking like a theater programme that had been stepped on by a wet overshoe. Pani testified he paid $1,000 in cash to Rendigs on the night of November 6, and had deposited the check to his own account.

There was a strained silence as the determined lawyer walked to the stand to testify for himself. He gazed about the court-room, his head lifted high. Then he looked squarely at the jurors, as though reading the minds of each and every one. Attorney Shanahan led the witness down to the time of indict-ment. Fallon said he had applied to Colonel Hayward, United States Attorney, for permission to appear before the grand jury.

"I was willing to waive immunity," Fallon said, "but Colonel Hayward declined to permit me to appear."

Shanahan then questioned Fallon about Eidlitz. Fallon an-swered questions in an even, unhurried voice. This afforded a complete contrast to his pugnacious, stormy cross-examination of Federal witnesses. He seemed perfectly serene and self-contained. The court-room crowd waited expectantly. From every angle, here was the old Fallon, resourceful, sparkling, ver-satile in attack and defense. A champion. He outlined, bit by bit, and in a most convincing manner, allegations of organized persecution and intrigue, intended, he declared, to bring about his ruin. In support of the conspiracy charge, he declared he had received a confession from Eidlitz in the apartment of Billie Bennett, an actress, and in the presence of Miss Bennett, Walter O'Neill, and Mrs. Mona Lewis.

Eidlitz's purported confession to Fallon had to do with the former's journalistic visits with the editor of The *American*. Fallon described Eidlitz as in tears when talking to his old-time boss, "Pill." He pictured Eidlitz as having confessed that he had been forced by reporters for The *American* to attack the defend-ant. Eidlitz said, according to the Fallon testimony, that he was threatened with arrest for forgery unless he appeared against Fallon.

"I asked Eidlitz to make an affidavit covering his confession," Fallon said. "But he refused, protesting that he would imme-diately be arrested for perjury. I then advised Eidlitz to go to Prosecutor Millard to make his confession, but Eidlitz evaded this with a plea that he was too ill and upset. He then went to Montreal for a rest. He went away promising to go to Millard's office and make his confession as soon as he returned."

Asked if he had given Eidlitz $2,500 to leave the country, Fallon replied:

"I couldn't give him that, because I didn't have it. I didn't give him a cent at that time."

Fallon testified that Eidlitz revealed how E. M. Fuller, W. F. McGee, Charles W. Rendigs and two other men had met at McGee's home for the purpose of involving Fallon with Rendigs. He said the plan had failed when two of the potential plotters refused to have anything to do with the scheme.

Fallon said he had defended without fee Alfred De W. Blum in the Durrell-Gregory mail-fraud trial in 1922, in which case Rendigs was a juror.

Q: Did you know Rendigs at that time? A: I never saw the man in my life, nor any man on that jury, before that date.

Q: When did you meet the Gregory brothers (of the Durrell-Gregory firm)? A: Not until the opening of their trial; and I never spoke to them, with one exception, and that was when Rhode H. Gregory came to see me.

Q: What conversation did you have with him then? A: Blum brought him to see me. He asked me how I thought the trial was going on, and I said I thought it was going along very well.

Q: Did you ever meet Rendigs at the Woodmansten Inn, or at the home of W. Frank McGee? A: No. I never met him before we were arrested on the bribery charge.

Q: Did you ever give Rendigs $1,000 on the stairs of the Woodmansten Inn? A: No, nor at any other place. In fact, I never even heard of him until he was indicted.

The storm broke when Fallon testified concerning other parts of the purported Eidlitz confession:

"Eidlitz said to me that he told Watson (editor of The American) he was fearful he would be arrested, and that he (Eidlitz) knew I had the birth certificates of the children of a moving-picture actress, and that I knew Mr. Hearst had sent a woman, who pretended to be a countess, to Florida to get evidence against his wife. He said he had told Watson that I intended to use that information to blackmail Mr. Hearst."

The court-room was electrified. The witness continued:

"Eidlitz said he told Mr. Watson that I had the number of the car and the name of the man who went to Mexico with the same party, the same moving-picture actress. He said a few days later Hearst communicated with Watson, and said to Watson: 'Fallon must be destroyed.' "

Mr. Millard had a slightly deflated expression as he rose to cross-examine. His questions were remarkably brief. There was one angry exchange of words between witness and prosecutor—the first time Fallon departed from his easy, even recital. That came when Millard asked concerning the whereabouts of the defendant's wife. He characterized her as "poor Mrs. Fallon."

Fallon sat up in the chair. "She's not *poor* Mrs. Fallon, and you can have her here any time you want her!"

The court intervened. "You gentlemen both should know, as lawyers, that the defendant's wife could not testify."

The Fallon testimony was given on August 6. On August 8 it was evident that the sensational case was nearing its close. Comptroller Charles L. Craig appeared as the last witness for the Prosecution's rebuttal. Fallon clashed with the court when he sought to link the silver-haired and rosy-cheeked Comptroller with the Fuller Construction Company, which was building the new county court-house. Mr. Craig was chairman of the building committee until the Board of Estimate removed him. After the tilt between the judge and Fallon, the latter shouted angrily for a mistrial. He stood rather close to the bench while raising his voice. The judge checked Fallon repeatedly as he asked numerous questions concerning the Fuller Construction Company's contract. (This company in no way was connected with the bucketing firm of Fuller & McGee.)

The court said sharply: "I told you that was out of this case. I want you to understand that you can't *do* these things. You can't run *this* court!"

Fallon then asked concerning the resignation of Walter J. O'Neill from the Comptroller's office. O'Neill had been one of Fallon's witnesses. The question was so framed that the court understood Fallon to be misstating the Comptroller's direct testimony.

Judge McClintic appeared extremely annoyed. "You are twisting the facts, which no honest man would do."

Fallon's face turned white. He screamed: "I except to the court's comment, and demand the withdrawal of a juror!" This would have meant a mistrial.

The Judge shouted back: "You can object and shut up!"

Fallon again screamed: "I object to *that* remark."

The Judge pounded his desk with a gavel. "You can object, but I tell you that *I'm* running *this* court-room."

Fallon folded his arms. "I again object and except."

"You can except; that's easy to do."

Fallon now had gained control of himself. He thought he saw a valuable opening for grounds for appeal. He pressed his opportunity with all his old-time ability for getting on the nerves of the bench. He said: "Of course it's easy to do, and in view of your attitude, I ask that a juror be withdrawn."

The judge was enraged. "You can't make a joke out of this court!"

Fallon seized on the word "joke." "There are lots of things about this case that are a joke." He looked meaningly at the jury. "But it's no joke to me. In view of your remarks about making a joke of this case, I again demand the withdrawal of a juror."

The judge refused to declare a mistrial. He ordered Fallon to proceed with the cross-examination. The Comptroller had said that O'Neill had been discharged as *his* employe. O'Neill had testified that he had "resigned."

Mr. Fallon asked the Comptroller if O'Neill hadn't told him

that Grover Whalen (then Commissioner of Plant and Structures), was angry because O'Neill had gone into the bus business and was hurting Whalen's departmental buses. The Comptroller denied this.

Q: Didn't you *ever* have a conversation with O'Neill on the subject of buses? A: Yes.

Q: Do you remember saying to O'Neill that you were politically ambitious, and that the Hearst powers might start out after you? A: No.

Craig accused O'Neill of receiving Jules C. Rabiner, bucket-shop operator, in his office, and of accepting $310,000 for alleged services to a water-main contractor.

Mr. Fallon shouted: "You got $350,000 from the Fuller Construction Company, didn't you?"

Mr. Craig's pink face turned to a magenta shade. "I didn't get $350,000 or 350 cents, and you know that better than anyone else!"

Mr. Fallon then referred to Mr. Craig's commitment by Federal Judge Julius M. Mayer for contempt of court. Mr. Millard arose to ask the witness:

"You are *still* the Comptroller?"

"Yes."

"Well, he won't be long," Fallon piped, as Mr. Craig got from the stand.

With Craig as the final witness, the hour arrived for summing up. The most bitter fight of Fallon's spectacular career now was in its closing stages. Not only his professional honor, but his liberty was at stake. If he had aught of eloquence or persuasive powers, here was a time when The Great Mouthpiece needed them most urgently. The room was full; bailiffs were shouldering the outside crowd away from the doors. Mr. Fallon advanced to the jury-rail.

The clear, vibrant voice of the defendant rose against the silence of the room. It was twenty minutes before noon when Fallon got to his feet for his final innings. He spoke until one o'clock, and then the court declared a recess for lunch. After lunch

Fallon returned to his oratorical task. Certain advisors had counseled him against splitting his speech, saying the full import of it might be lessened through interruption; that the second part might appear an anti-climax.

"Don't worry about your anti-climaxes," said Fallon. "I'll save the real fireworks until afternoon, when the jurors will have returned from dinner, their stomachs full."

He spoke for two hours in all, building bit by bit the supposed journalistic vendetta, and leading up to thunders of accusation against his prosecutors. It seemed as though they, and not Fallon, were being given a burden of guilt and asked to purge themselves. The Broadway Cicero limned an array of Catilines.

The court had told Fallon that his "back was to the wall." At the outset he said, calmly but forcibly:

"I am *not* with my back to the wall, as the court has said." He pointed his finger. "I am right in the front line. I have faced every accuser, and when I shall have finished, I believe that you will find that there is absolutely no truth or foundation for the charges brought against me."

Fallon warmed to his theme. He made a striking figure. He commanded interest. He had the attention of every juror. Often in his court-speeches of other trials he had given an appearance of playing to the gallery; of showing off, almost, for the benefit of thronged court-rooms. Now, however, he was patently engrossed in cheating prison, in fending off disgrace. He spoke only to the jury:

"If you think I have been impetuous during this trial," he said, "let me say it is not easy for a man who has stood here and defended others, to stand here and defend himself. But I have done so. I could look every one of my accusers in the eye and tell them they were not telling the truth. Who of you could stand up and face your accusers without being impetuous and overbearing? If you heard men lie, and knew they were lying, wouldn't your animosity be aroused?"

He leaned forward, almost across the rail of the jury-box. He was tremendously in earnest.

"You twelve men stand as the bulwark, under our system of jurisprudence, between me and an unjust conviction. I don't care about prisons. Reputation is what everyone holds dear."

He now repeated the conspiracy charge. It had been the main theme of his defense. He again alleged that employes of William Randolph Hearst had entered a plot to destroy him. And now came an added sensation. He pressed his hand to his breast-pocket.

"I have here in court the actual birth certificates of the illegitimate children of a certain motion-picture actress!"

He then attacked the testimony of The *American's* editor. He accused the editor of lying when he said there had been a meeting in the journalist's home; that the meeting had been had to persuade Fallon to plead guilty and move for his own disbarment.

"You gentlemen can guess why Watson (the editor) wanted to see me. You know it wasn't, as Watson said, to see if I would involve others in this case. You know they wanted what I had. What Eidlitz saw I had. What Watson lied about. They knew what I had, and that I got it to protect my clients. I got information no one else could ever get."

He charged that the testimony of Eidlitz and Rendigs had been concocted; that the alleged plotters had been unable to make their stories coincide.

Mr. Fallon now began to shout. "Eidlitz told his story before Rendigs told his. That's why they are so widely divergent. I ask you to pay special attention, gentlemen, to the character of the witnesses who have testified against me here. If you had a brother or a father on trial, with his everything at stake, would you believe the testimony against him of the witnesses who have testified against me here? We find strong reasons why they were all testifying against Fallon.

"Who would take the word of a McGee, confessed bucketeer and robber of millions of poor people? Who would believe Rendigs, the juror, that miserable creature who faces ten years under a conviction for perjury? He is now in The Tombs. I believe he

at first said to himself that he would not further disgrace himself by testifying against me, but a few weeks of a cell have had
their effect. He saw ten more years in prison ahead of him.

"Doesn't the fact that Eidlitz, my former employe, was discharged for forging checks refute his testimony against me? I
say to you now, and I say it is the truth, that The *American*
deliberately started out to destroy Fallon, and if I were like
Watson, I would prove it to you in one second. You don't think
he invited me to his apartment that day to suggest that I con-
fess and give him information about some others, do you? You
don't think that I would say anything against any one? I now
say to you publicly that I don't know anything about anybody,
any big politician, or any big gambler that would ever put them
in jail."

The speaker said the story that the prosecution originally intended to present was different from the case put in against him.
He added that Becarris, the Woodmansten Inn waiter, who testified he took Fallon upstairs to Rendigs, when the bribe-money
was passed, was frightened into testifying against him.

"Becarris was in the liquor business and the Government could
raid him every half-hour."

Mr. Millard rose to interject: "There's nothing in the evidence of that sort!"

Mr. Fallon was happy to have the Government defend its in-
tegrity as to liquor violations. He retorted: "It is a matter of common knowledge, and the jury can judge as to that for itself."

The court now joined in. "Gentlemen of the jury, that's not
true. We're trying this case on the evidence."

Mr. Fallon closed with these words:

"All that the whole world means to me, I now leave in
your hands."

He stood there for twenty or more seconds, his eloquent
hands outstretched. He stood in silence, watching the effect of
his appeal. Then he bowed slightly, went slowly to the counsel
table, drew a deep breath, squared his wide shoulders and sat
down. Gene McGee shook his hand.

Prosecutor Millard began to sum up immediately after Fallon sat down. He characterized Fallon's testimony as "glib, arrogant, and pure lying."

"The defendant," said Mr. Millard, "is guilty of corrupting an American juror. I ask you to place a shield between the sanctity of the jury-box and the pillars of our courts of justice. Fallon's main defense has been that William Hayward, United States Attorney; Joab Banton, District Attorney; and two judges have conspired to destroy him. Was ever such consummate rot submitted to the intelligence of an American jury?"

Mr. Fallon popped up. "I object. I said The *American* manufactured evidence, and gave it to these people."

The judge took an hour and ten minutes for his charge. He explained that the court was allowed to discuss with the jury certain parts of the testimony in order to aid the jurors in arriving at a verdict. He added it was "a very sad, sorrowful duty" for him to try a lawyer charged with the crime named in the Fallon indictment. Every lawyer, he explained, had to swear "to honestly demean himself" before beginning practice. The judge then spoke concerning the conspiracy allegation.

"There has been a great deal said about an alleged conspiracy of the New York *American* to get Fallon. Newspapers have aided public authorities before, and their motives are of no consequence if the man should be found guilty. There is no evidence in this case to show improper motives of the *American*.

"I have admitted certain papers alleged to have been written by Ernest Eidlitz. Statements relative to Fuller & McGee, in these papers, are not evidence in this case. There is no evidence, either, proving that the *American* paid Eidlitz $9,000.

"There was no evidence that any promise of immunity was given to Fuller, McGee, or Rendigs. There is no evidence that they were convicted. I can't believe that the United States District Attorney, as a responsible government officer, would do anything improper to get their testimony in this prosecution."

The jury retired. It was eight minutes after 5 o'clock. At

7:20 o'clock word came from the jury-room that the twelve had been unable as yet to reach a conclusion. It was rumored they then stood 9 to 3 for acquittal. The court directed that the jurors be taken to dinner. They went in the care of United States Marshals. Special police kept back a crowd as the jurors filed out. They returned an hour later, and again were locked in their chamber.

Fallon stayed at the Federal Building, not caring to eat. He smoked and chatted with friends. He said to Gene McGee: "They said they would agree in half an hour, but it looks as though they'll be a while longer."

Fallon seemed confident. His spirits were excellent.

At ten minutes after 10 o'clock, the jury reached a verdict. Judge McClintic had gone to the theater. A call was sent to him. He arrived at court in less than an hour and the jurors came in. He warned the spectators against a demonstration. The crowd in the court-room included many notable Broadway figures.

Gertrude Vanderbilt was not there. She had said she was too nervous, too concerned to be present. She might break down, no matter what the verdict. She would await word at her home.

Hyman Rosing, foreman, announced that the jury had found Fallon *not guilty* on both counts of the indictment.

There was a tremendous cheer. The gavel sounded. Judge McClintic immediately adjourned court.

Fallon stood for a moment, smiling at the jurors. Then he stepped forward quickly and shook hands with each of them. The crowd in the court-corridors now took up the shout. Fallon started out, but had difficulty getting through the cheering men and women that surrounded him. He paused at reporter Ferber's place at the press table. He leaned over and said:

"Nat, I promise you *I'll never bribe another juror!*"

Someone asked Fallon what he was going to do. He said he might take a trip to Europe. A group of Broadwayites and attorneys rescued Fallon from the mob that now gathered outside, as well as inside, the Old Post Office Building. People danced in the court-corridors. There was a shouting throng in the triangle south of City Hall Park. Word swept uptown that Bill Fallon had won his own case. Broadway celebrated as only Broadway can. It seemed an election jubilee. Champagne bottles appeared in mysterious plentitude on café tables. Fallon again was hero.

Fallon stayed on the water wagon during his entire trial. He had signed another pledge. Now he began to hoist a few in the Knickerbocker Building. He made several telephone calls—to women—and assured each one that she was the *first* to whom he had told the news.

The celebration at the Knickerbocker was a strictly stag affair Fallon had promised not to bring any women. When one of his lady-friends appeared, one of the revelers hurled a whiskey bottle at her. She ducked.

The Great Mouthpiece began to feel ill shortly after the trial. The strain had been great. He had exerted himself to the full. He sought relief by drinking. His digestive tract was mis-behaving. A physician warned him. He suggested that Fallon stop drinking.

The day after his victory, Fallon attended a baseball game at the Polo Grounds. The Giants were playing the Cincinnati Reds. Fallon occupied a box on the first-baseline. He rooted for the Giants and watched the nimble Captain Frankie Frisch, a Ford-ham product, cavort all over the infield. Many men and women recognized Fallon and cheered him.

The newspaper men wanted to know of his plans. Fallon re-plied good-humoredly: "I don't know what I'll do. I've had only one case, a small one, since my indictment in 1923. I may go to Europe. Later I'll get an office in Fifth Avenue and resume practice."

Fallon now came home again to his wife. He again was full of promises and reform. He said he was going to quit criminal practice and take up civil cases only. He was photographed with his wife at her home, No. 146 West Seventy-seventh Street. Mrs. Fallon's capacity for believing him was infinite.

The photographer poised his camera. "Would you smile a little, Mrs. Fallon, please?"

"It's about time I went over to Fifth Avenue," said Fallon, "and left Broadway flat. According to some persons, Fifth Avenue is more desirable than Broadway. Oh, Broadway is all right. It's as good a friend as any. They are all up when you are, and down when you are. After all, what did Broadway ever do to me? I can return to it as long as I can pay the cover charge. I'm not very different from anybody else in that respect."

"Describe Broadway," suggested a reporter for The New York *World*.

The Great Mouthpiece shrugged. "I couldn't describe it *all* to you. It wouldn't do for your paper. I found Broadway just as it remains. There's no change whether I'm there or not, and I left it just as I found it. Broadway was perfectly satisfactory to me. Why, haven't you ever seen the lights and the people on Broadway? Not very near-to, perhaps. Not close enough, eh? The only difference is that when you are near, the lights are brighter. Well, even the brightest grow dim."

He thought for a while. "Why do you think I know anything about Broadway?"

"You used to train around with Peggy Joyce."

"Ah! Then why don't you get *her* to tell you of Broadway. Doubtless she knows a lot more than I do."

"But she's out of town."

"Well, find her latest husband and you can always find Peggy. A lot of people might contest for the title of knowing most about Broadway. Peggy is on the other side of Broadway. There *are* two sides. . . . No, the lights don't look any dimmer to me now than they always did. You see, I don't turn them on, and neither do I know when they are turned off. Remember, it's never difficult to find Broadway. It's more difficult to miss it."

"I guess you don't *want* to tell *all* that you know concerning Broadway."

"Nonsense. I'm not holding anything back. Didn't I almost go to jail for keeping secrets?"

In this interview, Fallon said his favorite pugilists were Jack Dempsey and Benny Leonard. "One is a good Irishman and the other a good Jew. . . . No, I don't think I'll stop practicing law. You see I entered the profession casually, just as I do everything else. I'm a casual fellow. If I ever stopped to think, I'd get into trouble. I'm seriously opposed to all manner of thinking."

Juror Charles W. Rendigs (indicted in 1923 with Fallon) pleaded guilty in July, 1927, and received a *suspended sentence* of two years. Judge Harry Anderson imposed this sentence in United States District Court at the request of Assistant United States Attorney Thomas T. Cook. Rendigs' testimony against Fallon was accepted as the reason the suspension of sentence.

Chapter Twenty-Five

THE GRAY INTERLUDE

THE GREAT MOUTHPIECE emerged from his triumph with tattered banners. The hours of elation died like the thunders of distant clouds. He had risen to his greatest emergency, hurling Dead Sea apples at his censors. His battle concluded, Fallon retired to his wife's apartment—too weak in body to lick his wounds, too spent of soul to make-believe.

The aftermath was cruelly draining. There were times when Fallon seemed on the way to regain his former bouncy spirit, but always a shadow hovered above him. There was a vigorous movement—mysterious in origin and relentless in purpose—to force Fallon's disbarment. He brooded over this. He seldom had brooded over anything, in all his gay, almost desperate career of challenging the prim virtues of the world. But now he brooded. He became obsessed by a belief that everyone was bent on persecuting him. Life itself was a plot. Civilization was a hangman. The World was a hangman's house.

His liver was hardening. Bile filtered into his bloodstream, making him moody and often unable to rationalize. But his pride dimmed not one bit. He carried his handsome head with a fierce and burning pride. He would neither borrow nor beg. When important clients took their business elsewhere, he made no complaint. He was not a cry-baby.

Fallon's first appearance in court, following his acquittal, was in October, 1924. It was a trivial case. He won it, but the insignificance of this sort of routine disgusted him. He withdrew more and more inside himself.

An ephemeral return to his old spunk and agility was manifest in the Fall of 1924, when Fallon appeared as attorney for Alvin J. ("Cozy") Dolan, former baseball player and assistant coach of the New York Giants. Judge Landis, Czar of Baseball, had outlawed Cozy from organized baseball for participating in an alleged plot to bribe Shortstop Heine Sand of the Philadelphia National League Club. Fearing another upheaval, similar to the Black Sox scandal, the good Judge fumed and fretted, grew hot and bothered. It was an all-around tempest in a teapot. Fallon sought to gain for Cozy a share of the World Series money. It had been denied him when he ran afoul of Judge Landis.

I shall not detail the dumb plot, but it is sure that Cozy Dolan never bribed anyone, nor attempted to do so. He was merely a clumsy jester, and the worst thing he ever did was to acquire a habit of stuffing his mouth with BB shots and spitting them slyly at bewildered strangers.

Fallon started off with his usual fanfare and got the Czar of Baseball rather dizzy with insulting statements. Indeed, during the series between the Giants and Washington, and with Mr. Coolidge tossing out the first ball, the Judge was howling advice for the whole world to "keep its shirt on."

Fallon soon behaved like a faulty automobile tire. He neglected the Dolan case and lasped into his "persecution" mood. He kept thinking of the threat of disbarment.

Mr. Dolan, exiled from baseball, went to Florida. He engaged in the racing of whippets. Mr. W. O. McGeehan, the eminent sports writer, discovered Cozy among the Florida dogs, and blowing a few BB shots for the sake of artillery practice.

"This dog-racing is on the up-and-up," Cozy confided to Mr. McGeehan. "You see, they ain't no jockeys on the dogs' backs. The dogs think the rabbit they chase is a *real one*, and they do their best to ketch up with it."

Mr. McGeehan is a cynic, as well as a deputy sheriff of some county or another in Connecticut. "But suppose one of the dogs *should* catch the rabbit? What then?"

Mr. Dolan looked embarrassed. "Well, to tell the truth, one of our best dogs *did* ketch the bunny onct. After that, he was no good for racing at all. Every time we tried to race him after that, he'd just set there on his haunches and watch the other dogs do the running. He got wise, you see. I never saw a dog so disgusted in all my life. He give his owner an awful dirty look. He had been made a sucker of."

Physicians again warned Fallon of drinking. One glass of whiskey seemed to affect him immediately, making his tongue thick and his step uncertain. He wandered the streets, mumbling about his becoming an actor.

"Belasco is going to put me in a play," he would tell his friends. "I'm going on the stage."

When Gertrude Vanderbilt went abroad in 1925, Fallon seemed to lose his grip entirely. He had been straying again from his home, and now he didn't seem to want to return to his wife. He felt, perhaps, that he was too tired to make the usual excuses, to give his customary promises of reform. He was out of answers. Sick in body and soul, he went to the home of his elder sister in Mamaroneck.

For a while, the familiar sights in this sanctuary of his boyhood soothed his tortured spirit. But not for long. He was put to bed and lay there for weeks, much of the time in delirium. When he heard boats whistling on the Sound, he would rise to his elbow, stare with feverish eye and say:

"She's coming now. I hear her boat whistling. I must hurry and get down to the dock in time."

So ill was Fallon that the family desired a priest to administer the last rites of the church. Fallon opposed this. He stoutly maintained that he was not going to die.

"I'll get up from here," he said. "I can't have the priest

now. It wouldn't be right. I would have to give up the woman I love, were I to receive the last rites. And in my soul I know I'll never give her up. When I get well, I'll go right back to her. She's all that matters."

Finally, however, and to please those dear to him, he quit protesting, and the last rites were administered. It looked as though he could not live for many hours. But he smiled and said: "I'll live two more years." To his younger brother, who adored him, and who called Fallon "Peabody," he said:

" 'Tots,' they all think I'm dying. Well, I'm not. I'm going to die sometime. Sure. And why not? But I'll get up from here and I'll live another two years. Then I'll die. I'm gamer than they think."

And he did get up.

He seemed a walking corpse. But still his pride burned fiercely. It was perhaps the strongest part of him. He set to work to forestall disbarment. He seemed better in mind and body for a time, what with a new fight on his hands.

The Bar Association brought proceedings to have him disciplined by the Appellate Division, mentioning the case growing out of the defense of Fuller, as well as another action, in which Miss Carolyn Connor brought suit for $1,000,000 against Isaac H. Dickinson. The latter was a Lancaster, Pennsylvania, banker. Miss Connor, a nurse, alleged that Dickinson had promised her $1,000,000 if she would devote herself to him for five years. She also was to receive $1,000 a month. She sued for alleged breach of contract. The case, in which Fallon was counsel for the nurse, was dismissed in Supreme Court.

Fallon personally defended himself against the charges brought by the Bar Association. In his address, he said:

"No attorney ought to be harassed or annoyed by the bringing of such proceedings as this, based upon no substantial violation of any of the canons or ethics of any of the various associations."

As he spoke, the pallor of illness left his face. He was himself again, if only for the passing hour.

On March 26, 1926, the Appellate Division decided that

Fallon had violated none of the ethics of his profession. They dismissed the charges.

In August of 1926, Fallon came into public print in a grewsome manner. He had been on a protracted spree in the Hotel Belleclaire. A woman friend had spent some of her time with him. Other acquaintances had dropped in for a visit.

Fallon was partly undressed and was pouring himself a drink of gin. The bellboy had come with ice and had neglected to close the door. As Fallon turned from his bottle, he saw one of his most jealous women admirers at the entrance to his room. He bowed and said:

"If you don't mind, would you call some other time?"

The intruder saw Fallon's blonde companion, and began to hurl invectives at her. Then she put her hand in her bag and brought out a vial. Fallon sensed that the visitor was going to do something desperate. He leaped between the two women. As he did so, the wrathy caller hurled acid. It struck Fallon in the face. He groped for the table on which the gin bottle was standing. He took a handkerchief and soaked it with gin. He wiped away the acid as best he could with the gin-soaked cloth. Then he collapsed, blinded and faint with pain.

Dr. John Munz responded, and treated Fallon for the burns. By this time there were several women and men in the room. Fallon lay on the bed, writhing. The right side of his face and his right eye were affected. Someone told Dr. Munz that the injured man's name was "Clarkson."

Fallon remained at the hotel overnight, refusing to go to the hospital. In the morning he was in such great pain, and so likely was the danger of his becoming permanently blind that he consented to go to Polyclinic.

The agonized man kept saying: "Don't tell the police. Don't let it get in the papers."

The miracle was that Fallon not only recovered his sight,

but there was not a single scar to show where the acid had seared his handsome face.

Although Broadway at last voted that Fallon was through as a counselor, and on his way to Bryant Park, where the stumble-bums sit and stare, his fame yet persisted in the courts. The man himself now seldom appeared before the bar, but his shadow was there—and it was feared.

When Dandy Phil Kastel was arrested after a five-year search by Federal and up-State authorities, certain judges felt that Fallon was in the background of the defense. Kastel had been sought in connection with one of several swindles. Fallon had nothing to do with his former client's case, but the presence of Joe Shalleck, a one-time Fallon associate, at the Kastel counsel table, made certain observers believe that Fallon was guiding the defense.

Kastel was under $10,000 bail in the Federal Courts on a bucketing charge. When he failed to appear for trial, Judge John C. Knox declared the bail forfeit. Not until afternoon was it learned that a confusion in dates had been responsible for the non-appearance of the defendant. The next day Judge Knox set aside the bail-forfeiture.

Frederic R. Coudert, Jr., son of the international lawyer, and Ralph Koenig, son of Samuel S. Koenig, Republican political leader, were the Assistant United States Attorneys who prose-cuted Kastel. The defense attorneys were Joe Shalleck, James W. Osborne, and Clark L. Jordan. The jury disagreed. There were whispers that "Fallon is in the background." United States Judge Colin Neblett discharged the jury, after it was learned that they stood 11 for conviction and one for acquittal (the old Fallon "score"). The court set the date for an immediate re-trial.

In the second trial, and after the jury had deliberated for twenty-six hours, there was another disagreement, again by the score of 1 to 11.

In discharging the second jury, Judge Neblett, visiting Judge from New Mexico, told the jurors he was unable to understand *why* they had been unable to reach a verdict. The court regarded it as significant that during both trials over which he had presided, the corridors had been infested with denizens of the underworld.

The Judge had spent much of his time on the bench, waiting for the second jury to come to a conclusion. He learned that the jurors were sitting in bored silence, with one man holding out steadfastly.

During this long deliberation, there was a flurry in the corridor. The underworld mugs were disturbed no little when United States District Judge A. N. Hand, from another court, ordered a squad of marshals to go through the fifth floor and clear the place of loiterers.

Judge Winslow, sitting in still another court, also seemed to feel the presence of an "overshadowing menace." He was completing the trial of Vincent Fidele, charged with selling narcotics. It had been a most disturbing case. Fidele was not in court. He had failed to reappear after the noon recess. A bench-warrant was issued for his arrest, and his bail declared forfeit. Although Fidele was adjudged a fugitive, his trial went ahead after Assistant United States Attorney D. W. Whitney submitted decisions upholding the legality of proceeding without the defendant's presence. It was insisted by Fidele's attorney, Joseph Weber, that such a course was unique in American jurisprudence. He flatly refused to sum up for his absent client. The jury returned a verdict against the missing defendant in seventeen minutes.

Fresh from this experience, Judge Winslow summoned the grand jury before him. He charged them to undertake an investigation of the existence, causes, and possible remedies for the presence of underworld characters in the corridors of the building.

"The work of a judge in the court-room," said Judge Winslow, "is largely nullified, so far as the real furtherance of justice is concerned, if every defendant, when he steps from the court-room, becomes the prey of evil and sinister characters, who are as ready to defeat justice as those in the court-room might be to preserve it. A member of the trial jury in the Fidele case has just reported to me that he caught a man in the act of picking his pocket in the wash-room across the hall from the court. The man got away after a short struggle. There is inadequate policing."

United States Attorney Buckner spoke to the Grand Jury concerning the presence of jury-fixers and witness-tamperers in the corridors.

With the whole place buzzing with rumors that Fallon's shadow was hanging over the Old Post Office Building, Judge Neblett fixed the date for a third trial for Kastel. In discharging the jury, he said:

"There will be a new trial Tuesday morning. If necessary, I shall remain here all summer. You are discharged."

Eleven of the twelve jurors now crowded about the bench. What they said to the judge could not be heard. But they were plainly indignant. The Judge took the eleven men to his chambers, where they were closeted for some time.

In the third trial, with United States Attorney Buckner prosecuting, the jury was out for twenty-three hours. This trial was presided over by Judge A. N. Hand, the transfer having been made after Attorney Osborne complained that Judge Neblett had showed bias. The jury found Kastel guilty on one of six counts in the indictment. They recommended clemency.

In sentencing Kastel to serve three years at Atlanta, Judge Hand said if it had not been for the recommendation of clemency, he would have given Dandy Phil a full five-year term for "this flagrant case of bucketing."

Fallon admitted to friends that he was not feeling well. He was warned repeatedly that if he continued drinking, he need not expect to live. He compromised—as he put it—by placing raw eggs in sherry and drinking that concoction.

"Eggs are food, aren't they?" he asked, with something of the old-time mischief in his eye.

He was often in the company of Gertrude Vanderbilt, who seemed a last link between him and his fellow men. On a Friday preceding Easter Sunday, 1927, Fallon took Gertrude for a walk in Central Park. He seemed in better spirits today, and spoke of a new start.

"A lot of people owe me money," he said. "I've got at least $20,000 that I ought to collect. Of course there are hundreds of thousands that never will be paid. Just think of the people I've defended for nothing. I spent my own money in the Inch case. I got nothing from Fuller & McGee except a stab in the back. All I got out of Nicky Arnstein, you could put in a gnat's eye. But the past is gone and dead. Why speak of the past?"

"If you'll only take care of yourself," Gertrude said.

"Some day I'll pay you back, Baby. You've spent a lot on my account."

"You are welcome to everything I have."

"I know. I know. But we'll get all straightened out, and then we'll go to the mountains for a rest."

They came into Fifth Avenue and walked down town. Both liked to look into shop-windows. Suddenly Fallon began laughing. He acted as though he had a great and ludicrous secret. Gertrude knew what it was. She had a *run* in her stocking. Usually a fastidious dresser, she had said nothing about the run, not wanting to bother Fallon. He would have insisted on returning immediately to her home for fresh stockings.

Gertrude pretended she didn't know what Fallon was laughing at. When they reached the apartment, Fallon laughed again. "Well, I've got a good one on you, Baby!"

"What?"

"You had a run in your stocking, and didn't know it. You and your immaculate legs!"

She pretended to be very much put out. "You should have told me."

Fallon then called up the home of an art-dealer. He pretended he was a detective. "I know that you're palming off fake works of art," he telephoned. "And I'm out to get you." Fallon laughed as the art-dealer sputtered.

Then, as they sat down to tea, Fallon began to tell anecdotes. But all his jokes and his stories were not up to par. They were simple things, like the run in Gertrude's stocking, somehow lacking point. Gertrude sensed that Fallon was far from well; that he was trying to bluff her into believing he was in good spirits.

Finally she said: "Billy, I want you to spend Easter Sunday with your children. I'm going away for the week-end."

"I thought we were going to spend the week-end together?"

"No. I'd rather you went away for Easter."

"When are you leaving?"

"I'm going to the Steiners' for the week-end, and I want you to go on home."

"You wouldn't kick me out this way?"

"Don't talk like that. Nobody is kicking you out. Stay here for a while, and the maid will cook your dinner. I'm going to clear out now."

"Just as you say. Gee, but I hate to be alone!"

"Now don't stay here tonight. Remember. I'm trusting you. Go home."

"I'll call you up Easter morning."

When Gertrude Vanderbilt came down for breakfast Easter morning at the Steiner home, Mr. Steiner said: "There was somebody named Martin calling you at 2 o'clock this morning."

"Martin? I don't know anyone named Martin."

"That's what he said. He sounded a bit piffoed. I wasn't going to disturb you."

Miss Vanderbilt had a hunch. She called her home. Her maid answered.

"Yes, Miss Vanderbilt. Mr. Fallon didn't go home. He's having some breakfast now."

"Is he well?"

"I guess maybe he is."

"Have him come to the 'phone."

Before Miss Vanderbilt could lecture him, Fallon began. "Listen, Baby. Don't hop onto me. I know I shouldn't have stayed. But listen. I was so lonely and so sick. No, I didn't take much to drink. Just a couple. But I fell asleep right after dinner. Honestly. And then I had the most terrible dream. I can't shake it off. I had to call you. I was almost crazy. You've got to listen to the dream before you bawl me out. Please! I dreamed, Baby, that you were dead, and you were lying on some sort of slab, all naked. I could see your skin. It had a sort of dew on it. Then I saw your dog, Billy. And a lot of people came in to take you away and Billy wouldn't let them. He barked and I seemed powerless. I couldn't move. Billy and I were near you, and the people in the dream were beating Billy. I couldn't go home, Baby. I couldn't. I'm so afraid it means that something is wrong, that you might die and leave me."

"Nonsense. You go right on home."

"I'll do it."

"And don't let me find you when I come home tonight."

"I'm going as soon as I have my coffee."

"And no more drinking."

Miss Vanderbilt was upset. She felt that Fallon's dream *was* a sign of death. She was so unnerved that she cut short her visit with the Steiner family. She arrived home at noon to find Fallon lying on a couch, and half-seas over. She was furious.

"What *can* I do with you, if you don't behave?" she asked.

"Somebody had to take care of the cat and the dog," he said.

"You needn't try to joke about it. I'm dreadfully annoyed."

"I couldn't go home after that dream."

"Where did you get the liquor?"

"I sent out for some. It tasted as though a monkey-wrench had been mated with sulphuric acid."

"Now you go on home."

"Are you so mad at me, Baby?"

"Well, I think you might be more considerate. It hurts me when you abuse yourself."

"Don't be cross with me, darling. I just don't know any better."

The next day Fallon appeared in court on a minor civil matter concerning John McGraw, baseball manager. During an address to the bench, he suddenly collapsed. He was taken home to his wife's apartment, at the Hotel Oxford.

Gene McGee was notified of his friend's illness. He came at once to sit beside the bed of The Great Mouthpiece. They talked of the old Fordham days and of their later triumphs. Then Fallon lay back as though drowsy.

"I'm going," McGee said. "You've talked too much."

Fallon roused. "Don't go, Gene. Here, old friend, let me hold your hand a while. I'm not tired. I was just thinking."

"Thinking?"

"Yes. Of sin."

"I wouldn't bother about that sort of thinking. Let's think about baseball. Maybe you'll be well enough to attend the opener. The days go fast."

Although wasted by disease, Fallon roused from his pillow. A momentary fire and lust for life came again to his blue, Irish eyes.

"Yes, Gene, the days go fast. Almost as fast as the years. You know, Gene, I never really sinned at all."

"That's what I think."

"Everyone says I have sinned; that I'm paying the price of sin. That I tried to take Life by a *tour de force*. Let's confine ourselves to the issue and let's not depart from the law. The law of sin is explicit and simple. To sin, one has to premeditate the sin. I never premeditated a sin. I acted spontaneously, always, and as the spirit moved me."

He sighed and lay back quite still for a long time. He pressed McGee's big, powerful hand with his own white and shapely hand. His eyes were now closed, and one saw only the half-smile and the shock of apricot-colored hair—now darker than in the days he tossed his head with leonine virility—the hair he gloried in with the love of a narcist, barbering it himself and touching it with henna.

He sighed. "You see, Gene, I never really premeditated anything at all—not even death."

The next morning, at 11 o'clock, April 29, 1927, Fallon seemed in cheerful mood. He called his wife to his side. "Listen, dear, I'm not as badly off as the doctors say. What is a hardened liver or two between friends? I'm going to get up and put on my clothes."

Mrs. Fallon was excited. "You mustn't think of such a thing! Now you lie back and rest."

He smiled in his determined, headstrong fashion. "Do you think for a minute that I am going to lie here when I can go see the baseball game?"

"Please, Bill!"

"I'm going to the bathroom to shave. Don't bother to help me. I'll show you how Bill Fallon can walk and take care of himself. He's taken care of himself a long time."

Against Mrs. Fallon's advice, he rose and went to the bathroom. She heard a gasp and hastened to the door. She opened it. She was horrified. Fallon was on the floor. There was a brownish-red trickle from his mouth. He had suffered a gastric hemorrhage and a heart-attack.

Mrs. Fallon leaned over him, calling. She ran to the telephone. She summoned a physician. Then she went back. She didn't need a doctor to tell her what had happened.

The Broadway pilgrimage was done.

Chapter Twenty-Six

A BLACK WAGON ON THE BRIDGE

THE Church of the Ascension at One Hundred and Fourth Street and Amsterdam Avenue was crowded. A thousand notables sat or knelt there on the morning of May 2, 1927, to hear services for the repose of William J. Fallon's soul. There were beautiful women and important men among the mourners. Outside the church was a great throng that could not gain admittance. They craned their necks and talked about the man who lay dead.

Fallon was in a mahogany coffin that John McGraw had bought for his old friend. There were candles burning at the head and feet of the sleeper. The Reverend Father Donahue conducted the high requiem mass.

And now came a tribute unusual in the Roman Catholic Church. Eight mitred priests and acolytes gathered in black robes about the bier of the man who had defended gamblers, pimps, and confidence men. The clergy that clustered about the coffin were members of the Society of Jesus. They were his former Fordham teachers. They joined the Reverend Father Donahue in intoning the funeral chants. The air was heavy with incense. There were sobs. On the face of the handsome sleeper was an almost spiritual expression of peace and full acceptance.

The Fallon funeral represented New York. Broadway was there. The bench, the bar, the race-track, the sporting fraternity paid tribute and sent a fortune in blooms. Those outside the church stood bare-headed.

As services neared a close, there was an incredible bit of drama in the street. Once the chants had been sung and the candles were guttering, the choir boys sang "One Sweetly Solemn Thought." Then the pallbearers carried the body of the playboy-lawyer down the aisle and outside to the hearse. But before the black wagon started for Queensboro Bridge and Calvary Cemetery, and while a cortège of forty cars was being formed, a young man came to the doors of the church.

"My name," he said to an usher who sought to block his path, "is William J. Fallon. I'm the nephew of the man in there."

The usher was bewildered. He saw a young man, a truck-driver, who wore red sweater, a cap, and a license-tag on the visor of the cap. "I came from Trenton," said the young man. "I'm sorry I'm late. Uncle Bill was the whitest man in the whole world, and the smartest."

He went on, as though reciting from the catechism. "I didn't even know that Uncle Bill was dead until I tried to get in touch with him Sunday. I got in a pretty tight jam, you see, and I knew if anyone could help me out, it would be Uncle Bill. I was arrested in Trenton, and held in $1,000 bail by prohibition agents. They said they discovered a load of beer in one of my trucks. When I finally got out, I telephoned, and they told me Uncle Bill was dead. So I drove my other truck over. And there it is in the street. I'm going to drive it to the cemetery. Uncle Bill would like to have me do it that way. So you'll please see that I get a place in line."

Among the limousines of Broadway personages, the lone truck went across the bridge. At the cemetery, the young man stood beside the heavily veiled Mrs. Fallon, and looked down into the new grave. He plucked nervously at his red sweater. He heard someone say that Fallon was being buried beside an ancestor named Elias Fallon. He heard another man say:

"Do you know? When I looked at Bill, I was knocked for a goal. Why, he looked like some twenty-five-year-old kid!"

The Fire Island Baker saw a light burning from my window at first-dawn today. He dropped in and was glad to hear that the book was done.

"I tell you what," he said. "Me and you will take a trip some day to Calvary Cemetery. I'd give a lot just to stand and look at the monument on this here Fallon's grave."

"There is no monument on his grave," I said. "It's just bare."

The Baker was mystified. "The hell you say! No monument at all? And I've knowed guys that had tons of marble on their chests, and with wonderful lies all over the stone. . . . Well, I wish I could go out on the bay. They say the blue fish are running great again. But we got to do our work, don't we? The grease is hot, and I got to cook some sinkers. Come down in about an hour and have some sinkers for your coffee."